Steinbeck's Typewriter:
Essays on His Art

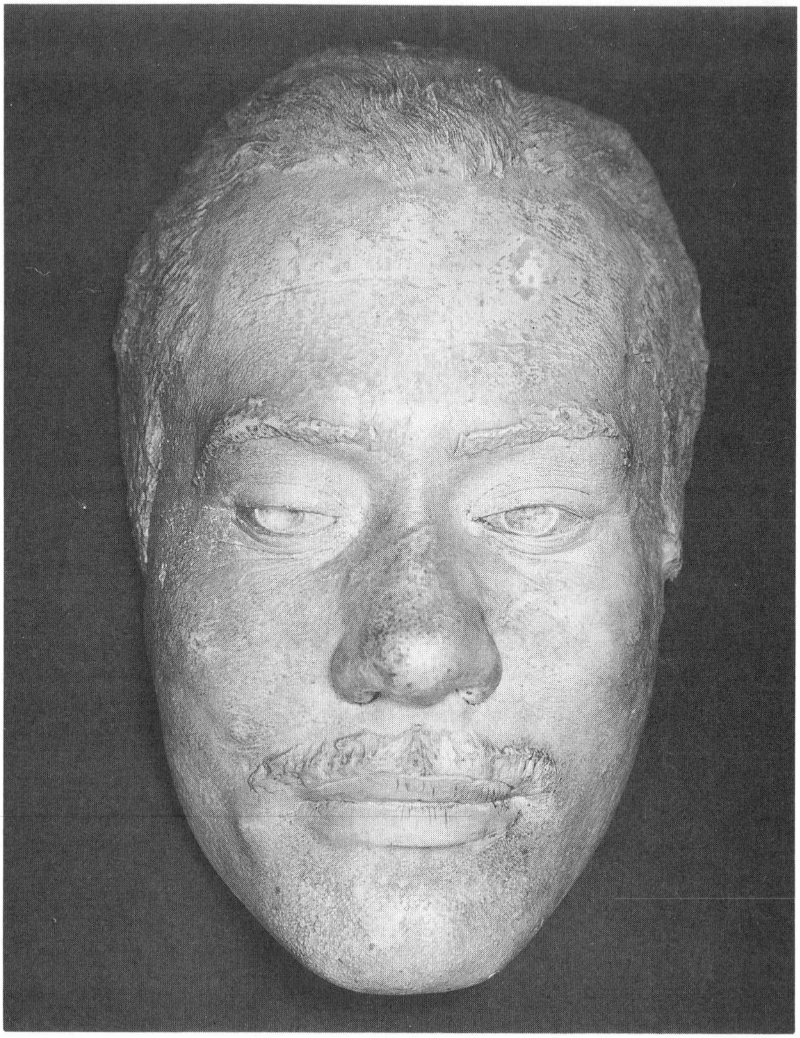

John Steinbeck life mask
by Ritch Lovejoy, early 1930s.
In his biography, *Steinbeck: The Good Companion* (1983), Carlton Sheffield recalled: "About that time, John and Carol became interested in some experiments with a plastic moulage process introduced to them by Ritchie Lovejoy . . . [who] had found a Swiss product named Negocol that opened up new techniques in making casts from almost any type of surface with amazing ease and flexibility. . . . So that was the start of the Faster Master Plaster Casters, an organization with no capital and almost unlimited potential. . . ." (153-54).
Courtesy of the University of Virginia Library, Charlottesville, VA.

Steinbeck's Typewriter:
Essays on His Art

Monterey, CA

Robert DeMott

For Bert Ring — we'll meet once again in Steinbeck country — Cheers,

Bob DeMott
3-22-97

The Whitston Publishing Company
Troy, New York
1996

Library of Congress Catalog Card Number 93-60806

ISBN 0-87875-446-6

Printed in the United States of America

For my mother, Colletta Helen Ventrella DeMott:

". . . all things in a single volume bound by Love,
of which the universe is the scattered leaves;
substance, accident, and their relation
so fused that all I say could do no more
than yield a glimpse of that bright revelation."

—Dante, *Paradiso,* Canto 33 (Tr. J. Ciardi)

By Robert DeMott

Books and Chapbooks

Steinbeck's Typewriter: Essays on His Art (1996)

News of Loss (1995) [Poems]

After "The Grapes of Wrath": Essays on John Steinbeck in Honor of Tetsumaro Hayashi (1995) [With Donald Coers and Paul Ruffin]

John Steinbeck: A Checklist of Books By and About (1987)

Steinbeck's Reading: A Catalogue of Books Owned and Borrowed (1984)

Mapping "East of Eden" (1981) [*Steinbeck Quarterly* special issue]

Artful Thunder: Versions of the Romantic Tradition in American Literature in Honor of Howard P. Vincent (1975) [With Sanford Marovitz]

A Concordance to the Poetry of Hart Crane (1973) [With Hilton and Elaine Landry]

Editions and Anthologies

John Steinbeck: "The Grapes of Wrath" and Other Writings 1936-1941 (1996) [With Elaine Steinbeck]

To a God Unknown (1995) [Penguin Twentieth-Century Classic]

John Steinbeck: Novels and Stories 1932-1937 (1994) [With Elaine Steinbeck]

The Grapes of Wrath (1992) [Penguin Twentieth-Century Classic]

Working Days: The Journals of "The Grapes of Wrath," 1938-1941 (1989)

Your Only Weapon is Your Work: A Letter by John Steinbeck to Dennis Murphy (1985)

From Athens Out (1974) [With Carol Harter]

Contents

Preface and Acknowledgements viii

Introduction xvi

Illustrations and Photographs xxiv

Abbreviations xxv

PART ONE: CREATIVE READING/CREATIVE WRITING

"Things that Happened to Me": Steinbeck's Varieties of Reading Experience 2

"A Great Black Book": *East of Eden* and *Gunn's New Family Physician* 55

"Working at the Impossible": The Presence of *Moby-Dick* in *East of Eden* 75

PART TWO: NEGOTIATING TEXTS

"Writing My Country": Making *To a God Unknown* 108

"This Book Is My Life": Creating *The Grapes of Wrath* 146

"One Book To a Man": Charting a Bibliographical Preface to *East of Eden* 206

PART THREE: INTERIOR DIMENSIONS

"The Girl of the Air": A Speculative Essay on Steinbeck's Love Poems 234

"Of Ink and Heart's Blood": Adventures in Reading Steinbeck 265

Steinbeck's Typewriter: An Excursion in Suggestiveness 287

PART FOUR: BIBLIOGRAPHY OF BOOKS BY AND ABOUT JOHN STEINBECK 319

Index 345

Preface and Acknowledgements

This book on John Steinbeck's writing (which I once thought would be called *"In Awe of Words": Steinbeck's Fictive Art*) has been evolving in stages for a long, long time. I have not only come to appreciate the teasing implications of Whitman's statement that certain projects are "creative" and have "vista," but I have also come to incur so many debts during this period of changes that it is impossible to tally them all. While most of the essays in *Steinbeck's Typewriter* have been relentlessly revised for this book, and so have come to inscribe a work of second and third and fourth chances—a gathering of renewals and elaborations—they are also products of well-traveled pasts and owe their existence to numerous conference organizers, and/or journal and book editors, to whom I am grateful for permission to reprint. I want to thank especially John Gross and Maria Orozco, past organizers of the annual Steinbeck Festival in Salinas, California, where several of these pieces were presented; Tetsumaro Hayashi (formerly of Ball State University, and now Graduate Professor of English at Yasuda Women's University, Hiroshima, Japan), long-time chief editor of the *Steinbeck Quarterly* (1968-1993) and co-organizer of the Second and Third International Steinbeck Congresses; and Michael Millman, Senior Editor, and Kristine Puopolo, Associate Editor, Viking/Penguin, for exceptional generosity, instigation, and encouragement.

For those interested in such matters, the lineage of the present selection of essays is as follows:

Chapter 1, "Things That Happened to Me": Steinbeck's Varieties of Reading Experience," was presented in briefer form at the Modern Language Association convention, San Francisco, December 1979; as lectures at Steinbeck Festival V and Second International Steinbeck Congress, Salinas, August 1984; as speeches at Ohio University, University of Windsor, Western Maryland

University, and Salisbury State University, in 1983 and 1984; as an address to the Roxburghe Club, San Francisco, in September 1985. Part of the essay was first published as "'Culling All Books': Steinbeck's Reading and *East of Eden*," *Steinbeck Quarterly* 14 (Winter-Spring 1981): 40-51; then as the introduction to the now out-of-print *Steinbeck's Reading: A Catalogue of Books Owned and Borrowed* (New York: Garland Publishing, 1984), xix-lxvi. The revised version here also incorporates some material from "The Interior Distances of John Steinbeck," *Steinbeck Quarterly* 12 (Summer-Fall 1979): 86-99; "*Steinbeck's Reading*: First Supplement," *Steinbeck Quarterly* 17 (Summer-Fall 1984): 94-103; and "*Steinbeck's Reading*: Second Supplement," *Steinbeck Quarterly* 22 (Winter-Spring 1989): 4-8.

Chapter 2, "'A Great Black Book': *East of Eden* and *Gunn's New Family Physician*," was presented as the keynote lecture at San Jose State University's College of Humanities and Arts Institute for Arts and Letters, March 1984; and to the Friends of The Gleeson Library, University of San Francisco, November 1985. It was published under the same title in *American Studies* 22 (Fall 1981): 41-57; reprinted in briefer form as "Steinbeck's *East of Eden* and Gunn's *New Family Physician*," in *The Book Club Of California Quarterly News-Letter* 51 (Spring 1986): 31-48; and again as "Creative-Reading/Creative Writing: The Presence of *Dr. Gunn's New Family Physician* in Steinbeck's *East of Eden*," in Cliff Lewis and Carroll Britch, eds., *Rediscovering Steinbeck: Revisionist Views of His Art, Politics and Intellect* (Lewiston, NY: Edwin Mellen Press, 1989), 35-57.

Chapter 3, "'Working at the Impossible': The Presence of *Moby-Dick* in *East of Eden*," was first presented as "Steinbeck, Melville, and the American Romantic Tradition in Fiction," the Centennial American Fiction Lecture, John Carroll University, October 1985, for which I was invited by James Magner and David LaGuardia; at the "Rediscovering Steinbeck" conference, University of Lowell, April 1986; and at the "Steinbeck and the Environment" conference, Nantucket, May 1992. A shorter version of the essay will appear in Susan Beegel, Wes Tiffney, and Susan Shillinglaw, eds., *Steinbeck and the Environment: Interdisciplinary Approaches* (Tuscaloosa: University of Alabama Press, forthcoming in 1996).

Chapter 4, "'Writing My Country': Making *To a God Unknown*," was delivered in abbreviated form as "Robinson Jeffers and John Steinbeck: Parts of a World," at Western

American Literature conference, Estes Park, Colorado, October 1991; and as the introduction, without footnotes and documentation, to Penguin's Twentieth-Century Classics edition of *To a God Unknown* (New York: Penguin Books, 1995), vii-xl. It also draws upon some elements first adumbrated in "Toward a Redefinition of *To a God Unknown*," *University of Windsor Review* 8 (Spring 1973): 34-53, which was reprinted in revised form as "Steinbeck's *To a God Unknown*," in Tetsumaro Hayashi, ed., *A Study Guide to Steinbeck: a Handbook to his Major Works* (Metuchen, NJ: Scarecrow Press, 1973), 187-213.

Chapter 5, "'This Book Is My Life': Creating *The Grapes of Wrath*," the longest piece, is here significantly updated and elaborated, and deserves a special explanation. It reflects a personal experiment in a kind of willfully expanding non-fictional discourse, an attempt to understand how—as my attitude toward this particularly complex and problematized novel changed from year to year in the past decade—those changes in perspective, depth, tone, or coloration are written into revised versions of a critical text. In working through these numerous stages and arriving at the present selected narrative (with yet another focal title and epigraphs), my result has not been mastery of the subject, but a humbling exercise in contingency and qualification; for me, what surfaces is a nagging sense of inadequacy at how much remains here unsaid about *The Grapes of Wrath*. This chapter is based on the introduction and bridging commentary sections to my edition of *Working Days: The Journals of "The Grapes of Wrath," 1938-1941* (New York: Viking Press, 1989). It was also presented in briefer form as talks at a panel, "Composing and Recomposing American Fiction," at National Council of Teachers of English conference, St. Louis, November 1988; at "*The Grapes of Wrath*, 1939-1989: An Interdisciplinary Forum," San Jose State University, March 1989; at Steinbeck Festival X, Salinas, August 1989; and as an abbreviated lecture at a week-long Soviet-American symposium on Steinbeck held in Moscow in October 1989, in conjunction with the Esalen Institute's Soviet-American Exchange Program, USSR Union of Writers, USSR Ministry for Publication, Print, and the Book Trade, and Moscow International Book Fair. In addition, earlier versions of the essay have been published as "'Working Days and Hours': Steinbeck's Writing of *The Grapes of Wrath*," in *Studies in American Fiction*, 18 (Spring 1990): 3-15; as the introduction, without notes and documentation, to Penguin's Twentieth-

Century Classics edition of *The Grapes of Wrath* (New York: Penguin Books, 1992), vi-lv; and as "'A Truly American Book': Pressing *The Grapes of Wrath*," in James Barbour and Tom Quirk, eds., *Biographies of Books: The Compositional Histories of Notable American Writings* (Columbia: University of Missouri Press, 1996), 187-225.

Chapter 6, "'One Book to a Man': Charting a Bibliographical Preface to *East of Eden*," was published in briefer form as "*East of Eden*: A Bibliographical Checklist," *Steinbeck Quarterly* 25 (Winter-Spring 1992): 14-28; then updated as "Charting *East of Eden*: A Bibliographical Survey," in Donald V. Coers, Paul D. Ruffin, and Robert J. DeMott, eds., *After "The Grapes of Wrath": Essays on John Steinbeck in Honor of Tetsumaro Hayashi* (Athens: Ohio University Press, 1995), 148-171.

Chapter 7, "'The Girl of the Air': A Speculative Essay on Steinbeck's Love Poems," was initially presented as a talk at the Third International Steinbeck Congress, Honolulu, May 1990; and published in briefer form as "After *The Grapes of Wrath*: A Speculative Essay on Steinbeck's Suite of Love Poems," in Tetsumaro Hayashi, ed. *John Steinbeck: The Years of Greatness, 1936-1939* (Tuscaloosa: University of Alabama Press, 1993), 20-45.

Chapter 8, "'Of Ink and Heart's Blood': Adventures in Reading Steinbeck," was first given as a talk at Steinbeck Festival XI, Salinas, August 1990; then published in *Connecticut Review* 14 (Spring 1990): 9-21, as "'Of Ink and Heart's Blood': Adventures in Reading *East of Eden*."

Chapter 9, "Steinbeck's Typewriter: An Excursion in Suggestiveness" was originally given as a brief panel presentation, "'A Fine, Crazy Consistency': *Sweet Thursday* and *Li'l Abner*; or Steinbeck's Comic Book: The Influence of Al Capp on *Sweet Thursday* (An Exercise in Tentativeness, Understatement and Suggestiveness)" for American Literature Association conference, San Diego, June 1990; and as a talk for Steinbeck Festival XIII, Salinas, August 1992. The essay was first published in briefer form as "*Sweet Thursday* Revisited: An Excursion in Suggestiveness," in Donald V. Coers, Paul C. Ruffin, and Robert J. DeMott, eds., *After "The Grapes of Wrath": Essays on John Steinbeck in Honor of Tetsumaro Hayashi* (Athens: Ohio University Press, 1995), 172-196.

The final section, "A Bibliography of Books By and About John Steinbeck," is a much expanded version of a limited edition chapbook, *John Steinbeck: A Checklist of Books By and About*, published by Robert F. Hanson's Opuscula Press in Bradenton, Florida, in 1987.

I am grateful to the appropriate conference organizers and journal and book editors and publishers, including Viking/ Penguin, Farrar, Straus and Giroux, Paul S. Eriksson, Garland, Edwin Mellen, Random House, University of Missouri Press, University of Alabama Press, University Press of Mississippi, and Ohio University Press, for permission to use this material again.

***

During the past fifteen years, when the various parts of this book have been in the chute, I have created some special debts, which require more than the usual acknowledgment. Elaine Steinbeck's unsurpassed generosity, support, and friendship has been a blessing; she has opened many doors and continues to keep them open. Thom Steinbeck, too, was ever-gracious and accommodating. I am also indebted to Eugene Winick and Julie Fallowfield at McIntosh and Otis, exclusive agents for Elaine Steinbeck and Steinbeck's literary estate, who have not only granted permission to quote from Steinbeck's numerous unpublished writings and his non-Viking Press publications, but have cleared paths that might have otherwise remained tangled with undergrowth. And Florence Eichen at Penguin Books has generously granted permission to quote liberally from Steinbeck's published writings.

I also wish to thank Margaret Cohn, former Dean, Ohio University Honors College, for 1993-1994 and 1995-1996 Research Internship Awards; Harold Molineau, interim Dean, Ohio University's College of Arts and Sciences, for a Dean's Research Award, Spring 1995; Betty Pytlik, Chair, Ohio University's Department of English, for numerous felicities; Susan Crowl, Director of Graduate Studies in English, for repeated encouragement and support; Mickey Bugeja, Ohio University's E. W. Scripps School of Journalism, for publishing advice; William Owens, Ohio University's Department of Classics, for electronic research assistance; Lois Vines, Ohio University's Department of French, for a key translation; Ohio University's Research Committee for a couple of discretionary grants; Jason Puskar, my Honors College Research Intern in 1993-1994, and Steve Jain, my Honors College Research Intern in 1995-1996; and to these doctoral students—Cornelius Browne, Russell Chamberlain, Tracie Church

Guzzio, Lisa Lundstedt, John Marsden, and Patrick Smith—all of whom, either in English 775, my American literature seminars, and/or in English 716, my Apprenticeship in Teaching Literature course—have consistently presented the right kinds of challenges at the right times and have reinforced daily my belief in teaching's central place in the scheme of things. At long last, I thank Jean Goode, President, Whitston Publishing Company, for her unflagging encouragement and patience during the interminable spell while this book was repeatedly delayed.

As with *Steinbeck's Reading* and *Working Days*, this book depends in great part on the previously unknown Steinbeck, the Steinbeck of unpublished manuscripts, ledgers, and correspondence; once again I would not have gotten far without superior archival assistance in and among the largest and most bountiful of Steinbeck collections. I can not count the number of times my requests for information or for copies of Steinbeck materials have been promptly—and cheerfully—provided by Susan Shillinglaw, Director, Steinbeck Research Center, San Jose State University, San Jose, CA; Mary Jean S. Gamble, chief Steinbeck Librarian at the John Steinbeck Library, Salinas, CA; Margaret J. Kimball, Head, Department of Special Collections, and Linda J. Long, Public Services, Department of Special Collections, at Stanford University Library, Stanford, CA; Robert E. Parks, the Robert H. Taylor Curator of Manuscripts, Pierpont Morgan Library, New York City; and the directors and their staffs at the Manuscripts Division, Library of Congress, Washington, DC; Harry Ransom Humanities Research Center, University of Texas, Austin, TX; Rare Book and Manuscript Library, Columbia University, New York City; and Clifton Waller Barrett Library, Rare Books and Manuscript Library, University of Virginia, Charlottesville, VA. I am deeply indebted to the directors and trustees of all these libraries for their courtesy and permission to employ primary Steinbeck documents and related items.

I have also been fortunate to benefit from the encouragement, example, and advice of these Steinbeck experts, all of whom I count as friends: Jack Benson (San Diego State University); Don Coers (Sam Houston State University); Warren French (Tallahassee, Florida); Brian Railsback (Western Carolina University); Roy Simmonds (Billericay, England); and especially John Ditsky (University of Windsor), and again Sue Shillinglaw, both of whom have read, reread, and commented on various parts of this book in recent years. Although I cannot be positive about where their ideas end and my own begin, I can say with certitude that I have profited from the work of a number of other fine Steinbeck scholars, including Pascal Covici, Jr. (Southern Methodist University), Mimi Gladstein (University of Texas, El Paso), Robert Morsberger (California State Polytechnic University, Pomona), Louis Owens (University of New Mexico), John Timmerman (Calvin College), and Thom Tammaro (Moorhead State University). That nine out of thirteen of these scholars teach Steinbeck's works at a public university, as I do, or at a private liberal arts college, reinforces my sense that the novelist's reputation crosses numerous gender, cultural, and academic barriers.

The announcement of a comprehensive *John Steinbeck Encyclopedia* (edited by Brian Railsback, forthcoming from Greenwood Press in 1997) and especially the recent addition of Steinbeck's works to the Library of America's ongoing publishing project—itself a kind of extended pragmatist literary program under the guidance of Richard Poirier—further indicates that, as the centenary of his birth approaches in 2002, Steinbeck is still being sought out by an increasingly demanding and discriminating body of readers. And when I think of discriminating readers and writers, I think of Jim Aton, Susan Beegel, Kevin Bezner, Maggie Cook, John Haines, Kathy Mangan, Jack Matthews, Mark Rollins, Dave Smith, Michael Waters, and Nancy Zane—as well as the Library of America's Gila Bercovitch and Geoffrey O'Brien—all of whom, while they might not know it, have lent something significant to this production, but are not to be held responsible for its shortcomings. The same goes for Ruth Nuzum, Maureen Pastine, Pauline Pearson, Virginia Scardigli, and the late Chase Horton, Pare Lorentz, Elizabeth Otis, and Carlton Sheffield, all of whom taught me much about generosity. Before donating his incomparable Steinbeck collection to Princeton University last year, Preston Beyer, dean of all Steinbeck bibliophiles, happily provided copies of scarce, fugitive items on the shortest possible notice; so did California bookmen James Johnson and Jim Dourgarian.

***

I was fortunate enough to fly fish through much of the making of this book. In this way sanity and an incalculable sense of process and humbleness were maintained ("reading" a trout stream is not all that different from interpreting a written text, for in both instances the medium is the language, and the language is embarrassingly slippery). I thank Stan and Mike Horton at Staley Springs Lodge on Henry's Lake, Island Park, Idaho, for their attentiveness; and Jackie and Craig Matthews and John Juracek at Blue Ribbon Flies, West Yellowstone, Montana, for good advice on trouting and earnest talk on extra-literary matters. My outdoor compatriots closer to home—Lars Lutton, Rod Lyndon, Mike McCollister, John Mitchell, Jaimie Roederer—wisely refrained from asking about the intricacies and progress of this book and so allowed me to focus on sporting matters at hand instead.

My father, James, my daughter, Elizabeth, and especially my wife, Andrea, have been steadfast supporters all along, as have my in-laws, Carl and Ildiko Berger. They have all given new meaning to Dezso Tandori's lines in his poem "Hommage II"—"After a while the past always works out. / It becomes later, all that it could have been. . . ."

Finally, this book is dedicated to my mother, Helen, for with her have resided the profoundest sanities of all—intelligence, compassion, faith, courage, and love.

August-December, 1995
Island Park, Idaho & Athens, Ohio

Introduction

We work in the dark—we do what we can—we give what we have. Our doubt is our passion and our passion is our task. The rest is the madness of art.

—Dencombe to Doctor Hugh, in Henry James's "The Middle Years" (1893)

For we work in our own darkness a great deal with little real knowledge of what we are doing. I think I know . . . but it still isn't much.

—John Steinbeck to Pascal Covici, 23 April 1951, in *Journal of a Novel* (1969)

I have come belatedly to regard *Steinbeck's Typewriter* as the final work in a trilogy. It began with *Steinbeck's Reading* (1984), which reconstructed Steinbeck's composite library of more than nine hundred books he read and/or borrowed during his lifetime (a significant number of entries include his comments on or reactions to specific books). My annotated edition of his *Grapes of Wrath* journal, *Working Days* (1989), provided an inside narrative of the multiple forces, historical events, and personalities that entered the composition and controversial aftermath of Steinbeck's most powerful and famous novel. I am disposed to think that *Steinbeck's Typewriter* not only extends my involvement in the complexities and contradictions of Steinbeck's writerly life by addressing the creation, reception, and interpretation of several of his books, but does so according to his own preferred life-long attitude of acceptance and understanding.[1]

By continuing my habit of letting his published and unpublished texts speak as often as possible for themselves, I hope some light will be thrown on Steinbeck's interior spaces and his creative habits, which I believe have been not only seriously underestimated but woefully ignored. As in my previous two books, this one employs a mode of homemade, improvised genetic criticism, which is to say that in seeking out the generative dimensions of Steinbeck's writing and his mode of inscription as process, my method of focusing on patterns of emergence relies more on enthusiastic advocacy and descriptive alertness than on rigorous critique or dispassionate analysis. I have taken as a constant Steinbeck's definition of process, his rationale for authorial work: "I feel good when I am doing it—better than when I am not. I find joy in the texture and tone and rhythms of words and sentences, and when these happily combine in a 'thing' that has texture and tone and emotion and design and architecture, there comes a fine feeling—a satisfaction like that which follows good and shared love. If there have been difficulties and failures overcome, these may even add to the satisfaction" ("Rationale," 309). I am content in this attentive writerly enterprise, therefore, to look at Steinbeck's focal texts in their state of becoming, in their motion toward what is, rather than in their devolving toward the opposite, toward what isn't. It is a position I see suggestively limned in Ritch Lovejoy's arresting and unsettling life mask of Steinbeck (see frontispiece)—which is to say that the condition of coming-into-being, the erotics of process, is perhaps what really matters most for this writer.

In addressing the uncertain, slippery elements of textual origination and evolution, and in writing toward the ground of writing itself (one of the ineluctable American literary themes), I find myself, like a character in a Paul Auster novel, less and less able—or willing—to hew to a straight critical account that obeys the rules of homogeneous analytical methodology. As a result, *Steinbeck's Typewriter* is not at all a traditional scholarly monograph (in the heroic sense of that term) with a clearly developed thesis and commensurately uniform presentation; instead this book is a loose federation of essays that (dramatically for me anyway) circle around a few obsessive themes, scenes, habits, and texts in John Steinbeck's career as a writer and reader. If such motivation produces an overlapping, crescive approach that runs the risk of sounding like enthusiastic literary talk or an informal classroom lecture rather than elevated or rarefied intellectual dialogue, then, after three decades as a teacher, it is a risk I am willing to take. The result of such risks, as G. Douglas Atkins says, "need not be waywardness, recklessness, indulgence. That the choice is no simple either/or is a lesson of theory. Theory and life: they are involved, one with another."[2]

Working outside the traditionally sanctioned master plot of literary analysis (which I have felt is necessary in order to expand the boundaries of critical conversation on Steinbeck) has had formal implications, too, for some of these chapters spread out the (re)presentation of factual information in such a way as to intentionally defer readerly gratification and to postpone evaluative insights until my audience, ideally, through his or her own investment, has the whole essay in mind. In their juggling of multiple elements, in their seesawing back and forth, and in their give-and-take seriality, several of these pieces are more akin to an acrobatic seminar presentation than to a spiffy, well-mannered mode of discourse. In their orchestration of particulars, they are indebted to current trends in contemporary fiction and creative non-fiction; in that some of these essays employ a certain degree of internal disruptiveness, I think of them more as assemblages than as monolithic pronouncements.

Although I have occasionally lost the thread or forgotten the shape of the pattern, my purpose throughout this three-book narrative of immersion and engagement (in so far as hindsight helps clarify such intentions) has been to show the ways Steinbeck's imagination worked and was worked upon, and to construct a loosely linked biography of his creative process based on an elaboration of the way he sought to engage his sources, influences, and experiences. Certainly, for a writer long thought to be little more than a naive realist, he spent an inordinate amount of real time and psychic energy attending to, reflecting on, and recording his own daily compositional strategies, and even more time working out the implications of what it meant to be "creative," to enter the zone of making, the arena of doing. In seeking the cumulative, textual implications of this old-fashioned but nonetheless intriguing topic, I have tried to strike a pragmatic balance between traditional and revisionary ways of considering the author's role. If it is no longer possible to believe naively in the full-blown autonomy of artistic genius, with its heightened rhetoric of transcendence and sovereignty, neither is it possible to accept unhesitantly the opposite posture—that a writer is a bloodless integer, utterly determined by uncontrollable, unconscious forces of language, politics, race, gender, and class.[3] Instead, I have positioned Steinbeck at an intersection between these poles of idealism and skepticism, abandonment and discipline, appropriation and passivity, practice and theory, action and repose.

That is, I have tried to honor Steinbeck's sense of being a self-willed writer who prized the shaping, authorizing power of imagination (however tenuous and imperfect that proved to be), but I also have tried to show how a welter of contextual details and intervening events gave direction to his writing life, ultimately contributing density and thickness to his published work. "I, as a novelist," he once declared, "am a product not only of my own time but of all the flags and tatters, the myth and prejudice, the faith and filth that preceded me. . . . A novelist is a kind of flypaper to which everything adheres. His job then is to try to reassemble life into some kind of order" (*SLL*, 591-592). A number of Steinbeck's texts, especially his later ones, such as *East of Eden, Sweet Thursday*, and *The Winter of Our Discontent*, enact this uneasy (but no less real) choreography between expression and construction, reflexivity and mimesis, self and world. Indeed, in some of these later works the struggles of the writing/reading life becomes a ground of presence for Steinbeck, and writing—conceived of in its largest sense as a mode of narration, a style of perception, and a habit of mind—becomes a way of being and acting in the world.

My approach in these three books, and especially in this selection of essays, has been to locate Steinbeck not so much as a sovereign master of those "flags and tatters," but as a partner in an uncertain dance with them, a negotiator of inner vision and outer resources, a mediator between internal compulsion and external forces, synthesized in the image of Steinbeck's portable typewriter which closes the penultimate chapter of the book. My project here—perhaps ultimately impossible to attain—has been to find a way to view Steinbeck's elusive creativity by bridging certain aspects of expressivism and determinism, individual volition and marketplace pressure. "I think that writing may be simply a method or technique for communication with other individuals; and its stimulus, the loneliness we are born to. In writing, perhaps we hope to achieve companionship. What some people find in religion, a writer may find in his craft or whatever it is,—absorption of the small and frightened and lonely into the whole and complete, a kind of breaking through to glory" ("Rationale," 309). In trying to situate Steinbeck in a reciprocal—and receptive—middle point between text and context, between operative utterance and myriad localized forces, between wholeness and fragmentation, I am attempting to portray his scriptive authority, his authorship, not as a closed system of autonomy, but as contingent, problematized, and negotiable within a field where individuality, discipline, resilience, and craft still matter. Furthermore, the critical notoriety and commercial success of *The Grapes of Wrath* shows that Steinbeck, a man in and of his time, occasionally rose spectacularly above it, too, which is, I suppose, a means of simultaneously validating and negating competing hegemonic theories. In any event, such a moment when a work of fiction—whether by deft authorial design, or by the brute conjunction of other determinants—accomplishes its duty in the aesthetic, affective, *and* political realms ought to warn us against making the mistake (even when well-intentioned) of assuming, or presuming, too much where Steinbeck is concerned. "Let us treat our authors (and our texts as well), Emerson might have said, as if they were real. Perhaps they are."[4]

The essays gathered in *Steinbeck's Typewriter* resume the music of the dance. The pieces collected here have had prior lives, especially those that began as invited lectures, speeches, or talks, and then subsequently appeared elsewhere in print. I want to make clear, however, that the bulk of these nine essays, while maintaining a more or less responsible and recognizable relationship to their roots, are not simply being reprinted from previous venues, but have turned into revised, expanded, updated (and sometimes intermingled) versions of their original selves. That is, this is not an anthology of reprinted offerings, but a freshly shaped collection. The result is that, in most cases, the essays are not simply retitled, but feel to me like altogether new writing that will, I hope, work in concert with each other. In working over these chapters during the past year, and in teasing out and elaborating some aspects that heretofore eluded me, I have come to understand—maybe truly for the first time, maybe at last once and for all—how literary criticism is itself a kind of enabling fiction, in the sense that it becomes the story of our obsessions, the tale of what haunts us, the shape of our unconscious desires. It is an equation Steinbeck certainly understood, as when he told Ed Sheehan in 1962, "I have known for years that criticism describes the critic much more than the thing criticized. That's as it should be" (*CJS*, 101).

Although these pieces differ in tone and execution, all of them are intensely personal, by which I mean they either echo thematic resonances in my own life, or, in the case of the essays grouped in section three, exhibit my direct intervention into the text itself. This personal stamp (which I hope will not be regarded as a license for arrogance, or as a ticket to distort Steinbeck's texts beyond recognition), is also especially relevant to my repeated focus on *East of Eden*, which I realize now is the key work in the following pages, and one which, in a manner of speaking, has become the cornerstone of my reading of Steinbeck's later career. In particular, I keep returning, as though haunted, to events surrounding Steinbeck's divorce from his second wife, Gwyn, in 1948, to his period of isolation and upheaval in 1948 and 1949, and to his eventual rebirth after 1950 when he married again (happily to Elaine Anderson Scott) and launched into his new domestic life at the same time he began composing *East of Eden*, a kind of fiction he had never practiced before. Besides the fact that *Eden* has many uncharted depths worthy of serious attention, the whole saga of its background and writing has seized me as a parable of renewal, perhaps even of a certain kind of salvation.

Having confessed to the appeal of that concept, though, I am quick to add that it is not possible to establish conclusively which event exerted prior influence—Steinbeck's life change or his decision to write in a new mode of representation. It is more helpful, I think, to consider the two events as coterminal and interlaced, which further indicates that this period of Steinbeck's life can also be understood as a reflective symbol for his creativity, relying as it does upon the interdependence of biographical events, extra-literary elements, and shaping intention. In any event, mindful of my life-long experiences as a fly fisherman in pursuit of leader-shy trout, I have preferred to approach Steinbeck's texts throughout with as light a doctrinal touch as possible, avoiding where possible heavy-handed critical vocabulary, specialized jargon, or convoluted syntax (the bane, it seems to me, of much contemporary academic writing). In any event, theory of one persuasion or another is inescapably part of our literary, critical, and cultural landscape now, as I believe these essays will demonstrate; the trick as I see it, is to achieve a suitable balance of sustained discovery without bludgeoning a reader's sensibility or patience. At least one way of doing so, as I have indicated above, is to return meaningful personal emphasis to critical writing, to advance what Tzvetan Todorov (following Mikhail Bakhtin) terms a "dialogic criticism" that speaks "to" and "with" literary works.[5]

The view of Steinbeck's art that issues out of the following pages (especially in "Interior Dimensions") is, finally, my responsibility, and is as much the result of my reading of *his* texts as it is of *my* own preoccupations, predelictions, and impositions (I think often of Steinbeck's refusal in *The Log from "Sea of Cortez"* to be seduced by the "myth of permanent objective reality"). Central to my interpretative narrative, however, is Steinbeck's unswerving participation in the vitally contested scene of writing. Again, I find myself moved by his commitment and by his faith in the process of writing artfully, in a knowing and willing sense, even if—or when—it meant working in darkness. To me, and to everyone I know who reads and writes or who teaches reading and writing, that constancy, that humility, that honesty, that attentiveness to the wor(l)d, ought to make all the difference for our own tasks wherever and however we find them.

Notes

[1] See Steinbeck's two *Saturday Review* pieces, "Critics, Critics, Burning Bright" (1950) and "Critics—From a Writer's Point of View" (1955), which are reprinted in *Steinbeck and His Critics: A Record of Twenty-Five Years*, eds. E. W. Tedlock and C. V. Wicker (Albuquerque: University of New Mexico Press, 1957), 43-51, and especially his "A Postscript from Steinbeck," 307-08, and his "Rationale," 309 (hereafter cited as "Rationale").

[2] *Estranging the Familiar: Toward a Revitalized Critical Writing* (Athens: University of Georgia Press, 1992), 157.

[3] The tangled and contested history of current theories on authorial agency and displacement, the function of poetic imagination, and debates over the legitimacy of source hunting and usage is laid out in a timely, challenging collection of essays (all influenced by Russian critic Mikhail Bakhtin, French theorist Roland Barthes, and Bulgarian-born French feminist Julia Kristeva), *Influence and Intertextuality in Literary History*, eds. Jay Clayton and Eric Rothstein (Madison: University of Wisconsin Press, 1991). Especially valuable for my project in *Steinbeck's Typewriter* is Susan Stanford Friedman's summary statement in chap. 6, "Weavings: Intertextuality and the (Re)birth of the Author," 173: "At its 'birth,' intertextuality [coined by Julia Kristeva in 1966] by its self-definition denied its origins in the discourse of influence. But as the term spread intertextually, the author whose death it had proclaimed insistently returned, particularly as intertextuality was transposed into American critical discourses. We have come full circle, back to the fabric of a text, this time an intertextual web of critical discourses that are endlessly woven and rewoven. Central to this (intertextual) reweaving of the critical discourses of intertextuality is the reinsertion of the author, along with some of the biographical and historical methodologies of influence studies, back into the pattern of

the fabric." In another way, the fabric itself—the total accretion of real and latent presences, authorial investments and writerly negotiations, interior dimensions and external appropriations, the work and its work site—make up the characteristic Steinbeckian literary architecture ("Rationale," 309), or better yet, *architexture*, if I may be allowed to merge and modify Steinbeck's term with that of a recent narratological theorist. See Gerard Genette, *The Architext: An Introduction*, trans. Jane E. Lewin (Berkeley: University of California Press, 1981), 81-83, for insight on a term I use here and in later chapters of *Steinbeck's Typewriter*.

[4] Tom Quirk, "Sources, Influences, and Intertexts," *Resources for American Literary Study*, 21, no. 2 (1995): 255. Quirk also states that "the match between text and intertext, between author and work, is never exact . . . and we must continually adjust private conviction to an ever-shifting body of demonstrable fact and a fuller comprehension of historical occasion."

[5] *Literature and its Theorists: A Personal View of Twentieth-Century Criticism*, trans. Catherine Porter (Ithaca, NY: Cornell University Press, 1987), 161. See also Atkins, "The Return of/to the Personal," chap. 6 of his *Estranging the Familiar*, 82-84, and especially 95-97, where he records his yearning for a responsive "personal criticism" that illuminates literary texts and reading experiences by defamiliarizing habitual critical methods. The boundary-crossing subjective criticism Atkins calls for is now finding a significant place for itself in the current critical landscape. For a lively and informative conversation on the pros and cons of this New Belletrism, consult the essays by Diane P. Freedman and others collected in H. Aram Veeser, ed., *Confessions of the Critics* (New York and London: Routledge, 1996). In his "Introduction: The Case for Confessional Criticism," Veeser states: "Autocritography takes us across a threshold: there was scholarship before it, and after it, and they are not the same" (xxiii).

Illustrations and Photographs

Steinbeck's Hermes typewriter ....dust jacket cover

John Steinbeck life mask by Ritch Lovejoy....................frontispiece

The Steinbeck family reading at home 8
Steinbeck's letter to Paul Caswell..29
John Steinbeck on the set of *O. Henry's Full House*......................34
Steinbeck's letter to the Pierpont Morgan Library..........................39
Title page of Steinbeck's copy of *Prince Otto*..................................109
Autograph manuscript page of Steinbeck's
Grapes of Wrath journal..147
Steinbeck's postcard announcing title of
The Grapes of Wrath... 158-159
First page of *The Grapes of Wrath* manuscript............................171
Elizabeth Otis's Western Union wire to Steinbeck 181
First page of *The Grapes of Wrath* typescript.................................187
Steinbeck on cover of *Saturday Review* 210
Carol Steinbeck in 1941..237
Publicity photograph of Gwyn Conger...241
Judith Diem's oil painting of John Steinbeck.................................256
Ellwood Graham's charcoal sketch of Steinbeck............................257
Steinbeck's Hermes typewriter 286

Abbreviations

All references to these frequently utilized standard primary and secondary works will be abbreviated as shown below and noted parenthetically in the following essays in *Steinbeck's Typewriter*. Wherever possible I have used the current trade editions of Steinbeck's texts, in nearly all cases available exclusively from Penguin Books as a regular Penguin paperback or in Penguin's Twentieth-Century Classics format. For complete publishing information consult the final chapter, "A Bibliography of Books By and About John Steinbeck."

CJS Thomas Fensch, ed., *Conversations with John Steinbeck* (1988).

EE John Steinbeck, *East of Eden* (1952; reprinted 1992 as Penguin Twentieth-Century Classic with introduction by David Wyatt).

LTE Florian Shasky and Susan Riggs, eds., *Letters to Elizabeth* (1978).

S&C Thomas Fensch, *Steinbeck and Covici: The Story of a Friendship* (1979).

SCSU Susan F. Riggs, *A Catalogue of the John Steinbeck Collection at Stanford University* (1980). [Quotations of Steinbeck's unpublished letters and manuscripts at Stanford are transcribed directly from the originals; paranthetical references to Riggs's annotated catalogue are included to provide provenance, chronology, and location.]

SLL Elaine Steinbeck and Robert Wallsten, eds., *Steinbeck: A Life in Letters* (1975; reprinted 1992 by Penguin).

SR Robert DeMott, *Steinbeck's Reading: A Catalogue of Books Owned and Borrowed* (1984).

TAJS Jackson Benson, *The True Adventures of John Steinbeck, Writer* (1984; reprinted 1992 by Penguin).

WD John Steinbeck, *Working Days: The Journals of "The Grapes of Wrath,"* ed. Robert DeMott (1989; reprinted 1990 by Penguin).

JN John Steinbeck, *Journal of a Novel: The "East of Eden" Letters* (1969; reprinted 1990 by Penguin).

PART ONE: CREATIVE READING/CREATIVE WRITING

"There is then creative reading as well as creative writing."
—Ralph Waldo Emerson, "The American Scholar" (1837)

"I seem to have had a fortunate childhood for a writer. My grandfather, Sam'l Hamilton, loved good writing, and he knew it too, and he had some bluestocking daughters, among them my mother. Thus it was that in Salinas, in the great dark walnut bookcase with the glass doors, there were strange and wonderful things to be found. My parents never offered them, and the glass doors obviously guarded them, and so I pilfered from that case."
—John Steinbeck, *Travels with Charley* (1962)

"In one way or another, then, all writers are forced to enter into a dialogue or debate with their predecessors, recycling bits and pieces of earlier texts, giving them a fresh application, a nuance of redefinition, a radically new meaning, a different function, an unanticipated elaboration. Since antecedent texts can neither be ignored nor repeated verbatim . . . this process of infinite combination and permutation of texts, of 'simultaneous activation' of texts, is ineluctable in the making of literature."
—Robert Alter, *The Pleasures of Reading in an Ideological Age* (1990)

"Things that Happened to Me": Steinbeck's Varieties of Reading Experience

> "Every book is a quotation; and every house is a quotation out of all forests and mines and stone-quarries; and every man is a quotation from all his ancestors."
> —Ralph Waldo Emerson, "Quotation and Originality" (1859)

> ". . . our theory should allow that a book may well be a revelation in spite of errors and passions and deliberate human composition, if only it be a true record of the inner experiences. . . ."
> —William James, *The Varieties of Religious Experience* (1902)

> "'It's almost impossible to read a fine thing without wanting to [write] a fine thing.'"
> —John Whiteside, in *The Pastures of Heaven* (1932)

From that decisive moment in childhood when he resolved to unlock the "secret" language of Sir Thomas Malory's *Morte d'Arthur* and again later as a teenager when he read Sir Walter Scott and Robert Louis Stevenson on his own and vowed to become a writer, John Steinbeck set in motion an energetic, appreciative disposition toward writing, the world of books, and the act of reading that remained linked in varying degrees of engagement for the rest of his life. In a career which had its share of personal and artistic triumphs and failures, Steinbeck's reading, his residence in the creative habitation of books (to extend his own "home" metaphor), comprised an abiding and ineluctable activity. At times, his passionate involvement not only demanded as much of his attention as his writing but even threatened to eclipse it. For Steinbeck, reading and writing constituted the creative life: at their fullest, as an ideal synergy and a more or less unified field of endeavor, both were compelling acts; furthermore, in the latter stages of his career, they became redemptive processes as well.

Steinbeck's reputation (earned mainly from his fictional achievements of the 1930s) as the impersonal, objective reporter of striking farm workers and dispossessed migrants, or as the escapist popularizer of primitive folk, has needlessly obscured his intellectual background, literary interests, and artistic methods. He was an author who read to write—one who frequently depended on various kinds of documents to supply, augment, highlight, or temper his reconstruction of personal experience and to contextualize his view of cultural reality. To think of him simply as an exponent of primary, empirical experience—a naive realist in inspiration and a straightforward journalist in execution—is to disregard his attitude not only toward the complexities of his art but toward an entire arena of vicarious experiences. No less abundantly than physical reality, scientific observation, or oral legends, the world of books provided Steinbeck with a relational matrix of imaginative enrichment, intellectual sustenance, and practical resources. Indeed, he often read so intently that the traditional distinctions between primary and secondary experience disappeared. "Certain books," he told Ben Abramson in 1936, "were realer than experience—*Crime and Punishment* was like that and *Madame Bovary* and parts of *Paradise Lost* and things of George Eliot and *The Return of the Native*. I read all of these things when I was very young and I remember them not at all as books but as things that happened to me" (*TAJS*, 23).

Steinbeck's admission has come to stand as his most celebrated comment on his reading, yet it has also been treated more or less as an anomaly, as though many of his critics refused to believe that he had a deeply reflective intellectual side. Consequently, with the exception of a few important critical/biographical studies published in the past two decades, Steinbeck's confession has been valued more for its list of specific titles than for the larger issue—the causal relationship between reading and Steinbeck's mind and art. Steinbeck's cultural and literary appropriations—not arrived at without struggle and debate—are still subjects worthy of continuing interrogation. Compared to the analytical work on his contemporaries Hemingway and Faulkner, so few of the antecedent "echoes" in Steinbeck's texts have been scrutinized that much remains to be pursued before a full view of his creative patterns can emerge.[1] Steinbeck was thoroughly implicated in most facets of his reading life so that his relationship with his literary past was not innocent but was in fact so tangled that it calls into question many previously held attitudes about the extent and employment of his borrowings. His involvement further problematizes the traditional view of his imagination which was more opportunistic, even cannibalistic, than many scholars allow.

Beginning in the early 1920s, with his derivative short stories, poems, and drama (a sequel to George Bernard Shaw's *Caesar and Cleopatra*), and extending through even the most original of his publications during the next four decades, Steinbeck's reading informed and enriched his art. It was informed, that is, in the widest sense, ranging from oblique suggestions and resonant echoes to direct influences and even some "shameless" borrowings (*SLL*, 95). This is not to accuse him of mean-spirited, out-and-out plagiarism, which he consciously avoided to the best of his knowledge and characteristically abhorred.[2] It is, rather, to say that being "informed" signals a wide range of interpretative possibilities for his art and admits an enormous latitude of interaction between the ground of reality and his fictive imagination, between agent and subject. Obviously he never intentionally set out to steal another writer's work or slavishly duplicate what had already been done by someone else. However, as his manuscripts, letters, and journals attest, in the act of composition he was vulnerable to every type of influence without always being able (or willing) to discriminate their origins. Like so many other American novelists working in the expressive tradition whose imaginative appetites were rapacious—Hawthorne, Stowe, Melville, Twain, Wharton, Hemingway, and Faulkner come to mind—Steinbeck was not above pilfering from the library of available material, the storehouse of literary artifacts. Generally—and this is what matters most—he transmuted those appropriated elements, not always without struggle, in such a way that in most cases they became his own fictive property, subsumed in the particularities of his narrative voice. Texts acted on him, of course, but he acted on them, too, and the result was dialogic, a dance of give and take between the acts of quoting and inventing.

Whether Steinbeck borrowed directly from his sources, which he once proposed to Berton Braley was how "literatures are built," or whether he steeped himself in the atmosphere and "texture" of his preparatory research, reading had a "profound" effect on his work.[3] In fact, for a writer who has traditionally been considered an heir to the rigorously mimetic strain of realism in American literature, it is important to note that nearly all of Steinbeck's thirty full-length books include references or allusions to other works of literature. They also show a frequent orientation toward literary models and categories and portray a large gallery of characters in the act of reading (or commenting upon) literature (*Tortilla Flat, Of Mice and Men,* and *The Red Pony* are chief exceptions) or less specific cultural texts. Steinbeck's gaze in this regard is reminiscent of Henry James's, for there is something hauntingly modernist—even postmodernist—in his gestures. Taken together, these strategies open up endless corridors of reference, allusion, echoes, linkages; they constitute an important aspect of Steinbeck's signature as a self-willed author. Such markers were his way of inhabiting the interior dimensions of his fiction, not only by creating a verifiable realm of historicity and intellectual immediacy, but also as a means of indulging his role as a literary outlaw and exercising his delight in fictive play. Even *In Dubious Battle,* Steinbeck's most sustained nonteleological fiction, contains a self-portrait of the artist as reader: Jim Nolan's acquaintance with the key works of Plato, Herodotus, Gibbon, Macauley, Schopenhauer, and others reflects his enrollment in Steinbeck's own curriculum of vital knowledge and provides a layered dimension of relevance, a further twist on the young Nolan's "education" in the school of hard knocks.

What differs from book to book, however, is the visible emphasis Steinbeck placed on his sources, the degree of inspiration or guidance he acknowledged from them, and the tonal effect he wished to achieve. Generally, the objective quality, contemporary social/economic content, and omniscient point of view that—together or in part—characterizes his writing through the early 1940s camouflaged or minimized the *apparent* presence of his borrowings. (The comedic tone of *Tortilla Flat* certainly disguised its parallels with *Morte d'Arthur*; the polyphonism of *The Grapes of Wrath* thoroughly subordinated Tom Collins's helpful migrant camp reports.) And although the textual choices of characters in the act of reading were drawn from Steinbeck's own preferences, they often served ironic effects. Inordinately "bookish" characters—James Flower in *Cup of Gold* and Elizabeth McGreggor in *To a God Unknown*—are satirized as inept or judged to be unprepared for the harshness of "real" life. The reading habits of others, including Junius Maltby and Richard and John Whiteside in *The Pastures of Heaven*, are portrayed as individually salutary but held to be suspicious by the community because they defer physical action or promote daydreaming. In these latter instances, Steinbeck portrayed his own attraction to an outlaw sensibility; ostensibly harmless, reading becomes nothing less than a revenge against middle-class complacency, an indictment of straight-laced righteousness.

However, in Steinbeck's later writings, from *Cannery Row* onward, there is more overt dependence on literary influences and occasions, as well as several testimonies of indebtedness. The whole drama of tradition is fittingly climaxed in the last book of his life, *America and Americans*, which extolls the virtues of reading and creates, in effect, a public forum for Steinbeck's own lifelong private beliefs. Such artful acknowledgements represent a culmination of his interest and provide evidence that Steinbeck—perhaps as a bold way of compensating for his attenuated artistic power—elevated reading to symbolic and even moral and political levels in the best of his postwar books. It was with good reason that, when he joined William Faulkner, Saul Bellow, Donald Hall, and other American writers on President Eisenhower's People to People campaign in late 1956 to come up with ways to counteract Soviet propaganda in Eastern European countries, Steinbeck suggested sending books that show Americans as they truly are, with faults, weaknesses, and all; such books, Steinbeck knew from his own experiences behind the Iron Curtain, would be "revered . . . treasured . . . distributed" (*TAJS*, 802).

1

Steinbeck's sensitivity to the alluring world of language and gesture which he encountered in books awakened his artistic temperament and helped sustain his decision to become a writer. Beth, his older sister, remembered that the Steinbeck house on Central Avenue in Salinas was "full of books" that were always available. "The choice was ours," she said, "and there were no pressures ever put on us—for or against." Her recollection is corroborated by Steinbeck's statement in *Travels with Charley*, but his version also reveals another twist. He judged that he "had a fortunate childhood for a writer," because "in the great dark walnut bookcase with the glass doors, there were strange and wonderful things to be found. My parents never offered them . . . and so I pilfered from that case."[4]

Thievery only heightened the moment, for reading already made up a living legacy in the Steinbeck family. It was an intellectual heritage, a qualitative factor almost atmospheric in character, that distinguished Steinbeck's childhood and provided artistic capital he drew on for the rest of his career. It has been widely acknowledged that his "bluestocking" mother, Olive Hamilton Steinbeck, affected his early choices (*TAJS*, 18). She had been a country school teacher whose eclectic taste in literature was later replicated by Elizabeth McGreggor in *To a God Unknown* and Miss Molly Morgan in *The Pastures of Heaven.* To her influence must be added that of his father, John Ernst Steinbeck, who passed on to his son a love for Greek and Roman classics. Steinbeck affectionately dramatized that legacy in the penultimate chapter of *The Pastures of Heaven.* John Whiteside "always remembered how his father read to him the three great authors, Herodotus, Thucydides, Xenophon." *The History, The Peloponnesian Wars,* and *The Anabasis* contained "everything mankind is capable of. . . ." Similarly the Bible and *Pilgrim's Progress* were in the air around him, and his uncles "exuded Shakespeare" (*AKA*, xi). With his sisters, especially Mary, Steinbeck read and discussed Malory's *Morte* and spent long hours with their other favorite, Homer's *Iliad*.[5] Behind his immediate family stood the tutelary presence of his grandfather, Samuel Hamilton. His love for and knowledge of "good writing" (*TWC*, 37) affected all of his children and inspired the future novelist. Steinbeck was an infant when his grandfather died in 1904, but he was such a powerful legendary figure on the maternal side of the novelist's family that Steinbeck resurrected him as the mythic hero of *East of Eden.* In that novel (the closest Steinbeck ever came to writing sustained autobiography), Samuel is portrayed as an exemplary reader, and the Hamiltonian habit of mind, its hunger for sacred books, is explicitly established as Steinbeck's rightful heritage.

Thus, by the time Steinbeck graduated from Salinas High School in 1919, he had an unusually good background in world literature. Besides the Bible, Malory, and Shakespeare, he had a solid grounding in ancient classics, including Tacitus, Virgil, and Suetonius (later remembered as a "joy"). He also had read widely in poetry, including Wordsworth, Keats, Shelley (he was especially fond of "To a Skylark"), Robert Browning, Longfellow,

John Steinbeck, with his mother and father and a sister, reading in the living room of the Steinbeck house, 132 Central Avenue, Salinas, CA, 1918. John Steinbeck was about 16 years old at the time.

Courtesy of Valley Guild, Salinas, CA, and the John Steinbeck Library, Salinas, CA.

Whitman (especially "Song of Myself"), and Tennyson (never one of his favorite poets because he was too prim for Steinbeck's taste), as well as Californians Edwin Markham and Joaquin Miller. His interests in fiction and prose generally ran toward adventure and romance: Sir Walter Scott, Marco Polo, Alexander Dumas, Jack London, James Branch Cabell, Zane Grey, Robert Louis Stevenson, Jules Verne, Mark Twain, and fugitive items like *A Tramp's Life*. He also read Poe, Booth Tarkington, Gertrude Atherton, Harold Bell Wright, David Grayson, and acted the minor part of Justin Rowson in the Salinas High School commencement production of Harry Smith's comedy, *Mrs. Bumpstead-Leigh*. In addition, numerous periodicals were regularly available in the Steinbeck household, including *Youth's Companion, National Geographic*, and *Century Magazine* (*TAJS*, 18).

Steinbeck entered Stanford in September 1919 and left after the spring semester of 1925, without having earned a degree. The first half of his academic career was dismal. Out of eight possible academic semesters from spring 1920 through fall 1923, he was enrolled twice in a total of eight courses. He withdrew from all of them, preferring instead nomadic stints as a laborer and farm hand in the country below Salinas. His second stab at college was more consistent and respectable. From the winter semester of 1923 through spring semester of 1925, he was enrolled seven out of ten possible semesters and earned grades or credit in thirty-two of thirty-five courses. His recent abortive attempts at writing, however, brought home to him the need for a firmer knowledge of literature and writing techniques. Accordingly he enrolled in eleven English courses (these included several in Journalism, such as News Writing, and Feature Articles; and in Composition, such as Essay Writing, Narrative Writing, Exposition, and Oral Debate), and three Classical Literature courses, including the History of Rome, and Greek Tragedy.[6] Along the way he encountered some memorable and inspiring classes: Margery Bailey's English 10, a literary survey; Professor William Herbert Carruth's English 35, Versification (one of Steinbeck's six A's at Stanford); and Edith Mirrielees's English 136, Short Story Writing, which he later remembered as one of the best he ever took (*TAJS*, 58). Under the enthusiastic direction of Professors Bailey and Mirrielees, Steinbeck added Boswell and Dickens, Chekhov, and especially Maupassant to his store of formal reading. The latter's "The Piece of String" was, Steinbeck felt, a model of deft short story construction, and several years later he recommended imitating it as a tonic to George Albee, a struggling writer (*SR*, 162).

Even in his reputable phase, however, Steinbeck did not let Stanford dictate the terms of his real education. Like Melville, he swam in libraries; like Faulkner, college did not prevent him from pursuing his vocation. That vocation was writing and, the older Steinbeck grew, the more committed he became to building a suitable background for the task. His incipient notion of creative doubling—the bonding and mirroring of reading and writing—gained enormous impetus in Bailey's and Mirrielees's classes and carried over to his own experience. In the first half of the 1920s, when he wasn't working odd jobs or on the lam from Stanford, he was reading voraciously and writing, though not always with definite direction. "I went flibberty geblut," he recalled to Pascal Covici, "and got to going to the library and reading what I wanted to read instead of what was required" (*JN*, 102). In one "maniacal" span in 1924, for instance, he devoured *The Book of the Dead* and works by Molière, Vincente Ibañez, Katherine Gerould, Rebecca West, Casanova, Pushkin, and Turgenev (*SLL*, 8). A little later, between 1924 and 1926, according to his Stanford classmates Carlton Sheffield and Robert Cathcart, Steinbeck plowed through some unspecified novels by Ouida (Marie Louise De La Ramee), which he thought "comic stuff," studied books on magic and alchemy from Stanford University's library, read Normal Douglas's *South Wind*, Ben Hecht's *Count Bruga*, fiction by Carl Van Vechten, and was already aware of Hemingway's influential style (*SR*, lviii). In the spring of 1926, having left Stanford for good and temporarily living in New York City, Steinbeck read *The Magnificent Idler*, a newly published fictionalized biography of Walt Whitman by Cameron Rogers and James Branch Cabell's *The Silver Stallion* and *The Heart of Black Papua*.

In practice, though, his writing was not very successful. He could analyze "fine" writing (and, as a member of Stanford's English Club, discuss it *con brio*), but he could not yet produce it himself. Throughout the 1920s and into the early 1930s, his fiction showed a pronounced subservience to popular literary models. His youthful efforts, such as "A Lady in Infra-Red" (the germ of *Cup of Gold*) and "The Gifts of Iban" (by "John Stern"), were indebted to the literary fantasies of Cabell, Donn Byrne, James Stephens, and Arthur Machen. In *Cup of Gold* he began to outgrow the "Cabbelyo-Byrneish preciousness" (*SLL*, 17), substituting instead echoes of Synge's lilting language, the descriptiveness of Alexander Esquemeling's *Buccaneers of America*, and the allure of Welsh legendary tales like *The Red Book of Hergest*. But it took several years for Steinbeck to expel the patently formulaic strain from his system, and even after several revisions the effects of imitation still linger. In this apprentice period, Steinbeck's work manifests the unconscious struggle for authority between his own sensibility and those values which he acquired through reading. Both aspects, both competing stresses, exist simultaneously in *Cup of Gold* and in the unpublished "Murder at Full Moon." In the latter, Steinbeck's struggle with opposing tendencies is clearly exemplified.

This 233-page hack novel was written, Steinbeck boasted, in "nine days," ostensibly to discharge a "debt" (*SLL*, 32).[7] The debt was financial, though in a symbolic sense it was also literary, because "Murder" is one of those miscarriages a young writer has to endure in order to reach a higher stage of development. The plot is youthful and thoroughly manufactured; its style is wooden and blatantly literary. The novel is slavishly influenced by Poe (Steinbeck wrote it under a *nom de plume*, "Peter Pym"), Jung's *The Psychology of Dementia Praecox* (1909), and the formula detective fiction of S. S. Van Dine (Willard H. Wright), J. S. Fletcher, Edgar Wallace, and others popular in the early 1930s. This morbid amalgamation—Benson calls it "Jungian-flavored mumbo jumbo" (*TAJS*, 207)—is partly rectified, however, by the narrator's self-parodying tone (Steinbeck called it "burlesque"), which indicates that he was not only attuned to the gothic aspects of Poe's fiction but also to the hoax-like posture of his narrative voice and the appropriating grasp of Poe's borrowings. In making fun of the conventions of literary consciousness, formula fiction, and self-reflexiveness, Steinbeck probably achieved a better understanding about the slippery nature of attribution and influence. In making the novel's protagonist, Maximilian Sergius Hoogle, a perceptive critic of crime literature, Steinbeck also limned the first of several reader-heroes in his fiction, characters like Mayor Orden in *The Moon Is Down*, Doc in *Cannery Row*, and Samuel Hamilton in *East of Eden*, all capable of acting meaningfully on their knowledge.

Concurrently, then, Steinbeck's perceptions were changing. In *To a God Unknown*, his reliance on myth (via Sir James Frazer's *The Golden Bough*) and the psychology of the unconscious (via several of Carl Jung's books) is still pronounced, but it became a functional aspect of characterization rather than an imposed structural device. Between 1929 and 1932, in addition to reading in those related areas of anthropology and deep mythology (aided and abetted by his lively discussions with Joseph Campbell), Steinbeck wrote constantly. In the face of frequent rejections from publishers and an increasing "disgust and lack of faith" in his own work (*SLL*, 45), he forged ahead. "In the last year and a half," he told Amassa Miller in December 1931, "I have written the Dissonant Symphony, the detective story, six short stories, part of a novel that is too huge for me just now and "The Pastures of Heaven" (*SLL*, 51). One of those six unpublished stories, "The White Sister of Fourteenth Street," is set in New York City, where Steinbeck had done a stint in 1925 and 1926 (*SCSU*, 142). Jackson Benson suggests it is "a pretty good attempt at light comedy" (*TAJS*, 98), but arguably the story more readily shows Steinbeck's increasing facility with a stringent strain of realism and an ironic point of view. In a letter of 22 May 1929, to Katherine Beswick, Steinbeck already had adumbrated a view of tragedy that could be applied to common characters. He had discovered elements in the fiction of Theodore Dreiser (Elsie in "White Sister" is reminiscent of Carrie Meeber), O. Henry, Aldous Huxley, and Ring Lardner more compatible with his emerging sensibility than the traditional Aristotelean concept, in which, he claimed, "only high persons and high causes can make high tragedy" (*SCSU*, 9). In addition, his recent reading of other serious artists, like Joseph Conrad, Sherwood Anderson, and Ernest Hemingway, was beginning to pay dividends for his sense of theme, characterization, and dialogue, and—in the story cycle or composite novel form of *The Pastures of Heaven*—dividends for his execution of structure as well. Certainly, Steinbeck's critical eye had sharpened. He vilified the pulp writers who lived in nearby Carmel, announced to George Albee that Beverly Nichols's fiction made him "sick" (*SLL*, 49), and looked with disdain on his own "feeble and childish" productions (*SLL*, 51).

In 1930 Steinbeck had married Carol Henning, moved with her to Pacific Grove, on California's Monterey Peninsula, and began the most momentous epoch of his life. He entered the 1930s as a novice, despite his one published book, but ended the decade as one of its most acclaimed writers. Along the way he dedicated himself completely to the development of his art.

Even though, in the Depression, books were among the first things people did without, he continued to write anyway, managing (after the publication of *The Pastures of Heaven* and *To a God Unknown*, in 1932 and 1933) to rekindle his faith and persevere through extremely pinched personal and economic conditions.

He also managed to launch the most intensive reading program he had ever undertaken. It was a process of education that profoundly affected his writing for the next two decades. He didn't add much to his private library until after 1935, when, with the publication of *Tortilla Flat*, his novels began making money, so he depended on the Pacific Grove Public Library and the remarkable collection of Edward F. Ricketts, whom he had met in 1930. Marine biologist, ecologist, owner of Pacific Biological Laboratories on Cannery Row, and later co-author of *Between Pacific Tides* and *Sea of Cortez*, Ricketts was a man of enormous intellectual energy, enthusiasm, and knowledge. Before a fire destroyed his business in 1936, his library contained the most impressive collection of marine texts in the area and also reflected his related interests in foreign languages, anthropology, myth, philosophy, travel, poetry, drama, and fiction. In short, Steinbeck found not only a soul mate but also a resource for books equal to his own omnivorous habits. As one respected observer stated, "The first time I saw John Steinbeck, he was reading a book at Ed's lab."[8]

In their periods of intellectual intimacy, from 1933-36, and again in 1940-41, Ricketts encouraged Steinbeck's interest in new vistas of scientific thought. Thus he became the first of several intellectual mentors Steinbeck looked to not so much for blind guidance but for fertile discussion and debate during generative research periods (Joseph Campbell, Chase Horton, and Eugene Vinaver were others). For instance, when Steinbeck developed his encompassing theory of the social phalanx or group unit in 1933, Ricketts served as a sounding board for the writer's ideas and contributed much biological documentation (especially the organizational patterns from W. C. Allee's 1931 study, *Animal Aggregations*) necessary to establish the theory's legitimacy. On Steinbeck's part—and this would remain true all his life—he took those leads enthusiastically and burrowed into not only books on economics and sociology but also works on geography, anthropology, myth, and physics. What Steinbeck unearthed from these seemingly disparate sources was "gratifying": Ellsworth Huntington, Oswald Spengler, Vladimir Ouspenski, Carl Jung, Robert Briffault, Erwin Schrödinger, Max Planck, Neils Bohr, Albert Einstein, and Werner Heisenberg, he reported on 30 June 1933 to Carlton Sheffield, "have all started heading in the same direction . . . toward *my* thesis. This in itself would indicate the beginning of a new phalanx or group unit" (*SR*, 57; *TAJS*, 270; my emphasis). With additional documentation from Harold Lamb, and from the holistic treatises of John Elof Boodin and William Emerson Ritter, Steinbeck built a solid foundation of knowledge, a thick context for his chosen area. In the years from 1933 to 1936 he worked furiously to translate his knowledge "into the symbolism of fiction" (*SLL*, 76). When philosophical thought and artistic structure finally did cohere, in "The Vigilante," "Leader of the People," *In Dubious Battle*, and *The Grapes of Wrath*, he completed the circuit of his intentions and added a new literary dimension to the phalanx unit he had drawn upon.

While Ricketts was an incomparable instigator and even performed midwifery for Steinbeck's ideas at this stage, it is erroneous to think that Steinbeck oscillated solely in Ricketts's rainbow, for his fiction of the 1930s shows other distinct literary bearings, other tropisms. For all his originality as a thinker and scientist, Ricketts was not a creative writer. His exciting, but eclectic, philosophical essays and his notes for *Sea of Cortez* show that he was generally more concerned with theme and content than with the nuances of structure, motivation, language, and texture necessary for the complexities of fiction. As a scientist, Ricketts used his sources differently from the way Steinbeck did as a novelist.

The poetry of Robinson Jeffers is a case in point. The famous line from "Roan Stallion"—"Humanity is the mould to break away from, the crust to break/through"—instigated Ricketts's essay on transcendence, "The Philosophy of 'Breaking Through.'" Where it serves a didactic purpose for Ricketts, the same concept of breaking through (or "keying into") which Steinbeck employed in *In Dubious Battle, The Grapes of Wrath,* and *Cannery Row*, became an organic experience, embedded in the particular visions of fictive characters. Again, in "A Spiritual Morphology of Poetry," Ricketts ranked Jeffers (on the evidence of "Signpost") as "*an all vehicle mellow* poet" (his highest category), because the poem expressed the "heaven-beyond-the-world-beyond-the-garden."[9] To regard Steinbeck's knowledge of

Jeffers as simply another instance of adopting Ricketts's perspective distorts the picture by reducing an occasion of creative tension to third-hand borrowing. Steinbeck discovered Robinson Jeffers—and in the full implications of that act read him with awe and trepidation and not a little Bloomian anxiety—in 1932, around the time of his final revision of *To a God Unknown*, in which Steinbeck boldly recycled Jeffers's lyrical style in order to one-up him in representing California's mythic landscape.

A similar argument can be made regarding Steinbeck's premier achievement, *The Grapes of Wrath*, which is a work of such originality and power that it extends far beyond the axis of Ricketts's ideas and personality. First of all, Steinbeck espoused a more teleological and processional view of life than Ricketts was customarily comfortable with. Second, Steinbeck went farther afield in his reading of philosopher Boodin than Ricketts did. Where Ricketts preferred Boodin's 1931 *A Realistic Universe*, Steinbeck ultimately found important holistic statements in Boodin's 1934 *Three Interpretations of the Universe* which informed his novel (especially chapter 14). Third, Steinbeck relied heavily on the Bible for texture, diction, and rhythm, rather than the texts of oriental religion which Ricketts seemed to prefer. Fourth, Steinbeck's dependence on Tom Collins's government reports for much of the details, action, and incidents (especially chapters 22 to 26) represents a dimension of social and institutional dynamic in which Ricketts showed little interest. But perhaps most importantly, Steinbeck's achievement in that book had more to do with its radical technical conception than with the employment of a theme which he had worked over for the previous six years. His structural accomplishment in the novel was also conditioned by his reading of fiction, a genre Ricketts was simply less attuned to than was Steinbeck.

Steinbeck's awareness of what other writers had achieved in style and form created a model context he could depart from, and, by adding to his store of fictive alternatives, increased the confidence and freedom with which he handled his own techniques. For Steinbeck, the world's novels were benchmarks for his own fictional concerns, primary signposts in the inexhaustible multiplicity of the textual universe. (Theorists of literary influence often overlook this kind of significance.) Without belaboring the point, Malcolm Cowley's testimony is important here. Cowley was prescient in claiming that, while *The Grapes of Wrath* "is not an imitative book, it could not have been written without a whole series of experiments" to guide Steinbeck: Dos Passos's *USA*, Faulkner's *As I Lay Dying*, and Caldwell's *Tobacco Road*, to name but three prominent American examples.[10] Add to the mix these other elements: the psychological power of Dostoevsky's *Crime and Punishment*, whose "characters are the essence of mankind," Steinbeck told Martin Bidwell in 1933 (*WD*, 146-47); the epic scale and panoramic movement of Tolstoy's *War and Peace*, which Steinbeck considered his favorite novel (*SR*, 176); the metaphor of the spiritual journey in Bunyan's *Pilgrim's Progress*, which he mentions in chapter 9; and the fluid linguistic resources of John Hargrave's experimental 1935 novel *Summer Time Ends*, which Steinbeck read repeatedly, because it was "a book from which writers can learn" (*SR*, 51). Considering all these diverse sources and subtexts brings a fuller realization of just how far Steinbeck's greatest novel not only transcended the immediate sphere of Ricketts's scientific influence but also transmogrified its own literary precursors.

Steinbeck paid an enormous price for the success of his novel, however. Writing *The Grapes of Wrath* exacted a psychic toll unprecedented in his earlier experience. (The harrowing strain is recorded in the final third of *Working Days*, the day book which he kept during the novel's composition.) The effort temporarily exhausted both his sources and his resources; he admitted to Carlton Sheffield in November 1939 that he had "worked" the "clumsy" novel form as far as he could "take" it and needed to "make a new start" (*SLL*, 194). The opportunity for a fresh departure immediately presented itself in two forms, both closely associated with Ricketts. The first was a project to create a handbook to the marine ecology of the San Francisco Bay area (the book never got beyond preliminary stages); the second was *Sea of Cortez: A Leisurely Journal of Travel and Research*, which eventuated from the Steinbeck/Ricketts collecting trip on a rented purse-seiner called *The Western Flyer* to the Gulf of California in March and April of 1940. Ricketts was the presiding genius behind both these endeavors, but once again, Steinbeck did his homework enthusiastically. "I've been studying harder than I ever did in school and doing some independent research also," he told Sheffield (*SLL*, 197).

Where he had been on familiar ground in his recent fiction, here he was aware of intruding into another professional discipline. Ricketts's expertise was already established with *Between Pacific Tides* (1939), but Steinbeck had yet to "build some trust in the minds of biologists." In preparation he told Elizabeth Otis, "I have a terrific job of reading to do" (*SLL*, 196). In Los Gatos, in early 1940, then later, when he was back in Pacific Grove and working at Ricketts's lab in 1941 (separated from his first wife, Carol, and romantically involved with Gwyn Conger), Steinbeck scoured marine biology books with an eye toward establishing an encompassing ecological pattern of action and investing his own text with multiple dimensions, "four levels of statement" (*S&C*, 31).

Whether Steinbeck actually read the hundreds of recondite sources listed in the "Annotated Phyletic Catalogue and Bibliography" (covering pages 320-578) of the original edition of *Sea of Cortez* is unknown. It is certain, however, that he was thoroughly familiar with the books taken aboard *Western Flyer* and with the seven-page "General References" section of *Sea*'s first edition, for which he may have provided some annotations himself. Indeed, in July 1941, Steinbeck informed Pascal Covici that he had ". . . found a great poetry in scientific writing," which he had tried to emulate (*S&C*, 31). In the collaboration between Ricketts's journal notes and his essay on non-telological thinking (in the "Easter Sunday" chapter of *Sea of Cortez*), and Steinbeck's renewed poetical awareness that the language and structure of fiction could be transposed to accommodate an explicitly scientific subject, the result was a nonfictional prose work of startling originality and vigor, nothing less than "a new kind of writing" (*S&C*, 31).

In the wake of Steinbeck's search for a new kind of discourse for *Sea of Cortez*, he further developed his belief that reading was not an "escape" from reality but an entrance into another—usually heightened or layered—degree of reality, such as one finds in "the rich reality of Tolstoy" or in "the glowing emotion of a poem." From 1939 on, Steinbeck always claimed emphatically that his books had at least four—and, in the case of *The Grapes of Wrath*, five—levels of "statement" or meaning. Each reader's intellect and emotion "keys into" the text and allows active "participation" in its imaginative experience. "No one has ever read Treasure Island or Robinson Crusoe objectively," he wrote, because "the chief characters in both cases are . . . the skin and bones of the reader. The political satires of Gulliver have long been forgotten but the stories go on. The message . . . of a story almost invariably dies first while the participation persists."[11] Steinbeck already had created this affective quality and multidimensional level in his realistic earlier fiction, notably *Of Mice and Men, The Red Pony,* and *The Grapes of Wrath,* as well as in parts of the nonfictional *Sea of Cortez.* In the mid-1940s, however, motivated by a series of sweeping personal and psychological changes in his life, including a violent reaction against the "crap" journalism he had written as a war correspondent for the *New York Herald Tribune* in 1943 (published in 1958 as *Once There Was a War*), Steinbeck became disenchanted with a predominantly mimetic and objective approach to fiction (*SLL,* 268-81).

The idea of achieving a permanent dimension of subjective transaction between reader and writer became a central goal in his aesthetic program and propelled him to experiment with a heuristic concept of writing that combined fabular, moral, and personal elements. The multiple levels of *Cannery Row,* designed so that "people can take what they can receive out of it" (*SLL,* 273), signified a culminating turn in Steinbeck's technique toward the use of reflexive structures to express consciously artistic values. Cannery Row is, of course, an historical section of Monterey, California; more importantly for Steinbeck's aesthetic purposes, however, it is a piece of fictive geography, "a poem, a stink, a grating noise, a quality of light, a tone, a habit, a nostalgia, a dream," which is to say it is a textual site that not only invites, but demands, each reader's imaginative participation.[12] "The Word," he writes, "is a symbol and a delight which sucks up men and scenes, trees, plants, factories, and Pekinese. Then the Thing becomes the Word and back to Thing again, but warped and woven into a fantastic pattern" (*CR,* 17). The metaphor, a kind of *mise en abyme,* could as easily serve to describe Steinbeck's view of the creative process.

Not surprisingly, Steinbeck situates the figure of Doc (based on Ed Ricketts), a model reader and interpreter of texts, at the center of that imaginative geography, a site of historical referentiality and imaginative representation whose dimensions change so quickly that it requires active participation to remain abreast. In his "library" at Western Biological Laboratory, Doc habitually reads not just "books of all kinds" (*CR,* 29), particularly the Sanskrit poem *Black Marigolds,* which moves him to tears (*CR,* 184-85), but musical texts and natural texts, too—the tides and the weather. His ability to read all manner of encoded signs and texts empowers Doc in certain ways and only makes more ironic his transcendent loneliness. In short, Doc becomes a practitioner of reader-response criticism, long before such concepts were widely broadcast or codified by theorists. In creating the necessity for readers to negotiate the spatial *architexture* of the novel, Steinbeck became a precursor of postmodernist fictive tendencies.

During the next few years, though he was called down for being frivolous by influential socially-minded critics and reviewers, Steinbeck moved increasingly toward private issues of creative choice, individual consciousness, and inherited legacy. Exemplary figures such as Jesus Christ, Joan of Arc, and Mexican revolutionary Emiliano Zapata, the subject of his 1951 filmscript for Elia Kazan, or allegorical characters such as Juan Chicoy in *The Wayward Bus* and Juana and Kino in *The Pearl,* captured his interest as literary subjects as sites of intense psychological struggle. His new projects helped crystallize his belief, espoused in a letter to John O'Hara on 8 June 1949, that the writer's main duty is to "preserve and foster the principle of the preciousness of the individual mind." Responding as much emotionally to the twin 1948 disasters of Ricketts's death and his divorce from Gwyn as he was intellectually to the global threat of Soviet hegemony in the Cold War era, Steinbeck abandoned his theories of phalanx: "The group ungoverned by individual thinking is a horrible destructive principle" (*SLL,* 359-60). At the turn of the decade Steinbeck's reading and writing was a vital force in his individual growth and a personal political rebuke to "the creeping paralysis that is coming out of the Kremlin, the death of art and thought . . ." (*SLL,* 403).

While he was planning "Salinas Valley," the novel that would eventually become *East of Eden,* Steinbeck increasingly came to regard reading as a lodestone of his own turmoil and as a means of personal catharsis. His reaction to T. E. Lawrence's 1937 edition of Charles Montague Doughty's *Travels in Arabia Deserta* (1888) was a case in point. "I am glad to have it," he told Pascal Covici, on 22 January 1949. "I think that it is the greatest secular prose in English that I know. Doughty makes the language a great stone with designs of metal and diamond and obsidian. It is good to have it here to see what can be done with the language. I do not think it was easy for him to write. No such sense of ease and flow ever came without great and tearing effort" (*SLL,* 347-48; *S&C,* 105). To help with his own tearing effort, Steinbeck asked Covici to get him "complete catalogues of Everyman, Random House and other libraries" so he could replace the books he needed which Gwyn refused to relinquish. "Isn't it odd," he continued, "that having stripped me of everything else, she also retains the tools of the trade from which she is living?" (*SLL*, 349). During the following couple of months, Covici dutifully sent Steinbeck catalogues of Random House's Modern Library, Dutton's Everyman Library, Oxford's Classical Library, and of course Viking's Portable Library, from which the novelist could choose selected titles (*S&C*, 112, 128-30).

The reconstruction of his personal library and the habit of mind that regarded books not simply as material possessions, but as essential to his trade and to the well-being of his soul, stands in large part behind the best of Steinbeck's remaining writing. Whereas in the past, Steinbeck's reading served a generally supportive function in his novels, now, with his acceptance of a new set of narratological values, the act of reading itself became a thematic subject in his work and formed a stratum of "deeply personal" (*SLL*, 360) truth no less important than outward reality. This subjective, or reflexive, interior dimension was especially important in *East of Eden*, Steinbeck's major achievement in the post-World War II years. An examination of how his reading figured into that novel should help clarify its purpose and provide an anatomy of Steinbeck's hungry imagination at work.

2

Beginning with his reflexive tonal use of *Black Marigolds* and his thematic employment of the *Tao Teh Ching* in *Cannery Row*, Steinbeck's attitude toward reading as a way of apprehending the world and as a means of framing and refracting experience not only became more assertive but took on an almost numinous cast. In 1951, while he was writing *East of Eden*, he published a brief essay, "Some Random and Randy Thoughts on Books." Aside from humorous and occasionally prophetic statements about commercial marketing procedures, Steinbeck also observed that a book is "sacred"—"one of the few authentic magics our species has created."[13] The sacrosanct nature of books and the creative tradition of reading formed a seductive impulse in Steinbeck's imagination during the *East of Eden* period and provided him with various direct sources to sustain his all-important resurrection of an earlier era, as well as the inspiration to conceive the novel in a self-conscious fictive tradition that he saw extending from Cervantes through Melville, Sherwood Anderson, André Gide, and himself. His frequent excursions into reading produced a heightened sense of purpose in *East of Eden* that complemented his desire to continue the survival of his family's intellectual legacy and helps to explain why he wrote the novel as though it were his "last book," a synthesis of "all styles, all techniques, all poetry" (*JN*, 8). "This is not a new nor an old fashioned book," he wrote on 20 March 1951, "but my culling of all books plus my own invention" (*JN*, 31). With that revealing announcement, emphasizing the dialectical gestures of "culling" or careful consideration and sifting on one hand, and "invention" or open creativity on the other, the binary nature of Steinbeck's project proclaimed itself. When the doors of Steinbeck's imagination swung open, they opened as wide toward his own personal history as they did toward a library of antecedent texts. "Original power," Emerson says in "Quotation and Originality," "is usually accompanied with assimilating power."

Because of its autobiographical nature, *East of Eden* announced a metamorphosis in Steinbeck's fictional vision, technique, and temperament. He was, in a sense, beginning all over, reinventing himself as a writer and as a person. His concept of fictional propriety evolved toward a more open, expressive form as a vehicle to address a new range of personal convictions. He refused to bow any longer to the tyranny of omniscient technique, and he insisted that in *East of Eden*, "I am in it and I don't for a moment pretend not to be" (*JN*, 24). For Steinbeck, being "in" his book meant that a whole vista of artistic freedoms had opened up. The technical license implicit in his bold departure also included his right to appropriate suitable materials from his readings. In his hunger to fulfill the daunting obligations of *East of Eden*'s epical design and subject, Steinbeck summoned a variety of literary and documentary sources which he employed to express his attitude toward characters, to discharge his thematic purpose and formal design, to provide factual information, and to extend the novel's pietistic consequences.

Literary allusions and references clarify Steinbeck's method of characterization in *East of Eden* and offer commentary on the direction and meaning of its plot. Not all Steinbeck's choices underscore cultural continuity, however. For example, Cathy Ames's entrance and exit in the novel are purposely associated with her fractured reading of Lewis Carroll's *Alice's Ad-*

ventures in Wonderland, a work of fantasy which symbolizes her habits of secrecy and isolation and lead her to escape into the fantasy of suicide (*EE,* 552). Joe Valery reads Harold Bell Wright's enormously popular melodrama, *The Winning of Barbara Worth,* his attention held by the novel's optimism (*EE,* 555). These examples of literary misprision underscore each character's distorted self-concept. In the same vein, Aron Trask's eventual demise is prefigured in his quirky, unexamined vision of university life, which he probably got "from the [Gustav] Doré illustrations of Dante's *Inferno* with its massed and radiant angels" (*EE,* 523).

More often than not, however, Steinbeck's allusions to prior works function positively to provide a kind of link to generative scenes from his past. The books associated with Samuel Hamilton, Steinbeck's maternal grandfather, indicate a surprising depth of character, spiritual vitality, and intellectual curiosity commensurate with his role as *East of Eden*'s mythic hero. Besides his self-sufficiency and practical expertise, Samuel's uniqueness stems from his love of books and his ability to use them. Samuel pursues his reading with zeal and, by borrowing books from his wealthy neighbors, "had read many more of the Delmars' books than the Delmars had" (*EE,* 39). Samuel's worldly poverty belies his imaginative wealth. True to Steinbeck's longstanding activist belief, Samuel's reading is even considered a potentially dangerous and suspect act, but it is necessary for his survival, because survival must be regarded as more than the ability to be financially successful, or to "bring in a crop or keep a scrap of cloth on his children's backs." Even this most original of characters, however, is given to "quoting," to use Emerson's term for the mind alive with written traditions; in a refracted sense, Samuel functions as a metonym for Steinbeck's reclamatory project.

Among the books Samuel owns, Steinbeck refers explicitly to *Dr. Gunn's Family Medicine,* William James's two-volume *Principles of Psychology,* Marcus Aurelius's *Meditations,* and the Bible. In a capacious sense, all four works minister to human survival. Each book speaks to a vital part of Samuel's temperament: Gunn for his body, James for his mind and senses, Marcus Aurelius for his moral and ethical will, and the Bible—his preeminent text—for his soul. The most enduring legacy within the novel revolves around Samuel's interpretation of the Bible: "'Give me a used Bible and I will, I think, be able to tell you about a man by the places that are edged with the dirt of seeking fingers'" (*EE*, 267). His knowledge of the Old Testament, especially his fascination with the Cain-Abel story in Genesis, literally provides him with names for the Trask twins and helps establish a fragile bond between the Hamiltons and the Trasks. Symbolically Samuel confers existence on Adam's children by granting them the gift of identity, for which survival becomes a choice: "'Caleb and Aron—now you are people and you have joined the fraternity and you have the right to be damned'" (*EE*, 272). In centering the Bible as an embedded text within *East of Eden*, Steinbeck sought to echo its primary resonance of sacredness and to keep alive traces of its purity, insofar as it is possible to do so in a fallen state.

Samuel, of all the characters, is best able to balance these words and texts. Indeed, his assimilation of the precepts and knowledge contained in those works is transmitted to others in a kind of genealogy of gift-giving. After Samuel dies (in chapter 24), his presence is continued through the influence of his reading and is commemorated through the legacy of his books—a dual heritage Steinbeck was aware of when he told Covici, "we won't lose him" (*JN*, 117). After his death, however, Samuel's vision of the world (based on intellect, imagination, and effective action) can no longer be fully assumed by any other single character, although Lee (the Trask family's Chinese servant) keeps the process of reading alive by adding to it in his own way.

Lee, Steinbeck's spokesperson, is Samuel's ally in intellectual matters, for he too understands the necessity of reading as a way of knowing and inhabiting the world. Meditative Lee shares Samuel's love for books and even dreams of owning a bookstore, though commerce is an arena he is admirably unsuited to enter (*EE*, 166). He has, among the "thirty or forty" books in his possession, *Psychology: a Briefer Course* (1892), the one-volume textbook version of James's *Principles of Psychology* (*EE*, 188). Lee's catholic taste and his scholarly disposition allow him to approach the Bible as comparative mythology. Together, in Adam's presence, Lee and Samuel converse on the meaning of Genesis before the latter names Adam's two boys. It is Lee who understands the participatory dynamics of reading—"'If a story is not about the hearer he will not listen'" (*EE*, 270)—which aptly reflects Steinbeck's reflexive technique in *East of Eden* and his new belief that only the "deeply personal and familiar" makes a "great and lasting story" (*EE*, 270). Lee is also the one who rescues the Cain-Abel story from a strict parochial interpretation and places it in psychological perspective (again epitomizing Steinbeck's approach) by calling it "the symbol story of the human soul," an "old and terrible story" important "because it is a chart of the soul" (*EE*, 270). If Lee lacks Samuel's worldly experience and his capacity for action, he surpasses him in academic diligence, and this is sufficient to qualify him as Samuel's intellectual heir. The story of Cain and Abel "bit" so "deeply" into Lee that he studied it "'word for word.'" In his belief that *timshol* (Steinbeck spelled it improperly as *timshel*) means "Thou mayest" and gives humans some choice in their actions, Lee, too, rediscovers the sacred word and the originating power of language which releases Samuel toward "an ending wonderful" (*EE*, 308) and finally allows Adam to bless Caleb, his wayward son (*EE*, 602), thereby completing the onomastic covenant that Samuel initiated earlier.

Still later, "consciously searching for some reassurance" (*EE*, 565) in a time of impending crisis for the Trasks, Lee reads passages from Marcus Aurelius's *Meditations*, which he had stolen from Samuel. As a whole, Marcus Aurelius's stoicism fits Lee's rational sensibility better than Samuel's. In this instance, however, its contents are less inspiring than Lee's intuition that Samuel would have understood his thievery: "Suddenly Lee felt good. He wondered whether Sam'l Hamilton had ever missed his book or known who stole it. It had seemed to Lee the only clean pure way was to steal it. He still felt good about it. His fingers caressed the smooth leather of the binding as he took it back and slipped it under the breadbox. He said to himself, 'But of course he knew who took it. Who else would have stolen Marcus Aurelius?'" (*EE*, 565-66). The piety contained in Lee's ceremonial gesture enlarges the archetype of legacy in *East of Eden* and echoes Steinbeck's Hermes-like trope of stealing books mentioned earlier. In light of the priority books, reading, and textual hermeneutics assume in this novel, Lee's continuation of Samuel's intellectual tradition was as valuable to Steinbeck as the ethical and moral tradition embodied in the *timshol* doctrine. And given Lee's awareness of the ironies apparent in the major monetary legacies—Adam "living all his life on stolen money" and Aron "living all his life on the profits from a whorehouse" (*EE*, 583)—Steinbeck resolves that not only will a world without literature be a much diminished world, and survival a far more agonizing process, but also that a person can do far worse than pilfer a book.

As with his composition of *The Grapes of Wrath,* Steinbeck's background in reading helped focus *East of Eden*'s technique. *Journal of a Novel* reveals his conscious awareness of other writers as a measure for Steinbeck's own novel and for his creative process. There is nothing exactly unitary in his examples, but in aggregate they illuminate Steinbeck's need to assess his own progress according to competitive standards. He invokes Twain and Whitman in his musing on the relationship between bodily comfort and writing conditions (*JN*, 6). Melville's *Moby-Dick* is offered as a comparison for the reception Steinbeck expects for *East of Eden* (*JN*, 29). In the same paragraph, he says "in pace [*East of Eden*] is much more like Fielding than Hemingway," an idea repeated later when he writes, "Its leisure derives from 18th-century novels, but it goes from that to the intense" (*JN*, 174). He also considered Sherwood Anderson and Cervantes inventors of the modern novel (*JN*, 124, 179) and *The Book of the Dead* "as good and as highly developed as anything in the 20th century" (*JN*, 9). On 2 July 1951, a little more than halfway through his writing, he said, "I am not going to put artificial structures on this book. The real structures are enough, I mean the discipline imposed by realities and certain universal writers" (*JN*, 118).

Steinbeck has left some clues to those "universal writers." First and foremost, the story of Genesis not only provided the novel's title (*JN*, 104) but also exerted a profound influence on the symbolic nature of *East of Eden,* especially its conceptual dualism. The verses concerning Cain and Abel, the Garden of Eden, and Adam and Eve's fall from grace provided the central, generative mythos. Around this "key to the story" (*JN*, 104), Steinbeck developed a contemporary perspective toward the dramatic, ethical, and psychological implications of the eternal contest between good and evil that dominates the novel. The imprint of Genesis pervades the theme and plot of *East of Eden,* figures prominently in Steinbeck's alignment of characters according to C-A initials (though this does not exclusively dictate their individual roles), and echoes in the rhythm of some of his prose. In his utilization of *timshol* into *timshel,* Steinbeck found the ideogrammic lever to move the burden of the novel's moral weight. And though Steinbeck has been accused of appropriating and translating *timshol* improperly (he uses *timshel* to mean "Thou mayest" rather than "Thou shalt"), it should be remembered that Steinbeck was writing fiction, not scriptural exegesis (*JN*, 109). Given his invocation of Cervantes in the original dedication to *East of Eden* (*JN*, 179) and his explicit reference to Herodotus which opens chapter 34 (*EE*, 413), Steinbeck's real consistency was his adherence to the artist's freedom to write in any manner he wished, which included his right to distort facts for artful purposes, as well as his propensity to reinvent the message of his literary precursors. Harold Bloom's pronouncement is germane here: "to imagine is to misinterpret. . . ."[14]

One of the most controversial and least explored issues in *East of Eden* concerns form and structure. For Steinbeck, who was not an erudite literary theorist, form was "organic" only in the sense that a single consciousness wrote through from beginning to middle to end: "Write freely and as rapidly as possible and throw the whole thing down on paper," he told Robert Wallsten in 1962 (*SLL*, 736). What occurs in between or afterwards was often subject to the author's tangents or swervings. In such a "field" theory of composition, even seemingly unrelated elements intersect and resonate with the main narrative. The intercalary chapters in *The Grapes of Wrath*, the mobile form of *Cannery Row*, and later, *Sweet Thursday*, with its explicit chapters on "hooptedoodle," are all examples of this open compositional method. In *East of Eden* the editorial chapters create tonal variations for the narrative that support the dramatic, literary, or historical thrust of the book and keep alive the fictive voice of the doubly mirrored and shape-shifting narrator. Whatever corroboration for such "formless" form (*JN*, 112) Steinbeck found in those antecedent works in which the teller is apparent in his tale—*Don Quixote, Tristam Shandy, The Counterfeitors,* and especially *Moby-Dick* (treated in a later chapter of *Steinbeck's Typewriter*)—his conception of morphology in *East of Eden* also was aided by classical sources.

Early in *East of Eden* Steinbeck was already thinking of it as a "kind of parallel biography" (*JN*, 15), a term often applied to Plutarch's *Lives*. Like Plutarch, Steinbeck evinced an interest in the moral dimensions of individual characters and employed a contrapuntal design to structure his book. In a sense, the Hamiltons can be considered Steinbeck's Greeks, the Trasks his Romans. Their "biographies," invested with exemplary stature, constitute his version of the decline of the mythic world and the birth of the mundane—an intention clarified in Steinbeck's comment of 2 July 1951, that Samuel's death marked the "end of an era" (*JN*, 117).

Steinbeck also referred to *East of Eden* as "history": "You will notice my methods of trying to create the illusion of something that really happened—in this book. I think it can properly be called not a novel but a history. And while its form is very tight, it is my intention to make it seem to have the formlessness of history. History is actually not formless but a long [view?] and a philosophic turn of mind are necessary to see its pattern. And I would like this to have that quality" (*JN*, 17).[15] Steinbeck did not think of history in its rigidly documentary sense; rather he thought of it the way the Greeks often did, with emphasis on *story*, the encompassing idea of logos which J. A. K. Thomson applied in 1935 to Herodotus in *The Art of the Logos* (*SR*, 110). Under the rubric of Herodotus's cosmogonal intention, all the information he gathered about the known world was brought into play—a comprehensive spirit of inquiry echoed in Steinbeck's own belief that his book "should contain everything that seems to me to be true" (*JN*, 24). One of the main structural features of Herodotus's work is its use of digression, and one of its notable characteristics (frequently attacked by orthodox historians) is impressionism. To the degree that he also hypostatized the concepts of East and West, creating conflicting moral, ethical, and political orders within which humans must choose, Herodotus exerted not only a lasting formal impression on Steinbeck but a thematic one as well. Jackson Benson's contention that Steinbeck had "a strong sympathy for the ancient Greek world view" (*TAJS*, 234) is not only valid but deserving of far deeper investigation.

This twofold emphasis is apparent in chapter 34 of *East of Eden*. It is itself a digression from the main narrative. Steinbeck refers directly to the Greek historian's "Persian War" and selectively employs a truncated version of Croesus's decline and fall (told fully in Book One of Herodotus's *Histories*). Although Croesus was not burned to death "on a tall fire" (*EE*, 414) but was saved and honored by Cyrus, Steinbeck is chiefly concerned with what he considered the central aspect of Croesus's decline from favor. This was his eleventh-hour recognition that Solon's wisdom had proven true: a man's life cannot be judged fortunate or unfortunate until after he has died.

Just as Steinbeck's idiosyncratic interpretation of *timshol* grants man freedom of choice between good and evil, his interpretation of Croesus's situation further illuminates that major preoccupation, which the narrator couches in a contemporary mode: "It seems to me that if you or I must choose between two courses of thought and action, we should remember our dying and try so as to live that our death brings no pleasure to the world" (*EE*, 415). Steinbeck's focus is not only on the operation of good and evil in the universal world of political and economic reality but also serves as the basis for his literary procedure. Like Herodotus, Steinbeck considered human action the nexus from which history-as-story was made, and he felt, too, that the art of the storyteller cannot be separated from the tale itself.

From ancient Greece to contemporary California, the lineage of *East of Eden* also extends to Steinbeck's research and source material. Even though he transformed primary and literary materials with a certain amount of latitude and bravado, Steinbeck was nevertheless scrupulous about verifying basic facts. Several letters, written in 1948, testify to his distrust of "old timers" (*SLL*, 304) and his desire to make his material "right and correct" (*SLL*, 308). In regard to concrete details about local history, political offices, and the cultural and economic flavor of the Salinas area, Steinbeck originally planned to utilize back files of the *Salinas Californian*, and on 2 January 1948 wrote to its editor, Paul Caswell, of his intention to do so (*SLL*, 303). By the time Steinbeck actually wrote the novel three years later, he was out of touch with his native state, making his need for documentation especially acute. The plan to photocopy back issues of the newspaper was abandoned as excessively expensive and burdensome. Instead, Max Gordon, a staff reporter, agreed to answer Steinbeck's questions (nearly two hundred of them) and supply pertinent data.[16] Information about Adam Trask's lettuce shipping venture and about wages and prices current at the turn of the century came to Steinbeck through Gordon's professional research and saved Steinbeck from potential embarrassment.

Steinbeck was not so scrupulous about crediting all of his sources, however. Although he "worked and studied and made research" (*JN*, 92) for the scene in chapter 20 where Kate gains control of Faye, he still wondered if he had stolen the idea (*JN*, 93) and worried about being accused of plagiarism. Such confusion is obviously an occupational hazard for any writer, especially one who believed that literature is sometimes built on "borrowing." In fact, as if to highlight the slipperiness of his acquisitive memory, incautiously close parallels are to be discerned between *East of Eden* and three books which Steinbeck had en-

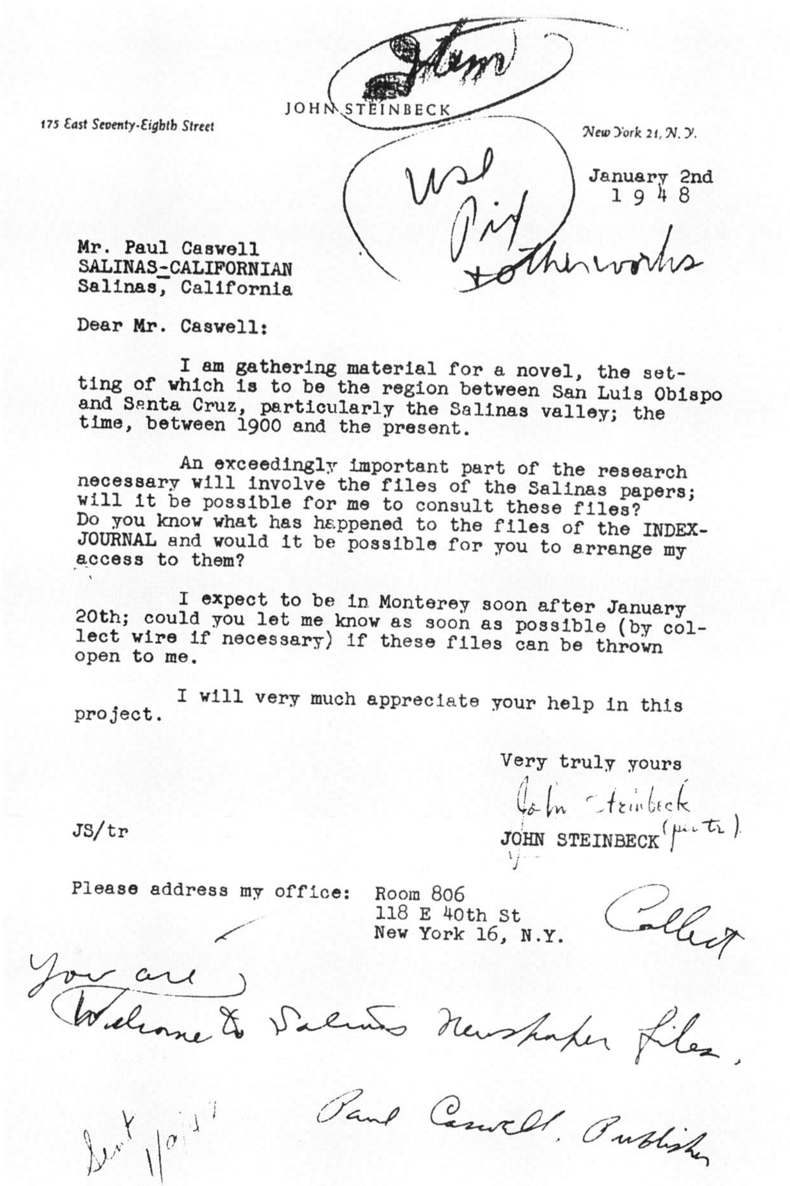

JOHN STEINBECK

175 East Seventy-Eighth Street

New York 21, N. Y.

January 2nd
1 9 4 8

Use
Pix
& other works

Mr. Paul Caswell
SALINAS-CALIFORNIAN
Salinas, California

Dear Mr. Caswell:

I am gathering material for a novel, the setting of which is to be the region between San Luis Obispo and Santa Cruz, particularly the Salinas valley; the time, between 1900 and the present.

An exceedingly important part of the research necessary will involve the files of the Salinas papers; will it be possible for me to consult these files? Do you know what has happened to the files of the INDEX-JOURNAL and would it be possible for you to arrange my access to them?

I expect to be in Monterey soon after January 20th; could you let me know as soon as possible (by collect wire if necessary) if these files can be thrown open to me.

I will very much appreciate your help in this project.

Very truly yours

John Steinbeck

JS/tr

JOHN STEINBECK

Please address my office: Room 806
118 E 40th St
New York 16, N.Y.

Collect

You are Welcome to Salinas Newspaper files.

Paul Caswell. Publisher

Sent 1/10

Steinbeck's letter to Paul Caswell
Courtesy of John Steinbeck Library, Salinas, CA.

countered: Raoul Faure's 1948 novel *Lady Godiva and Master Tom*, Erich Fromm's 1950 *Psychoanalysis and Religion*, and John Gunn's antiquated *New Family Physician*, already referred to above as *Dr. Gunn's Family Medicine*. Faure's scathing novel fit right in with Steinbeck's postdivorce anger, bewilderment, and grief. The misogynistic portrait of Lady Godiva as fickle, treacherous, and sexually unfulfilled—Steinbeck judged it a "really blistering study of a woman" (*SLL*, 334)—aided his physical portrait and psychological treatment of Cathy/Kate (also based on ex-wife Gwyn) and probably inspired her identity as a "monster," though Steinbeck's utilization of that term goes far deeper than Faure's.[17] Moreover, Steinbeck's shift toward the primacy of individual psychology, his humanistic interpretation of original sin and the fall from Eden, as well as his portrayal of Samuel Hamilton as a "pillar of fire," were all directly inspirited by Fromm's "brilliant" monograph, which, Steinbeck reported to George Albee on 19 December 1950, was "all the things we have thought about, but stated clearly and well" (*SR*, 44, 148).

Finally, as I demonstrate in the next chapter of *Steinbeck's Typewriter*, the novelist positively reveled in Gunn's massive treatise, from which he begged, borrowed, stole, and otherwise alchemized numerous utilitarian elements. Steinbeck's employment of Gunn brings us back to his belief in the personal and cultural efficacy of books and the transactional power of reading. Gunn's volume once belonged to the real-life Samuel Hamilton, and Steinbeck imaginatively reclaimed it as a talisman which symbolized a legitimate connection with his family's capacity for survival and his grandfather's archetypal love of books and reading. In this way, mediated by narrative, Samuel passed the originating legacy of participation to other Hamilton descendants: toward the novel's narrator, "John Steinbeck" (the intratextual recipient of Samuel's beneficence), and toward the author, John Steinbeck, who (in an extratextual convolution performed by walking through *East of Eden*'s narratological looking glass into *Journal of a Novel*) passes on everything he has rescued to his own sons, Samuel's grandchildren.

3

"Mr. Steinbeck read widely," his literary agent Elizabeth Otis recalled, and while at any given time his "favorite" reading could range from dictionaries (especially the *OED*, which he considered "the greatest book in the world") and reference works to classic literature, "it spread out every which way from there."[18] The spread of Steinbeck's reading during the final epoch of his life was exceptionally wide and deep, but it was also marked by uncertainties and reservations, as well as seductions and dead-ends (the latter chiefly in regard to his work on the Arthurian legend which I will examine shortly). At times during this era his reading paralleled the erratic shape of his writing career and reflected his movement toward resuscitating a personal brand of romanticism. After failing to complete his modern rendition of Malory's *Morte d'Arthur*, a project with which he wrestled unsuccessfully for several years, Steinbeck found a way to achieve an imaginative resolution in *The Winter of Our Discontent* and an imperative one in *America and Americans*. By the 1960s Steinbeck's artistic powers had clearly waned (in 1967 he admitted to Elizabeth Otis that he had been "worked out" for a long time), and although neither book is vintage Steinbeck, each one has much to recommend it, especially for the purpose of articulating his reflective judgments on the significance of reading.

Before arriving there, however, it is necessary to indicate the kinds of reading and writing that occupied Steinbeck's attention in the 1950s and 1960s. Naturally, he kept up his interest in classic writers—Homer, Herodotus, Plutarch, Thucydides, Marcus Aurelius, Petrarch, Malory, Shakespeare, Rabelais, Voltaire, Cellini, Rousseau, and Smollett all earned his praise for their ability to remain fresh, exciting, and instructive. Since his "discovery" of Cervantes's *Don Quixote*, in 1945, that wonderful shape-shifting book remained one of Steinbeck's literary touchstones through the 1950s, until its presence was largely effaced by his involvement with Sir Thomas Malory. Indeed, Steinbeck was so impressed by Cervantes's achievements as a writer (not only in *Don Quixote* but later in the *Exemplary Novels* as well) and was so moved by Cervantes's experience as a prisoner (part of Steinbeck's intense attraction to Malory stemmed from similar impulses) that in 1954 he talked of traveling to La Mancha to chronicle "all of the places Cervantes wrote about" in preparation for a book he planned to write "that parallels Don Quixote" (*TAJS*, 745-46).

Like several other projects during these years, that "written and photographed" account never materialized. Yet Steinbeck's habit of utilizing his favorite reading remained consistent, if somewhat refracted and deferred. The spirit of Steinbeck's proposed quest later informed his cross-country American odyssey in *Travels with Charley*, a "Project Windmills" carried out with his poodle, Charley (a diminutive Sancho Panza), in a pickup truck/camper named "Rocinante" in homage to the don's horse. This is admittedly a kind of honorific connection and another of Steinbeck's exercises in literary play. But the deliberate burlesque should not mask his deeper attraction to Cervantes's book, which was both a criticism of formulaic romance and a celebration of its individual spirit. For all of its realistic contemporary focus, its exposure of the synthetic face of American experience, *Travels with Charley* also is embedded in the expressive values of introspection and process which Steinbeck held increasingly dear in the second half of his career. Like *The Winter of Our Discontent* and *America and Americans*, *Travels* is a "reading" of America as large-scale text.[19]

Besides Cervantes and the other authors read, mentioned, or quoted from in *Travels* (he took 150 pounds of books on the trip), including Thomas Wolfe, C. E. S. Wood (his former neighbor in Los Gatos in the late 1930s), Sinclair Lewis, and William Shirer (*The Rise and Fall of the Third Reich*), Steinbeck also invoked Herodotus, Marco Polo, and Sir John Mandeville to lend a fabulous air to his journey. "I am happy to report," he wrote after passing through Fargo, North Dakota, "that in the war between reality and romance, reality is not the stronger" (*TWC*, 136). In the pressing matter of introducing himself to his readers—who are "more interested in what I wear than what I think, more avid to know how I do it than in what I do"—Steinbeck borrowed a convention from the "Master" Joseph Addison by opening *Travels with Charley* with his own digressive "History" (*TWC*, 38-40). And from Elaine Steinbeck's reference to Robert Louis Stevenson's *Travels with a Donkey* (1879), Steinbeck discovered his title (*SLL*, 676).

The duality Steinbeck uncovered in his "wandering narrative" is an apt metaphor for his reading experiences during this period of his life. From the early 1950s until the late 1960s he discovered some new reading interests and intellectual vistas, but they were not always as satisfying or as lasting as his experiences with traditional authors. In the August 1952 issue of *Collier's*, Steinbeck called Albert Guerard's *France: A Short History* a "beautiful little history." A month later, delighted with Ernest Hemingway's comeback novella, *The Old Man and the Sea*, Steinbeck told Carlton Sheffield that it was "a very fine performance" (*SLL*, 457), and in December he told a *New York Times* reporter that he would like to be able to write the "terse, parched electrical prose" Hemingway had captured. That year, too, Steinbeck appeared on camera to introduce and narrate a film, *O. Henry's Full House*, which included renditions of five of William Sydney Porter's most famous short tales (*SR*, 86, 166). In 1958 Steinbeck was instrumental in getting Dennis Murphy's first novel, *The Sergeant*, published by Viking Press. He also wrote a rare dust jacket blurb: "A remarkable book. It has none of the faults of a young first novelist, faults which took me many years to overcome because I thought they were virtues. I mean verbosity, ornamentation, and a lack of compactness. . . . Most impressive is his ability to put believable people on paper and then to relate them in scenes which happen. There is a great deal of truth and beauty in this book." His friendship with Edward Albee drew out his curiosity about absurdist drama, and his natural tendency to identify with the dispossessed found a practical outlet in his support of Budd Schulberg's Watts Writers' Workshop and its first publication in 1966, *From the Ashes* (*SR*, 99; *TAJS*, 985-87).

He also kept abreast of current trends in prose and followed *Paris Review*, *Publishers Weekly*, and *Saturday Review*. He maintained his belief that Hemingway and Faulkner were his two "favorite" contemporaries—"Hemingway's short stories and nearly everything Faulkner wrote," he claimed in 1962 (*CJS*, 79). That same year he told a British interviewer that he considered Joseph Heller's *Catch-22* "one of the best war books ever written, and a lot less of a fantasy than many people seemed to have thought," and singled out James Baldwin, James Purdy, Jack Gelber, and Robert Lowell as American writers with talent to watch (*CJS*, 82). At other times he praised John O'Hara's *From the Terrace*, Barnaby Conrad's *The Matador*, Jack Kerouac's *On the Road*, and Frank Conroy's autobiographical *Stop-Time*, but he could never finish Boris Pasternak's *Dr. Zhivago* and he remained puzzled by the "despairing brilliance" of J. D. Salinger's *Franny and Zooey* (*LTE*, 106).

Even three established voices in American fiction struck leaden chords with him: Katherine Anne Porter's *The Ship of Fools* seemed "removed from reality"; Mary McCarthy's *The Group* was "duller than ditch-water," and Thornton Wilder's *The Eighth Day* he judged "tedious." In his last years Steinbeck read with "interest and admiration" fiction as diverse as Philip

Steinbeck on the set of *O. Henry's Full House* (1952), a five-part anthology film, for which he provided introduction and commentary
Courtesy of John Steinbeck Library, Salinas, CA.

Roth's *Goodbye, Columbus,* J. F. Powers's *Morte D'Urban,* William Faulkner's *The Reivers,* John Updike's *Rabbit, Run* and *The Centaur,* and Truman Capote's "nonfiction" novel *In Cold Blood,* but he realized that his "eye for fiction [had] changed its focus" (*LTE,* 106). He seemed increasingly content to look to the past for substantive enrichment. In February 1962, for example, making yet another journey through the *Peloponnesian Wars,* he wrote Elizabeth Otis from Capri, "One of the nice things about this time is the re-reading of old things and the re-evaluating. Some things I admired have fallen off but others have become far greater. Walter Pater, whom I used to adore, has slipped way back for me, while Thucydides has gone up. They haven't changed—I have" (*SR,* 111; *TAJS,* 907).

That change in temperament had been coming for several years. After his fortuitous marriage to Elaine Scott in December 1950, Steinbeck began to assemble a working library, a "staunch bastion" comprised mainly of books on words and a large selection of reference works (to replace those lost after divorcing Gwyn). The new volumes satisfied his renewed passion for words. "The crazy thing about all this," he informed Carlton Sheffield on 10 September 1952, "is that I don't use a great variety of words in my work at all. I just love them for themselves" (*SLL,* 457). His statement emphasizes the pleasures of reading and research and indicates a relaxed, if not indulgent, preference for the process of study rather than its eventual product. Within a few years, it was not just books on words and the American language that captivated Steinbeck's attention but a nearly obsessive commitment to expanding his library with everything he could get his hands on that dealt with Sir Thomas Malory's *Morte d'Arthur.* By the late 1950s Steinbeck had accumulated a first-rate library on the subject and a scholar's knowledge of the field but had managed only an incomplete translation of Malory's great book into modern American.

In fact, after the burst of creativity between 1950 and 1954 which had resulted in "About Ed Ricketts," *Burning Bright, Viva Zapata!, East of Eden,* and *Sweet Thursday* (whose relational affinities with Al Capp's *The World of Li'l Abner* is discussed in the title chapter of *Steinbeck's Typewriter*), Steinbeck published only one other book in that decade—*The Short Reign of Pippin IV,* whose "spiritual father" was Voltaire's *Candide* (but which lacked its bite). Many other publications in the 1950s can be classed as journalism. There were frequent appearances as a contributor to *Saturday Review*, travel essays, and political dispatches commissioned for the Louisville *Courier Journal*, and a collection of occasional prose pieces, *Un Américain à New York et à Paris*, published in a limited edition in Paris in 1956. One of his short stories, "How Mr. Hogan Robbed a Bank" (*Atlantic Monthly*, 1956), became a partial basis for *The Winter of Our Discontent*, while the earlier Poe-like "The Affair at 7, rue de M—" (*Harper's Bazaar*, 1955) was incorporated in the first posthumous edition of the *Viking Portable Steinbeck*, edited by Pascal Covici, Jr., and published by Viking Press in 1971. For the most part, though, Steinbeck's publications between 1955 and 1959 had the air of being occasional efforts, interesting as chatty social critiques and useful for charting his personal and cultural attitudes.

It was also a time of false starts and unrealized dreams. Besides the Cervantes project and one on Christopher Columbus (*SLL*, 476), he also abandoned a proposed (and partly researched) book on the Caribbean when he read Alec Waugh's *Island in the Sun*. "If I did not know about this book," he told Elizabeth Otis, "it would be all right because it is not likely that we could write exactly the same kind of account. But the fact that I do know about it before my own work is completed puts an entirely new face on the matter. I will have to abandon my plans" (*LTE*, 61; *SR*, 179). His disappointment was almost a harbinger of his next three years' work.

And yet to say that Steinbeck *accomplished* little else during this period is not accurate either, for one of those unfinished dreams called for an effort as monumental and single-minded as Steinbeck ever undertook. As a reader, Steinbeck's engagement with the research and acquisition of books necessary to prepare his novelization of Malory's *Morte d'Arthur* was unprecedented, approached only by his phalanx reading in the 1930s; as an artist, however, the Arthurian research bore fruits of a different kind. Like *The Grapes of Wrath* and *East of Eden*, Steinbeck conceived *The Acts of King Arthur and His Noble Knights* as another of his "big" books, the third in a trilogy of huge undertakings, and the capstone of a lifetime of devoted building. Steinbeck seems as much to have chosen Malory's text as he was chosen by it (he discovered the Caxton version of Malory's *Morte* when he was nine years old); it was another of those deep possessions the novelist could not refuse to embrace no matter how unforseen or overwhelming the consequences. The trouble, though, Steinbeck said, was his "ignorance" about a text that had become sacred to him and which, given his capacity for humility and reverence, compelled him to "know everything . . . about what Malory knew and how he might have felt" (*AKA*, 316). That humility, however, soon took on a competitive edge.

In the years from 1956 to 1959, when he was researching, then writing, his modern rendition of the *Morte*, Steinbeck hungrily consumed "hundreds" of books and documents related to the history, language, and literature of Malory's fifteenth century and its parallels in the twentieth century (*AKA*, 317). Along with the major literary sources and cultural antecedents of Malory's book, Steinbeck scoured "the scholarly diggings and scrablings" not only of "Chambers, Sommer, Gollancz, Saintsbury" (*AKA*, xii), but also of Rhys, Hicks, Kittredge, Vinaver, Newstead and a host of other experts (see *SR*, 55, 66, 84, 94, 115). He branched out from there in every direction: "Since Christmas I have been reading, reading, reading and it has been delightful, like remembered music," he told Pascal Covici on 7 January 1957. "I've been back into Gildas and into the Anglo Saxon Chronicle, into Bede, and back into histories of Roman Britain and Saxon Britain and into the whole field of [Greek, Buddhist, and Jungian myth] . . . and into the twelfth and thirteenth and fourteenth century in England" (*S&C*, 198).

Maintaining the voracious appetite his desire for authenticity imposed on him would not have been possible without the advice and assistance of Chase Horton, owner of the Washington Square Book Store in New York City. Like Ed Ricketts years earlier and Eugène Vinaver a little later, Horton served as an enthusiastic, patient guide through the forest of scholarship and bibliography. Horton not only supplied Steinbeck with books, both here and abroad, but sometimes, as with Robert Grave's *The White Goddess* and Ivan Margary's *Roman Roads in Britain*, he also marked out key passages ahead of time to make sure Steinbeck did not miss them (*SR*, 48, 77).[20] But Steinbeck's passion for the quest was so strong, so erotic and addictive, that the reading process itself became a self-generating fetish, endlessly proliferating and incapable of being fulfilled, as he did his part zealously, pushing himself and Horton to new limits of determination and acquisition. For the first time in his life, Steinbeck began to take real pleasure in the physical appearance—the look and feel—of books (especially Iris Origo's *The Merchant of Prato* and Armando Sapori's *Merchants and Companies in An-*

cient Florence). "We are going to have a rather formidable library before we are finished," he wrote Elizabeth Otis on 19 April 1957, "and I couldn't be happier about this" (*AKA*, 303). Throughout this period he continued to read avidly on his own (in one brief stretch, despite his admittedly slow reading pace, he managed to devour six books by C. G. Coulton and all three volumes of *The Reign of Henry the Fifth* by James Hamilton Wylie [*SR*, 30, 124]), as well as in the Pierpont Morgan Library and in what he thought would be the untapped resources of libraries in Florence and Rome, especially The Vatican, the most "exciting" library he ever saw (*SLL*, 552).

After six months of research, which began in November 1956, Steinbeck lost the thread of his design, bludgeoned by the sheer weight of the endeavor. Then, almost miraculously, he discovered it again one morning in Rome in late April of 1957. His major breakthrough, a "dizzying inductive leap," which he hoped would cancel all the scholarly "inconsistencies and absurdities," centered on a twin recognition: first, that the *Morte* should be considered "the first and one of the greatest novels in the English language"; and second, that Malory should be considered essentially a romantic novelist, "a rearranger of nature," who makes "an understandable pattern" (*AKA*, 304-05). This linked insight gave Steinbeck some leverage in his wrestling match with his precursor's originary text. By defying objective historical precedent, and by reading backward from himself and his own times to Malory and his times, Steinbeck's "revisionary compensation" granted him a great deal of freedom and breathing room in his treatment.[21] This new view deliberately brought Malory and the *Morte* into a recognizable fictive realm, an arena where Steinbeck initially felt comfortable because he was able to codify his affinity: "If Malory could rewrite Chretien [de Troyes] for his time, I can rewrite Malory for mine," he announced boastfully to Elizabeth Otis on 9 July 1958 (*AKA*, 321). In a very real sense, then, Steinbeck's proposed re-writing was an attempt to participate in the primacy of Malory's own reinscribed text.

However, it also led to a major aesthetic dilemma Steinbeck never solved. The novelist's "self-character"—the "one chief or central character in the novel" (*AKA*, 304) invested with the writer's own virtues and faults ("You will find one in every one of my books," he confessed)—cannot conclusively "win" the quest for the Grail. For Malory, whose self character was Lance-

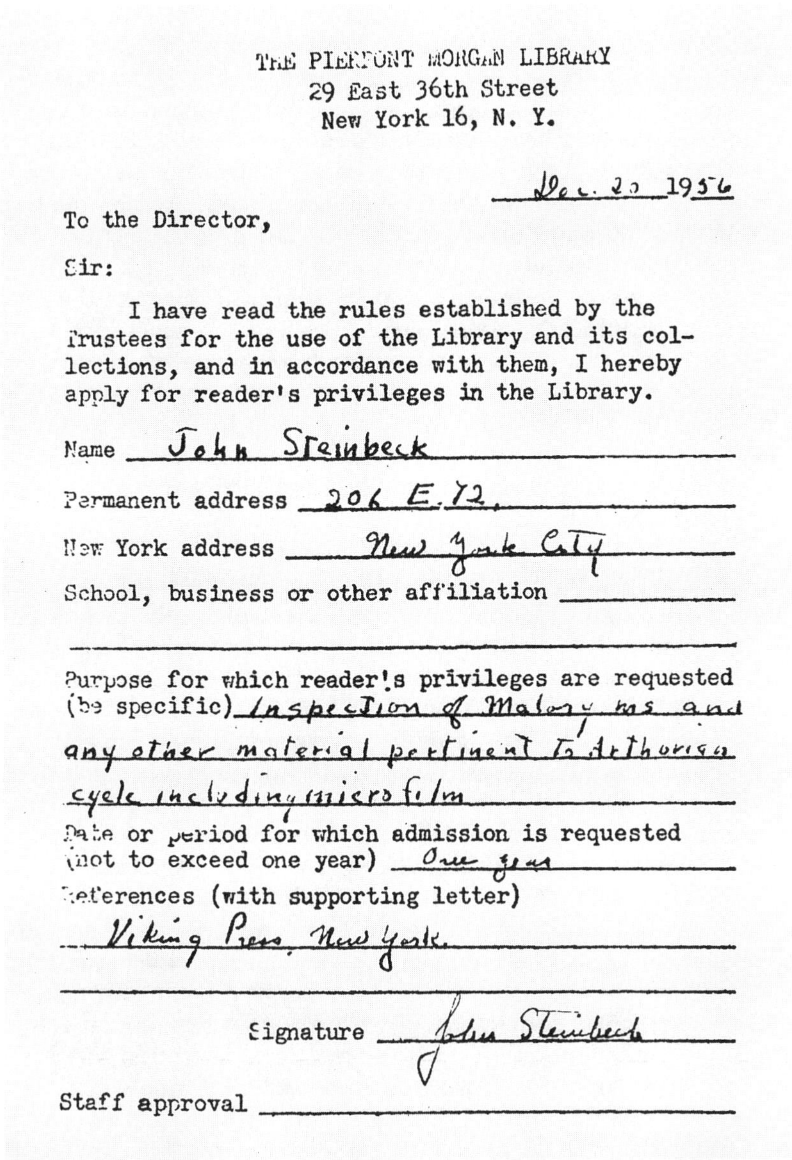

THE PIERPONT MORGAN LIBRARY
29 East 36th Street
New York 16, N. Y.

Dec. 20 1956

To the Director,

Sir:

I have read the rules established by the Trustees for the use of the Library and its collections, and in accordance with them, I hereby apply for reader's privileges in the Library.

Name John Steinbeck

Permanent address 206 E. 72.

New York address New York City

School, business or other affiliation

Purpose for which reader's privileges are requested (be specific) Inspection of Malory ms and any other material pertinent to Arthurian cycle including microfilm

Date or period for which admission is requested (not to exceed one year) One year

References (with supporting letter)

Viking Press, New York.

Signature John Steinbeck

Staff approval

Steinbeck's reader's application to the Pierpont Morgan Library.
On 18 January 1957 Steinbeck told Alexander Frere, "working on the Malory is a thing of great joy to me, like coming home. The Morgan Library has opened its arms and its great manuscripts to me. . . ." (*SLL*, 548)
Courtesy of Pierpont Morgan Library, New York City.

lot, this meant that Lancelot could not achieve the Grail, but his son Galahad could because only he was "unsoiled" and pure enough. For Steinbeck, whose self-character was a combination of both Malory and Lancelot, this configuration led to a cruel irony, for he had to be at once in the impossible posture of being "the writer who must write the writer as well as the Morte" (*AKA*, 316). Although at the time he was encouraged by his belief that the "Malory-Lancelot" double could indirectly fulfill the quest, it soon became apparent that in Steinbeck's hands the search could never be finished and his Grail (in this case the finished book) could never be attained. Perhaps Steinbeck, who habitually feared ending a book as much as he hated beginning one, allowed himself to be swayed by an immediate conviction—that the achievement of perfection he sought could be sublimated to the process of the creative quest, "unfinished" at last (*SLL*, 859). The book, he had reminded Elizabeth Otis earlier, "is much more Acts than Morte" (*AKA*, 298).

Steinbeck was so fired by justifying his fabular approach (a line-by-line collation of Eugène Vinaver's Winchester text of the *Morte* with Steinbeck's *Acts* shows the novelist's emphasis on mythic continuity, symbolism, and psychological motivation) that he eventually became intimidated by its infinitude. Normally a fairly strong reader in regard to making use of his antecedent texts, in this case Steinbeck's competitive survival quotient failed him. The pressure to transform a legend which had persisted in his imagination since childhood led Steinbeck into so much primary and secondary research, so much hair-splitting of individual words, names, places, so much resuscitation of thick context, that he never recovered the creative balance between culling and invention, reading and writing, necessary to complete his task. The competitive desire to prove himself at least worthy, if not masterful, in a traditional literary and historical area changed rather quickly from aggression toward the "frightened" academic scholars to a genuine admiration for their work: "I'm having a hell of a fine time with the books," he reported to Chase Horton at a period when he was "staying away from Malory" (*AKA*, 311). For one of the few times in his career (the other notable instance occurred when he was researching Joan of Arc in the mid-1940s), the seductive pleasures of his study preempted his writing: "I've been doing some concentrated reading—a lovely thing," he told Alexander Frere at Heinemann's, his British publisher. "To read and read in one direction night and day; to pull an area and a climate of thinking over one's head like a space helmet—what a joy that is!" (*SLL*, 548). "I have read until I am blind with reading," he confessed to Eugène Vinaver fourteen months later on 10 March 1958 (*SLL*, 578).

Steinbeck's ironic admission can be considered unintentionally prophetic—he had indeed been blinded by Malory. Despite a year of concentrated writing at Discove Cottage, Somerset, England, in 1958-59 (he even experimented by writing with a goose quill pen he had modified for his long hours at the desk [*SLL*, 638]), and the unflagging encouragement of Elaine Steinbeck, Chase Horton, and Eugène Vinaver—enthusiasm, however, not fully joined by Otis and Covici, who both doubted the commercial value of his venture and preferred that Steinbeck produce something like T. H. White's *The Once and Future King* or fluff like *Camelot* (*TAJS*, 811)—Steinbeck never finished his fictionalization. If his struggle with "The Winchester Manuscripts of Sir Thomas Malory and Other Sources" ended in personal frustration and disappointment for Steinbeck, it was not because of the quality of his work nor the depth of his understanding of the material, but because the subject proved to be far more vast, complicated, and demanding than he had anticipated. Ironically, in refusing to write the "popular" book which Otis and Covici wanted and holding out for a "permanent" one instead (*AKA*, 343), he was stymied by his own passionate pursuit of knowledge and his own scrupulous standards of novelistic conduct. "This perplexity is like a great ache to me," he confided to Vinaver on 27 August 1959. A writer, he said, "must believe himself capable of perfection even when he fails. And that is probably why it is the loneliest profession in the world and the most lost. I come toward the ending of my life with the same ache for perfection I had as a child" (*TAJS*, 857).

4

The other side of blindness, however, is insight. In several important ways, Steinbeck's research was not wasted but only deferred. In a writer so ecologically minded as Steinbeck, this postponement was not a bad thing. After abandoning *Acts* in 1959, Steinbeck was frequently assailed by fears of his decline as a writer. In the spring and summer of 1960, when he was writing *The Winter of Our Discontent* (and already planning the

American journey which would result in *Travels with Charley*), he spoke of the necessity to "save [his] life and the integrity of [his] creative pulse" (*SLL*, 669). Through symbolic transference, Steinbeck's pressing need for artistic salvation influenced *Winter's* survival quotient. And by once again elevating the act of reading to a generative function, Steinbeck found a way to redeem his failure with the Arthurian fiasco and (even though there is nothing overtly Arthurian in the novel) to transmute some of his acquired knowledge into the elements of fiction. "*Arthur*," Jackson Benson reports, "acted as a first draft for . . . *Winter* . . ." (*TAJS*, 858). Steinbeck's anecdotal story, "How Mr. Hogan Robbed a Bank," suggests one of the possible directions *The Winter of Our Discontent* might have taken, but it will simply not explain what Steinbeck created in the novel; in the years between 1956 and 1960 his experiences in deep reading intervened in such a way as to make all the difference in execution, theme, and resolution.

Like *East of Eden, The Winter of Our Discontent* is an intensely personal, experimental novel, but it is also a problematic novel because of its reliance on two distinct points of view and competing narrative voices. Although few critics agree on the quality of Steinbeck's achievement in *Winter*, none dispute its indebtedness to a variety of sources (*TAJS*, 875). It is a veritable orchestra of subtexts and allusions. Besides Shakespeare's *Richard III*, which supplied his title, Steinbeck ransacked the New Testament Gospels (especially Matthew and Luke), Caedmon's Genesis, Boethius's *Consolation of Philosophy*, Holinshed's *Chronicles*, Henry Clay's speeches, Hans Christian Andersen's fairy tales, Lewis Carroll's *Alice in Wonderland*, Frank Baum's *The Wizard of Oz*, T. S. Eliot's *The Waste Land*, and Boodin's *A Realistic Universe*—to name the most significantly evoked and embedded texts—for everything from thematic and structural parallels, symbolism, imagery, and elements of characterization to dialogue, stylistic echoes, and direct quotations. As usual, Steinbeck handled these materials with a mixture of scrupulous integrity, dramatic irony, and—in the case of some garbled quotations—with a certain amount of conscious impressionism.[22] Despite their striking differences and elliptical presences, however, nearly all of these bookish elements contributed to Steinbeck's awareness that the only worthwhile subject for a writer in any age is the dilemma of individual conscience, human suffering, and existential choice—an awareness, moreover, which underlies the thorny plight of Ethan Allen Hawley, the novel's protagonist and occasional first-person narrator who is himself, like his author, often mastered by history, by the burden of the past.

If the disparateness of these sources argues for a patchwork job, a rough-stitched combinatory assemblage, rather than a seamless construction, it should be remembered that Steinbeck utilized them purposely to reflect Hawley's divided sensibility, not necessarily his own. *The Winter of Our Discontent*, he informed the Loessers on 25 May 1960, is "part Kafka and part Booth Tarkington" (*SLL*, 666), which is to say it is part surrealistic nightmare, part sharp social commentary. The division in Hawley's mind between social requisites and individual propriety overarches the entire novel. The Tarkingtonian aspect of *Winter* is associated with the social value system of New Baytown (and by extension, all of America) which, as it enters a sophisticated technological age, Steinbeck criticizes for its moral and spiritual backsliding, its abdication of traditional mores, and its neglect of nurturing human actions. This realistic dimension, characterized by epochal changes in contemporary humanity's tolerant attitude toward corruption, greed, and hypocrisy, occasions the novel's desultory plot and supplies its external action.

Steinbeck's reference to Kafka provides a pathway to a lower level and suggests a key to Hawley's conflicted sensibility. ("It's not a novel like any I have seen or read or heard of," Steinbeck told Covici [*SLL*, 676].) Large sections of *The Winter of Our Discontent* are devoted to Hawley's explorations of his own interior distances. He is fascinated with his "night thoughts" and the compelling (and often confusing and contradictory) force of his own mental and emotional processes. His self-revelatory accounts are tinged with surrealism and, furthermore, they are organized to produce significant metamorphoses in his psyche and character. "It's as though, in the dark and desolate caves of the mind, a faceless jury had met and decided" (*WOD*, 109) the direction his life should take; in doing so, that "Congress in the Dark" supported his contention "that a man is changing all the time," though not necessarily for the better (*WOD*, 111).

Hawley witnesses moral decline everywhere around him and decides to get his piece of the action. Unlike Mr. Hogan in Steinbeck's story, Hawley's plans to rob the New Baytown bank are scotched, but not before he has gained possession of Marullo's store (where he works as a clerk) and the rights to valuable land (formerly owned by his childhood friend, Danny Taylor) that will be the site for New Baytown's airport. The verdict of his inner voices justifies Hawley's ignoble and Judas-like decision to abnegate his "normal" past, which he now considers a "failure," to turn his back on "habits and attitudes" which he used to consider "moral, even virtuous" (*WOD*, 111), and, through chicanery and deceit, to pursue a course of financial and personal aggrandizement: "Once I perceived the pattern and accepted it, the path was clearly marked and the dangers apparent. What amazed me most was that it seemed to plan itself; one thing grew out of another and everything fitted together. I watched it grow and only guided it with the lightest touch" (*WOD*, 240). In Hawley's abdication of free will to justify his villainous plan, Steinbeck is clearly distancing himself from his protagonist and is using him instead as a representative vehicle for rampant, self-induced follies and cruelties of his age. In this sense, *Winter* is a postmodernist allegory of loss, fragmentation, and betrayal.[23]

Steinbeck's separation from Hawley's amorality does not mean a complete dissociation from all facets of his protagonist/narrator's character, however. In fact, Hawley serves the same function Steinbeck had earlier conceived for Malory and Lancelot; that is, Hawley is in some respects Steinbeck's "self-character." If Hawley is at times treacherous, hypocritical, and supercilious, he is also reflective, inquisitive, and perceptive. In some declarative ways, his habits of mind are closely linked to Steinbeck's: "So many old and lovely things are stored in the world's attic, because we don't want them around us and we don't dare throw them out" (*WOD*, 89). What Steinbeck refused to throw out of his novel was the entire realm of myth, which had been the major by-product of his Arthurian studies. His immersion in the works of Carl Jung, Joseph Campbell, Jessie Weston, Robert Graves, Stith Thompson, and others exerted a profound influence on *Winter*'s tone and atmosphere. Steinbeck's reading confirmed his insistent belief in the synchronism of psychological processes, the continuity of mythic and symbolic forms of action, and the eternal return, so to speak, of the desire for originating experiences.

As his earliest fiction shows, Steinbeck had always believed that "the body of myth . . . changed very little in its essence" from generation to generation (*AKA*, 316), but in the period from 1956 to 1960, the individual ramifications of that awareness came back to him with special force and reaffirmation of purpose. Besides supplying his collateral concern with witchcraft, folklore, and superstition, the body of myth and various texts in comparative religion and anthropology formed the novel's essential emphasis on archetypes, including light/dark imagery, water symbolism, withdrawal/return patterns, and totemic icons, especially sexy Margie Young-Hunt's Tarot cards and the Hawley family talisman, a "strange" and "magic" "translucent stone," brought back from China by his ancestors. These latter function as the novel's ultimate symbols of fluid process and indeterminacy, encoding an entire range of textual/sexual responses (*WOD*, 161). Drawing on the familiar echoes and latent allusions of Jungian psychology, Steinbeck evoked the mysterious recesses of the unconscious mind, that "secret and sleepless . . . spawning place" deep inside Hawley, which, fittingly, he envisions as "a great library" where he can read "everything" pertaining to his life (*WOD*, 109). Once again, reading as an activity—a site for and a scene of hunger and satiety—functions as a trope that initiates a cycle of induced blindness and liberating insight.

The continuous, "durational" feeling of myth (*AKA*, 326) that Steinbeck wished to achieve in his treatment of *Morte d'Arthur* carried over to *The Winter of Our Discontent* and tempered its contemporary realism, linked it to the remote past and to the world of Hawley's ancestors (especially his Great Aunt Deborah, a woman of "curiosity and knowledge" who, like Samuel Hamilton a decade earlier, dove deeply "into books"), and conditioned Hawley's sensitive predelictions for the nether world, the "uncharted country" of dreams, the felt world of visitations. "Like most modern people," he says, "I don't believe in prophecy or magic and then spend half my time practicing it." In a sense, then, like Joseph Wayne in *To a God Unknown*, the Harvard-educated Hawley stands figuratively between ancient and modern values, pagan and learned knowledge, rigorous critical intelligence and mythic perception. If he is hampered by his age's moral relativity and his own debilitating and puritanical self-scrutiny, his eventual refusal to be sacrificed is rooted in a much more ancient monomyth—the secular hero's return from the dark underworld toward the living light, a pattern of resurrection Hawley specifically enacts when he leaves his secret Place on Old Harbor for the last time. Moreover, as Steinbeck's self-character, Hawley is not pure enough to complete this wayward version of the Grail quest for himself. He can, however, turn his weaknesses to strengths by utilizing his knowledge of the quest's process to ensure its survival in Ellen, one of his children, the new "owner" of the Hawley talisman, the new bearer of the family "light" (*WOD*, 358).[24]

Ever since his original experiments with the parable form in *The Pearl* fifteen years earlier, Steinbeck had moved toward a poetic mode which would allow apprehension of, and participation in, the wondrous quality of experience. "A story must have some points of contact with the reader to make him feel at home in it," Hawley says, echoing Lee in *East of Eden*. "Only then," he continues, "can he accept wonders" (*WOD*, 89). In *Winter*, an essential approach to the numinous—and indeed the whole evanescent tradition which light signifies—is conveyed through the presence of books and the persistence of knowledge. Steinbeck's recent period of intensive research awakened his fascination for what, by 1960, must have seemed a fairly inscrutable and tenuous bond between the act of reading, the formation of consciousness, and the role of the writer in authorizing the past. Steinbeck was surely aware more acutely than ever of the disruptions to his creative authority—a "state of confusion," he named it in late 1959 (*SLL*, 656)—when his imagination was too deeply immersed in a welter of competing, dissonant written sources.

Steinbeck's response to this ongoing crisis of signification was partly compensatory and partly celebratory and led to one of the most resonant passages in his fiction, Ethan Allen Hawley's attic revery. In the attic of Hawley's ancestral home, the books, which represent both the cumulative intellectual heritage of his family as well as everything they would like to throw out, "sit . . . waiting to be rediscovered." Hawley recollects "scrambling among the brilliants of books"—not only the ringing political speeches of Lincoln, Webster, and Clay, and the intensely expressive writings of Emerson, Thoreau, and Whitman (*WOD*, 38), but these other titles in their museum-like setting,

> tinted with light, the picture books of children grown, seeded, and gone; *Chatterboxes* and the Rollo series; a thousand acts of God—*Fire, Flood, Tidal Waves, Earthquakes*—all fully illustrated; the Gustave Doré Hell, with Dante's squared cantos like bricks between: and the heartbreaking stories of Hans Christian Andersen, the blood-chilling violence and cruelty of the Grimm Brothers, the Morte d'Arthur of majesty with

> drawings by Aubrey Beardsley, a sickly, warped creature, a strange choice to illustrate great, manly Malory. (*WOD*, 88-89)

Taken in its entirety, this scene dramatizes how far Ethan Hawley has fallen from intimations of primary experience and psychic wholeness. It also illuminates the dichotomy in Hawley's mind between the current demands of practicality and the desire for nostalgia and permanence, as well as the contest between violence and innocence which defines his particular stance throughout the novel. By evoking a potentially living tradition centered in this oddly eclectic selection of books, Steinbeck simultaneously deepens the pathos of Hawley's complicitous amorality and foreshadows the entire realm of consciousness that has a chance to survive when Ethan decides not to kill himself at the end of the novel.

The scene's self-reflexive and *architextural* implications are potent: in this static setting, the titles are dead objects, relics of a repressed or outmoded past, neglected, abandoned, consigned to attic limbo. But as books they are also waiting to be rediscovered, picked up, handled, entered into; waiting, that is, to be vivified by an active appreciator, an aggressive reader, perhaps a devourer of texts and an assimilator of quotations, who will use them knowingly according to their nature and kind, and who will, in a sense, bring them into the present and redefine their originality. Viewed in a wider perspective, then, this syncretic passage, with its steady gaze into a place of ambient textuality, goes way beyond the ruptured mind of Ethan Allen Hawley and can be considered Steinbeck's mature testimony to the generative, inspirational, and potentially curative power of books.

Conceived in this way, the scene is a kind of apologia for a lifetime of reading and being sustained—in all the overlapping and even contradictory implications of that word—by and through books. Like his protagonist, held back from fulfilling his desire by seduction, rationalization, betrayal, and self-created obstacles, Steinbeck turned the process of searching into a suggestively redemptive gesture, a symbolic statement that such knowledge need not be lost or consigned solely to the oblivious past. In the sense that Ethan Allen Hawley is temporarily seduced by the lure of popular morality and meretricious alternatives (and by the debasement of language which accompanies such choices), Steinbeck dramatized his own perilous artistic condition (*SLL*, 653). Just when the situation seemed bleakest, however, he turned apparent failure into a kind of affirmation by joining the investiture of myth with the presence of a creative tradition he truly embraced. With good reason, Emerson said in "Quotation and Originality," "In every man's memory, with the hours when life culminated are usually associated certain books which met his views. . . . What but the book that shall come, which they have sought through all libraries, through all languages, that shall be to their mature eyes what many a tinsel-covered toy pamphlet was to their childhood, and shall speak to the imagination?" Not for nothing, Elaine Steinbeck once said of her husband, "he gobbled up books—all kinds of books" (*SR*, ix).

The act of reading, a kind of hungry seeking "through all libraries," became a deeply justifiable imperative for Steinbeck, not just because it was a recuperative process, but because it was a "projective" art.[25] Reading could engender understanding, insight, critical awareness, compassion, relatedness, and continuity: in short, admirable qualities human beings could aspire to even if they could not reach them. Given the depth of Steinbeck's commitment to the cause of intellectual and creative sanctity and his belief in the typology of reading, it is a short but direct route from the private codes of *The Winter of Our Discontent* to the public pronouncements of *America and Americans*, the last book published in his lifetime and the final avatar of his readerly theme. In his chapter on literature, "Americans and the World," Steinbeck constructed a version of American literature's "two-fold" growth, and emphasized the necessity of reading our best native literature, even though it is "no more flattering than Isaiah was about the Jews, Thucydides about the Greeks, or Tacitus, Suetonius, and Juvenal about the Romans."[26] As might be expected for a white male writer of his time and place, his sketchy survey of the "great ones" of American letters is extremely selective, so that no African-American writers are represented (though there is an entire chapter on racism in America) and only one woman novelist—Willa Cather, his favorite—is mentioned (in 1935 Steinbeck had considered Cather the "best" prose writer in America [*SR*, 24]). The sketch is also highly impressionistic, as evidenced in Steinbeck's decidedly imperfect knowledge of Stephen Crane.

But Steinbeck was not speaking as an authoritative scholar about his subject. Rather, he adopted the voice and point of view of an artistic communicant, a believer in the ontological benefits of reading fiction. He speaks here as an advocate, a participant in a traditional literary canon whose thematic objectives he fundamentally adopted, just as he frequently and self-absorbingly transmuted its technical resources. If critical appraisal of his position in that American literary tradition is bound to be unsettled, given the shifting ground rules of literary history and academic taste-making, Steinbeck himself was far less confused about the issue, though for discretionary reasons he was circumspect. By this late in the game, however, if we have been sensitive to the reflexive, inward-gazing dimensions of his readerly theme, it should come as no surprise that he implicitly suggests his rightful place in the American literary tradition belongs not with thinly disguised reportage or journalism, but with the infinitely varied mode of modern symbolic fiction. *Huckleberry Finn, An American Tragedy, Winesburg, Ohio, Main Street, The Great Gatsby,* and *As I Lay Dying* (*A&A*, 135) comprised enduring treasures for many general American readers, but they were equally compass points for the individual American writer of Steinbeck's era. In 1938, when he was forging his grandest achievement, *The Grapes of Wrath,* into "a truly American book," such novels were part of his creative landscape (*WD*, 29). Three decades later, they were present again as landmarks in that fictive geography he wished to imagine himself inhabiting.

Books of all kinds occupied a momentous position in Steinbeck's life and art. The poetics of reading—whether for inspiration, creative atmosphere, general background, specific information, allusion, reference, elaboration, spiritual sustenance, pure pleasure, or any number of other ineffable and less well defined reasons—significantly shaped and enhanced Steinbeck's sense of artistic place, as well as his creative and personal identity. "Home," he announced to Carlton Sheffield in 1964, is "only that place where the books are kept" (*SLL*, 798). In the resonant implications of that statement, Steinbeck fulfilled a condition he had been working toward all of his life: reading/writing was nothing less than a way of living and acting in the world.

Notes

[1] During the past four years, in providing annotations for the first two volumes of the Library of America's edition of Steinbeck's works (which includes his major books from *The Pastures of Heaven* through *Sea of Cortez*) I was struck by how comparatively little sustained referential and informational ground work has been done by scholars in identifying and analyzing the writer's literary, philosophical, historic, artistic, scientific, and cultural borrowings. It seems more relevant than ever to say that to read Steinbeck meaningfully is to read him reading. Notable recent exceptions to the habit of relegating Steinbeck to the dumb ox school of writing are Richard Astro, *John Steinbeck and Edward F. Ricketts: The Shaping of a Novelist* (Minneapolis: University of Minnesota Press, 1973); Jackson J. Benson, *The True Adventures of John Steinbeck, Writer* (New York: Viking Press, 1984); John H. Timmerman, *John Steinbeck's Fiction: The Aesthetics of the Road Taken* (Norman: University of Oklahoma Press, 1986), and his *The Dramatic Landscape of Steinbeck's Short Stories* (Norman: University of Oklahoma Press, 1990); and Brian Railsback, *Parallel Expeditions: Charles Darwin and the Art of John Steinbeck* (Moscow: University of Idaho Press, 1995). The imagery of literary borrowings operating like musical "echoes" from one text to another is developed in an intriguing study by John Hollander, *The Figure of Echo: A Mode of Allusion in Milton and After* (Berkeley: University of California Press, 1981).

[2] In Terry G. Halladay's "'The Closest Witness': The Autobiographical Reminiscences of Gwyndolyn Conger Steinbeck" (MA thesis, Stephen F. Austin University, 1979), 66, Steinbeck's second wife, Gwyn, states that her husband "was horrified of plagiarism." F. Scott Fitzgerald once called Steinbeck a "cagey cribber," though it is better perhaps to see Steinbeck's manner of borrowing as a survivalist technique. John H. Timmerman, in "The Shameless Magpie: John Steinbeck, Plagiarism, and the Ear of the Artist," in *The Steinbeck Question: New Essays in Criticism*, ed. Donald R. Noble (Troy, NY: Whitston Publishing, 1993), 276, "lays to rest charges of plagiarism" by showing how Steinbeck's imagination dominated his materials. In any event, Steinbeck's habit of acquisitive reading was sufficiently wide and deep (and at times aggressively so) to justify considering issues of influence in a larger framework than simply categorizing specific images, ideas, and themes that he found in his predecessors, though of course that is part and parcel of the current attempt at demonstrating what Louis A. Renza calls "affiliative relations." See his "Influence," chap. 14 in *Critical Terms for Literary Study*, eds. Frank Lentricchia and Thomas McLaughlin, 2nd ed. (Chicago: University of Chicago Press, 1995), 186. Though Steinbeck does not fit well into the complex (and elitist, because essentially canonical) multistage, esoteric, psychological scheme of influence ("Six Revisionary Ratios") laid out by Harold Bloom in *The Anxiety of Influence: A Theory of Poetry* (New York: Oxford University Press, 1973) and elaborated in its companion volume, *A Map of Misreading* (New York: Oxford University Press, 1975), as well as in *Agon: Towards a Theory of Revisionism* (New York: Oxford University Press, 1982), it is nearly impossible to consider issues of literary influence at all in our time without resorting—even loosely, obliquely, and impurely (which of course proves the very thesis of misreading postulated in his books)—to many of Bloom's key terms and tropes (*appropriate, belated,*

misprision, misreading, revisionary, swerve, etc.). But adopting his terminology, even on an occasional or limited basis, also requires qualifying his pronouncements, at least in one's own purview. "Weaker talents idealize," Bloom says categorically in *The Anxiety of Influence,* and "figures of capable imagination appropriate for themselves" (5). In fact, though, Steinbeck, who was by turns reverential and ruthless, candid and duplicitous, in his use of sources, demonstrated both imaginative capacities, sometimes in the confines of a single work. It is a balanced valuation I try to keep open in the following pages. In this I have been inspired by Emerson's bountiful essay "Quotation and Originality," which valorizes the combinatory power of the quoting mind, elevates quoting beyond mimesis to generative status, and redefines originality according to its debt to tradition. See his *Letters and Social Aims,* vol. 8 of the Centenary Edition of *The Complete Works of Ralph Waldo Emerson,* ed. Edward Waldo Emerson (Boston: Houghton Mifflin, 1904), 175-204. I also recommend as useful Robert Alter, "Allusion," chap. 4, in *The Pleasures of Reading in an Ideological Age* (New York: Touchstone, 1990), 111-40.

[3] Steinbeck's letter to Braley, dated 26 June 1934, appears in the latter's novel, *Morgan Sails the Caribbean* (New York: Macmillan, 1934), vii-viii; his observation about "texture" appears in a letter to Elizabeth Otis, written 4 March 1958, published in the appendix to *The Acts of King Arthur and His Noble Knights,* ed. Chase Horton (New York: Farrar, Straus and Giroux, 1976), 311 (hereafter cited as *AKA*). The closer Steinbeck approached an individual voice and stance of his own, the more uneasy, even defensive, he became about being compared to or considered in debt to other writers. He often claimed not to have read much contemporary literature and in a typical disavowal told Robert Ballou in 1932 that he didn't "like fiction very much." While it is certainly true that he tried to keep himself "immaculate" (*SLL,* 25) from conscious imitation, his categorical denials of reading novels or "recent books" or even of giving advice to young writers are simply not true and may have had more to do with his self-fashioned public persona than with his actual private habits. Asked in 1938 by Merle Danford, an Ohio University graduate student, to respond to a private questionnaire—"You read little fiction, but you like Thackeray's work"—Steinbeck fired back: "Sure I like Thackeray, but I like a hundred others" (*CJS,* 24). See also my preface to *Your Only Weapon Is Your Work: A Letter by John Steinbeck to Dennis Murphy* (San Jose, CA: Steinbeck Research Center, 1985).

[4] Elizabeth Ainsworth's comment was contained in a letter to me written on 5 October 1979. Steinbeck's version of the recollection is in *Travels with Charley in Search of America* (New York: Viking Press, 1962; reprint, New York: Penguin Books, 1986), 37-38 (hereafter cited as *TWC*). A few years ago, shortly before his untimely death, John Steinbeck IV recalled that his father used a similar ploy on young John and his older brother Thom: "Correctly suspecting he had given birth to a petty thief, my father encouraged me to read by locking in a leaded glass-front bookcase books that he thought were essential—the *Iliad,* Lao-Tse's *Tao Te Ching,* Mark Twain, the Bible, King Arthur. . . . Then he hid the key where he knew I would find it and threatened me within an inch of my life if he ever caught me in there. Needless to say, I learned to read rapidly" (quoted in Judith Moore, Abe Opincar, and Bob Shanbrom, "John Steinbeck Was My Father," *San Diego Weekly Reader* 30 March 1989, 26).

[5] With such extensive exposure to classic works at an early age, it should be no surprise that in his later life all of Steinbeck's "big" books, including *The Grapes of Wrath, East of Eden, The Acts of King Arthur,* and even *The Winter of Our Discontent,* were constructed around or in some way occasioned by or deeply responsive to one or more significant, world-renowned texts. The Bible, *Moby-Dick,* and *Morte d'Arthur,* respectively, annexed Steinbeck's imagination and affection—perhaps because they each represented the pinnacle of achievement in their respective genres and therefore a standard of originary excellence the writer felt obligated to be judged by or to attempt to elaborate upon.

[6] Information on Steinbeck's college career is taken directly from his Stanford University transcript.

[7] The unpublished typescript is among the extensive John Steinbeck Works collection in the Pascal Covici Papers at the Harry Ransom Humanities Research Center at the University of Texas, Austin.

[8] Joel Hedgpeth, telephone interview by author, 16 May 1979.

[9] Ricketts's essays, unpublished in his lifetime, are printed in Joel Hedgpeth's *The Outer Shores, Part 2: Breaking Through* (Eureka, CA: Mad River Press, 1978), 69-79, 80-89. See Richard Astro, *John Steinbeck and Edward F. Ricketts,* 34-42, for an appraisal.

[10] "A Farewell to the 1930's," in *A Casebook on "The Grapes of Wrath,"* ed. Agnes McNeill Donohue (New York: Thomas Y. Crowell, 1968), 23.

[11] Steinbeck's comments are contained in what is undoubtedly one of the oddest documents in the Steinbeck archive at the Harry Ransom Humanities Research Center. It is a three-page autograph manuscript that accompanies a letter to Pascal Covici, written in September 1942. The manuscript is in Steinbeck's handwriting but is titled "Introduction by Pascal Covici." It was apparently meant to serve as a general introduction to Covici's edition of the first *Viking Portable Library Steinbeck* (New York: Viking Press, 1943). Covici must have thought better of that idea, for he eventually wrote his own, quite different, preface to the anthology. Steinbeck's emphasis on the lasting effects of "participation"—a key concept in his aesthetic program—are also echoed in his brief piece, "In Awe of Words," which appeared in *The Exonian* in March 1954 (*SLL,* 523), and in his interview with Diana, Lady Avebury, published as "Healthy Anger" in *Books and Bookmen* 4 (October 1958): 24 (*CJS,* 67).

[12] John Steinbeck, *Cannery Row* (New York: Viking Press, 1945; reprint, with introduction by Susan Shillinglaw, New York: Penguin Books, 1994), 5 (hereafter cited as *CR*). Kevin Hearle's "'The Boat-Shaped Mind': Steinbeck's Sense of Language as Discourse in *Cannery Row* and *Sea of Cortez,*" in *After "The Grapes of Wrath": Essays on John Steinbeck in Honor of Tetsumaro Hayashi,* eds. Donald V. Coers, Paul D. Ruffin, and Robert J. DeMott (Athens: Ohio University Press, 1995), 101-12, makes a significant contribution to understanding Steinbeck's self-conscious use of language in this novel.

[13] In *The Author Looks at Format,* ed. Ray Freiman (New York: American Institute of Graphic Arts, 1951), 32, 34.

[14] *The Anxiety of Influence,* 93.

[15] Steinbeck's free definition of history and his sense that historical writers "from Homer to Toynbee" have all constructed speculative interpretative narratives is borne out in an excised section of the typed manuscript of

America and Americans, housed at the Harry Ransom Humanities Research Center: "History," he said, "is based largely on fiction, opinion, and speculation" (137).

[16] Paul Caswell, letter to author, 1 April 1979.

[17] A more complete account of Steinbeck's appropriations from Faure appears in my essay, "Cathy Ames and Lady Godiva: A Contribution to *East of Eden*'s Background," *Steinbeck Quarterly* 14 (Summer-Fall 1981): 72-83.

[18] Elizabeth Otis, letter to author, 25 February 1979.

[19] Following Louise Rosenblatt's categories in *The Reader, The Text, The Poem* (1978), Geralyn Strecker writes, "Steinbeck is primarily an aesthetic reader in *Travels with Charley* with an artistic appreciation for the country without any driving concern for order. In *America and Americans*, he is an efferent reader, looking for patterns, order (teleology), and scientific knowledge about his country and its people." See her "Reading Steinbeck (Re)-Reading America: *Travels with Charley* and *America and Americans*," in *After "The Grapes of Wrath,"* 215.

[20] Chase Horton, interview by author, 20 August 1979, New York City. Horton was extremely modest about his role in helping Steinbeck "build a background" (*AKA*, 312, 318) for his book and his efforts should not be underestimated. On the day I interviewed Horton at his Manhattan apartment he gave me a meticulously typed list of books that Steinbeck had read or researched for *Acts* (I entered more than eighty of them in the main catalogue of *Steinbeck's Reading*) and a copy of an unpublished 1957 letter from Steinbeck about the allure of his Arthurian reading. See my "In Memoriam: Chase Horton (1897-1985)," in *Essays on Collecting John Steinbeck Books*, ed. Preston Beyer (Bradenton, FL: Opuscula Press, 1989), 27-31.

[21] Harold Bloom, *A Map of Misreading*, 62.

[22] John Steinbeck, *The Winter of Our Discontent* (New York: Viking Press, 1961; reprint, New York: Bantam Books, 1970) (hereafter cited as *WOD*). See Reloy Garcia's section on Steinbeck's background debts in "Steinbeck's *The Winter of Our Discontent*," chap. 14 in *A Study Guide to Steinbeck: A Handbook to His Major Works*, ed. Tetsumaro Hayashi (Metuchen, NJ: Scarecrow Press, 1974), 244-45. On Steinbeck's confusion of passages from Luke and Matthew, see John Ditsky, "The Devil Quotes Scripture: Biblical Misattribution and *The Winter of Our Discontent*," *San Jose Studies* 15 (Spring 1989): 19-28. Both Richard C. Bedford in "The Genesis and Consolation of Our Discontent," *Criticism* 14 (1972): 277-94, and Hassell A. Simpson, "Steinbeck's Anglo-Saxon 'Wonder-Words' and the American Paradox," *American Literature* 62 (June 1990): 310-17, unravel Steinbeck's garbled use of primary sources caused by his collapsing of lines from the Old English poem *Genesis A* and Boethius's *Consolation of Philosophy*. Earlier critics condemned Steinbeck for such textual and linguistic slip-ups, but in our time, as these commentators show, misprision is artful and deepens the interior significances and abiding paradoxes of one of Steinbeck's most misunderstood and unfairly dismissed novels.

[23] Michael J. Meyer, "Transforming Evil to Good: The Image of Iscariot in *The Winter of Our Discontent*," *Steinbeck Quarterly* 26 (Summer-Fall 1993): 101-11, examines in close detail Steinbeck's "revisionist expression" and "syncretic" doubling of the Judas myth in Ethan Hawley's portrayal: "Steinbeck's literary alchemy merges the wavering images of Judas and Christ to create . . .

a subtle warning to the modern age" (111). Meyer continues his scrutiny of the multilayered polarities in this novel in "Citizen Cain: Ethan Hawley's Double Identity in *The Winter of Our Discontent*," in *After "The Grapes of Wrath,"* 197-213.

[24] Steinbeck's obsession with the dynamics of family life—especially the tenuous and conflicted relationship between fathers and children—and the recurring use of what Peter Valenti calls "motifs of change" ("masks, ventriloquism, slipped snakeskins, and plagiarism") became constitutive metaphors for most of his fiction between 1950 and 1961. See Valenti's "Steinbeck's Geographical Seasons: *The Winter of Our Discontent*," *Steinbeck Quarterly* 26 (Summer-Fall 1993): 111. A pattern of quest and failure, death and rebirth, quotation and invention, which Steinbeck felt deeply in his own life and art at this time, gave an immediacy to the self-consciously "modern" texture and bifurcated point of view of *The Winter of Our Discontent*. Even with that much at stake, though, the paragraphs on Hawley's optimistic decision to save himself and his emphasis on familial continuity were late additions to the novel. Scrutiny of the second draft of *Winter*, housed at the Pierpont Morgan Library, New York City, shows that the final thirteen sentences of the novel were not in the autograph manuscript but were added by Steinbeck to the next stage, the typescript, then capped by a final comment (which was later deleted from the published text): "And I hope this time it's clear. I really do hope so" (443). The Morgan Library typescript also contains much philosophically disturbing material, including a large section of Hawley's cynical sermon to the canned goods at Marullo's store (181-84), and an entire chapter of dark musings on human sexual warfare and on gender differences between Ellen and Allen Hawley (276-81). Steinbeck later excised these sections completely, perhaps because they were too pessimistic.

[25] Joseph N. Riddel, *Purloined Letters: Originality and Repetition in American Literature*, ed. Mark Bauerlein (Baton Rouge: Louisiana State University Press, 1995), 102. See also Michael Cohen's affecting essay, "(T)Reading for My Life," his chapter on "Constructing Gender" in Emory Elliott, gen. ed., *The Columbia History of the American Novel* (New York: Columbia University Press, 1991), especially 543, where he links "imagining-as-reading" with "reading-as-imagining" as a particularly powerful kind of creativity.

[26] John Steinbeck, *American and Americans* (New York: Viking Press, 1966), 134 (hereafter cited as *A&A*).

"A Great Black Book": *East of Eden* and *Gunn's New Family Physician*

"Dr. Gunn's Family Medicine . . . told you all about what to do if a body was sick or dead."
—Mark Twain, Chapter 17 of *Adventures of Huckleberry Finn* (1885)

1

John Steinbeck's reading habits often brought him into contact with intriguing and useful texts of all kinds that had a way of eventually becoming an embedded part of his own work. Mark Twain's comic dismissal aside, Dr. John Gunn's book had yet another appearance to make in an American novel. In *East of Eden* Steinbeck substantively employed a later version—*Gunn's New Family Physician*—as a means of deepening the artistic portrait and creative legacy of his maternal grandfather Samuel Hamilton (who owned a copy of Gunn's book), as a source for several kinds of information, and as a model for certain aspects of human behavior which he hoped to preserve for his children. Gunn's treatise was instrumental in filling out Steinbeck's portrayal of an earlier historical era; it was one of those nonliterary works he often resorted to that give texture and depth to a period by providing a kind of handbook to its cultural context and social codes. In the sense that Samuel Hamilton was imagined to be a man beautifully balanced in and of his times, he represented to Steinbeck a model of intelligence and behavior. The novelist represented Samuel as a hero, a "pillar of fire," not because he was superhuman, but because he was an inventor capable of imagining a way of living meaningfully beyond his limitations without denying their validity or significance.

East of Eden, a consciously autobiographical novel, announced a marked change in Steinbeck's way of writing. From

Cannery Row in 1945 through *Burning Bright* in 1951, Steinbeck had turned away from much of the formal restraint and coherent totality of the mimetic novel. Parables and fables offered Steinbeck basic structures and styles that would allow him to express a disguised human moral and at the same time create a maximum quality of readerly participation, "a little play in your head."[1] It was a short leap from getting his audience involved in the experience of his fiction to involving himself in its architectonics. As a result of his experiments as a fabulist in the late 1940s, Steinbeck moved toward a more open, expressive form to address a new range of personal convictions. He would not accept any longer what he considered the prevailing "technique" of realism—"the squeamishness of not appearing in one's own book"—and insisted that in his new venture, *East of Eden*, "I am in it and I don't for a moment pretend not to be" (*JN*, 24). In 1953, in response to Charles Mercer's interview questions, Steinbeck claimed that he did not "set out to break down an established novel form. It just occurred to me that the author has become so absent from the modern novel, he's so careful never to get into the act, that it's actually becoming a stereotype. I felt I could tell *East of Eden* better by being in it myself" (*CJS*, 57). For Steinbeck, "being in" his novel was, like setting up shop at home, an assault on absence; as a result of his move, a whole new range of attitudinal freedoms opened up for him. In his daily writing diary he emphasized to Pascal Covici, his Viking Press editor and the dedicatee of *East of Eden*: "I said the teller would be opinionated. . . . And as for my comments on the story . . . I feel that it is more direct and honest to set it down straight than to sneak it in so that the reader will not know or suspect it as opinion. As you will have discovered . . . the technique of this book is an apparent lack of technique and I assure you that is not easy" (*JN*, 60).

Entering the distant world of his own ancestors, Steinbeck needed to grant himself license to explore the psychological and moral implications of individual actions and personal destinies (dramatized in the contiguous lives of the Hamiltons and the Trasks), to experiment with modulations of first- and third-person points of view (injecting numerous subjective statements on personal, ethical, and cultural values) and to trace the historical course (in which history serves the dominant imaginative and mythical purposes of fiction) of his native area—California's Salinas Valley—from fabled Eden in the mid-nineteenth century to its emergence at the end of World War I on the brink of a less glamorous but more realistic age. The new novel would be, he said, "the story of my country and the story of me" (*JN*, 3). The associational freedoms implicit in his bold departure—his linkage of past and present, history and autobiography, text and context—also included his right to appropriate suitable materials from his readings. Faced with filling *Eden*'s huge canvas, Steinbeck drew on numerous literary and documentary sources for structural and thematic corroboration, for elements that added ballast to his fictive speculations, and for authenticity to correct otherwise misapprehended accounts and dimly recollected memories of Salinas Valley life.[2] His aim was not to produce a photographically perfect and minutely "detailed account" but to get the right "impression of the Valley" (*JN*, 15) by attending to the small, ubiquitous but often overlooked things that not only comprise but actually help explain social life in a past era. In Steinbeck's archeological hunting trip through the layered accumulation of his ancestral past, in his excursion toward giving *East of Eden* a palpable air of imaginative reality and a sustained specificity, Gunn's book became a chief (re)source.

2

Jackson Benson, Steinbeck's biographer, believes that where *East of Eden* is concerned, Steinbeck was "too damned literary" (*TAJS*, 681), by which he means the novelist was too deeply afflicted by high-flying literary models. Rather, immersed in the process of revisiting the past, Steinbeck did not discriminate between high and low cultural artifacts. Indeed, democratic through and through, he embraced all kinds of works, from the Christian Bible to the intellectually elite *Moby-Dick* to the populist *Dr. Gunn's Family Medicine*. Capable of being utterly pragmatic and ruthless as a writer, Steinbeck found allegiances wherever he could. For instance, Steinbeck always had a penchant for medical and pseudo-scientific texts. The twenty-fifth edition of Gray's *Anatomy of the Human Body* (1948) was part of his working library (*SR*, 48). On 22 January 1949, he asked Pascal Covici to order books to "fill out" his library, including "a Pharmacopea (can't even spell it). This should be a new one because of the many new drugs . . ." and "the best standard volume in Toxicology" (*SLL*, 346-47). But at other times in his life he was intrigued by Albert Hayes's *The Science of Life; or Self-Preserva-*

tion (1868), George Hall's *Plain Points on Personal Purity* (1892), and Mark Graubard's *Man the Slave and Master* (1938) (*SR*, 47, 50, 52). In its comingling of text and discourse, Gunn's book fits this quotable persuasion.

The popularity and wide distribution of Gunn's treatise rested as much on its explicit and practical self-help medical text ("Arranged on a new and simple plan by which the practice of Medicine is reduced to principles of Common Sense," according to the "12th edition" of 1838), as on its patently moralistic prefatory material.[3] The encyclopedic "Medical Part" comprises approximately three-quarters of Gunn's book (later editions were over a thousand pages long). Written in "plain language," the huge text covers causes, symptoms, and recommended treatments—preferably herbal or natural—for a host of human diseases, complaints, complications, wounds, and illnesses, including everything from asthma to ulcers. The prefatory matter (preface, introduction, remarks, and a major section, "The Passions") includes discourses on psychology, morality, and ethics (which also punctuate the medical text), frequently interrupted by Gunn's situational sermons on the religious temperament and discipline necessary to remain healthy in this life and to ensure smooth passage to the next.

Behind Gunn's zealous fundamentalism, however, Steinbeck found a holistic approach close to his own. Gunn's insistence on knowledge "*founded upon truth*" (*NFP*, 635) displays the same bias as Steinbeck's entry in his *East of Eden* journal: "a book—at least the kind of book I am writing—should contain everything that seems to me to be true. There are few enough true things in the world. It would be a kind of sin to conceal any of them" (*JN*, 24). Gunn's rudimentary explanations of the psychological influences on human behavior were precursors of Steinbeck's contemporary personal and fictional concerns. The *New Family Physician*'s mixture of personal observation, anecdotes, case studies, and empirical information also presented an analogue for *East of Eden*'s eclectic and "unorthodox" morphology (*JN*, 60). "Since this book is about everything," Steinbeck told Pascal Covici, "it should use every form, every method, every technique" (*JN*, 43). And, perhaps most importantly, because Gunn's book was once owned by Samuel Hamilton, it was further distinguished in Steinbeck's mind by pietistic imperatives.

The difference between Twain's humorous use of Gunn

and Steinbeck's serious use, then, is a matter of attitude and tone. Twain's recollection of life in the Mississippi River area of his youth was compounded by the increasingly critical tone and unrelenting satirical posture which the *Adventures of Huckleberry Finn* assumed during its long composition. In *East of Eden* Steinbeck's re-creation of the Salinas Valley of his boyhood (and earlier) is no less socially oriented in its attention to critical factors which changed American life since the nineteenth century; however, due to the often positive quality which adhered to some of those memories, Steinbeck's novel is, at turns, both expository and personal, its tone engaged and reverent. It is especially reverent in the first half of the book because of Steinbeck's partly fictive, partly biographical creation of Samuel Hamilton (*TAJS*, 679).

Steinbeck emphasizes two linked traits that define Samuel's stature as a "huge figure of folklore" (*JN*, 111) in the California landscape.[4] First, Samuel's role as skilled, self-reliant man: he is equally adept creating tools at his forge, locating and drilling for water (except, ironically, on his own dry land), or delivering babies. "The few overworked doctors of the county," Steinbeck writes, "did not often get to the ranches for a birth unless the joy turned to nightmare and went on for several days. Samuel Hamilton delivered all his own children and tied the cords neatly, spanked the bottoms and cleaned up the mess" (*EE*, 10). Second, Samuel's lyrical sensibility separates him from the run of people in the Salinas Valley. His poetical imagination and personal sensitivity allow him to participate in a world of correspondences and intimations closed to his neighbors and even to Liza, his utterly pragmatic and dour wife. In spite of the anti-intellectual cast of California's frontier life, part of Samuel's uniqueness, his sense of cultural difference, stems from his love of books and his ability to use them—attributes Steinbeck considered memorable: "Then there were his education and his reading, the books he bought and borrowed, his knowledge of things that could not be eaten or worn or cohabited with, his interest in poetry, and his respect for good writing" (*EE*, 39).

Among the books Samuel prizes, Steinbeck refers directly to Marcus Aurelius's *Meditations*, William James's *Principles of Psychology*, and Dr. Gunn's *Family Medicine*. In a commanding sense, all three have to do with survival. The first two reflect Samuel's inquisitive, philosophical temperament, the exceptional accommodation of his mind, and his need to see into the springs of human motivation according to the oldest and newest wisdom. The *Meditations* and James's *Psychology* are kept hidden from Liza, which testifies to their illicit intellectual appeal and increases their personal value. The medical text, too, qualifies as part of the equipment necessary for survival. Its telelogy coincided with prevailing religious beliefs and therefore would not have offended Liza, who had a "finely developed sense of sin" (*EE*, 11).[5] In a telling paragraph Steinbeck establishes the utility of Gunn's book and suggests reasons for the Hamiltons' ability to survive and flourish on their barren farm:

> Samuel had a great black book on an available shelf and it had gold letters on the cover—*Dr. Gunn's Family Medicine*. Some pages were bent and beat up from use, and others were never opened to the light. To look through *Dr. Gunn* is to know the Hamiltons' medical history. These are the used sections—broken bones, cuts, bruises, mumps, measles, backache, scarlet fever, diptheria, rheumatism, female complaints, hernia, and of course everything to do with pregnancy and the birth of children. The Hamiltons had either been lucky or moral for the sections on gonorrhea and syphilis were never opened. (*EE*, 10-11)

The description of Gunn's emblematic book was written on 9 May 1951, less than three months after Steinbeck began his novel. In the original manuscript, this passage is more detailed and appears much later in the narrative—at the point where Cathy Trask waits out her pregnancy (pp. 184-85 of the published novel) until she can abandon her husband Adam and her family. (She eventually changes her name to Kate and becomes the proprietor of a brothel in Salinas.) Thus the description was occasioned primarily, but as a kind of aside, by Cathy's impending delivery and the dramatic necessity for Samuel to preside over the birth scene.

In establishing his authority for Samuel's obstetrical ability, Steinbeck also said of Gunn's book, "I have it still"; but later deleted that line, as part of his general reworking of the entire section (*Ams*, 106/216).[6] Sometime in late 1951 or early 1952, during his revision of the enormous manuscript (*SLL*, 431, 432, 434), Steinbeck trimmed the paragraph on Gunn from 151 words to 102 (see quotations above). He then moved it and the lines, "The few overworked doctors . . . for several days" (quoted earlier) and "When his youngest . . . take over for himself" (quoted below), both of which had also been written on 9 May 1951, forward to chapter 2 (*EE*, 10). Steinbeck orchestrated this later material with a section written on 20 February 1951, in which he described the necessity for Samuel to deliver his own children, the sureness and gentleness of his hands, and the effect of his voice on children (*EE*, 6; *Ams*, 15). As a result Steinbeck created a symbolic context for Gunn's book rather than a merely referential one. Cathy's birth scene was inherently dramatic enough to warrant Steinbeck's rescuing the Gunn passage and utilizing it earlier. In so doing, the novel's contrapuntal tension between the Hamiltons and the Trasks gained specific focus and increased gravity and resonance.

Though the symbolic effect was achieved later, from the outset Steinbeck was aware that Gunn's book constituted an important connection between himself and his family's past. This is attested by an entry in *Journal of a Novel*: "This [*East of Eden*] is a personal book and every now and then I have to yank it back to the personal. . . . And at the same time I want it to be believed as a record of past truth" (*JN*, 80). In the context of the original manuscript (journal entry on the left page; novel on the right page), this otherwise oblique notation refers to Steinbeck's satisfaction at having introduced Gunn's treatise into his novel. He had just finished writing the passage on Gunn when he made this assessment; clearly, he considered Samuel's copy of Gunn a way of sustaining the "personal" integrity of his novel, as well as a means of presenting "past truth."

While Dr. Gunn's text is the source for medical information, Samuel's ability to use that knowledge properly is brought into a much larger arena. It signifies his innate correspondence with the forces of life and occasions at least one triumph over death: "When his youngest was born with some small obstruction and began to turn black, Samuel put his mouth against the baby's mouth and blew air in and sucked it out until the baby could take over for himself. Samuel's hands were so good and gentle that neighbors from twenty miles away would call on him to help with a birth" (*EE*, 10). By consciously transposing the Gunn/Hamilton nexus, Steinbeck simultaneously deepened Samuel's mythic personality and used the Hamiltons' medical history to inform the larger history he had written (see also *JN*, 17). The "bent and beat up" pages of the *Family Medicine* symbolize the vulnerability and resiliency of the Hamiltons. They are a compellingly human and "well-balanced family" (*EE*, 44) against whom the Trasks will be judged. The Hamiltons' freedom from venereal disease is opposed to Cyrus Trask's clap, Samuel's self-sufficiency is opposed to Adam Trask's dependency, the Hamiltons' acceptance of pregnancy and childbirth (they have nine children) is opposed to Cathy's determined resistance, and their innate morality is opposed to the Trasks' learned ethicality—all of these personal and ontological juxtapositions are initiated and sustained in Steinbeck's synecdochical passage on Gunn's book.

3

Yet, like the buried meteorite in chapter 17, the full dimensions of Gunn's presence in *East of Eden* remain to be uncovered. This is less a matter of influence than of confluence and intertextual linkage. Nevertheless, there are three categories of echoing similarities between *East of Eden* and *Gunn's New Family Physician* which are worth discussing because of the light they shed on some aspects of Steinbeck's creative process.

At the most elementary level Steinbeck depended on Gunn for specific contemporary medical information that added verisimilitude to his rendering of nineteenth-century life. In most of these cases Steinbeck followed Gunn's material faithfully. Alice, the young girl who becomes Cyrus Trask's second wife (his first wife and mother of his son, Adam, had committed suicide), "knew perfectly well that she had what was called consumption" (*EE*, 19). Gunn's section on consumption provided Steinbeck with the symptomatic deep cough, perspiration, and flushed cheeks he used to describe Alice's disease (*EE*, 19, 33): "Consumption often begins with a dry, hoarse cough, which gradually increases, and continues for months." It is accompanied by "Hectic Fever" which comes and goes during the day, but "returns again in the evening or at night, and goes off with what are known as Night Sweats. Upon each cheek of the Consumptive person there will be, during the fever, a bright red spot" (*NFP*, 271).

Steinbeck used Gunn's information on pregnancy and midwifery, especially for medical lore and common sense knowledge current during the last century. For details to substantiate his account of Cathy Trask's delivery (*EE*, chapter 17), Steinbeck followed the fifth division of Gunn's treatise—"Diseases of Women." Steinbeck's comment that a "woman gave a tooth for a child" (*EE*, 184) was suggested by Gunn's description of "the toothache, so often complained of by pregnant women" and his recommendation that the tooth "ought not to be drawn during Pregnancy, unless urgently required" (*NFP*, 542). Cathy's "strange taste" for the carpenter's chalk (*EE*, 184-85) is indebted to Gunn's statement about "Green Sickness" which causes an "unnatural craving" for "clay, chalk, and the like" (*NFP*, 546).[7] When Samuel is summoned to attend Cathy's delivery, he counsels forebearance (*EE*, 191). Gunn says, "But in every instance, let me impress on your mind *patience*; and let Nature alone, for she will accomplish the labor" (*NFP*, 526). Samuel reflects this latter admonition too in his comment to Adam: "'The birth happened before I was ready. Popped like a seed'" (*EE*, 193). Shortly afterward, Cathy bears a small child. Samuel "worked fast and as with the first the birth was incredibly quick" (*EE*, 194)—a reasonable approximation of Gunn's reminder to midwives: "In most cases of twin children, the second is quickly and easily born" (*NFP*, 534). Despite the ease of Cathy's deliveries, Samuel's presence is necessary to advance the novel's dramatic action. Samuel's celebrated proficiency as a midwife sets up a direct confrontation with Cathy. He comes away literally wounded, forever conscious of her demonic nature. When Samuel returns home with fever and illness brought on by the vicious bite Cathy inflicts on his hand, Steinbeck marshalls a subtly humorous counterweight to the grim scene, as well as an acknowledgement of a folk cure corroborated by Gunn:

> Hence, Soups, Broths and nutritious Teas will constitute a large proportion of the proper diet for the sick. Chicken Soup is one of the most common as well as most useful and beneficial kinds of Soup. (*NFP*, 970)

> And Tom brought [Samuel] chicken soup until he wanted to kill him. The lore had not died out of the world, and you still find people who believe that soup will cure any hurt or illness. (*EE*, 198)[8]

The most numerous borrowings from Gunn are associated with details which amplified characterization or which set the stage for dramatic episodes. Steinbeck ranged freely through Gunn's book, picking and choosing elements which either enriched his notion of a character's personality or confirmed his intuition toward that character's role. For example, Dr. Wilde owes certain attributes to Gunn. Steinbeck's deft sketch—"he was a combination doctor, priest, psychiatrist," with true humility and a proper sense of "the mystery of death" (*EE*, 243)—agrees with Gunn's qualities for successful ministration set forth in his preface, introduction and remarks. Lee, the Trasks' Chinese servant who becomes the novel's *raissoneur*, was intended to be a "philosopher" (*JN*, 73), which is to say, he was supposed to be reasonable, detached, forbearing, and compassionate. In the ten years since Cathy abandoned Adam and the twins, the responsibility for taking care of Aron and Caleb, running the Trask household, and looking after the ineffectual Adam fell to Lee (*EE*, 304). Indeed, while Steinbeck might have conceived Adam's decade of self-pity from Gunn's remark that in "comparison with the loss of a wife, all other earthly bereavements are trifling" (*NFP*, 91-92), the qualities which distinguish Lee were at least partly indebted to Gunn's belief that "the highest attainable virtue" lies in possessing "a mind which will not lose its tranquility in the severest adversity . . . a mind that is capable of enjoying the blessings of wealth and favor, or of being happy without them" (*NFP*, 91-92).[9]

Gunn's account of the tranquil mind certainly parallels Steinbeck's conception of Samuel's temperament as well, though Samuel is less consistent in this regard than Lee. However, Gunn's book offered Steinbeck other clues for his characterization of Samuel. The following quotations were written on 20 February 1951, shortly after Steinbeck began *East of Eden*. The borrowing indicates that Steinbeck was already employing Gunn's book to augment his own admittedly "hazy" recollections (*EE*, 8) of the Hamiltons (see also *JN*, 63). Samuel is one of Steinbeck's purest heroes, "one of those pillars of fire by whom little and frightened men are guided through the darkness" (*JN*, 115). It is fitting, then, that his noble attributes are consistently supported with material from Gunn that manifest innate efficacy. Gunn's operative belief in the vital conjunction between "virtuous regulation of the moral feelings, and the health of the body" (*NFP*, 98) found expression in Steinbeck's appraisal of Samuel: "And just as there was a cleanness about his body, so there was a cleanness in his thinking. Men coming to his blacksmith shop to talk and to listen dropped their cursing for a while, not from any kind of restraint but automatically, as though this were not the place for it" (*EE*, 11). Again, from a section on management of children, Steinbeck employed Gunn's observations to symbolize the effects of Samuel's voice—a distinctive feature of his appeal and his uniqueness:

This is one other means [of governing children] seldom regarded. I refer to the human voice. . . . We are by no means aware of the power of the voice in swaying the feelings of the soul. . . . blessed is that parent who is endowed with a pleasing utterance. What is that which lulls the infant to repose? It is no array of mere words. . . . It is the sound that strikes its little ear that soothes and composes. . . . A few notes, however, skillfully arranged, if uttered in a soft tone, are found to possess a magic influence. Think ye that this influence is confined to the cradle? No, it is diffused over every age. (*NFP*, 630)

Samuel had no equal for soothing hysteria and bringing quiet to a frightened child. It was the sweetness of his tongue and the tenderness of his soul. (*EE*, 11)

Samuel always kept a foreignness. Perhaps it was in the cadence of his speech, and this had the effect of making men, and women too, tell him things they would not tell to relatives or close friends. (*EE*, 11)

With nearly everything he appropriated from Gunn, Steinbeck reinscribed the original (by compression or expansion), avoided Gunn's sentimental language and rhetorical flourishes, and extracted the spirit of Gunn's passage to fit his conception of characterization. The limberness of Steinbeck's fictive imagination, his need to seek out the implications otherwise buried in declarative details, is evident in his transformation of Gunn's pedestrian account on melancholy. Steinbeck's covenant is with the language of fiction, and toward that end he re-ordered Gunn's material into the imagistic diction and crisp vernacular associated with his best writing. In Gunn's catalog of mental disaffection, Steinbeck saw the potential for a devastating portrait of Cyrus Trask's first wife, whose psychological quirks and aberrant religiosity eventually destroy her:

Melancholy is a purely mental disease. . . . The patient shuns society and seeks to be alone: is low-spirited, fretful, suspicious and inquisitive; has a distaste for everything. . . . Indeed, the disease can often be traced to some sudden misfortune as the cause, such as the death of a friend, or member of the family, disappointed affection, matrimonial difficulty. . . . So tormenting are these imaginary fears sometimes, that the unfortunate sufferer seeks every opportunity to end his troubles by self-destruction, or suicide. (*NFP*, 383-84)

Mrs. Trask was a pale, inside-herself woman. No heat of the sun ever reddened her cheeks, and no open laughter raised the corners of her mouth. She used religion as a therapy for the ills of the world and of herself, and she changed the religion to fit the ill. . . . Her search was quickly rewarded by the infection [gonorrhea] Cyrus brought home from the war. . . . Her god of communication became a god of vengeance. . . . It was quite easy for her to attribute her condition to certain dreams she had experienced while her husband was away. But the disease was not punishment enough for her nocturnal philandering. Her new god . . . demanded of her a sacrifice. She searched her mind for some proper egotistical humility and almost happily arrived at the sacrifice—herself. (*EE*, 15)

Steinbeck's attraction to Gunn's psychologizing extended to his conception of other characters, too. The condition of Tom Hamilton's mind in the moments before his suicide (*EE*, 407-10) suggests an affinity with Gunn's observations on hypochondria: "As in Melancholy, the mind is greatly disturbed, and the person is troubled often with imaginary evils." These symptoms are accompanied by "absurd and ridiculous fancies and apprehensions" (*NFP*, 384).

Some of the interior motivations for Steinbeck's characters, then, were suggested by Gunn's book. The melancholic mind Gunn describes above was, with some transmutation, brought into play for Steinbeck's treatment of Adam's reaction to Cathy's desertion. Adam's traumatic response (this from a man who had earlier escaped a prison chain gang) also owes some of its atmosphere to Gunn's remarks on the "bitter consciousness" that results "when we are wakened from our long-cherished confidence in that being whom we devotedly loved, and know that from henceforth it may never be indulged again" (*NFP*, 79). Cathy is important because she embodies evil.[10] But simply making her a "monster," Steinbeck said, was not sufficient justification for her appearance in the novel (*JN*, 42). He was equally interested in her effect on others: "since she had the most powerful impact on Adam and transmitted his blood to her sons and influenced the generations—she certainly belongs in this book" (*JN*, 42). In fact, the transmission of familial traits is one of Steinbeck's preeminent subjects in *East of Eden*, and is symbolized by the thematic refrain that the sins of the parents will be visited upon their children. It is also among Gunn's favorite subjects (*NFP*, 586). In its purest form, of course, this is a biblical injunction. But Steinbeck was not promulgating theological doctrine, he was writing a novel (*JN*, 104-05). Gunn's otherwise patronizing notions concerning the influence of the mother ("How all-powerful, for good or evil, is the influence of the mother" [*NFP*, 113]) and his observations about the "hereditary descent of intel-lectual and moral qualities" (*NFP*, 586) helped fill out the "psychological sign language" (*JN*, 27) necessary to sustain the Trasks' dilemma through three generations.

Similarly, a paragraph on anger (from "Of the Passions") supplied some working attributes to particularize another generative mythos—the Cain-Abel story.[11] In chapter 3 Steinbeck initiates the breach between Charles and Adam Trask when the enraged, irrational Charles nearly murders his brother (*EE*, 29-32). This powerful scene, instigated by Charles's jealousy over Cyrus's preference for Adam, is saliently represented in Gunn's assertion that "Anger is a violent emotion of the mind, arising from an injury whether real or imaginary, which openly vents itself against the offending party" (*NFP*, 61). That Steinbeck had Gunn at hand when he described the effects of Charles's rage appears more than merely coincidental in light of Gunn's remarks:

> The passionate man under its influence becomes incapable of distinguishing right from wrong. As an idiot or a madman, he is carried away by the impulse of the moment, a caprice of the imagination; as violent as a gust of wind, he rashly determines his conduct, and hur-

> ries to the perpetration of actions. . . . Behold that countenance under the influence of passion; it wears the strongest and most visible marks of uncontrollable power. (*NFP*, 61)

Given this heritage of psychological abnormality, most of the dysfunctional Trask family is damned in the process (Mrs. Trask, Cyrus, Cathy/Kate, Charles, Aron), one is saved (Caleb), and Adam wins a belated reprieve. He does so by overcoming the paralyzing effects of Cathy's abandonment, then later in the novel, by tacitly forgiving Caleb for his transgressions. The first of these breakthroughs occurs when Adam finally confronts his estranged wife. For years he has wallowed in self-pity and inactivity, but upon the death of Samuel Hamilton he realizes he must overcome his lethargy. In chapter 25 Adam visits Kate's notorious Salinas whorehouse to test his cherished and wholly invented memory of her against the reality she presents. After a shocking exchange, Adam acknowledges Kate's arrogance and hatred and is able to walk away with his dignity intact. In the opening section of chapter 26, Steinbeck begins to lay the foundation for the new Adam, apparently aided by a suggestion from Gunn. This borrowing once again demonstrates the alchemical quality of Steinbeck's imagination. In his discourse on joy, Gunn confines himself to its salutary physiological effects, while Steinbeck wants a stronger emotion—ecstasy—to signify the depth and degree of Adam's rebirth:

> This emotion is founded on delightful occurrences and causes a universal expansion of vital action. The blood, under its animating influence, flows more liberally through the whole system, the countenance becomes expanded, its expression brightens, and the whole surface acquires the ruddy tint and genial warmth of health. The body feels bouyant and lively. There is a consequent disposition to quick and cheerful muscular motions . . . In short, every function

> And again there are mornings when ecstasy bubbles in the blood, and the stomach and chest are tight and electric with joy. . . . Out of the gray throbbing an ecstasy arose. He [Adam] felt young and free and filled with hungry gaiety. He got off the train at King City, and, instead of going directly to the livery stable to claim his horse and buggy, he walked to Will Hamilton's new garage. (*EE*, 327)

> would *seem to be gladdened by the* happy moral condition. (*NFP*, 79)

Thematic and conceptual parallels comprise the third category of similarities between *East of Eden* and the *New Family Physician*. Steinbeck's borrowings in this sphere can be attributed to an awareness of kindred elements in Gunn. It is not overstating this connection to say that the usefulness of Gunn's book was heightened by its encompassing example. In Gunn's comprehensive system of knowledge—which addressed man's temporal condition and prepared him for spiritual salvation—Steinbeck recognized affiliations with his own cosmogonal intentions. Gunn's holistic ministration to the physical and metaphysical ailments of mankind arises from his unproblematized belief that humans are capable of action based on right reason, enlightened judgment, and faith (*NFP*, 506). Furthermore, Gunn's use of plain language (generally free from Latin phrases and erudite explanations) became the vehicle for expressing simple and basic truths (*NFP*, 5).

Both this instructional quality and urgent tone are evident in *East of Eden*, though with an often ironic, self-aware tone. A compelling convergence of symbolic antecedents and personal experiences occurred in Steinbeck's mind when he wrote the novel. It was originally conceived and written for his young boys, Thom and John (by his second wife Gwyn), who no longer lived permanently with him. He proposed to tell them who they were by explaining their genealogy and geographical background (*SLL*, 590) and to prepare them for their future's by relating "perhaps the greatest story of all—the story of good and evil . . ." (*JN*, 4). *East of Eden* was many things to Steinbeck, among them a way of accommodating his absentee parenthood by creating a paradigm of responsible human behavior. Because the book was written in plain language ("it will be necessary to speak very straight and clearly and simply," he told Pascal Covici [*JN*, 41]), he hoped to make it accessible to his children when they grew older, and provide a "background in the world of literature" (*JN*, 4). In this way, *East of Eden* is a kind of "manner book," a guide to ethical conduct and moral deportment passed on from elders to children (*JN*, 40). Just as Gunn's book was passed down to Steinbeck, so *East of Eden* completed the pietistic continuity and imaginative legacy of the Hamilton line.

Eventually, numerous direct passages addressed to the Steinbeck boys were excised from the published version. However, the extant expository sections and the manifold emphasis on parent-child relationships remained intact enough to carry the weight of Steinbeck's familial preoccupations. The frequently pernicious effects of Trask parents on their children (Cyrus and his wives on Charles and Adam; Adam, Charles and Cathy on Aron and Caleb) are balanced by the generally fortuitous example of the Hamiltons. The differences between the way the Trasks and the Hamiltons treat their children was illumined by Gunn's recommendations for parental governance, a condition much in the estranged Steinbeck's mind during the composition of *East of Eden* (*JN*, 11, 12, 25-26, 40, 41, 49, 50, 87, 114):

> The laws which govern children from the commencement should be simple, plain, reasonable, and firm. To govern properly, you must always govern yourself. Let your own example enforce the precepts you inculcate. To train up a child in the right way, you must walk in the right way yourself. Children are close observers. Beware of partiality; it has been the ruin of hundreds of children; they quickly perceive it, and become envious, which eventually destroys all the finer feelings of affection and respect (*NFP*, 604).

This quotation also has direct bearing on young Adam Trask's discovery of his father's tyranny, ironically exercised through Cyrus's partiality for Adam over Charles: "When a child first catches adults out—when it first walks into his grave little head that adults do not have divine intelligence, that their judgments are not always wise, their thinking true, their sentences just—his world falls into panic desolation. The gods are fallen and all safety gone" (*EE*, 19).

Walking in the right way, that is, exercising the freedom and ability to choose between right and wrong, good and evil, is both the predominant theme and the motivating humanistic purpose of *East of Eden*. Following the proper path is linked, of course, to Christian concepts. The Cain-Abel antithesis, and the central importance of the *timshel* doctrine (freedom of choice over sin) constitute the symbolic Biblical archetypes Steinbeck invested with psychological vitality and contemporary realism. While he certainly gained his major impetus from a fresh reading of Genesis (*JN*, 104), he also saw these concepts mirrored in Gunn's book.[12] The range of human emotions have a common source in the "probability of good and evil" (*NFP*, 39), an idea that is echoed in Steinbeck's "net of good and evil" (*EE*, 413) which snares all humans. The *timshel* doctrine, finally uttered by the dying Adam Trask as a means of forgiving his wayward son (*EE*, 602), has a parallel in Gunn's section on "Forgiveness," which "is not to be practiced by God alone, [but] is enjoined upon man by Divine precept as well as Divine example" (*NFP*, 82).

4

Beside these related elements, there is a shared affinity between Steinbeck's belief in the writer's "duty" to "lift up, to extend, to encourage . . ." (*JN*, 115) and Gunn's declamation that "Progress in moral and intellectual excellence is our duty, our honor, and our interest" (*NFP*, 12). However, where Gunn looks to God as the final solution of man's dilemma, Steinbeck considers the field of human activity, especially the nature of good and evil, to be the province of the writer:

> Thanks be unto God, where good is brought into operation, the evil must wear out, but the good never. If goodness, that is, the obedience of faith, working by love, were not omnipotent, society would never be improved—for propensity to sin, or to act from selfish impulse alone, is psychologically proved to be unavoidable and irresistable, unless the spirit of holiness be imparted. But experience also demonstrates that immorality does not necessarily continue; the entrance of true light, through the mercy and goodness of God, gives new power and direction to the soul. . . . (*NFP*, 589-90)

> We have only one story. All are built on the never-ending contest in ourselves of good and evil. And it occurs to me that evil must constantly respawn, while good, while virtue, is immortal. Vice has always a new fresh young face, while virtue is venerable as nothing else in this world is. (*EE*, 415)

This is the point where Gunn and Steinbeck part company, one returning to "the gem Religion!" (*NFP*, 13), the other embracing the personal "miracle of creation"—"the preciousness" in "the lonely mind of man" (*EE*, 132). Steinbeck's mind was receptive and alive to the nuances of experience, even those already textually recorded in other places. Appropriately, in a novel which was supposed to be "about everything," there are "venerable" resonances from a lifetime of reading, personal experiences, and memories. As part of his intervention into his own familial past and as part of his preparation for his writing—his "culling of all books plus my own invention" (*JN*, 31)—Gunn's *New Family Physician* was among the inset texts that helped Steinbeck construct the allusive circuit of *East of Eden* and aid the "little play" he hoped would be created in everyone's head.

Notes

[1] John Steinbeck, "The Novel Might Benefit by the Discipline, the Terseness of the Drama . . .," *Stage* 5 (January 1938): 50. For a seminal discussion of Steinbeck's experiments with fables and parables and a consideration of *East of Eden* as a "massive parable," see Lawrence William Jones, *John Steinbeck as Fabulist*, ed. Marston LaFrance, Steinbeck Monograph Series, no. 3 (Muncie, IN: John Steinbeck Society of America/Ball State University, 1973), 25-28. In his introduction to *Steinbeck: A Collection of Critical Essays* (Englewood Cliffs, NJ: Prentice-Hall, 1972), 9, Robert Murray Davis states flatly that "closer examination of the whole body of Steinbeck's work . . . shows that he was not often a realist in method and never wholly realistic in mode. Instead he consciously employed what Robert Scholes and Robert Kellogg [in *The Nature of Narrative* (1966)] call *fictional* as opposed to *empirical* forms." John Ditsky, in a speech at Steinbeck Festival X, held in Salinas in August 1989, carries on ways of reading Steinbeck's fabular project that highlight its disenchantment with traditional mimesis. See the revised speech in "The Late John Steinbeck: Dissonance in the Post-*Grapes* Era," *San Jose Studies* 18 (Winter 1992): 20-32.

[2] An overview of Steinbeck's borrowings is available in my "'Culling All Books': Steinbeck's Reading and *East of Eden*," *Steinbeck Quarterly* 14 (Winter-Spring 1981): 40-51.

[3] Gunn's book, first published in 1830, was originally called *Gunn's Domestic Medicine; or, Poor Man's Friend, in the House of Affliction, Pain, and Sickness*. Steinbeck used a later version, first titled *Gunn's New Domestic Physician*, then—according to the editions I examined at Yale University School of Medicine Library—from about 1865 on, titled *Gunn's New Family Physician: or, Home Book of Health; Forming a Complete Household Guide*. In his preface to an 1860 edition of *New Domestic Physician*, Gunn asked patrons to "bear in mind that this is not a new edition of the old work 'Gunn's Domestic Medicine,' which was published thirty years ago, but an entirely new work, first published in 1857, and now enlarged and perfected." Samuel Hamilton ar-

rived in California around 1870, so it is reasonable to assume he could have had a version of the newly revised and enlarged 1865 edition. In a passage from *East of Eden* quoted later in this essay, Steinbeck refers to the book as *Dr. Gunn's Family Medicine* and notes specifically that it was a black book with gold letters—as far as I can determine, the characteristic binding for *Gunn's New Family Physician.* All direct references will be to John C. Gunn, *Gunn's New Family Physician*, 100th ed., rev. and enl. (Cincinnati: Moore, Wilsatch and Baldwin, 1865) (hereafter cited as *NFP*.) Twenty years earlier Steinbeck had mentioned Gunn's book in *The Green Lady*, an unpublished novel on which *To a God Unknown* was based. In the typescript, which can be examined in the extensive John Steinbeck Collection at Stanford University's Department of Special Collections, Steinbeck stated that teacher Beth Willets, "a strong and subtle woman," "had read with care and interest every page of Doctor Gunn's Family Medicine" (4).

4 A good discussion of Samuel's mythic dimensions and his centrality to the novel are available in Richard Peterson, "*East of Eden*," in *A Study Guide to Steinbeck, Part II*, ed. Tetsumaro Hayashi (Metuchen, NJ: Scarecrow Press, 1979), 76-78. Recently Louis Owens pointed out that in Samuel's growth toward "symbolhood," Steinbeck is allowing us "to see the free inventive play" of his novelistic imagination. See "*East of Eden*," in *A New Study Guide to Steinbeck's Major Works, With Critical Explications*, ed. Tetsumaro Hayashi (Metuchen, NJ: Scarecrow Press, 1993), 78-79.

5 In the original autograph manuscript of *East of Eden* (1951), on the double-numbered folio page 5/13, Steinbeck was explicit about the differences in Liza's and Samuel's reading habits: "In all her active life she read only two books: The Bible and Pilgrim's Progress. But when she was very old and alone she read one other—a novel named Mother, by Kathleen Norris. And whereas all his life Samuel read starvingly every book he could buy or borrow, his wife never raised her small bright eyes from his Bible and Pilgrim's Progress." The manuscript is part of the Steinbeck Works archive at the Harry Ransom Humanities Research Center, University of Texas, Austin (hereafter cited as *Ams*).

6 Except in the sense of imaginative possession, Steinbeck did not have his grandfather's copy of Gunn's tome. In a letter to me on 30 November 1979, Steinbeck's sister, Elizabeth Ainsworth, recalled the "big and thick black book," but remembers distinctly having presented it to her son, after whose death the book unaccountably disappeared. Elaine Steinbeck has told me on a couple of occasions that several attempts to find Gunn's book among her husband's belongings and library have failed. As Steinbeck's references to Gunn and his borrowings from Gunn are generally accurate (the sections listed in the passage on page of *East of Eden* occur primarily in the fifth, sixth, and seventh divisions of Gunn's book (*NFP*, 522-698]), Steinbeck either had another, similar copy at his disposal in 1951, talked with someone in his family who remembered the book accurately, or sometime earlier had himself taken careful notes.

7 Steinbeck used another of the symptoms for green sickness—"feet and ankles often become swollen" (*NFP*, 546)—to describe Kate's "thickened" legs and feet (*EE*, 316). The entire episode about Kate's gradual dominance over and eventual murder of Faye (chapters 20-22) necessitated research by Steinbeck (*JN*, 92). In conjunction with other toxilogical sources, he might also have con-

sulted Gunn's section on medical flora for information on poison (nux vomica, or strychnine—*EE*, 248; *NFP* 837) and purgative (croton oil—*EE*, 249; *NFP*, 837) which Kaye gives Faye.

[8] In a letter to me on 3 December 1979, Elaine Steinbeck underscored the totemic nature of Gunn's book for her husband's family and confirmed Gunn's usefulness as a source for medical information in *East of Eden*, but she emphasized that the chicken soup cure was also a longstanding Steinbeck family joke.

[9] Lee's equanimity and poise bear striking resemblances to a character in Raoul Faure's 1948 novel *Lady Godiva and Master Tom*, which Steinbeck had read, perhaps with some glee (*SLL*, 334; *SR*, 41). Ezra, Sir Leofric's adviser and treasurer, has a predeliction for philosophy and an affinity for management similar to Lee's. For more on Lee, see Tetsumaro Hayashi's informative "The 'Chinese Servant' in *East of Eden*," *San Jose Studies* 18 (Winter 1992): 52-60.

[10] It has become a staple of biographical interpretation to claim that Steinbeck's portrayal of Cathy/Kate was modeled on his ex-wife, Gwyn. It was a realization Pascal Covici made years ago (*S&C*, 166) and one Jackson J. Benson reestablishes in *Looking for Steinbeck's Ghost* (Norman: University of Oklahoma Press, 1988), 95-96, as does David Wyatt in his introduction to Penguin's Twentieth-Century Classics edition of *East of Eden* (xi). But as Mimi Reisel Gladstein notes in "The Strong Female Principle of Good—or Evil: The Women of *East of Eden*," *Steinbeck Quarterly* 24 (Winter-Spring 1991): 32, Cathy is "more than" an allegorical embodiment of "Steinbeck's hostility" to his ex-wife. The portrait of Kate also had literary antecedents. For example, for the parallels with Satan's serpent imagery in Milton's *Paradise Lost*, see John H. Timmerman, *John Steinbeck's Fiction: The Aesthetics of the Road Taken* (Norman: University of Oklahoma Press, 1986), 226-28. Roy S. Simmonds provides a contemporary parallel with William March's *The Bad Seed* in "Cathy Ames and Rhoda Penmark: Two Child Monsters," *Mississippi Quarterly* 39 (Spring 1986): 91-101.

[11] For an illuminating reading of Steinbeck's complex use of the Cain-Abel saga/theme, see Ricardo Quinones, *The Changes of Cain: Violence and the Lost Brother in Cain and Abel Literature* (Princeton: Princeton University Press, 1991), 135-44.

[12] Steinbeck's use of the Bible and his Christological references and allusions in *East of Eden* have been documented by Peter Lisca in *The Wide World of John Steinbeck* (New Brunswick, NJ: Rutgers University Press, 1958), 261-63, and with special dexterity by Joseph Fontenrose, in *John Steinbeck: An Introduction and Interpretation* (New York: Barnes and Noble, 1963), 120-24. Recently John H. Timmerman has written a convenient overview of the whole subject in "John Steinbeck's Use of the Bible: A Descriptive Bibliography of the Critical Tradition," *Steinbeck Quarterly* 21 (Winter-Spring 1988): 24-39.

"Working at the Impossible": The Presence of *Moby-Dick* in *East of Eden*

"A good writer always works at the impossible. There is another kind who pulls in his horizons, drops his mind as one lowers rifle sights. And giving up the impossible he gives up writing. Whether fortunate or unfortunate, this has not happened to me."
—John Steinbeck, *Journal of a Novel* (1969)

"The writer who writes within . . . the modern romance tradition may not be writing novels which in all respects partake of novelistic orthodoxy; but as long as those works have vitality, as long as they present something that is alive, however eccentric its life may seem to the general reader, then they have to be dealt with; and they have to be dealt with on their own terms."
—Flannery O'Connor, *Mystery and Manners* (1961)

1

"No one is his own sire."
—Herman Melville to Evert Duyckinck (1849)

The following event is such an intriguing example of serendipity that it might as well have been invented. On 23 January 1857, John Steinbeck's patrilineal great-grandfather, Walter Dickson, and his wife, Sarah Eldredge Dickson, two Massachusetts Seventh-Day Baptists who had undertaken agricultural and missionary work in the Middle East, entertained Herman Melville during the writer's extended recuperative journey through the Holy Land (Melville's travel cure proved nearly as tiresome as his ailment). "I walked out to see Mr. Dickson's place. About an hour from Joppa Gate. . . . At the house we were . . . introduced to Mrs. D. a respectable looking elderly woman. . . . They have two daughters married here to Germans,

& living near, fated to beget a progeny of hybrid vagabonds. —Old Dickson seems a man of Puritanic energy, and being inoculated with this preposterous Jew mania, is resolved to carry his Quixotism through to the end. . . . The whole thing is half melancholy, half farcical—like all the rest of the world," Melville confided that day.[1]

It takes a Quixote to know one: in sketching Deacon Dickson, world-weary Melville, who believed he might have written the "Gospels" in his century (most recently *The Confidence-Man*, his bitter vision of human gullibility), projected some of his own obsessiveness, morbidity, and frustration into the portrait. Beyond that, he unintentionally penned the earliest notice of the future author of *The Grapes of Wrath* and *East of Eden*, because though Steinbeck rarely spoke publicly of his paternal line, he clearly inherited the Dickson's puritanic energy and evangelistic mania (Walter Dickson contributed fanatical letters to the Seventh-Day Baptists' organ, the *Sabbath Recorder*), if not for preposterous tasks like farming the desert and reaping wayward souls before the millennium, then surely for the equally arduous work—"the ancient commission"—of writing books with which to reach minds and hearts: "Man himself has become our greatest hazard and our only hope. So that today, Saint John the Apostle may well be paraphrased: In the end is the *word*, and the word is *man*, and the word is *with* man," Steinbeck testified in his Nobel Prize Acceptance Speech in Stockholm on 10 December 1962.[2]

In what must surely be among the most unusual of American literary visitations, Melville's words, it might be said, touched Steinbeck from before the cradle as well as from beyond the grave. Although Steinbeck was aware of his family's tragedies and misfortunes in the Holy Land as early as 1945 (*SLL*, 278), it was two decades later before news of Melville's visit to his ancestors reached him. In Haifa in 1966, on a tour through the Holy Land, Steinbeck was presented with the journal entry which had been published eleven years earlier in a scholarly edition of Melville's *Journal of a Visit to Europe and the Levant* (*TAJS*, 979). Steinbeck immediately wrote to his agent, Elizabeth Otis: "Oh! there are lovely things in the Melville account of the Dicksons. I wonder why we have never found it before."[3] And yet the implications of Melville's visit had started converging at least a decade and a half earlier, for Steinbeck had long been aware of the "lovely things" to be found in Melville's prose—

particularly *Moby-Dick* (1851), "one of his favorite novels" (*TAJS*, 667)—which Steinbeck discovered with full force a year or so before its centenary, when a spate of Melville biographies, critical studies, and editions of *Moby-Dick* attracted public attention between 1949 and 1950.[4]

While at first glance—compared, say, to his contemporaries, Thomas Wolfe and William Faulkner—John Steinbeck might seem an unlikely benefactor of Melville's expressive romantic strain, the fact is that Steinbeck became passionately attracted to *Moby-Dick* and carried on a conversation with it until his death, so that this chapter can be considered a trope of that referentiality, a doubloon reflecting various facets of belated engagement and literary inheritance. Steinbeck's reading of Melville's great book was more than simply a coincidence, an expediency, or a vicarious exercise, but another instance of something profound that "happened" to him like a gifted presence he could not refuse that entered the environment of his awareness, "the warp and woof of . . . consciousness" (*EE*, 413). "The older text," Robert Alter claims, "is not just something the poet reads but something that *possesses* him, and the recreation of the old work in the new is an effort to make sense of that experience of possession, to explain what cultural memory means."[5] Though far different in many respects, *East of Eden* is, like *Moby-Dick*, a searching, questioning, speculative fiction (*TAJS*, 667-68) which points up the difficulties of positing a coherent ideology about the mass American experience. Melville's ship of state (presented through his inflating rhetoric of democratic tragedy) and Steinbeck's garden of Eden (presented through its conflating language of sexual pathos) function as powerful tropes precisely because they are rendered in ironic ways, and in ways that fit in their authors' politics and the shifting aesthetic tempers of their respective eras.[6]

Besides interrogating the deepest psychological implications of malevolence in the universe, as well as exploitation, anger, misogyny, and silence, both novels enact drastic statements on the abuse of power and the nature—and limits—of parental and literary authority. And yet beneath—or in spite of—the overarching mythology of corrupt national and personal identities (expansionism and capitalism, tyranny and dynastic destiny) that imbues both books, Melville and Steinbeck arrive at a humanistic (and hermeneutical) consensus. Just values, they suggest, reside in finely balanced personal gestures of sacramental or imaginative communication that acknowledges Otherness: Ishmael narrating his story that honors language and blesses whales, even as it accommodates their essential slipperiness and unknowableness; Steinbeck's narrator culminating his tale with Adam Trask's deathbed blessing that honors individual integrity even as it underscores the communal burden of complicity. To arrive at these moments, Melville and Steinbeck produced unconventional "hybrid" fictions—self-reflexive but not necessarily solipsistic—with which to address the meaning of meaning and to lay bare the truth-making process.[7] Indeed, once tentatively completed, that process begins again: Ishmael revisions (and in chapter 54, "The Town-Ho's Story," rehearses) his own drama before telling it; Cal Trask appears at the threshold of revising the sinful tales of his parents. The trajectory of each narrative at once decenters meaning and defers closure in a constant process of reinventing itself.

Keeping in mind that an inevitable distortion occurs in cases of creative inheritance and appropriation arrived at through reading, this essay focuses primarily on *East of Eden* as a work which receives and reinscribes some key Melvillean echoes, resonances, parallels, and strategies. In seeking out these textual affinities and intertextual entanglements with Melville's central book, and in proposing ways in which these realities endure in a modulated way in Steinbeck's work, my purpose here is interpretative and descriptive rather than traditionally evaluative, and is holistic and ecological rather than patently critical. Regarding these avenues of inheritance, I do not think that the scene of Steinbeck's writing was situated in a murderous field of Oedipal warfare, as Harold Bloom has so dramatically proposed, but in a middle ground of transference, an arena of debate between Steinbeck's unmediated dream of originality (which he never realized) and the local restraints of his own imaginative (re)sources (which were always apparent to him.)[8] Of course, *East of Eden* became the site of a certain amount of inevitable struggle, not just between precursor Melville and latter-day Steinbeck, but also between Steinbeck's nostalgia for being nurtured by the past and his desire to transform it. Steinbeck's insistence on reclaiming the operation of free will (never fully attainable but never fully abdicated either) can be considered a metonym for his newly engendered authorial self, which paradoxically wanted to stretch its artistic limits at the same time it sought to accommodate (and disguise) constraints imposed by Melville's text, the boundaries of literary tradition, and of course Steinbeck's own writerly abilities: "My god this can be a good book if I can only write it as I can hear it in my mind" (*JN*, 42).

2

"Great writing has been a staff to lean on, a mother to consult. . . ."
—John Steinbeck, *Journal of a Novel*

When, in January 1951, after several years of gestation and false starts, John Steinbeck sat down to begin concentrated work on the book he had been preparing for all his life, he was at a crucial artistic moment. Steinbeck realized the necessity for a thorough transformation in his writing style, narrative technique, and subject matter. Besides the influence of Cold War politics, personal upheavals occurred in 1948 to propel Steinbeck toward his revolution—he grieved for his closest friend and former collaborator, Edward F. Ricketts, who died in a May train wreck, and he was devastated that summer (and for a long time to come) by a bitter divorce from his second wife Gwyn, mother of his two children (*TAJS*, 614-22). This collision of events turned him inside out: his emotional and psychological wounds figured in his treatment of Samuel Hamilton's death and in his searing portrayal of Cathy Ames Trask's womanhood. A novelist most famous for the objective documentary style, phalanx (group-man) theory, nonteleological philosophy, and proletarian bent of his late 1930s fiction, Steinbeck took a headlong dive into uncharted waters by consciously abandoning the dictates of prevailing literary realism that had marked his most successful earlier novels. He deliberately turned away from the "squeemish" [sic] mimetic mode, "the modern fashionable method" (*JN*, 43) that emphasized tightly controlled movement, circumscribed characterization, seamless omniscient narration, and fidelity to the aesthetic illusion of social realism.

Instead, like Melville leaving behind the mannered successes of *Redburn* and *White-Jacket* and launching into the treacherous philosophical depths of *Moby-Dick*, at a similarly conflicted moment of personal and national crisis, Steinbeck gave up his secure routine and embraced a comparatively naked presentation of self in looser, grander, more expressive mode of fiction.[9] In this crisis of authority, this moment "of profound readjustments" (*SLL*, 359), he realized there was much on the line: "The craft or art of writing is the clumsy attempt to find symbols for the wordlessness. In utter loneliness a writer tries to explain the inexplicable. And sometimes if he is very fortunate and if the time is right, a very little of what he is trying to do trickles through—not ever much. And if he is a writer wise enough to know it can't be done, then he is not a writer at all. A good writer always works at the impossible" (*JN*, 4). *East of Eden* was meant to embody Steinbeck's deepest beliefs in the sanctity of individual dignity, the "glittering instrument" of the human soul, and his advocacy toward the power of language to effect communication if not outright transformation. For Steinbeck as well as for *Eden*'s characters, such changes began in utter loneliness and ended in spiritual humility where language might "establish a relationship of meaning, of feeling, of observing" (*SLL*, 523).

East of Eden is Steinbeck's partly historical, partly fictional epic tale, based on the Cain-Abel story, of several generations of fictional Connecticut Trasks (Steinbeck took their name from "a friend of my father's—a whaling master named Captain Trask" whose family lived near Paso Robles) and quasi-real-life Hamiltons (Steinbeck's matrilinear family) whose lives run parallel, then contiguously, in a sixty-year period from 1862 to 1918, mostly in California. (Each successive generation of Trasks is fated to repeat the sins of its fathers.) At one pole of this counterpoised novel Steinbeck has situated his semifictional, larger-than-life grandfather, Samuel Hamilton, who stands, like Ishmael, for everything potentially sacramental in the fallen world. Against this pragmatic yeoman savant (William James is his favorite philosopher)—and against everyone else in the novel for that matter—Steinbeck sets up Adam Trask's wife, Cathy Ames Trask, the mother of their two children, Caleb and Aron (whom she abandons after she shoots Adam and leaves him for dead). Kate, as she comes to be known, is a seducer, a murderer, the vicious madame of a Salinas brothel, and a moral "monster" of the first order who dominates the book. Adam Trask is ranged between Samuel and Kate. This patently American Adam (conceived several years before R. W. B. Lewis gave the literary type a name) is naive, guileless in the ways of heterosexual love, and fatally determined to create a dynastic farm on his land. If Kate is the axle of the novel, Adam is its hub. He fails the edenic ideals of his quest, but he becomes the instrument through which emphasis on free will—a conditional situation symbolized by the word *timshel* (meaning "Thou mayest") —permits human beings (his wayward son Caleb first and foremost) to gain the potential to triumph over sin and to return to the wellsprings of their integrity.

This quick plot sketch, however, does little to capture Steinbeck's initial enterprise. In its original form, *East of Eden* boldly departed from tradition. In fact it was a startlingly innovative, double-voice, cross-referential work. On the left hand page of a large (10 3/4 x 14 inch) lined ledger book Steinbeck wrote daily warm-up letters. This became a kind of running workshop journal addressed to Pascal Covici, his esteemed Viking Press editor, who had, in a sense, filled in for the deceased Ed Ricketts as Steinbeck's latter-day compatriot. These entries formed an informal, personal commentary on Steinbeck's daily artistic processes and his intentions for the novel. Across from the journal, on the right hand page of the ledger book, Steinbeck composed the chapters of his novel, which was initially addressed specifically to his sons, Thom and John, aged six and four: "I am choosing to write this book to my sons. . . . They have no background in the world of literature, they don't know the great stories of the world as we do. And so I will tell them one of the greatest, perhaps the greatest story of all—the story of good and evil, of strength and weakness, of love and hate, of beauty and ugliness. I shall try to demonstrate to them how these doubles are inseparable—how neither can exist without the other and how out of their groupings creativeness is born" (*JN*, 4). The novel's essential dualism was not only thematic, then, but formal as well.

Unfortunately, the published novel represents a truncated version of Steinbeck's "inseparable" conception. All of the journal entries were dropped (later to be published posthumously in 1969 as *Journal of a Novel*) and many of the direct homilies to his children were dropped as well, so *East of Eden* is a good deal tamer and leaner than Steinbeck planned.[10] Nevertheless, the published version along with the integrally linked journal (it too was slightly edited for publication) retains enough traces of Steinbeck's initial informing vision and spirit to show that he was working at a level of discourse far different from his previous fiction. "In considering this book and in planning for it I have thought of many great and interesting tricks. I have made new languages, new symbols, a new kind of writing: and now that the book is ready to go, I am throwing them all away and starting from scratch" (*JN*, 6). In the process of reexamining the ontological ground of his past work, Steinbeck worked hard to achieve a perspectival position with *East of Eden*, which, he felt, combined "all forms, all methods, all approaches" into a unique order. "I am not going to put artificial structures on this book," he said. "The real structures are enough. I mean the discipline imposed by realities and certain universal writers" (*JN*, 118), of whom Melville—with his deep sense of Manicheism, his abiding awareness of philosophical and aesthetic dualism, and his use of alternating narrative and cetological chapters in *Moby-Dick*—was surely one.

Throughout 1951, as Steinbeck worked at his "impossible" task of finding "symbols for the wordlessness," Melville's masterpiece was a model type and forerunner of his bold experiment: "The admired books now were by no means the admired books of their day. I believe that Moby Dick, so much admired now, did not sell its small first edition in ten years. And it will be worse than that with this book" (*JN*, 29).[11] *Moby-Dick* exemplified the nonlinear narrative and dramatic "pace" (*JN*, 29) Steinbeck sought to revive in contemporary form. Steinbeck's newly adapted technique would allow him to develop his characters not only through the contemporary means of dialogue and exposition but through the older method of personal analysis as well (*JN*, 43). The technique also would allow the writer to slip in and out of his triple role as an implied narrator, editorial speaker, and actor in his own novel. "For many years I did not occur in my own writing. . . . But in this book I am in it and I don't for a moment pretend not to be," he said (*JN*, 24). Steinbeck's eclectic method—"neither new nor old fashioned" (*JN*, 43)—drew inspiration from Melville's phenomenological version of the American romance, with its go-for-broke style, exemplified by mythopoesis, philosophical dualism, self-referential artifice, processive narration, multiple authorial roles/voices, and symbolism.[12]

In this breach *Moby-Dick* became an empowering book for Steinbeck because, while it could not set him utterly free, it represented the fully orchestrated symphony of effects, the encyclopedic canvas, and the atmosphere of mystery and probability that Steinbeck set out to resuscitate in 1951, the hundredth anniversary of *Moby-Dick*'s publication. Thom Steinbeck, the novelist's eldest son, recalled his father first introducing him to *Moby-Dick* that centennial year by reading it aloud in hopes of firing his eldest son's appreciation for reading. He pointed specifically to his father's continued enthusiasm for the novel's "elegant form"—its dazzling layered construction, and its bold, rhythmic, energetic language, and its abundant symbolic technique, characterization, and setting. Steinbeck considered *Moby-Dick* to be a "sacred" text, an exemplary story of human conduct—at once an enduring American culture myth, a profoundly magical journey, and a moving drama of redemption. The tragic story of unrepentant Captain Ahab's doomed, vengeful quest aboard the *Pequod* to slay the white whale, narrated in the alternatingly chatty, philosophical, comical, ironical, lyrical, scientific, literary, and theatrical voices of survivor Ishmael, is a supreme literary achievement, one of "the great stories of the world," the older Steinbeck claimed.[13]

Moby-Dick is also a testament to Quixotic obsessiveness on at least three levels—Ahab's monomaniacal hunt for the beast, Ishmael's countering sacramental desire to poeticize the living whale, and of course, beyond that, the driven Melville's need to create a capacious fictive structure—part epic, part stage drama, part anatomy, part lyric poem—that would incorporate these antagonistic, extreme modes of perception, cognition, and being without trivializing any one of them: "To produce a mighty book, you must choose a mighty theme," Ishmael announces (*MD*, 456). Mighty *Moby-Dick* is a cosmogony, an entire world within the covers of a single work. That world was panoramic, comprehensive, epic, and encyclopedic in its reach and in its sweep and depth of knowledge. *Moby-Dick* attempts to explain ("Let me explain," Ishmael says over and over) the deepest wonders of the human and natural world to Melville's audience: "life—the cosmos and everything in it taken as a microcosm—confronts man as a compelling but insoluble mystery."[14] Steinbeck's obsessive intention in *East of Eden* was similar: he began the novel to explain the world's Manichean bipolarity and sexual mysteries to his two young sons and to introduce them to their roots via his recollection of their ancestors. In his imaginative reconstruction of California's Salinas Valley, Steinbeck chronicled the evolution of his personal cosmogony as surely as the *Pequod* portrayed Melville's on the *Acushnet*.[15] In anatomizing that world—in attending to details about individual characters, geography and setting, as well as the large motions of historical and social forces—Steinbeck too exhibited his own brand of encyclopedic knowledge: "The kind of book I am writing should contain everything that seems to me to be true" (*JN*, 24).

3

"It is with fiction as with religion: it should present another world, and yet one to which we feel the tie."
—Herman Melville, *The Confidence-Man* (1857)

While *East of Eden* can be considered a "poetic answering" of *Moby-Dick*, obviously they do not fit like hand and glove; the latter is not a slavish knock-off of the former, and it is simply not true that "*Moby-Dick* is referred to repeatedly in the *East of Eden* letters."[16] There is actually only one direct reference in *Journal of a Novel* and, more often than not, Melville's book is latent in *East of Eden*, lurking in the shadows behind and below Steinbeck's private and public texts, which is to say at the informing edges of his consciousness, where it waits to be transformed, revised, reinvested. Its proximity is enough, however, to color a great deal of Steinbeck's novel on everything from the pursuit of artistic form to the achievement of enabling beliefs, as I hope the following section will illuminate.

Both writers were so inflamed by their topics that their enthusiasm cascaded into private realms. Perhaps because they were aware that their respective manuscripts were extremely unorthodox (despite their nominal subjects, both books are as much "about" creativity and the resources of language as anything else), both men seemed to require a specific, trusted audience to explain their efforts. In 1850 and 1851 from his venues in New York City, then in Pittsfield, Massachusetts, Melville provided an inside narrative of his intentions by penning some of his most brilliant letters, first to Evert Duyckinck, but then especially to his Lenox neighbor, soul mate, and confidant, Nathaniel Hawthorne. Melville's letters have a sweep and energy characteristic of his restless, questioning mind; they manifest an air of impassioned self-rehearsal as he ranges from news of domestic particulars to talk of "ontological heroics" (*C*, 196). Melville dedicated *Moby-Dick* to the older Hawthorne, "In token of my admiration for his genius." When the novel was published, Hawthorne's reaction (his letter unfortunately is not extant) overjoyed Melville: "A sense of unspeakable security is in me this moment," he exclaimed in November 1851, "on account of your having understood the book" (*C*, 212).

Steinbeck built his self-confidence and focused his attention by journalizing; his daily letters to Covici, also full of explanatory fervor, ranged in subject from such quotidian tidbits as his preference in pencils to arcane philosophical disquisitions. Through it all he addressed the elder Covici as a mentor and confidant. Steinbeck too wrote his novel in New York and in Massachusetts, where, during the summer of 1951, he also crafted by hand for Covici a special mahogany box to hold the autograph manuscript of his novel. *East of Eden,* of course, is lavishly dedicated to Covici in "gratitude and love." (In his spare time Steinbeck amused himself by fishing and boating with his boys, whittling wooden sperm whales, and visiting the Nantucket Whaling Museum.)

Both books enact a retrospective view of the historical, personal, and literary past. *Moby-Dick* and *East of Eden* rise primarily from autobiographical ground, from acutely felt personal awarenesses and closely observed experiences. Filtered through the symbolic distance created by memory, those experiences are further augmented, if not in fact shaped, by research. Melville reprised his *Acushnet* whaling experience of a decade past; Steinbeck recreated his native California from Manhattan and Nantucket, two eastern islands a continent away from the main geographical setting of his book. Additionally, the opening chapters of *East of Eden* function like Melville's "Loomings" because they evoke through memory Steinbeck's generative past. As with the conflicting "wild conceits that floated" into Ishmael's "inmost soul" (*MD*, 7), Steinbeck's "rich" past looms both beautiful and terrible and becomes an ominous introduction to the book's bittersweet action. Steinbeck's incantatory refrain—"I remember"—announces on *East of Eden*'s first page as surely as *Moby-Dick*'s catchy opening—"Call me Ishmael"—a journey into a world of imaginative proportions vivified by the shape-shifting teller of the tale (who defies narrational propriety); it is a magical world signaled by the most basic and inviting of narrative licenses: "Once upon a time. . . ." In this vein, for Melville "true places" are never "down in any map" (*MD*, 55), while for Steinbeck, the storyteller "must name a thing before you can note it on your hand-drawn map" (*EE*, 6).

If these intensely felt books embody the primal energy and turbulence of geographical space, they also are enriched by literary artifice and allusions. Both Melville and Steinbeck read to write, to use Charles Olson's phrase, so that each book reflects its author's literary researches and preferences. Melville ransacked more extensively than Steinbeck but probably no more shamelessly. Melville's inspired transformation of his literary, historical, and cetological sources is but one example of Ishmael's contention that he "swam through libraries" (*MD*, 136).[17] Steinbeck's borrowings—his quoted and inset texts—were similarly functional and aesthetic. *East of Eden*—his "culling of all books plus my own invention" (*JN*, 31)—draws upon works by Herodotus, Plutarch, Marcus Aurelius, Dr. John Gunn, Lewis Carroll, William James, and Erich Fromm (*SR*, xxxii-xliii). Both novels center on and exploit embedded biblical texts for their own ends—the typological Old Testament parables of Jonah (*Moby-Dick*) and of Cain and Abel (*East of Eden*) are central to plot, theme, and characterization in each. Plurality—what Melville playfully termed a "higgledy-piggledy" quality (*MD*, xvii)—is further encoded in the many literary styles and discourses; although Melville resorts far more frequently than Steinbeck to puns, jokes, and extravagant metaphors, both writers mix graphic realism with soaring philosophical flights and discursive exposition with rapturous, lyrical passages.

Both writers also create plots which strain plausibility and therefore require our willing suspension of disbelief. This is especially true of characterization as well. In Ahab, Queequeg, and Fedallah, as well as in Sam Hamilton, Cathy Trask, and Lee, Melville and Steinbeck invented characters who are more often allegorical or exotic than physically or socially normative. Many characters have crippled or missing body parts (Ahab's leg, Moby Dick's deformed lower jaw, Captain Boomer's arm, Cyrus Trask's leg, Kate's hand, "wrinkled as a pale monkey's paw" [*EE*, 324]), or they are scarred in significant, emblematic ways (Ahab's lightning scar, Queequeg's tattoos, Charles Trask's and Kate's Cain-marked foreheads), under-scoring their links to the nether world of grotesque experience—the "speechlessly quick chaotic bundling of a man into Eternity" (*MD*, 37) and the interminable hell of the Trask family's conflicted relationships.

Kate is Steinbeck's most diabolical example. She is a demented isolato, a female tyrant, who sometimes out-Ahabs Ahab in her cold-heartedness, selfish pursuit of power, and calculating disregard for the sanctity of human life. The similarities between these two sensational gothic characters seem more than coincidental, as Warren French noted thirty-five years ago.[18] Ahab's inordinate pride, his overbearing hubris, and the "sultanism" of his brain (*MD*, 147)—"'I'd strike the sun if it insulted me. . . . Who's over me?'" (*MD*, 164)—is echoed in Steinbeck's portrayal of Kate—"'I'm smarter than humans. Nobody can hurt me,'" she says (*EE*, 323). Both Ahab and Kate are driven by fate; Ahab's soul, grooved to run on iron rails, has its equivalent in Steinbeck's statement that "Whatever she had done, she had been driven to do" (*EE*, 552). Both are reclusive and isolated; bear-like Ahab in his "caved" cabin "sucking his own paws" (*MD*, 153) is echoed by cat-like Kate in the "cave" lean-to of her brothel feeding on her own enmity, anger, and silence (*EE*, 474). Furthermore, both dissemble to advance their secret agendas and both necessarily employ Ahab's "external arts and entrenchments" (*MD*, 148) to consolidate their power over underlings. In addition, both debase the process they are in charge of fostering. Ahab selfishly undermines the economic purpose of the *Pequod*'s owners. In the world of Steinbeck's novel, where "the church and the whorehouse arrived in the Far West" at the same time (*EE*, 217), prostitution purportedly provides some redeeming social value, except at Kate's brothel, where bondage, sadomasochism, and blackmail make it a dirty commercial venture, fit only for revenge and extortion. Ahab's dream of revenge—to get even with Moby Dick for dismasting him—is reflected in Kate's admission to Adam that her deepest purpose is to get even with Mr. Edwards, the New England whoremaster who once disfigured her and left her for dead (*EE*, 323).

Just as Ahab, who, like some twisted latter-day Prometheus, vows to "spit his last breath" (*MD*, 572) at Moby Dick for mankind's sake, Kate too is totally consumed by hatred—ostensibly for Adam but also for the human race in general, which, in an equally perverse way, she hopes to disabuse of hypocrisy. At key points before their demise (to be discussed in section 4), Kate and Ahab both perform litanies that reaffirm the source of their demonism: Ahab's address to the "clear spirit of clear fire" in chapter 119 ("The Candles")—"'To neither love nor reverence wilt thou be kind; and e'en for hate thou canst but kill'" (*MD*, 507)—finds its cunning duplicate in Kate's gleeful assertion that only hatred, evil, and folly exist in the world (*EE*, 321-26). Partly Ahab, partly Moby Dick, then, Kate's function is central to the dramatic and moral action of the book. Like Ahab's doubloon or Ishmael's metaphor of philosophical whiteness, the depth of each character's personality is judged by his or her reaction to Kate's bottomless, inscrutable evil. But confrontation can lead to spiritual or psychological redemption: just as Ishmael was saved from his nightmare vision of complicity in "The Try-Works," first Adam is reborn from his "nightmare dream" vision and escapes Kate's cruelty, then their son Cal is redeemed as a whole person by knowledge of his mother's tainted nature and by his father's deathbed blessing (*EE*, 602).

Indeed, just as both books mingle mythic, psychological, or moral wellsprings of human motivation and conduct, aspects of characterization and setting overlap and blend into each other. In *East of Eden*, Lee, the Trask family's Chinese servant, is wise, gentle, and nurturing with both adults and children (Adam Trask acts like both at times). Far from being a stereotypical oriental character, Lee plays a variety of increasingly complex roles in the novel. And Lee is also Steinbeck's androgynous man, his feminized man who, in the tradition of Ishmael's "marriage" to Queequeg, remains committed to constancy in human relationships, not in an exotic world elsewhere but in the new frontier of human endeavor, the family of man, the place Ishmael himself prophesied as the sphere of "attainable felicity" (*MD*, 416). In his scholarly investigations into the meaning of *timshel*, Lee replicates the task of Melville's "sub-sub librarian" (*MD*, xvii) by providing the etymology of the book's central symbol word. Like Queequeg's hieroglyphic coffin, *timshel* can save lives by preserving free choice and moral duty and restoring love and integrity. Steinbeck's linguistic symbol empowers select characters to challenge sin by entering the full sacrament of their imperfect humanness, their mutual "joint stock company," to use Melville's apt phrase. Lee has some of Queequeg in him as well—paradoxically, though they are both nonwestern, they are the most Christian-like people in their novels—generous, forgiving, compassionate, and understanding.

Moreover, both works employ settings which reinforce symbolic aspects of characterization. Indeed, Thom Steinbeck singled out setting as one of *Moby-Dick*'s chief attractions to his father.[19] By this he meant that Melville had made the unfamiliar cosmos of the globe-circling *Pequod* "real" at the very same time he invested it with mystery, wonder, and terror. By setting *East of Eden* in California's agriculturally rich Salinas Valley, Steinbeck privileged its small-town past and sought to make real a world unfamiliar to an increasingly sophisticated and urban audience and to locate qualities of wonder and evil, sacredness and profanity, within its civic boundaries.

Both Melville and Steinbeck believed that their capacity to uncover life's deepest truths was necessarily limited in an indeterminate world, but artistic duty and personal curiosity demanded they try. Melville's operative belief that, "in this world of lies, Truth is forced to fly like a scared white doe . . . and only by cunning glimpses will she reveal herself" ("Mosses," 244) has its parallel in Steinbeck's statement that only "a little" of what the artist tries to do "trickles through" (*JN*, 4). Their narrators' pronouncements are often marked by honest self-doubt, demurral, or denial. Ishmael frequently stops short of the full disclosures warranted in his narrative office by admitting that some truths "would be to dive deeper than Ishmael can go" (*MD*, 187). "Dissect him how I may, then," he confesses of his attempts to capture the whale in prose, "I but go skin deep; I know him not, and never will" (*MD*, 379).

Where Ishmael must "explain" the compelling and indefinite "phenomenon of whiteness" otherwise all his "chapters might be naught" (*MD*, 188), Steinbeck's narrator seeks to plumb the equally mysterious phenomenon of sexuality, the heart of mortal inscrutability: "What freedom men and women could have, were they not constantly tricked and trapped and enslaved and tortured by their sexuality!" (*EE*, 75). Feline Kate becomes the focus of the narrator's didactic expositions—and increasingly indeterminate resolutions—on public and private evil, human fate, and the haunting spectre of genetic determinism. As much as Steinbeck wanted to be positive, getting at the truth "secreted in the glands of a million historians" (*EE*, 130) remains a puzzling and elusive task. Regarding his main character, Steinbeck literally deconstructs his intention by reversing direction in chapter 17: "When I said Cathy was a monster it seemed that it was so. Now I have bent close with a glass over the small print of her and reread the footnotes, and I wonder if it is true" (*EE*, 184). In this self-immolating fiction, even the vaunted certitude of the author's role is undercut.

This kind of disruptive flip-flopping appalled early critics of both novels who seemed unable to recognize that the novelists shared a propensity to improvise and were less concerned with the consistent ordering of a well-made fiction than the immediate compulsions of their creative consciousness. This was especially relevant for Melville's wandering act of composition. According to a letter written to his British publisher Richard Bentley on 27 June 1850, Melville first conceived of *Moby-Dick* as "a romance of adventure, founded upon certain wild legends in the Southern Sperm Whale fisheries" (*C*, 163), and while the *exact* chronology of the evolution and composition of his masterpiece is not known, it is true that the book grew substantially—even drastically—through at least three distinct periods, and that during those phases from August 1850 through the following summer, Melville was constantly adding, elaborating, and revising his text in a sometimes frenzied and haphazard way.[20] To take the most obvious of instances, Melville changed his initial whaling journey (still evident in the "shore narrative" section of the opening twenty-two chapters) into an epic tragedy as Ahab's role exerted more and more pressure on his imagination and his fresh reading of Shakespeare influenced his newly discovered tragic and philosophical bent.

Steinbeck did not build in quite such an obvious helter-skelter manner, but he too continually modified his novel.[21] Steinbeck was a writer who characteristically "thought out" his books repeatedly in his head before he wrote them (a process which sometimes lasted for years) or who in certain cases knew exactly where he was going before he started (for example, writing toward the scene of Rose of Sharon breast-feeding a starving man on the last page of *The Grapes of Wrath*). But in this instance Steinbeck found himself giving way to autochthonic impulses, especially in regard to characterization (his Cain/Abel paradigm did not hold up in all the ways he envisioned) and plot (his alternate Trask/Hamilton story lines became blurred and the Hamilton plot attenuated). "Dam it, this book gets longer, not shorter. Everything has pups. I never saw anything like the way it grows" (*JN*, 79). His working titles reflect the vicissitudes of his method. The book was called "Salinas Valley," then "My Valley," then "Cain Sign" (each title valorized a different fictive aspect). After he fully realized the psychological significance of the first sixteen verses of Genesis, Steinbeck found his permanent title, *East of Eden*: "my discovery of yesterday is sure burning in me . . . I think I know about the story finally after all this time," he noted on 12 June 1951 (*JN*, 104).

Both novels exist simultaneously on multiple levels of engagement, so that it is impossible to separate the layers of narrational and dramatic strands. Both books resist what Steinbeck called the easy formulations of plot; rather, they are themselves, which is to say they are unique architectural, spatial constructions, even if rough-hewn, unsymmetrical, and seemingly unfinished. From his upstairs study at Arrowhead, his Pittsfield home, Melville told Hawthorne on 29 June 1851, "I have been building some shanties of houses . . . and likewise some shanties of chapters and essays" (*C*, 195). Steinbeck too imagined that houses and books grew in similar ways (*JN*, 20), and he too characteristically found it difficult to write at all without first inhabiting a suitably comfortable and isolated workplace. Even their distrust of a perfectly finished product was similar: "God keep me from completing anything," Melville writes. "This whole book is but a draught—nay, but the draught of a draught" (*MD*, 145). And Steinbeck claimed flatly at one point, "I do not ever intend to finish it" (*JN*, 14). Melville's embrace of the organic method—"Out of the trunk, the branches grow; out of them, the twigs. So, in productive subjects, grow the chapters" (*MD*, 289)—is subtly paralleled in Steinbeck's narrative position not as an objective recording consciousness but as a convincing fabricator of characters and events from competing "hearsay," "stories told," and "memories" (*EE*, 8). Tracing out the "growth and flowering" of such sources takes the narrator in a variety of unpredictable directions surprising both to himself and, he guesses, to his audience (*JN*, 39, 116).

Clearly, *Moby-Dick* gave Steinbeck the courage to experiment with form, structure, and point of view. I use the word *experiment* with special emphasis because even though *Moby-Dick* was written midway in the nineteenth century it was also the first full-scale experimental novel in American fiction: it displayed a number of daring technical features which have only recently—in the past thirty years or so—become assimilated into postmodernist contemporary fiction. In updating Melville's organic form, artful digressions, and self-reflexivity (which includes frequent commentary on the process of making a book, especially important for the original version), Steinbeck was attempting to forge a fabular, metafictional novel.[22] *East of Eden* belonged not so much to the past or even to his own time but to the future of the children for whom he was writing the book in the first place. I don't think it is too much to claim that, because they turn so often on the hermeneutical implications of the metaphor of reading (Leviathan as text, Queequeg as a puzzling hieroglyphic volume, Father Mapple's sermon on Jonah; Samuel and Lee's central act of interpreting Genesis, and the narrator's own attempt to decode the "indecipherable" language of Kate's life), both *Moby-Dick* and *East of Eden* first challenged, then taught, their respective audiences to relearn the act of reading and therefore not only participate in "the drama of literary performance" but also perform a public function.[23] In the sense that they encourage readers to become not simply consumers of information, but participants in the construction of meaning as well, both are prophetic, perhaps even subversive, texts that have required the passage of time for audiences to catch up with them and to consider them more than "hideous and intolerable" allegories.

In *Moby-Dick,* Ishmael's conversion narrative (which reaches its psychological climax in chapter 96) and his ongoing cetological divagations cannot be subordinated to the dramatic trajectory of Ahab's quest for revenge against the white whale because they are all part of the same "warp and woof" (*MD,* 215) of consciousness, to be treated with "equal eye" (*MD,* 374); likewise, in *East of Eden* Steinbeck himself showed that the story of his country and the story of himself were so deeply intertwined that they were one and the same. Just as Herman Melville repeatedly crossed into the persona of fictive Ishmael, for instance in dating the composition of chapter 85 (at "fifteen and a quarter minutes past one o'clock P.M. of this sixteenth day of December, A.D. 1850" [*MD,* 370]), so Steinbeck did not curb his desire to break through to the other side of the artist's mirror. How else can we willingly accept that the fictional Adam Trask actually visits the real-life John Steinbeck at his parents' home on 132 Central Avenue in Salinas (*EE,* 385)? Whether we call such effects magical realism or poststructural ludism, Steinbeck and Melville were both ahead of their times.

In this jarring, metarealistic sense, both books are *scriptible* or *writerly* texts (to use Roland Barthes's terms) because they disrupt the normally passive posture of their audiences by employing self-conscious technique and interrupted literary form.[24] "There are some enterprises," Ishmael apologizes in chapter 82, "The Honor and Glory of Whaling," "in which a careful disorderliness is the best method" (*MD,* 361). Steinbeck's method, too, loops back and forth from the novel's traditional dramatic plot to a series of literary apologies or thematic advocacies of its subject matter. Chapter 13, ostensibly about Adam

Trask's purchase of the Sanchez farm from its current owner, Bodoni, begins with the narrator's justification of the honor and glory of the human mind, "the preciousness" in "the lonely mind of man," which in turn becomes a reflexive commentary on the process of the novel itself and the necessity of embodying "the freedom of the mind to take any direction it wishes, undirected" (*EE*, 132). To fill in the metaphoric silences and subtextual spaces calls for a suitably imaginative reader with an aggressively acrobatic attitude.

In their zigzag tack toward an ever-receding horizon of truth, both Melville and Steinbeck expressed their experiences in candid, brutal, and often shockingly irreverent terms. In September 1851, Melville warned his genteel Pittsfield neighbor, Sarah Huyler Morewood, not to read *Moby-Dick* because "Polar wind blows through it, & birds of prey hover over it" (*C*, 206); the merging diabolism in Cathy Trask prompted Steinbeck to claim that she would "worry a lot of children and a lot of parents" (*JN*, 46). It should come as no surprise that the former believed *Moby-Dick*, whose motto was "Ego non baptiso te in nomine patris, sed in nomine diaboli" (*MD*, 489), to be a "wicked book" (*C*, 212), while the latter felt *East of Eden* was "a terrible book" (*JN*, 156) which reflected the "shocking bad taste" Steinbeck associated with the greatest literature (*SLL*, 436). When their labors were done both writers felt similar reactions: each doubted the efficacy of his work, each admitted an enormous sense of relief, and, despite the sheer emotional commitment of living so long with their demanding offspring, each spoke of a follow-up—restless Melville's "Kraken" (*C*, 213), which turned out to be *Pierre* (1852), and Steinbeck's unwritten sequel, intended to cover the period from World War I to the Korean War. "In my book just finished I have put all the things I have wanted to write all my life," he told Bo Beskow on 16 November 1951. "This is 'the book.' If it is not good I have fooled myself all the time. I don't mean I will stop but this is a definite milestone and I feel released. Having done this I can do anything I want. Always I had this book wanting to be written. . . . There will be another one equally long. This one runs from 1863 to 1918. The next will take the time from 1918 to the present" (*SLL*, 431).

4

"The Pequod's sea wings, beating landward, fall/ Headlong . . . / Off 'Sconset. . . ."
—Robert Lowell, "The Quaker Graveyard in Nantucket" (1944)

I began with a little-known historical event; now I'd like to conclude with a quasi-fictive sequel, a fantasy of sorts. It requires "plenty" of Melville's ample "sea-room" ("Mosses," 246), as well as portions of Steinbeck's impossible horizons and undirected directions. My fantasy circles back on an event that I am not positive ever happened but certainly could have; an event which can't necessarily be proven by external facts or recorded history but seems nonetheless plausible, given the circumstances and the results.

On the afternoon of Wednesday, 15 August 1951, I imagine John Steinbeck could easily have traveled the six miles or so from "Footlight" (the Steinbecks' rented cottage on Baxter Road next door to the Coast Guard's Sankaty Point Light in Siasconset) to the Unitarian Church in Nantucket for the Historical Association's "Melville Memorial" Observance marking the one-hundredth anniversary of the publication of *Moby-Dick*. It was another "muggy and thick and foggy" day (*SLL*, 428), as it had been for over a week, and Steinbeck was playing hooky from the manuscript of *East of Eden*, which he had daily been composing since February, first in New York City, then from 18 June onward, in 'Sconset, where he was summering with his wife Elaine and sons Thom and John.

In true Melvillean style, Steinbeck had become a "fast fish," deeply hooked by his manuscript, as much pursuing it as he was pursued by it. Since his arrival on the island he had worked obsessively in the cottage's small upstairs back study. The window of his writing room faced inland, away from the distracting panorama of the ocean (the front of the cottage was no more than thirty feet from the high-flown edge of 'Sconset Bluffs). Steinbeck worked on his "big" novel right into the previous weekend, that is, through Sunday, 12 August. Then he took a few days off—"the longest layoff since I started the book" (*JN*, 145)—to prepare the Japanese lanterns and the twenty-one-gun salute from his new Abercrombie and Fitch marine cannon, as well as some other surprises for his wife's birthday party on Tuesday the 14th (*TAJS*, 689-90). The birthday celebration was clearly a success: "The birthday was fine," he noted on Thursday,

16 August (*JN*, 145). And to his agent, Elizabeth Otis, he boasted in a letter that same day that the party "was a humdinger and I think Elaine was happy with it" (*SLL*, 427).

That Thursday also, Steinbeck made a fairly long entry in his working journal in which he assessed his own mood and state of mind and indicated his plan of attack for the final section of the novel (emphasizing the realistic development of Cal Trask and Abra Bacon), though he did not actually write anything at all on the novel that day (*JN*, 145-46). In fact he took several more days off—that is, 17, 18, and 19 August—before launching into Book Four on Monday, 20 August (*JN*, 146). This much is known and recorded; meantime, mysteriously, Steinbeck said nothing at all about his whereabouts on Wednesday, 15 August.[25]

Now comes the speculative part of my tale, which concerns that lacuna, that conspicuous silence, upon which even his widow and his private diary could shed no light. On the 15th, I imagine, still a little tired from having completed Book Three of *East of Eden* on 12 August (that is, all the way through chapter 33, or more than two-thirds of the entire novel), Steinbeck treated himself to an extra day off; unmoored from his manuscript, but still in a celebratory mood, he took in—and I will qualify this by saying in thought if not in deed, spiritually, if not corporeally—the Historical Society's Melville Memorial Meeting which, as I said earlier, was convened to celebrate the centenary of *Moby-Dick*, and the ninety-ninth anniversary of Melville's first—and only—visit to Nantucket (Melville published *Moby-Dick*, with its eighty-eight references to Nantucket, before he had ever set foot on the island). Steinbeck too was already attuned to the significance of Nantucket as an historical, cultural, and literary site, for three months earlier he had written to Otis to discuss the feasibility of doing a "pet project—a set of informal but informative articles about the island of Nantuckett [sic]."[26] His requisite curiosity about the place and its cultural history was matched by his energetic sense of belonging: "This island is wonderful. I feel at home here. I wonder if it is my small amount (1/4) of my New England blood operating. . . . I never felt better about working" (*JN*, 107).

Steinbeck might have been aware of the Melville meeting since at least Saturday, 4 August, for the *Nantucket Inquirer and Mirror* ran this notice on its front page: "'Melville Memorial' To Be Held on Wednesday, Aug. 15th." And it might have been of interest to him that besides the main speaker, Wilson Heflin, two of Melville's granddaughters were slated to appear also—Mrs. Eleanor Melville Metcalf and Mrs. Frances T. Osborne. As it turned out, Melville's descendants were unable to attend (thereby scuttling an unimaginably spectacular ending to this essay), but the presentation by Professor Heflin on "Melville and Nantucket" went ahead as scheduled, as did historian Edouard Stackpole's introductory talk. The event was covered in the *Inquirer and Mirror* on Saturday, 18 August 1951 (p. 3); the report makes no mention of Steinbeck's being present, though he could have slipped in unnoticed. All in all, the celebration of Melville and his relations on the very island Steinbeck was then visiting, and especially the praise of Melville's most famous book—*Moby-Dick*—had a redoubled effect on Steinbeck.

If this fantasy about Steinbeck's "attendance" is so outrageous that it strains credulity, I am quick to counter that, in these revisionist times, his physical presence isn't the real point. For whatever reason, during that seven-day hiatus from his manuscript, Steinbeck dove back into his copy of *Moby-Dick* (Willard Thorp's edition, or maybe Leon Howard's), perhaps by reading passages to his sons and in other appropriate ways meditating about the life-and-death issues, the mysteries of iniquity, that Melville's novel raises but never quite answers. When Steinbeck resumed writing *East of Eden* again on Monday, 20 August, *Moby-Dick* manifested itself in the same way a submerged whale can suddenly breach and make its presence palpably known.

Chapter 34, one of Steinbeck's major discursive chapters, concerns the world's central story, the battle of good and evil, which is also one of *Moby-Dick*'s main themes. There is an interior signature at work that, if I read it properly, shows Steinbeck imitating Melvillean discourse in the penultimate paragraph of his newly penned chapter: "In uncertainty I am certain that underneath their topmost layers of frailty men want to be good and want to be loved" (*EE*, 414). That paradoxical diction—"uncertain certainty"—and that hierarchical valuation—"topmost layers"—are Melvillean syntactical constructions, signifying that Melville's text had merged into Steinbeck's present moment. Even Steinbeck's organizing strategy in chapter 34 simulates Melville's. In chapter 96, "The Try-Works," Ishmael's warning on the deadening effects of fire ("Look not too long in the face of fire, O man! Never dream with thy hand on the helm!"), is supported by his pointed reference to a classic text—

Solomon's *Ecclesiastes*—whose "fine hammered steel of woe" underscores the chapter's theme of human vanity and accountability (*MD*, 424).

These elements, substantially grounded and enriched by the sad tale of Perth, the *Pequod*'s blacksmith (chapter 112), are paralleled in Steinbeck's literary allusions to Herodotus's story of Solon and Croesus in *The Histories*. This becomes a cautionary tale that concerns the apocryphal issue of human vanity and good fortune and which in turn mirrors Steinbeck's own proposition on universal accountability: "It seems to me that if you or I must choose between two courses of thought or action, we should remember our dying and try so to live that our death brings no pleasure in the world" (*EE*, 415). In Steinbeck's drive toward resolving these knotty issues, the final paragraph of chapter 34 corresponds to the final paragraph of Melville's chapter 105, "Does the Whale's Magnitude Diminish?—Will He Perish?" In Steinbeck's line—"And it occurs to me that evil must constantly respawn, while good, while virtue, is immortal" (*EE*, 415)—there are resonances of Melville's belief that "Wherefore, for all these things, we account the whale immortal in his species" (*MD*, 462). *Moby-Dick* and *East of Eden* are hymns to the persistence of beneficence in whatever form it is to be found.

Further, the outrageous vanity of Ahab's realization—"'now I feel my topmost greatness lies in my topmost grief"—in chapter 135, "The Chase—The Third Day," is echoed in the hell-bent personal attitudes of two other tyrannical captains of industry, Rockefeller and Hearst, whom Steinbeck pillories in chapter 34 as grasping, satanic men incapable of proper human love. Moreover, Ahab's final condition—"'Am I cut off from the last fond pride of meanest shipwrecked captains? Oh, lonely death on lonely life!'" (*MD*, 571)—presages the demise of Kate, who becomes repentant for her dastardly actions only by default, only minutes before her untoward suicide.

Here we read Steinbeck reading Melville, but with an inevitable twist, a meaningful and willed reinscription. Where Promethean Ahab perishes in his unmediated final effort to penetrate the whale's imprisoning "wall" of "inscrutable malice," to thrust through the pasteboard mask of reality (believing he can still insinuate the ultimate purpose of the universe, can revenge himself—and therefore mankind—against the evil symbolized by the White Whale's agency), Kate penetrates through her "wall" of self and finds a principle of vacancy on the nether side of consciousness; this enervating emptiness is so horrifying that it decenters and stalls all questions of moral purpose or ethical behavior. If Kate gains a modicum of sympathy in the way Melville, for example, had briefly raised Ahab's humanity in chapter 132, "The Symphony," it is quickly subverted by the ironic legacy of her will: her son Aron would live "all his life on the profits from a whorehouse" (*EE*, 583), a figuration ultimately no less ironic and far-reaching than Ishmael's being saved from drowning by Queequeg's coffin. In this bizarre moment of climax, Kate too remains as lonely and isolated in death as she had been in life: "She was cold and desolate, alone and desolate" (*EE*, 552). After harpooning Moby Dick, Ahab dies a terrible death—partly willed, partly fated (in a sense, he too commits suicide)—garroted by the very whale line he has just thrown; yanked from the small boat, he disappears "ere the crew knew he was gone" (*MD*, 572). First Ahab, then the *Pequod* dissolve into nothingness, pass "out of sight" into the spinning vortex of the ocean. In much the same way Kate shrinks in terror to nothingness, too: "The gray room darkened and the cone of light flowed and rippled like water . . . as she grew smaller and smaller and then disappeared—and she had never been" (*EE*, 554). Both Ahab and Kate seem in the end to have been consumed by divergent aspects of a similar kind of monomania; their overweening sense of the difference of their differences collapses in on them, so that in their lust for destruction both can be said to deconstruct their identities before our eyes.

From first to last, *East of Eden* reveals that Steinbeck was alive to the multiple implications of Melville's theme, style, technique, and characterization. In the wondrous geography of the storytellers' world, for which we are required (at least briefly when entering the terrain of romance) to suspend our capacity for disbelief, anything can happen in the net of narrative: characters can be utterly good or blatantly evil; a ghostly Parsee can prophesy the future and aged Chinese savants can undertake the study of Hebrew in order to interpret a single word; a man, grievously insulted by the universe, can find in all the oceans of the world the lone whale which caused his treachery, while another man, wounded by marital treachery for ten years, can find the courage to redeem himself and his son by granting the gift of free will (like Ahab, Adam lacks the "low, enjoying power" and, through most of Steinbeck's novel, is "damned in the midst of Paradise!"); and finally, authors can perform dazzling feats of narrative sleights-of-hand that astound, perplex, and delight us.

In our daylight hours we might cavil at the apparent inconsistencies and flaws in both books (they are full of anomalies, factual contradictions, and lapses), but at night, say, when we take up *Moby-Dick* or *East of Eden* as we once might have done when we were younger and our reading intentions were perhaps purer or more accommodating, these books strike us as being resolutely unsubordinated to real life. Their consistency—their narrative logic—is closer to the world of dreams, which is to say it is internal, metaphoric, and poetical, because it is born out of and sustained by a continuing human need to tell and to hear stories which are frighteningly moving and finally somehow mysterious: "A child may ask, 'What is the world's story about?' And a grown man or woman may wonder, 'What way will the world go?'" (*EE*, 413). Certainly in originally addressing his book to his sons, Steinbeck—as John Ditsky claimed two decades ago—"knew what he was doing."[27] *East of Eden*—like *Moby-Dick*—is a book that in the very best sense is intended first for the child in all of us, then the grown-up. If, to jaded adult readers, *East of Eden* fails to be completely convincing, it is nevertheless a magnificent undertaking because again, like *Moby-Dick*, it is a book whose scope of vision, risk-taking technique, and assault on the impossible are not only huge, compelling gestures but are their own reasons for being. To read either of these scriptural texts in the right spirit of faith requires that we emulate "archangel" Hawthorne and look past "the imperfect body, and embrace the soul" (*C*, 213).

5

"He expands and deepens down, the more I contemplate him. . . ."

—Herman Melville, "Hawthorne and His Mosses" (1850)

In much the same way that Hawthorne's writings dropped "germinous seeds" into the "hot soil" of Melville's soul" ("Mosses," 250), so Melville's book continued to infiltrate Steinbeck's. And if Herman Melville penned the first review of the double-edged Steinbeckian character, Steinbeck himself continued to return the favor a century later. Besides his involvement in Sag Harbor's Old Whalers Festival and his help in founding the International Whaleboat Competition in which contestants attempted to harpoon "Mobile Dick" each year (*TAJS*, 953), Steinbeck never paid homage to Melville with more spritely gamesomeness than in his last novel, *The Winter of Our Discontent*, which is set in New Baytown, Long Island, a former East Coast whaling center modeled on Sag Harbor. Steinbeck's protagonist, Ethan Allen Hawley, descendent of whaling captains, tells Red Baker, an Irish setter: "Read *Moby-Dick*, dog. That's my advice to you."[28] Hawley's playful words echo this challenge in chapter 79, "The Prairie": "Read it if you can," Ishmael says as he meditates on the "wrinkled hieroglyphics" of the sperm whale's "sublime" brow (*MD*, 347).

As book and cultural icon, sublime *Moby-Dick* exerted more than mere literary influence on Steinbeck. It became a spiritual forerunner, a fountain of right knowledge, an enabling text, and a continuing reference point for Steinbeck's own headaches with the authority of critical valuation. Wounded by Arthur Mizener's front-page attack in the 9 December 1962 edition of the *New York Times Book Review*—"Does a Moral Vision of the Thirties Deserve a Nobel Prize?"—Steinbeck composed a ruminative, defensive letter to Pascal Covici invoking an analogy with Melville's reception: "You can almost hear . . . Mizener's guffaws of rage if a book should come out called Moby Dick." Twentieth-century reviews "would do just what the critics did when it was published," Steinbeck asserted facetiously (*S&C*, 230). Steinbeck's conception of *Moby-Dick*'s American reception (in Britain, *The Whale* fared far better) was in the main quite accurate, especially when one considers the myopic and fault-finding reaction of Melville's friend, Evert Duyckinck, editor of the taste-making *Literary World* (Melville canceled his subscription and satirized the journal and its editor in his next book, *Pierre*).

That there was something conspiratorial in *Moby-Dick*'s commercial and critical failure became a fixed idea with Steinbeck in the 1960s; it offered added proof that certain writers—despite their innate worth or worldly acclaim—remain outside the walls of literature's holy citadel. If it increased Steinbeck's contempt for critics, it also increased his regard for fellow writers, Melville first and foremost. Steinbeck's defensive posture is apparent in his sketch of American literature that appears toward the end of the nonfictional *America and Americans*, his last book: "At the time when the Golden Age of classic writing was flourishing in the East Coast centers of learning, when the accepted were members of an establishment endowed with keys to the heaven of literary acceptance, at this very time Herman Melville was writing *Moby Dick*, the first edition of which did not sell out for forty years" (*A&A*, 134). Melville's realization in "Hawthorne and His Mosses"—that all portraiture is self-portrayal (249)—subtly infuses Steinbeck's summary passage, so that its meaning cuts both ways—toward the melancholic and farcical, toward the Quixotic and puritanical, toward the past and present, toward the quick and the dead, toward quotation and invention. Thus Steinbeck's signification—at once his "little lower layer" of homage and lament—was his way of completing the circuit of Melville's vested presence and fulfilling his long sojourn of "working at the impossible."

Notes

[1] Herman Melville, "Journal 1856-57," in *Journals*, ed. Howard C. Horsford with Lynn Horth, vol. 15, *The Writings of Herman Melville*, ed. Harrison Hayford, Hershel Parker, and G. Thomas Tanselle (Evanston and Chicago: Northwestern University Press and Newberry Library, 1989), 93-94. All references to Melville's works in this essay will be to the following editions. *Moby-Dick or The Whale*, ed. Harrison Hayford, Hershel Parker, and G. Thomas Tanselle, vol. 6, *The Writings of Herman Melville* (Evanston and Chicago: Northwestern University Press and Newberry Library, 1988) (hereafter cited as *MD*). "Hawthorne and His Mosses," in *The Piazza Tales and Other Prose Pieces 1839-1860*, ed. Harrison Hayford, Alma A. MacDougall, and G. Thomas Tanselle, vol. 9, *The Writings of Herman Melville* (Evanston and Chicago: Northwestern University Press and Newberry Library, 1987). (hereafter cited as "Mosses"). *Correspondence*, ed. Lynn Horth, vol. 14, *The Writings of Herman Melville* (Evanston and Chicago: Northwestern University Press and Newberry Library, 1993) (hereafter cited as *C*).

[2] John Steinbeck, *Speech Accepting the Nobel Prize for Literature* (New York: Viking Press, 1962), 10. Steinbeck's speech is reprinted in *The Portable Steinbeck*, ed. Pascal Covici, Jr. (New York: Viking Press, 1971), 690-92.

[3] John Steinbeck to Elizabeth Otis, 19 February 1966 (*SCSU*, 77). Steinbeck continued: "My grandmother certainly did marry a German and they did produce at least one hybrid vagabond, namely me." Although most of this account of the Melville-Dickson visit was available as early as 1951 in Jay Leyda's two-volume chronicle, *The Melville Log: A Documentary Life of Herman Melville* (New York: Harcourt, Brace, 1951), which Steinbeck owned but probably only browsed in (*SR*, 69), he did not learn of it until this moment in 1966, when a staff member at the American Embassy showed him a copy of Howard C. Horsford's edition of Melville's *Journal of a Visit to Europe and the Levant, October 11, 1856-May 6, 1857* (Princeton: Princeton University Press, 1955). As early as 1962 Steinbeck expressed interest in writing about the Dickson group's

outrages in the Holy Land, where members of the family had been murdered and raped by marauding Bedouins, but the full saga never came to pass. See John Steinbeck, "Letters to Alicia," *Long Island Newsday* 12 February 1966, 3W, and his account in *America and Americans* (New York: Viking Press, 1966), 59, 65 (hereafter cited as *A&A*). For background on the Dicksons in Palestine and their significance—largely unremarked upon by biographers—see my "Steinbeck's Other Family: New Light on *East of Eden*?" *Steinbeck Newsletter* 7 (Winter 1994): 1-4.

[4] Newton Arvin, *Herman Melville* (New York: William Sloane, 1950); Richard Chase, *Herman Melville: A Critical Study* (New York: Macmillan, 1949); and Geoffrey Stone, *Melville* (New York: Sheed and Ward, 1949) are biographies that all appeared in this brief period. Howard Vincent's *The Trying-out of "Moby-Dick"* (Boston: Houghton Mifflin, 1949) was a full-fledged study of Melville's sources and his book's composition. Several editions of *Moby-Dick* were marketed too: by Maxwell Geismar (New York: Pocket Books, 1949); Sherman Paul (New York: Dutton [Everyman's Library], 1950); and Leon Howard (New York: Modern Library, 1950). It is not possible to tell precisely when Steinbeck first encountered *Moby-Dick*. It might have been prior to 1949 or 1950, but I have found no documentary evidence to support that contention. My surmise is that Steinbeck's introduction to Melville's book occurred as a result of the publicity preceding and surrounding the centenary of *Moby-Dick*'s publication in 1951. Around that time or a little afterwards, Steinbeck acquired Willard Thorp's edition of *Moby-Dick* (New York: Oxford University Press, 1947), Leyda's *The Melville Log*, and Leon Howard's *Herman Melville: A Biography* (Berkeley: University of California Press, 1951) (*SR*, 79).

[5] Robert Alter, *The Pleasures of Reading in an Ideological Age* (New York: Touchstone Books, 1990), 134. "We are as much informed of a writer's genius by what he selects as by what he originates," Ralph Waldo Emerson proposed in an 1859 essay. See "Quotation and Originality," in *Letters and Social Aims*, vol. 8 of the Centenary Edition of *The Complete Works of Ralph Waldo Emerson*, ed. Edward Waldo Emerson (Boston: Houghton Mifflin, 1904), 194.

[6] Ironically, *Moby-Dick*'s triumph as a work of art and the wholesale embrace of Herman Melville as a great writer belong more to our century than to his own. Melville's surge to fame as an American literary genius, the canonization of his formally innovative *Moby-Dick* as a central American text, and the growing critical acceptance of the romance as an indigenous and potentially hegemenous American literary form (because of, among other things, its antisociety values), were all occurring in the late forties. It seems reasonable to suggest that Steinbeck's 1949 decision to abandon the patently communitarian thrust of his early fiction in favor of the importance of creative individuality was not only occasioned by his own experiences in the Soviet Union in 1947 (documented in *A Russian Journal*, published by Viking Press in 1948) but also by the critical dynamics of the post-World War II era, including efforts to promote American exceptionalism and a "new liberalism" encoded, for instance, in critic/biographer Richard Chase's 1949 study of Melville (especially his preface). During the Cold War, then, phalanx organization and totalitarianism were out; individuality, free will, moral choice, native experience, and direct personal statements were in: "And this I believe: that the free, exploring mind of the individual human is the most valuable thing in the world. . . . And this I

must fight against: any idea, religion, or government which limits or destroys the individual" (*EE*, 32). Not surprisingly, Ishmael and Samuel Hamilton represent models of antiauthoritarian individuation; tyrannical Ahab and Kate go down to defeat. See Donald E. Pease's suggestive discussion of Melville and the Cold War, "Melville and Cultural Persuasion," chap. 7 of his *Visionary Compacts: American Renaissance Writings in Cultural Contexts* (Madison: University of Wisconsin Press, 1987), 235-75. Although he mentions Steinbeck only in passing, Thomas Hill Schaub's *American Fiction in the Cold War* (Madison: University of Wisconsin Press, 1991) presents a theoretical way of situating *East of Eden* in the era's quest for a "new liberalism" (vii). For an instructive critique of the romance tradition's privileged position at mid-century, see William Ellis, *The Theory of the American Romance: An Ideology in American Intellectual History* (Ann Arbor, MI: UMI Research Press, 1989), and especially William V. Spanos, *The Errant Art of "Moby-Dick": The Canon, the Cold War, and the Struggle for American Studies* (Durham, NC: Duke University Press, 1995), 12-36.

[7] Joseph N. Riddel, *Purloined Letters: Originality and Repetition in American Literature*, ed. Mark Bauerlein (Baton Rouge: Louisiana State University Press, 1995), 79. The introduction by Joseph G. Kronik and Mark Bauerlein states: "reflexivity remains a critical component of the [American] work, but totalization and closure are dismissed . . . as a fundamental misconception of writing" (15). Robert Alter notes such works consistently convey "a sense of the fictional world as an authorial construct set up against a background of literary tradition and convention." See his *Partial Magic: The Novel as a Self-Conscious Genre* (Berkeley: University of California Press, 1975), xi. For an ambitious reading of reflexivity in *Moby-Dick*, see A. Robert Lee, "*Moby-Dick*: The Tale and the Telling," in *New Perspectives on Melville*, ed. Faith Pullin (Kent, OH: Kent State University Press, 1978), 86-127; and on similar aspects in *East of Eden*, consult Louis Owens, "The Mirror and the Vamp: Invention, Reflection, and Bad, Bad Cathy Trask in *East of Eden*," in *Writing the American Classics*, eds. James Barbour and Tom Quirk (Chapel Hill: University of North Carolina Press, 1990), 235-57. On the issue of Melville's self-condoned narrative authority and the propensity among democratic writers for rhetorical structures, see Kenneth Dauber, who states in *The Idea of Authorship in America: Democratic Poetics from Franklin to Melville* (Madison: University of Wisconsin Press, 1990), 209, that "in *Moby-Dick* . . . Melville readdresses himself to the question of what authorizes an American book." The same could be said of Steinbeck's project in *East of Eden*.

[8] Not all of Harold Bloom's work is thoroughly committed to intertextual and inter-writer warfare. In *A Map of Misreading* (New York: Oxford University Press, 1975), 3, Bloom claims somewhat ethereally that "Influence . . . means that there are *no* texts but only relationships *between* texts. These relationships depend upon a critical act, a misreading or misprision, that one poet performs upon another. . . . The influence-relation governs reading as it governs writing, and the reading is therefore a miswriting just as writing is a misreading." Juggling similar issues of contestation and relatedness from a different perspective in *Purloined Letters*, the late Joseph Riddel has written: "If every quotation tropes, it does not necessarily vanquish or displace, or even sublate. . . . It renders, translates, transposes. And no law of genre can rule

quotation; it is fabulous, fabulating, carrying things away into their other" (29).

[9] On Melville at this crucial juncture, see Michael Paul Rogin, *Subversive Genealogy: The Politics and Art of Herman Melville* (New York: Knopf, 1983), 102-28; on Steinbeck, see John H. Timmerman, *John Steinbeck's Fiction: The Aesthetics of the Road Taken* (Norman: University of Oklahoma Press, 1986), 210-18.

[10] Mark W. Govoni, "'Symbols for the Wordlessness': The Original Manuscript of *East of Eden*," *Steinbeck Quarterly* 14 (Winter-Spring 1981): 15.

[11] *East of Eden*'s initial print run was more than 112,000 copies; the novel has never been out of print. Though *Eden* fared spectacularly, Steinbeck was intuitively correct in calling up *Moby-Dick* as a model for his "huge" unprecedented efforts. According to G. Thomas Tanselle, in *A Checklist of Editions of "Moby-Dick," 1851-1976* (Evanston and Chicago: Northwestern University Press and Newberry Library, 1976), 7, the first print run of the British edition of *The Whale* (published in London in three volumes by Richard Bentley in October, 1851, without, among other abridgements, the all-important "Epilogue" chapter) was 500 copies, and of *Moby-Dick*'s American edition, published in a single volume the following month in New York by Harpers Brothers, 2,915 copies. Overall, *Moby-Dick* sold about 3,700 copies in both editions between 1851 and Melville's death in 1891 (it was out of print during his last four years) and earned its author a little a little over $1,200. (See also "Historical Note," *MD*, 686-89.) Steinbeck's comments about *Moby-Dick*'s publishing history (he always spelled the title without a hyphen) are thematically similar to the introduction to Leon Howard's edition of *Moby Dick* (1950).

[12] There are as many variations on the definition of romance as there are critics who have written about it. Despite inherent problems in fixing this highly contested term and in spite of Steinbeck's protestation that *Eden* would not be a "romanza" (*JN*, 63), or light fantasy, what attractions Steinbeck may have found alluring in Melville's more weighty version of the form can be verified in studies by Richard Chase, *The American Novel and Its Tradition* (1957; reprint Baltimore: Johns Hopkins University Press, 1980); by Paul Brodtkorb, Jr., *Ishmael's White World: A Phenomonological Reading of "Moby-Dick"* (New Haven: Yale University Press, 1965); and by Richard H. Brodhead, *Hawthorne, Melville, and the Novel* (Chicago: University of Chicago Press, 1976), 9-25. Steinbeck, who mixed critical skepticism and mythic poesis, retained some elements of the form in *East of Eden* and dispensed altogether with others.

[13] Thom Steinbeck, telephone interview by author, 3 October 1985.

[14] Harrison Hayford, "'Loomings': Yarns and Figures in the Fabric," in *Artful Thunder: Versions of the Romantic Tradition in American Literature in Honor of Howard P. Vincent*, eds. Robert DeMott and Sanford Marovitz (Kent, OH: Kent State University Press, 1975), 122.

[15] See Warren French's treatment of Steinbeck's cosmogony, "*East of Eden*—California and the Cosmic California," chap. 10 in the revised edition of *John Steinbeck* (Boston: Twayne, 1975), 143. French uses John Milton and William Blake as touchstones for considering the cosmogonal realm of Steinbeck's novel. I have extended his implications to include parallels with

Melville. In a similar vein, see Lawrence Buell's essay, "*Moby-Dick* as Sacred Text," in *New Essays on "Moby-Dick,"* ed. Richard H. Brodhead (New York: Cambridge University Press, 1986), 53-72; and Jay Parini's *John Steinbeck: A Biography* (New York: Henry Holt, 1995), 351, which claims "*East of Eden* is an exercise in secular scripture."

[16] The dynamics of "poetic answering" are explored in John Hollander, *Melodious Guile: Fictive Patterns in Poetic Language* (New Haven: Yale University Press, 1988), 56. See Louis Owens, "The Mirror and the Vamp," 240, for his comment about *Moby-Dick* references.

[17] In his elliptical *Call Me Ishmael: A Study of Melville* (New York: Reynal and Hitchcock, 1947, reprint London: Jonathan Cape, 1967), 37, Charles Olson called Melville a "skald," who "knew how to appropriate the work of others. He read to write." Recently Susan Howe, borrowing Coleridge's term, dubbed Melville a "library cormorant." See her *The Birth-mark: Unsettling the Wilderness in American Literary History* (Middletown, CT: Wesleyan University Press, 1993), 5. The range of Melville's borrowings is dazzlingly deep and wide ("Historical Note," *MD*, 635-47). Besides Vincent's classic study of Melville's use of whaling documents, *The Trying-Out of "Moby-Dick,"* consult also Mary K. Bercaw, *Melville's Sources* (Evanston, IL: Northwestern University Press, 1987), and Merton Sealts, *Melville's Reading* (Columbia: University of South Carolina Press, 1988). Sealts's earlier version, *Melville's Reading: A Check-List of Books Owned and Borrowed* (Madison: University of Wisconsin Press, 1966) served as inspiration and model for my *Steinbeck's Reading: A Catalogue of Books Owned and Borrowed.*

[18] Warren French, "Patchwork Leviathan," in chap. 13 of his *John Steinbeck* (Boston: Twayne, 1961), 153. Both novels, French asserts, "concern the self-destruction of a monomaniac." After that, however, he notes that the similarity ends, "for the focussing upon a monomaniac that crystallized Melville's vision seems to have dissipated Steinbeck's."

[19] Thom Steinbeck, interview by author, 8 December 1985, Carmel, CA.

[20] Scholarship on the convoluted composition of *Moby-Dick* is itself detailed, conflicting, and complex ("Historical Note," *MD*, 648-49). The most persuasive account of the book's three stages of development is by James Barbour, "'All My Books Are Botches': Melville's Struggle with *The Whale*," in *Writing the American Classics*, 25-52.

[21] Roy S. Simmonds, "'And Still the Box is Not Full': Steinbeck's *East of Eden*," *San Jose Studies* 18 (Fall 1992): 60-63.

[22] See David Wyatt's introduction to Penguin's Twentieth-Century Classics edition (*EE*, xvi), and especially Steven Mulder, "The Reader's Story: *East of Eden* as Postmodernist Metafiction," *Steinbeck Quarterly* 25 (Summer-Fall 1992): 109-118. For a consideration of the link between nineteenth-century romance and contemporary metafiction, see Edgar A. Dryden, *The Form of American Romance* (Baltimore: Johns Hopkins University Press, 1988), 169-210. Dryden furthermore proposes to show "that the act of reading generates the enabling energy of American romance . . . the curious and troubling moment where the act of reading appears to mark and disturb the American novelist's passage from life to writing and to entangle experience with an intertextual system of relationships" (xi).

[23] See Stephen Railton, *Authorship and Audience: Literary Perfor-*

mance in the American Renaissance (Princeton: Princeton University Press, 1991), 7.

[24] Roland Barthes, *S/Z*, trans. Richard Miller (New York: Hill and Wang, 1974), 4-5. See also Steven Mailloux, *Interpretive Conventions: The Reader in the Study of American Fiction* (Ithaca, NY: Cornell University Press, 1982), 48 and 69, for more on the implications of disrupting reader passivity.

[25] In an interview with me on 14 May 1992 at the "Steinbeck and the Environment Conference" held in Nantucket, Elaine Steinbeck was understandably unable to recall her husband's specific activities that day forty years earlier. Another source proved futile as well. *The Standard Diary for 1951*, one of Steinbeck's recently unsealed personal ledger books (housed at the Pierpont Morgan Library, New York City), contains 209 pages of handwritten entries by Steinbeck but is almost entirely blank for the month of August 1951. "I have not kept day book because days too full," he noted on 6 August, with "all the million things of the summer." For more on Steinbeck's unpublished diaries, see "'One Book to a Man': Charting a Bibliographical Preface to *East of Eden*" later in *Steinbeck's Typewriter*.

[26] John Steinbeck to Elizabeth Otis, 21 May 1951 (*SCSU*, 49).

[27] John Ditsky, *Essays on "East of Eden,"* Steinbeck Monograph Series, no. 7 (Muncie, IN: John Steinbeck Society of America/Ball State University, 1977), ix. Howard Levant, in *The Novels of John Steinbeck* (Columbia: University of Missouri Press, 1974), 258, calls *East of Eden* "an admirably massive, essentially flawed narrative. . . . Steinbeck's great effort lies between these two poles, and there a critical judgment must take its abode if it is to be at all accurate." A less positive assessment is recorded by Louis Owens, who states that in "*East of Eden,* Steinbeck ventured resolutely into the forests of Hawthorne and Melville's great ocean, and he lost his way." See his *John Steinbeck's Re-Vision of America* (Athens: University of Georgia Press, 1985), 155. Again, see "'One Book to a Man'" for an overview of *Eden*'s critical reception.

[28] John Steinbeck, *The Winter of Our Discontent* (New York: Viking Press, 1961; reprint, New York: Bantam Books, 1970), 6.

PART TWO: NEGOTIATING TEXTS

"There must be long sullen hours of effort and the word written and thrown away. There must be purity of approach and purity of criticism. One must hunch down—really—not with humility but with quiet and one must beseech that secret part for strength. It seems to be there. There can be no lonely wife nor good handsome son nor bills nor responsibilities of making any one else happy or of making one's self happy for that matter. This does not mean that as so many young writers insist, that these cannot be, that one must leave one's home, abandon one's children and generally raise hell with one's little world. But during the hours of work—they must disappear for a while leaving nothing but the paper and the writer and there is nothing here that discipline cannot accomplish."

—John Steinbeck, *The Wayward Bus* journal (1946)
(Courtesy of the Pierpont Morgan Library, New York City)

"The discipline of the written word punishes both stupidity and dishonesty. A writer lives in awe of words for they can be cruel or kind, and they can change their meanings right in front of you."

—John Steinbeck, "In Awe of Words," in *The Exonian* (1954)

"If there is magic in . . . writing, and I am convinced that there is, no one has ever been able to reduce it to a recipe that can be passed from one person to another. The formula seems to lie solely in the aching urge of the writer to convey something he feels important to the reader. If the writer has that urge, he may sometimes, but by no means always, find the way to do it."

—John Steinbeck, preface to Edith Ronald Mirrielees, *Story Writing* (1963)

"Writing My Country": Making *To a God Unknown*

"'*Primus ego in patriam mecum . . . deducam Musas*'; for I shall be the first, if I live, to bring the Muse into my country. . . .' This was not a boast, but a hope, at once bold and devoutly humble, that he might bring the Muse . . . to his own little 'country'."

—Jim Burden on Virgil's *Georgics*, in Willa Cather, *My Antonia* (1918)

"This story has grown since I started it. From a novel about people, it has become a novel about the world. . . . The new eye is being opened here in the west—the new seeing."

—John Steinbeck in a 1932 journal

1

In the margin of an older sister's copy of Robert Louis Stevenson's *Prince Otto*, a very young John Steinbeck marked with pencil jottings his intention to be a writer (*SR*, xix). It was a startling proposal because, as Steinbeck later claimed in an early draft of *To a God Unknown*, "Artists and poets were not much thought of in western America. The artistic personalities of that period were hardly of the type to command respect from men of a hard and self reliant nature."[1] But at that time, when the definition of author seemed less ambiguous and contested (but no less fraught with dilemma) than it has become in our poststructuralist age, Steinbeck's desire would become a self-fulfilling prophecy, which he addressed with such undeflected intensity for the rest of his life that he often considered himself "monomaniacal": "when there is no writing," he remarked to George Albee in 1931, "I feel like an uninhabited body. I think I am only truly miserable at such times" (*SLL*, 48).

Steinbeck belonged to a turn-of-the-century generation of white male novelists for whom the act of writing would be con-

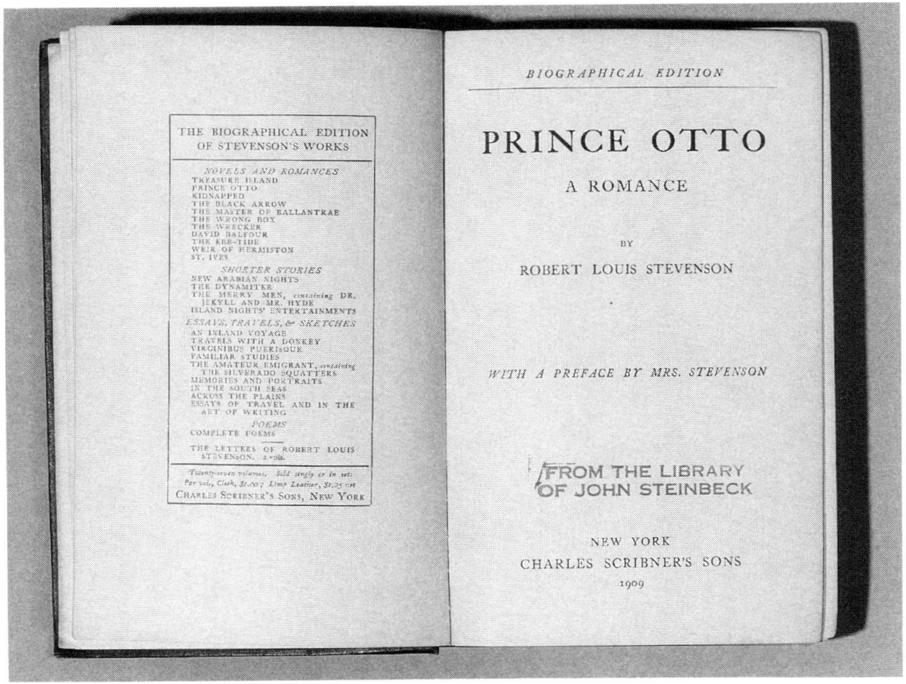

Steinbeck's copy of Robert Louis Stevenson's *Prince Otto*. It belonged originally to his older sister, Beth. According to his second wife, Gwyn, reading this book as a teenager galvanized Steinbeck's desire to be a writer.
Courtesy of Ruth Nuzum, Boulder, CO.

sidered an essential, even exalted, pursuit. (William Faulkner and Ernest Hemingway were his contemporaries; born within four years of each other, all three won Nobel Prizes in Literature.) For Steinbeck, as with many modernist-era writers, literary creativity took precedence over nearly all other life endeavors; this was so often the case that writing became an "addiction" (*TAJS*, 1). Steinbeck reached maturity in a period when becoming an author was a self-willed act with a romantic, rebellious aura to it, a way of managing the "clawed creature . . . tearing" in his "chest" (*TAJS*, 75); consequently, two of his first three books, *Cup of Gold* and *To a God Unknown*, feature larger-than-life heroes. More than that, however, throughout Steinbeck's life, writing was all things to him—a purely enjoyable activity, a sustaining addiction, a way of establishing and maintaining personal and economic identity, and perhaps most of all, a habit of being, a necessary condition of existence: "as long as [I] can eat and write more books, that's all I require," he stated to Edith Wagner in November 1933 (*SLL*, 90). In a sense, the desire to write well was Steinbeck's wound, the psychic engine that drove him relentlessly to create day in and day out for forty years.

Though occasionally insufferable when he played the role of Artist with capital *A*, Steinbeck was, more often than not, extremely humble and self-deprecating. Despite his shows of youthful cockiness, he learned early to distrust and even eschew the glamorous, celebrity side of authorship (with its emphasis on publicity and fame) and instead focused his energy on its private work-a-day side. If living so deeply in his fiction made him less than fully comfortable or agreeable in the social, domestic, and emotional spheres of ordinary life, it also provided therapeutic, compensatory benefits for a man who was known to be intensely shy and inward-looking. Novels "regulate our lives and give us responsibility," he claimed in 1930 (*SLL*, 25). Five years later, having tasted his first critical and commercial success with his fourth novel, *Tortilla Flat*, he confessed to the *San Francisco Chronicle*'s book critic, Joseph Henry Jackson, "The work has been the means of making me feel that I am living richly, diversely, and, in a few cases and for a few moments, even heroically. All of these things are not me, for I am none of these things. But sometimes in my own mind at least I can create something which is larger and richer than I am" (*SLL*, 119). Two decades later, Steinbeck was still espousing the priority of the life in art: in 1949 and 1950, escorting Elaine Anderson Scott around

Salinas and the Monterey area, Steinbeck told his wife-to-be that he could not remember a time when he didn't write; and a few years later he counseled Dennis Murphy, a young novelist and Salinas family friend, that "work is your only weapon" against whatever life has to offer.[2]

Writing was to become Steinbeck's ticket out of conservative Salinas, though once gone he remained in close contact with his family. (Like Joseph Wayne, Steinbeck always chafed between the competing desire to be "at home" and the need to be independent and court adventure; metaphorically and paradoxically speaking, writing fulfilled both urges.) His father hoped he would do something suitably practical with his life, such as be an engineer or lawyer, but he accepted his son's "ruthless" decision to become a writer. Beginning sporadically in 1929 he allowed John—and then after August 1930, and continuing for most of the next three years, John and his first wife, Carol—to occupy rent-free the family's three-room Pacific Grove cottage and also provided a $25 monthly living expense so that his son could concentrate solely on writing daily (*TAJS*, 147). From that time on, Steinbeck never held a steady outside job; working in words became his profession and vocation. Steinbeck's mother, never quite satisfied with her son's radical decision, hoped that, if he became a novelist at all, he would be like the successful Booth Tarkington (*JN*, 103), though as a young man Steinbeck himself preferred James Branch Cabell and Donn Byrnne as models.

Besides Steinbeck's marriage to the intrepid Carol, his acquaintance, begun in 1930, with Edward F. Ricketts—a philosophical marine biologist at whose Pacific Biological Laboratories on Ocean View Avenue in Monterey, Steinbeck spent countless hours of discussion and debate—would curb the mawkishness in his writing and enlarge his view of fictional taste and artistic propriety. In 1932, pressed to read Oswald Spengler's *Decline of the West*, Steinbeck perused the first chapter (Spengler preferred "the fine mind-begotten forms of a fast steamer, a steel structure, a precision-lathe . . . than all the pickings and stealings of present-day 'arts and crafts'"), but returned the book claiming he could not read it because it would "kill" his art (*SR*, 103, 173). Despite frequent lapses of self-confidence, however, on his way to becoming a full-fledged novelist Steinbeck relied upon little more than enormous dedication and commitment, unflagging endurance and independence, strong convictions, sincere intentions, an honest desire to improve, and a blistering capacity for self-criticism. To these aspects of his talent, he was fortunate to add the financial support of his family, the intellectual generosity and good will of several trustworthy friends, and the enabling capabilities of his wife.

Throughout the twenties in a succession of odd jobs in California and New York as surveyor, day laborer, carpenter's helper, bench chemist, ship's steward, journalist, and fish hatchery attendant, Steinbeck built a reservoir of practical experience (which he would draw upon for the rest of his life) and he continued writing stories and submitting them for publication, but without success. In 1927-28, seeking solitude to devote himself seriously to writing, he wintered at Lake Tahoe as an estate caretaker and began reworking "A Lady in Infra-Red," a story he had written while he was a student at Stanford in 1924. The result was his first novel, *Cup of Gold,* an historical novel (with strong fantasy elements) about the seventeenth-century pirate, Henry Morgan, set in Wales and Panama. It was published in August 1929 by the New York firm Robert M. McBride (which also optioned his next book). Steinbeck considered *Cup of Gold* "an immature experiment" necessary to purge a beginning novelist's enthusiasms and to sweep "all the Cabellyo-Byrneish preciousness out for good" (*SLL,* 17). As Steinbeck was soon to discover, however, *Cup of Gold*'s publication guaranteed nothing as far as mastery of his art was concerned. "It is an awful lot of work to write a novel," he reported to A. Grove Day, a Stanford classmate, in late 1929 (*SLL,* 15).

From 1929 through 1934, when Steinbeck was struggling to establish confidence and credibility and trying to perfect a tighter style, he wrote constantly but with mixed success; more often than not he wrote only for himself, but at other times he labored with an eye on the marketplace, such as it was in the early stages of the Depression. (Until *Tortilla Flat* succeeded commercially in 1935, Steinbeck earned less than a thousand dollars from his publications.) During this apprentice period, alternately dejected and elated by his progress and sometimes living hand to mouth, Steinbeck tried out different methods, forms, and styles but tried not to waver from his purpose: "Fine artistic things seem always to be done in the face of difficulties, and the rocky soil, which seems to give the finest flower, is contempt. Don't fool yourself," he informed fellow novelist George Albee in 1931, "appreciation doesn't make artists. It ruins them. A man's best work is done when he is fighting to make himself heard, not when swooning audiences wait for his paragraphs" (*SLL*, 34). Steinbeck had not yet reached the strategic sociological dimension that would become a hallmark of his greatest books (and whose acclaim would destroy his marginal status and put at risk all of his hard-earned credos about the writing life), but with *The Pastures of Heaven* and *To a God Unknown* he was on his way toward establishing a new fictional voice in California. Like Virgil, whose *Georgics* Steinbeck deeply admired (*SR*, 115), he too hoped, against great personal and cultural odds, to be the first of his generation to bring the Muse into "my country."

In this endeavor Steinbeck was not too different from Willa Cather in *My Antonia*, one of the American novels he admired most (*SR*, 24). Besides following Cather's achievement in poeticizing a distinct region of America, Steinbeck too was never fully comfortable with or in control of a strictly realistic mode. Like Pilon, a character in his comic *Tortilla Flat*, "the curse of realism lay uneasily" on Steinbeck, so his early admission to his Stanford classmate and fellow novelist, Carl Wilhelmson, is worth recalling when approaching many of Steinbeck's novels, especially *To a God Unknown*, which "leaves realism farther and farther behind. I never had much ability for nor faith nor belief in realism" (*SLL*, 87). It is, he added, just another "form of fantasy." That is to say, for Steinbeck, all modes of discourse, all enabling theories of writing, were equally fictive. Objectivity, which he adopted as a technical strategy, lay only in narrative distance and control (allowing him to establish irony and/ or ambiguity), not in absolute measure.

Steinbeck always distrusted realism's naive veneer. So he redefined it for his own purposes, made it up as he went, so to speak, and consistently nudged his readers behind or beyond the exterior face of reality to the contextual and constitutive factors—whether biological, economic, social, historical, emotional, mythical, or psychological—that impinge on the way his fictional human beings act (building a "wall of background" he later called it). The "profound and dark and strong" libidinous "streams" of the unconscious in every human being had become the locus of his interest, he admitted to Wilhelmson in August 1933 (*SLL*, 87). In *The Pastures of Heaven* and *To a God Unknown*, Steinbeck defined reality to include seen and unseen, physical and metaphysical, quotidian and psychological elements. In these style-conscious texts, his characters follow "a trail of innumerable meanings" toward what Joseph Wayne in chapter 10 tells his wife is "the undistorted real," the alluring reality behind reality.[3] This text, then, inscribes a related web in which the conscious life is affected by the unconscious, and the literal, denotative properties of language are repeatedly interpenetrated by symbolic, connotative values. Steinbeck's goal, writes his biographer, Jackson Benson, was to make people see the "whole" as it really is and "to see things as they are" (*TAJS*, 250).

By striking through outward masks, of course, Steinbeck also frequently bent the formal rules of realistic writing. In a loose sense, all his fiction—even his most naturalistic—has an allegorical dimension and can be considered fabular. (His propensity for writing parables has ensured Steinbeck's popular success but has hurt his reputation in the highest reaches of the critical academy—parables and fables, the argument goes, are not serious art). His favorite metaphoric gambit was to choose a microcosm to represent the drama of the world: fruit orchard in *In Dubious Battle*, bunkhouse in *Of Mice and Men*, Joad family's Hudson Super-Six in *The Grapes of Wrath*, and pre-World War II industrial cannery section on Monterey's Ocean View Avenue in *Cannery Row* are perhaps his four most recognizable examples of contested sites.

But Steinbeck also saw the macrocosm represented in the geographical space of his native country—California's Monterey County—and especially his home turf, the Salinas Valley. This entire region, which takes on a distinct life of its own in his fiction, was his equivalent of Faulkner's fictional Yoknapatawpha County in Mississippi and the rugged Carmel/Big Sur landscape of neighbor Robinson Jeffers's poems. From an early stage of his career, Steinbeck exhibited a special affinity with and—like Joseph Wayne—an enormous hunger toward this unique part of his native state (and, later, where Jeffers was concerned, he demonstrated a proprietary attitude that had a considerable impact on the final version of *To a God Unknown*). In 1933 Steinbeck told Albee, "I think I would like to write the story of this whole valley, of all the little towns and all the farms and the ranches in the wilder hills. I can see how I would like to do it so that it would be the valley of the world" (*SLL*, 73). Steinbeck's gaze covered an area from Santa Cruz and Watsonville on the north to King City and Jolon on the south; westward, Steinbeck's country was bound by the Pacific Ocean and the Santa Lucia mountains, and to the east, across the broad Salinas Valley, by the Gabilan Mountains. That slice of northern California is now popularly known as "Steinbeck Country."

Steinbeck's hunger, his compulsion to tell the significant stories of people situated in and on, but not apart from, this land, became one of his recognizable signatures as a novelist. In a 1932 journal (addressed privately to former Stanford roommate and close friend Carlton "Duke" Sheffield), Steinbeck noted of *To a God Unknown*: "The story is a parable, Duke, the story of a race, growth and death. Each figure is a population, and the stones, the trees, the muscled mountains are the world—but not the world apart from man—the world *and* man—the one indescribable unit man plus his environment" (*TAJS*, 260). Chronicling the lives of people in "the valley of the world" in such a way that they would be more than mere regional oddities, that they would represent an embedded part of the environment out of which they came, was Steinbeck's special achievement in *The Pastures of Heaven*, in the stories of *The Long Valley*, including *The Red Pony*, and of course in *To a God Unknown*, particularly in chapter 21, where Steinbeck's erotic ecological posture reaches a visionary level when he metaphorizes Joseph Wayne's body as a land mass, a "world-brain" with the power to destroy environmental "order" on a whim (*TGU*, 137). Philosopher John Elof Boodin's axiom that "the laws of thought must be the laws of things"—one of Steinbeck's favorite quotations from the philosopher's *A Realistic Universe* (*SR*, 16)—has special resonance here and underscores the novelist's view of the human body as text, the text as body, on which are written the defining struggles of desire, as well as the intricate difficulties of authorial representation. As with so many areas of Steinbeck's prose, reality and metaphor merge into each other in a corporeal whole.

When reading this unusual novel, then, with its oddly unsettling and strained combination of Christian and pagan, sacred and profane attributes—its earthiness and surreality, violence and pastoralism, pantheism and anthropomorphism, naturalism and lyricism—it is helpful to remember that Steinbeck invested his essential self in it, which is to say, he wrote it more like an extensive poem, or extended dream sequence, than like a traditionally mimetic or realistic novel. "I have the instincts of a minstrel rather than those of a scrivener," he informed Grove Day in late 1929 (*SLL*, 19). Thus, while *To a God Unknown* has an urgent, breathless fairy-tale quality and is, as critic Howard

Levant asserts, more "a series of detached . . . scenes," than "a unified . . . organic whole," it is not an incoherent concoction—"a rambling and improbable history," as Warren French calls it—that flies in the face of all sensible literary convention.[4] During its long gestation through different versions and multiple drafts, Steinbeck worked hard to create a palpable factual dimension that gives this otherwise arcane book a recognizable texture in regard to its geographical setting and landmarks (the moss-covered rock actually existed in the northern California town of Laytonville according to Steinbeck), its unusual characters (some of whom, like the Seer, Steinbeck claimed were based on living persons), and its feel for sharp details of nature and social life in Monterey County in the early part of this century. And yet throughout Steinbeck's work, observational detachment exists side by side with an attraction for archetypes, visionary experiences, and mythic patterns. The great live oak under which Joseph Wayne, the protagonist of *To a God Unknown*, builds his house has its counterpart in a "brother" pine tree the young Steinbeck planted next to the family's Monterey Bay summer cottage on Eleventh Avenue in Pacific Grove: "if the tree should die, I am pretty sure I should be ill," he claimed to Carl Wilhelmson in 1930 (*SLL*, 31).

Although Steinbeck is not normally considered an autobiographical writer during this phase of his career, the story of Joseph Wayne's pursuit reflects, up to a certain point, the story of Steinbeck; they are both obsessed with tracing out destinies and with seeking a generative place behind the reality of words and actions. *To a God Unknown* is driven by a kind of intense masculine poetic (symbolized by the phallic power of the totemic black bull in chapter 6) that thrives on competitiveness and seeks to attain primacy and mastery. But this poetic also is leavened by irony, skepticism, and employment of a "new eye in the west." Steinbeck relentlessly subverted California's populist image as a carefree golden land by pitilessly exposing its dichotomies, its mysteries, its unattainable felicities, as much for its citizens at large as for himself. Like those "twisted" madrone trees of chapter 2, whose "bright green and shiny" leaves appear only at the end of "horrible limbs" (*TGU*, 7), Steinbeck's imagination and his vision of himself as author were thoroughly implicated in these paradoxical critiques. Indeed, Joseph's drive toward the ineffable functions as a parable of Steinbeck's own struggle with his art, though where Joseph's solipsistic fetish, his sexual misalignment, and his dream of an unmediated vision of nature leads him back to the vortex of unconsciousness, which erases presence and the need for language, Steinbeck's expressive fetish thrusts him out of the unconscious toward a self-fashioned place in the vast geography of words, not so much a place of salvation as a mediated ground of being, a confluence of text and landscape. "You haven't any place you know until you make one," Steinbeck informed George Albee in the spring of 1932. "And if you make one, it will be a new one. Forget about genius and write books. Whatever you write will be you, no matter whether or not you rationalize it."[5]

2

On 12 September 1933, John Steinbeck received from Robert O. Ballou, his financially beleagured New York publisher, a small shipment of his newly printed *To a God Unknown*, with its dark green pictorial dust jacket designed by Steinbeck's artist friend, Mahlon Blaine. Editor Ballou had gone out on his own after the rapid, successive bankruptcies of Jonathan Cape and then Brewer, Warren, and Putnam (publisher of *The Pastures of Heaven*); although several houses eventually bid for *To a God Unknown* (including Simon and Schuster which would have promised more money), Steinbeck had remained loyal to Ballou's fragile, shoestring operation while the publisher sought the cash necessary to bring out his two fall list books—Steinbeck's and one by Julia Peterkin. "The books came this morning and I like them immensely. Thank you for doing such a fine job with them." They gave, he confessed, "more pleasure than I have felt for a number of months."[6] Steinbeck's casual reply has a restrained elegance that belies the protracted and delayed history of the book's development and production. In fact, in one form or another under three different working titles (marking various and sometimes overlapping stages of its progress), *To a God Unknown* occupied Steinbeck's attention and tested his artistic mettle and resources for over four years. Except for the posthumously published *The Acts of King Arthur and His Noble Knights* (1976), Steinbeck labored longer on *To a God Unknown* than any other book, including his two famous epics, *The Grapes of Wrath* and *East of Eden* (1952). "The book was hellish hard to write," he told Ballou succinctly in February 1933, and he admitted, without going into details, having worked toward it, counting research and note-taking and all, "for about five years" (*SLL*, 69).

The history of the making of *To a God Unknown* is worth elaborating upon, for the story behind the story (informed by a number of heretofore unpublished primary documents) makes an intriguing tale of its own, as well as a lesson in the felicities of endurance and dedication. Neither pure expressivism nor social construction can fully explain the creative act, which eludes final categorization. John Steinbeck was nothing if not resolutely single-minded. But the process by which the book grew was not so unitary, however, because forces of every kind from within and without kept entering his purview, altering his text, altering him. Even if all those factors were known—which is doubtful—it would still be impossible to establish their priority or present them fully, so what follows here is a working sketch, a narrative in and of process.

Steinbeck's novel had its roots in an unlikely source—an unfinished stage play called "The Green Lady" written in 1927 or 1928 by his Stanford University undergraduate classmate and boon companion, Webster "Toby" Street.[7] In the third and only extant draft of Street's play, the action "takes place in a front room of Andy Wane's ranch house in the hill country of Mendocino County, California" (1). Street's main characters include Andy Wane, "a tall, well-knit man of about fifty-five, or more, with the characteristic stoop of one who has made his way with his hands" (6); Mrs. Ruth Wane, "a woman about fifty" (1): and their three children—two sons, Luke and John, and one daughter, Susan, "a girl of seventeen or eighteen" (2). In addition, a neighbor, Milton, is a suitor for Susan's hand. The Wane family is gradually being torn apart by Andy Wane's pathological preoccupation with the trees on his land that make up "her"—the female forest, the "green witch" (2) of the natural world: "Seems like the whole outdoors was a green lady sometimes," Mrs. Wane complains bitterly (5). As the play progresses, the drama turns on Andy's nature worship but also on his selfish refusal to sell timber rights to raise the money necessary to send his daughter back to the University of California at Berkeley. Moreover, Andy conceives an illicit, unseemly attraction to Susie, confusing one form of natural beauty for another: "Men loves things 'cause they're like a woman, or 'cause they're pretty. They git 'em mixed up sometimes, an' don't know which is which," her jealous mother explains (4). According to Street's notes for the final act, in the end Andy is supposed to die in a raging forest fire.

Even though Webster Street was an active amateur playwright who "wrote all the time," by his own admission his work was "not very good." In the case of this unfinished play, his dialogue and gestures are wooden, his characterizations one-dimensional and unrealized. "I don't think it's anything like *To a God Unknown*, except that there is a pantheistic streak in it," he said in 1975.[8] And yet, despite Street's disclaimer, in protagonist Andy Wane's pantheism, his fatal attraction to natural and sexual forces, this otherwise uninspired melodrama does indeed contain the essential germ of Steinbeck's *To a God Unknown*, though it would be left entirely to Steinbeck to raise Andy Wane's aberrant behavior to the level of Joseph Wayne's tragic obsession in this novel.

Street, on the path to becoming an attorney (he earned his LLB at Stanford in 1928), recognized his friend's artistic ambitions and permitted Steinbeck to novelize the original treatment (which included a prologue and first act but only written suggestions for acts two and three). Although Steinbeck may have given thought to revising the play as early as 1927, it wasn't until mid-April 1928 that he told their mutual friend, Robert Cathcart (another Stanford classmate), that he was "preparing to write a novel around" Toby's play, which, he claimed, has "a fine thesis, and I do not know whether I have the power and acuteness and artistry to bring it out."[9] From that point on, even though it may have been intended as a collaborative effort, Steinbeck himself worked sporadically and mostly alone at "The Green Lady" for the next two years, marking the manuscript's uneven progress in frequent letters to his close friends of the time—Albee, Cathcart, Sheffield, Wilhelmson, poet Katherine Beswick, and lawyer Amassa Miller, who, until Steinbeck signed with literary agents Mavis McIntosh and Elizabeth Otis in 1931, served as the novelist's sole representative to New York publishing houses. All of them became sounding boards for Steinbeck's artistic concerns with this book.

In its first stage of composition the book seems to have languished during much of 1928 ("definitely shelved," he told Kate Beswick in September 1928 [*TAJS*, 142]) and into 1929—that is, for about a year after Steinbeck announced his intention to adapt Street's play. In February 1929 he traveled with Street to Laytonville and its environs in Mendocino County (north of

San Francisco) to visit the locale of the action and hoped to finish a draft by September. But over the next two months writing went very slowly and in early March 1929, he reported to Kate Beswick that he had temporarily fled Pacific Grove and headed for San Francisco, hoping to escape the "terror" of "The Green Lady" (*SCSU*, 8), by which he probably meant his own inadequacy at executing an inherited story, no matter how sympathetic he was to its basic premise. His hiatus, however, accomplished positive ends, in that it allowed Steinbeck to reassess his obligation to Street's original and to initiate important modifications, some of which would have long-range results. Around that time he reported to Cathcart that he was not as "afraid" of his "grand story" as he was a month or so earlier (*SCSU*, 14).

With fresh innovations in mind, around mid-April 1929, Steinbeck started "The Green Lady" again (*SCSU*, 9), this time so enthusiastically that in three weeks he reported to Beswick that he had finished eighty pages and had set his eye confidently on completing one hundred pages by June 1st:

> The Lady progresses pretty rapidly . . . and it seems to be improving in fluency and ease and in interest all the time. I am terribly anxious for you to have a look at it. I didn't make a carbon though. What shall I do? Shall I send you the first hundred pages heavily insured? Then if it were lost I would be repaid for doing it again. You see I write with a pen for five days of the week and on saturday and sunday I type and revise the pages I have written, so if the typed pages were lost all I would have to do would be to go through the typing and revising again. Or else I could wait and send you the third draft of which I shall make carbons. The only trouble is that I would like your criticism before I make the third draft.[10]

In his new version, Steinbeck began with a key decision to move the setting (except for the mossy rock and glade) from part of Mendocino County—about which he felt no emotional attachment or geographical familiarity—to an area near Jolon, in southern Monterey County, the writer's home county and thus a familiar landscape upon which to build his dynastic tale (as a child Steinbeck had spent summers on his uncle Tom Hamilton's ranch in King City, not far from Jolon.) The flat voice and slightly ironic tone registered in this characteristic early paragraph of "The Green Lady" indicates how declarative his approach was at this point: "Jolon is a large bowl in the earth in central California. It was watered in part by two large streams, the Naciemento and the San Antonio. It lies in the arms of the Coast Range mountains of which one rampart guards it from the ocean while a smaller ridge separates it from the long, fertile Salinas Valley. On one of the river's banks sat the old Mission San Antonio surrounded by its gardens and irrigation ditches, maintained by the Indians who, in return for their labor in making bricks, digging ditches and tilling the soil, received from the mission divine grace and cotton pants" ("GL," 2).[11]

Furthermore, instead of following Street's plan to begin *in medias res* in the present, Steinbeck started in 1850 (when the lure of easy money in California's gold fields was drawing men "westward like Hamlin's rats") which, he must have thought, would lend his version greater historical reach and sociological context. Steinbeck would also develop two generations of male Waynes: Joseph, the "strong" father, "born to be a patriarch," and husband to three successive wives, including his last, a Bible-reading woman named Carry, who never quite fits into the Wayne family regime; and Andy, Joseph's "strange," sensitive prodigal son (by his second wife, Beth Willets) who would become the protagonist of "The Green Lady" (and of "To the Unknown God"). The second half of the novel probably intended to chronicle Andy's domestic life with his new bride, Julia Seib. (In the third and final version of the novel Steinbeck would abandon the second half; he would also transpose the fledgling story of the Lopez sisters to chapter 7 of *The Pastures of Heaven.*)

Another element not mentioned by Street but added by Steinbeck was climatalogical: Steinbeck's version of "The Green Lady" incorporated the cyclical return of the dry years but did not elaborate upon its effect in determining character's actions. (One of the handwritten editorial comments on "The Green Lady" manuscript—perhaps by Street, or Beswick, or Sheffield—reads, "Must show effect of heat and dryness on Andy" ["GL," 45].) The basis for one aspect of *To a God Unknown*'s wasteland motif is evident here in the precursor draft:

> About every thirty years there have come periods of rainlessness to Central and Southern California. These desolating years seem to come creeping up out of the white desert to warn the west that it will one day die as the desert has died. They are like the Reminders of Death at an Egyptian feast. . . .
>
> And now the periodic drought had settled on the land. Little by little, year on year the water was

> sucked from the ground. The hills looked gaunt and hungry and pale. The bones of many thousands of starved cattle were whitening on the ground. Two families of Waynes packed up their possessions and drove away. Joe watched his dying land with terror and with loathing. ("GL," 42)

Several other basic elements in this originating version of "The Green Lady" would eventually be developed more fully in *To a God Unknown*: Joseph Wayne's preoccupation with fertility; a haunting "green grotto" in the mountains would become the published book's mysterious glade where much of the novel's key action occurs; Beth Willet's accidental death would be reprised in Elizabeth's death; and Andy's unconscious desire to "become one with the greenness" of the voluptuous forest would prefigure Joseph Wayne's attraction to the forest's "curious femaleness." Thus, from its roots in a circumscribed social and familial melodrama, Steinbeck was gradually broadening the work to a larger, more elemental scope; his characters and actions were proving to be no less bizarre than Street's original.

Steinbeck's impulse to elaborate continued. Six months later, in November 1929, Steinbeck told Beswick that "The Green Lady" was nearly finished (*SCSU*, 10). Later that year he sent her part of the manuscript to read and comment upon, planning to cut the "bad parts" with her assistance, though there is no proof that this collaboration actually occurred. At some point Webster Street may have read the typescript and made editorial comments, but given his work schedule as an attorney in Palo Alto, he probably had little time to do so, at least in any kind of sustained fashion (Street made no mention whatsoever of being involved in the novelized version of "The Green Lady" and for that matter never mentioned the manuscript at all in his 1975 interview with Martha Cox). So even though the title page of the manuscript read "*THE GREEN LADY* / a novel / by / John Steinbeck / and / Webster Street," Steinbeck was in the venture alone, and he was beginning to envision further changes that would make the material more congenial to his own imaginative and psychological demands, particularly in emphasizing Andy Wayne's delusional behavior.

Through the winter of 1929-30, Steinbeck kept at the book. His life meantime had changed significantly. In January 1930, he married Carol Henning, a remarkably strong and independent-minded person who not only encouraged his career as a writer but willingly shared the hard financial times of their early years together. In an effort to save both time and money, and because Carol was an incisive and effective editor (further removing Steinbeck's need to depend on Beswick and Street), in addition to her other jobs and duties (including a stint working at Ed Ricketts's lab), she typed Steinbeck's books, which freed the novelist to concentrate mostly on writing and revising. "Carol is a good influence on my work," he informed Carl Wilhelmson (*SLL*, 22). He agreed with Carol's suggestion that the ending of his book was "melodramatic" in places, but he felt that could be corrected in the next draft, in which, he told Wilhelmson on 30 March 1930, he would be "cutting several things out," including "all of that throw back about the childhood of Carry," which leads "off the interest from the main theme." Nevertheless, he continued, "I think it is a better book than I have done though that is not much to say for it. Certainly it has more effort in it that I have ever put in anything" (*TAJS*, 172).

Part of his effort at "amplifying and clarifying" certain places in the book involved seeking the right title. As early as January 1930, Steinbeck had wanted a new name for the second stage of his manuscript; by 10 March, he had titled his book "To the Unknown God." Writing from Eagle Rock, near Los Angeles, where the Steinbecks were living temporarily, he explained to Amassa Miller that the novel—projected to be about 375 pages or 110,000 words in length—"will be done and ready in about a month." He had "given it the title TO THE UNKNOWN GOD and am using some verses from the Vedic hymn of that title as a forepiece." Steinbeck wasn't sure that Robert M. McBride would want this book because, while it contained "nothing particularly sexual," it was "not a book that will please the great middle west."[12]

For the first time since he had begun working on the novel, however, he was able to follow the advice of Edith Mirriliees, his Stanford creative writing teacher, and reduce the novel's "thesis" to a single dispassionate statement: "It is a fairly close study of a paranoiac mind and of primitive instincts of a modern man. Whether or not there is any kind of race memory in paranoia is unimportant to me. I have recounted only that such a man reacted in a given manner. I have seen such reactions. And I have not drawn any conclusions from such reactions," Steinbeck told Miller in that same 10 March 1930 letter. And a few weeks later he admitted to Wilhelmson:

> Everything has been in a haze pretty much for the past

> three weeks. I have been working to finish this ms. and the thing took hold of me so completely that I lost track of nearly everything else. Now the thing is done. I started rewriting this week and am not going to let it rest. Also I have a title which gives me the greatest of pleasure. For my title I have taken one of the Vedic Hymns, the name of the hymn—
>
> TO THE UNKNOWN GOD
>
> You surely remember the hymn with its refrain at the end of each invocation "Who is the god to whom we shall offer sacrifice?" (*SLL*, 21-22)

Steinbeck's employment of the ancient hymn to Prajapati, supreme lord of creation, indicates that his story was exceeding regional concerns into a more profound and universal arena. His statement of artistic belief written around this time to George Albee speaks to his evolving "ambitious" vision: "I'd far rather under reach a large theme than wax redundant over a small one. I consider a magnitude of conception and paucity in execution far more desirable than a shallow conception with preciousness. [James Branch] Cabell painted the logical conclusion of that."[13] Although the novel was becoming increasingly his own property, he was still mindful of its origins in Street's play, however, so when Steinbeck sent Miller his finished manuscript in April 1930, he instructed that, should McBride accept the book, Steinbeck would write a short foreword "In which some mention of Toby Street should be made. . . . He has decided that he didn't do as much on this as he at first thought he did. But such a foreword is really necessary" (*SLL*, 23). (When *To a God Unknown* appeared, Steinbeck inscribed a gift copy: "For Toby—This isn't much like our old story and yet it is the same story many generations later" [*SCSU*, 148].)

As it turned out, however, his acknowledgment would not be needed because no publishing firm would take the novel, even though Steinbeck worked diligently in successive drafts to improve it by enlarging his characterization of the protagonist, another indication of the novel's growing reach: "I'm having a devil of a time with my new book," he wrote Albee on 27 February 1931, his 29th birthday: "It just won't seem to come right. Largeness of character is difficult. Never deal with an Olympian character" (*SLL*, 36). For fourteen months, from April 1930 to June 1931, Miller dutifully circulated drafts of "To the Unknown God" to numerous publishers, including McBride, John Day, Harper's, Farrar and Rinehart, Little, Brown, and others as well, all of whom rejected the manuscript. "The God must have been to ten publishers by now and has only received a decent note from one [John Day]," Steinbeck lamented in June 1931. "That is a pretty fair indication of its appeal" (*SLL*, 38). Part way through this disappointing period, in a letter postmarked "1-7-31," he registered his despair to Amassa Miller: "Rejection follows rejection. Haven't there ever been encouraging letters? Perhaps an agent with a thorough knowledge of markets would see that the mss. were not marketable at all and would return them on that ground. You see the haunting thought comes that perhaps I have been kidding myself all these years, myself and other people—that I have nothing to say or no art in saying nothing. It is two years since I have received the slightest encouragement and that was short lived" (*SCSU*, 26; *SLL*, 39).

Steinbeck got his wish: by May 1931, he signed on as a client with the new firm of McIntosh and Otis. "Carl Wilhelmson recommended me," he told Albee, and added humorously, if he had not known their method of doing business, he should be "very suspicious" of the "boundless enthusiasm" (*SLL*, 40). The upshot of this new arrangement on Steinbeck's side was a renewed vigor and confidence at a point when he most needed assurance and an abiding appreciation of and trust in McIntosh and Otis's professional abilities (they remained his agents throughout his life and still represent his estate). On 18 August 1931, Steinbeck confessed to Mavis McIntosh that "the imperfections of the Unknown God had bothered me ever since I first submitted the book for publication. In consequence of this uneasiness, your announcement of the book's failure to find a publisher is neither unwelcome nor unpleasant to me. If I were sure of the book, I should put it aside and wait. . . . But I know its faults. I know, though, that the story is good. I shall rewrite it immediately" (*SLL*, 45). Before undertaking his proposed rewriting, in late 1931 McIntosh submitted the manuscript of "To the Unknown God" one last time—to William Morrow (without success)—and Steinbeck, convinced more than ever of its unsalability, entered another "period of indecision and self-doubt," he told Wilhelmson on 1 September 1931. "I reread the Unknown God and was horrified at its badness as a whole. However I think I can make it pretty decent" (*TAJS*, 217).

Between bouts of anger at his inadequacy with this book and a growing entanglement with the stories that would comprise the linked chapters of *The Pastures of Heaven*, Steinbeck proposed a solution: "I guess I'll go back to the Unknown God," he informed Albee. "That title will have to be changed. Because the story will be cut to pieces and the pieces refitted and changed" (*SLL*, 50). And a little later he told Albee that the manuscript was "torn down like a Duzenberg having its valves reground" (*TAJS*, 221). It seems likely that, despite Steinbeck's repeated efforts at revision and elaboration, "To the Unknown God" was not substantively or stylistically different from its predecessor, and so something far deeper than mechanical patching and tinkering was necessary to keep it from reading "like a case history in an insane asylum" (*SLL*, 26), as he had once informed Miller. During the following year, however, Steinbeck made his greatest leap forward when a number of unanticipated elements spurred him to complete the novel we now have.

3

Nineteen thirty-two was the breakthrough year for *To a God Unknown*. In the previous version, Steinbeck treated Andy's paranoia, his "incurable ailment," too clinically, he told Amassa Miller, so that Andy's only options would be to commit "suicide" or to become a "homicidal maniac." Clearly, more complicated motivation was needed to make the new book succeed. Immediately Steinbeck reconceived Joseph Wayne as chief character, collapsing the roles of former patriarch (Joseph) and former protagonist (Andy) into one. In so doing, Steinbeck's character more deeply resonated aspects of the Old Testament Joseph (in Genesis), especially in his role as chosen brother and as dreamer and visionary; meanwhile, the epic cast of Joseph's westering journey to California's promised land echoed Biblical Joseph's removal to Egypt. As the book progressed, Joseph would increasingly—and rather heavy-handedly—recapitulate the overt messianic symbology of Jesus Christ and covert symbology of pagan sacrificial gods and primitive vegetation myth deities.[14]

Steinbeck also decided upon a new title: *To a God Unknown*. "The Unknown in this case meaning Unexplored," he said, so as not to confuse it with the "Unknown God of St. Paul" found in Acts 17: 22-29 (*SLL*, 67). Steinbeck later admitted to Ballou that he was writing a "religious" book (using the "pure and effective religion" of Bach's *Art of the Fugue* for inspiration and accompaniment as he wrote). But in finding a fictional form that approximated "the vehicle for the thought" of his time and in finding a way of expressing that "drive," Steinbeck was explicitly rejecting "mysticism," he further informed Ballou, by which he meant "bad vague thinking loosely stated" and "things that don't really happen."[15] His new twist on the Vedic hymn was extremely important because, as he later confided to Los Angeles book critic Wilbur Needham, the unknown god he employed was "that powerful fruitful and moving Unconscious." In his new version, the god Joseph sought was not manifest in the exterior world but resided inside himself. In directing Joseph's quest toward deep psychic recesses, Steinbeck was drastically changing the novel's thesis, altering its ground of being.[16]

Steinbeck's new version also would be enhanced by a contemporary historical event. He had incorporated the cyclical dry years into the fabric of the early versions, but it functioned as backdrop rather than as a controlling metaphor. Here the Jolon drought and its effects would create ambiance for Joseph's obsessive belief that only he can save the land, which would become the focus of the novel. (Joseph's brooding concern for the wasted land reflects the role of the mythological Fisher-King of Frazer's *The Golden Bough* and Jessie Weston's *From Ritual to Romance*—two works which stand prominently behind T. S. Eliot's 1922 poem, *The Waste Land*, as well as *To a God Unknown*.) On 25 January 1932, a couple of weeks before launching his final version, Steinbeck told McIntosh he no longer intended to merely patch up his book. "It would surely show such surgery. . . . I shall cut it in two at the break and work only at the first half, reserving the last half for some future novel." The reason for emphasizing the first half, he went on to explain, was "suggested by recent, and, to me, tremendous events":

> Do you remember the drought in Jolon that came every thirty five years? We have been going through one identical with the one of 1880. Gradually during the last ten years the country has been dying of lack of moisture. The dryness has peculiar effects. Diseases increase. . . . This winter started as usual—no rain. Then in December the thing broke. There were two weeks of downpour. The rivers overflowed and took away houses and cattle and land. I've seen decorous people dancing in the mud. They have laughed with a kind of crazy joy when their land was washing away. The disease is gone and the first delirium has settled to a steady jubilance. There will be no ten people a week

> taken to asylums from this county as there were last year. Anyway, there is the background. The new novel will be closely knit and I can use much of the material from the Unknown God, but the result will be no rewritten version. (*SLL*, 53)

"No rewritten version" is the key statement. Three weeks later, on 16 February, Steinbeck informed Amassa Miller that he had changed "the place, characters, time, theme, and thesis and name" of his new novel so "it won't be much like the first book" (*SLL*, 54). On 14 March he again wrote Miller, saying that he was "about a third finished with the first draft of the new version" and that he liked it "pretty well this time" (*SLL*, 61). His writing still went slowly (after reading in Spengler's *Decline of the West*, he was unable to work for three weeks), but at least it was moving toward a final shape.

For two years Steinbeck had enjoyed the company of an informal group of inquisitive, like-minded friends at Ricketts' Pacific Biological Laboratories. In early 1932, Carol started working for Ricketts, and the mutual relationship of all involved became deeper and more intense (*TAJS*, 224). Progressive, irreverent, free-wheeling discussions on every conceivable subject and a critical, bohemian attitude toward life were the order of the day. Steinbeck and Ricketts were especially compatible and launched the intellectual give-and-take that would eventually help Steinbeck formulate his phalanx, or group-man, theory, prominent in later works (there are moments of it in *To a God Unknown*—for instance when the dancers in chapter 16 join into one unit), as well as the shared philosophical tenets of "breaking through" and nonteleological thinking (already evident in its omniscient point of view and Joseph Wayne's live-and-let-live attitude), which would propel their 1941 collaborative nonfiction book, *Sea of Cortez* (Ricketts would also become the model for "Doc," the protagonist of *Cannery Row*, published four years later). Besides his metaphysical discussions with Ricketts, Steinbeck also enjoyed the use of the lab's excellent library. Steinbeck had already researched Celtic and Arthurian lore, Sir James Frazer's *The Golden Bough*, and Carl Jung's treatises on psychology and the unconscious, to cite but a few examples, and he continued to build a legitimate personal foundation of knowledge regarding what he called "psychological and anthropological" sources. Into this dynamic nexus of people, books, forces, and ideas, a couple of living rivals entered who would further transform the novel.

The first was Joseph Campbell. Later to become one of the world's most famous mythologists as a result of *The Hero with a Thousand Faces* (1949) and *The Masks of God* (1959-68), Campbell arrived in the Carmel/Monterey area in February 1932 and quickly gravitated toward Ricketts and his free-thinking cronies. Steinbeck had just started his revised manuscript and Campbell recalled hearing Steinbeck read aloud sections of his first four days' composition to him. Campbell thought the opening lacked "a sensuous, visual quality" and Steinbeck, impressed with the younger man's erudition and insight, decided to start over again with those qualities in mind.[17] For a while, Campbell and Steinbeck enthusiastically shared their parallel investigations into anthropology, ethnography, psychology, primitivism, mythology, comparative religions, and Arthurian romance. The hero's spiritual quest toward self-realization was to become one of Campbell's supreme subjects, so their discussions undoubtedly enlarged Steinbeck's view of Joseph Wayne's mythic dimension and the several stages of his progress, from his call to action through his transformation. In the poetical and by now more brilliantly visual, pictorial passages of the revised *To a God Unknown* that Steinbeck continued to read to him, and in Steinbeck's use of Joseph's rite of passage toward the sacred center of the world, Campbell discovered his and Steinbeck's mutual attraction to the "tendency" of "symbolism" as an essential way of apprehending, ordering, and understanding reality (*FM*, 169; Campbell later recalled that he had learned as much from Steinbeck as Steinbeck had from him).

In an ironic twist of life imitating art, both men, who believed they were two sides of the same personality, also shared an interest in the archetype of the eternal woman, the inspiring muse of creativity: Steinbeck writing Joseph Wayne's attraction to the "curious femaleness" of the forest of Our Lady paralleled in an uncanny way Joseph Campbell's belief in the importance of the feminine muse that leads the hero toward his destiny (*FM*, 167). This connection became extremely complicated for Campbell. He had met Carol briefly in Hawaii seven years earlier and now, reintroduced, fell deeply in love with her, resenting her marriage to John, who had "captured the girl" Campbell himself was "meant to have married" (*FM*, 186). The mutual attraction of Joe and Carol added yet another tangled dimension to Steinbeck's work. The ritual quest of the fictive Joseph became blurred by the flesh-and-blood Joseph Campbell, and the convolutions once more slowed down Steinbeck's work on his book. And although Steinbeck, like his main character, wanted to conduct his life above pity and therefore beyond teleological categories of praise and blame and good and bad (*FM*, 169), he could also be jealous, manipulative, and possessive. Ostensibly Steinbeck accepted the dalliance between the two platonic lovers but, stung a good deal more deeply than he cared to admit, John talked Carol into moving away to Montrose, near Los Angeles, for the next seven months.

Steinbeck also wrote his true reaction to the affair into *To a God Unknown*. The gay, alluring, lustful interloper Benjy Wayne (who earlier had nearly sung his way into the heart of Elizabeth before she married Joseph) is killed by Juanito for seducing his wife, Alice. If writing well was Steinbeck's best revenge for dispatching a rival, it could also be argued that the emotional strain of the affair between Campbell and his wife gave Steinbeck's novel a charged quality, a sexual reverberation, that earlier drafts probably lacked. The scene in chapter 21 in which Rama and the freshly widowed Joseph have intercourse out of "need" exemplifies this "furiously" lusty dimension (*TGU*, 138-39), and signifies Steinbeck's own need to write out of this renewed awareness of the human body. Around the time Campbell exited the scene, in the summer of 1932, the invigorated Steinbeck was having "the most fun" writing "eight pages a day," and considered the book "nearly half finished," he told Albee. "I am filled with excitement when I contemplate it. The plan is working so far and the pictures—as I see them at least, are sharp and deep. If I can go on I'll be finished in two months" (*TAJS*, 254).

In this final phase, then, Steinbeck discovered something about himself that would mark his writing career for the rest of the decade: he needed to feel a sense of competitiveness and urgency, needed to feel something threatening or annoying pushing back at him, creating internal stress as he composed. Campbell's involvement with Carol was one such transactional event that, by arousing Steinbeck's jealousy, injected a heightened sense of life into his novel and of course cannot be underestimated. However, a more lasting and palpable stamp on *To a God Unknown* came inadvertently from Robinson Jeffers, one of the chief American literary luminaries among the Ricketts lab bunch (*SR*, 60, 155). Beginning with *Tamar and Other Poems* in 1924 and continuing through six more volumes by

1932, Jeffers had created a unique poetry of enormous sweep and power centered around "continent's end," the California coastal landscape between Carmel and Big Sur, just a short drive from Monterey and Pacific Grove.

In his long fiction-length narrative poems, such as *Tamar, Roan Stallion, The Woman at Point Sur,* and *Cawdor,* Jeffers dealt obsessively with the seemingly aberrant and often violent behavior of contemporary people whose dramatic lives and actions resonated with mythological symbolism and erotic pantheism. Because Jeffers drew such exquisite attention to a nearby part of California, Steinbeck was bound to feel sad, nervous, threatened, even betrayed, in that deep-seated, anxiety-ridden way Harold Bloom has called attention to when he states that a poetical work contains a writer's "melancholy at his lack of priority. The failure to have begotten oneself is not the cause of the poem, for poems arise out of the illusion of freedom, out of a sense of priority being possible."[18]

Again, it was Carol Steinbeck who acted as major catalyst. The group was avidly reading and discussing Jeffers's work that spring when *Thurso's Landing* was published and the poet's photograph appeared on the cover of the 4 April 1932 issue of *Time,* establishing him as one of the most visible contemporary American writers. Carol discovered the central message of Jeffers's earlier poem, "Roan Stallion" (the title poem of his fourth collection, published in 1925), which states, "Humanity is the mould to break away from the crust to break / through, the coal to break into fire / The atom to be split. / Tragedy that breaks man's face and a white / fire flies out of it; vision that fools him / Out of his limits, desire that fools him out of his limits."[19] Ricketts and Campbell quickly realized the value of Jeffers's urge to push beyond the confines of the human ego. Jeffers was "one of the few poets that have ever really influenced my own thinking and style," Campbell admitted (*FM,* 180). And Ricketts, in developing two essays, "The Philosophy of Breaking Through" and "A Spiritual Morphology of Poetry," found that Jeffers penetrated to deep levels of "beyond" into realms of transhuman and natural beauty in his pessimistic poems.[20]

As a creative writer, however, and not a scholar or scientist, Steinbeck's reaction differed from theirs by being more affective. Where the others tended outward, Steinbeck tended inward. Highly respectful of Jeffers's ecological vision of the universe as an organic whole, Steinbeck also felt keenly the competitive sense, the anxiety of influence, the older man's poetry generated. An "effusive" five-page letter Steinbeck wrote in late 1932 to Ballou is the vital corroborating link here that explains what was at stake: he points out three times that Jeffers was not a native Californian but a transplanted Pennsylvanian, another interloper into his home country (Jeffers arrived in Carmel in 1914):

> My country is different from the rest of the world. It seems to be one of. those pregnant places from which come wonders. Lhasa is such a place. I am trying to translate my people and my country in this . . . book. The problem frightens me. Jeffers came into my country and felt the thing but he translated it into the symbols of Pittsburg[h]. I cannot write the poetry of Jeffers but I know the god better than he does for I was born to it and my father was. Our bodies came from this soil . . . our bones came . . . from the limestone of our own mountains and our blood is distilled from the juices of this earth. I tell you now that my country—a hundred miles long and about fifty wide—is unique in the world. . . . I've wanted to write this book for so long, and I've been afraid to. I've been too young, too ignorant, too thick headed. After the Roan Stallion, I thought Jeffers would do it but he hasn't. He got caught by Spengler and high school girls, and . . . Pittsburg[h] and the taboos of Pittsburg[h] to be rebelled against. He wrote the greatest poetry since Whitman but he didn't write my country. Perhaps he didn't want to.[21]

It does not matter how accurate Steinbeck's assessment of Jeffers is; what matters is that Steinbeck believed it. At once an apology and a credo, a hope and a boast, Steinbeck's self-confessedly "humorless" letter registers the gravity of his reaction to the intruder, the degree to which Jeffers was someone to be reckoned with, appropriated if needed, and even "surpassed," as Joseph Campbell characterized Steinbeck's attitude toward the poet.

At a crucial but undetermined point in his novel's development, Steinbeck began to *experience* Jeffers's poems in a haunting, visceral way (perhaps as much as a challenge as a threat); consequently, prone to borrow like a "shameless magpie" (*SLL*, 95), he transmuted something essential from them into his own text. In *To a God Unknown*, there are strong echoes of and parallels to Jeffers's overwrought and extremely demanding 1927 epic, *The Woman at Point Sur* in which Arthur Barclay, self-created prophet of a new religion, sacrifices himself.[22] But it wasn't simply Jeffers's subject matter, themes, characters, or setting Steinbeck was after, for he had been marking those areas out for himself for a number of years, perhaps even before having read Jeffers at all. Instead, it was the example Jeffers's work and life set as a standard of commitment to his art. If, as Steinbeck believed, poets and artists were still suspect in the American west, here was one who appeared as tough-minded as the country he wrote about. (A few years later Steinbeck told Lawrence Clark Powell, their mutual friend, that Jeffers should be awarded the Nobel Prize—"I don't know any American who can compete with him for it" [*SR*, 155].)

Despite our best theoretical abilities, we can never fully isolate or understand the influences that pass from one writer to another; practically speaking, Jeffers's muscular style apparently appealed to Steinbeck and helped elevate this book to a high level of intensity. For instance, in their sustained lyricism the last five chapters of *To a God Unknown* frequently show that Steinbeck internalized Jeffers's rhythmic style, such as evidenced in this passage in chapter 22 where Steinbeck's sentences easily break into the kind of sonorous line Jeffers favored and could be scanned with the same attention to the musical regularity of beat found in Jeffers's rhythm:

> He rode slowly home along the banks of the dead river.
> The dusty trees, ragged from the sun's flaying, cast very little shade on the ground.
> Joseph remembered how he had ridden out in a dark night
> and flung his hat and quirt to save a good moment out of a tide of moments.
> And he remembered how thick and green the brush had been under the trees,
> And how the grass of the hills bowed under its weight of seed. (*TGU*, 144)

And again, in this passage in chapter 25:

> At last they topped the rise and Joseph saw the houses of the ranch, bleached and huddled.
> The blades of the windmill shone faintly in the moonlight.
> It was a view half obscured, for the white dust filled the air, and the wind drove fiercely down the valley.
> Joseph turned up the hill to avoid the houses, and as he went up toward the black grove,
> the moon sank over the western hills and the land was

> blotted out of sight.
> The wind howled down from the slopes and cried in the
> dry branches of the trees.
> The horse lowered its head against the wind.
> Joseph could make out the pine grove darkly as he approached it. (*TGU*, 182)

Once again, as Joseph approaches the dark circle of pines for the last time, Steinbeck's cadence here creates a compelling tempo that reflects an inevitable march to the dark interior of Joseph's psyche. ("It's hardly the same book. Different feeling and rhythm," Steinbeck boasted to Kate Beswick.) Where Jeffers's Nietzschean inhumanism could strike readers as shrill, abusive, and defiant, Steinbeck exposed the potential for power inside man, especially at that threshold of relatedness, that vector of connection, where the human being and the landscape in all its physical and memorial attributes conjoin.

In that surreal epiphanic scene in chapter 21 referred to earlier in this essay, Steinbeck imagines Joseph's body as an extended trope of the earth, achieved by a doubling of self and world, made possible by both being inside and outside of language and memory at the same time: "And he thought in tones, in currents of movement, in color, and in slow prodding rhythm. He looked down at his slouched body, at his curved arms and hands resting in his lap. Size changed" (*TGU*, 136). The anatomy of the "world-brain" that follows in Joseph's "blue light" revery is unlike almost everything else in Steinbeck's writing (or in Jeffers's for that matter). A few chapters later, in Steinbeck's controversial climax when Joseph sacrifices himself to restore vitality to the land, Joseph is more Steinbeckian everyman that Jeffersian superman: "And yet he looked down the mountains of his body where the hills fell to an abyss. He felt the driving rain, and heard it whipping down, pattering on the ground. He saw his hills grow dark with moisture. Then a lancing pain shot through the heart of the world. 'I am the land,' he said, 'and I am the rain. The grass will grow out me in a little while'" (*TGU*, 184). In these deliberately antirealistic scenes Steinbeck attempted to surpass Jeffers by laying claim to the generative roots of "my country" and "my god" in a way that is indigenously organic, not philosophically superimposed. In this sense, then, Steinbeck's borrowing from Jeffers can be considered paradoxically both a homage and a challenge, a return and a breakthrough, a relinquishment and a possession.

4

Meeting the challenge from Jeffers helped Steinbeck finish his book. In December, a month after *The Pastures of Heaven* was published, he claimed that Robert Ballou had announced the new novel for spring release. Given the weak sales of *Pastures* (about 650 copies), Ballou's announcement was probably an incentive, and throughout January 1933, Steinbeck wrote quickly and steadily, completing the novel by 11 February. He and Carol were so poor that a friend volunteered to pay postage to New York (*TAJS*, 257-58). Steinbeck's final version displayed greater fascination for Joseph's stature as a "pattern breaker." Steinbeck had come a long way from his cold view of Andy Wane as a scientific oddity, a "close study of a paranoiac mind." This characterization of Joseph Wayne had fire because Steinbeck identified with him in a way he was unable to identify with Andy. In his private journal, he wrote: "Joseph is a giant shouldering his way among the ages, pushing the stars aside to make a passage to god. And this god—that is the thing. When god is reached—will anybody believe it[?] It really doesn't matter. I believe it and Joseph believes it" (*TAJS*, 260).

Herman Melville had created in *Moby-Dick*'s Captain Ahab a "grand, ungodly, god-like man" (Ahab's motto was "I baptize you in the name of the devil") and, afterwards, as he told Nathaniel Hawthorne in 1851, felt spotless as a lamb. So, too, Steinbeck was in the precarious position of presenting a character his readers might find zealous, imperious, and unlikeable, and whose life presented a tragic dichotomy between means and end. Writing to Robert Ballou on the day he had shipped the final manuscript, Steinbeck said: "It will probably be a hard book to sell. Its characters are not 'home folks.' They make no more attempt at being sincerely human than the people in the Iliad. Boileau [Nicolas Boileau-Despreaux in *The Art of the Poetic* (1674)] . . . insisted that only gods, kings and heroes were worth writing about. I firmly believe that. The detailed accounts of the lives of clerks don't interest me much, unless, of course, the clerk breaks into heroism" (*SLL*, 69). Joseph is monomaniacal, but he is also brave, energetic, inventive, and prophetic. As a transgressive, god-like hero, he has the courage of his convictions, even though they fly in the face of normative social and institutional values. It isn't stretching too much to say that, as a type of the artist (a "self-character" Steinbeck would later call such creations), Joseph not only creates himself but also reflects the young Steinbeck's sense of passionate commitment toward his own way of doing things and the necessity of sacrifice to break through to deeper levels of ecstasy or being.

Of course, where Joseph is ultimately restrained by the prison of self, even as he desires to reach an originary presence at the other side of reality ("the naked thing," he calls it in chapter 22) where words are "ridiculous" (*TGU*, 151), Steinbeck, pregnant with words, is constrained by the very limitations of the genre in which he is bound to work (it requires words to describe the symbolism of the "naked," unutterable presence). Joseph's covenental act of emptying himself of blood as a way of imagining that he can save nature and spiritualize himself symbolizes Steinbeck's own call to the complex improbabilities and conundrums of working in a medium that required him to empty himself of words, so to speak, and then, paradoxically, when he wasn't emptying himself, made him liable to feel dead, "miserable," and "uninhabited" (*SLL*, 48). That is to say, Joseph Wayne's tautological dilemma was Steinbeck's and vice versa: in a sense, the very thing that promised to sustain them also threatened to consume them, to defeat their aspirations, leaven their desires, deflate their identities. But as the two states—depletion and fullness, to give them tentative names—are linked, one cannot exist without the other; each thing is an index of everything else, Steinbeck became fond of saying.

Never a thorough-going inhumanist (as his attitude toward Spengler and Jeffers shows), Steinbeck was nonetheless uninterested in—and actually discouraged—a reductive humanistic interpretation of his book: "I have no intention of trying to explain my book," he told Ballou in February 1933. "It has to do that for itself" (*SLL*, 69). Rather, he was interested in the saga of creation and the process of interior passage for its own sake: "What the thing will be I don't care," he had told George Albee a bit earlier during the novel's composition. "The unspeakable joy of merging into this world I am building is more than enough" (*TAJS*, 252). Given what Louis Owens calls the book's "brilliantly sustained ambiguity," however, readers are free to perceive Joseph's salvation either as patently heroic (as priest of nature, his sacrifice causes the rain) or as ironic (as confused mystic, it is impossible for his death to have caused the rain). To choose the first is to choose an exotic, romantic reading in which Joseph's redemption is earned and Christianity is ridiculed, and which makes Steinbeck's artistic purpose seem silly, reductive, or naive. To choose the latter is to choose a serviceable, empirical reading in which Joseph's resolution is misguided and irrational and Father Angelo's point of view, secured by common sense, in turn makes Steinbeck's book a cautionary tale about the dangers of total immersion. Most scholarly appraisals of this novel fall into one of these camps.[23]

But privileging one interpretation over another violates Steinbeck's precariously balanced tensions. In fact, *To a God Unknown* is his version of Keats's negative capability in action. So before irritably reaching after the facts and reasons that we imagine will explain one reading or another, we must first accept that, for Steinbeck at that moment of his creative life, this poetical novel announced a new way of being in the world, one that was comfortable juggling uncertainty, mystery, and doubt, and one that balanced advocacy with skepticism. "The cult of so called realism is a recent one, and anyone who doesn't conform is looked on with suspicion. On the moral side, our moral system came in about two hundred years ago and will be quite gone in 25 more," he proclaimed to Edith Wagner in November 1933, a couple of months after the book was published (*SLL*, 89). What Steinbeck proposed in language had a consecration and validity all its own, so he did not feel obligated to resolve things for his audience in a traditionally moral or realistic manner. In mid-May 1933, while proofreading galley sheets of *God* that Ballou had sent, Steinbeck wrote in another notebook: "I read a few pages and found them fairly effective. The detached quality is there undoubtedly. Here and there I could see a word I would like to change were I better known and the fear of proof correction costs less fearful to me. But I was not cast down by the prose. It is ambitious. Perhaps in its thousands of lines there are one or two of pure poetry. The critics will scream at me but I do not care about that."[24]

Generally, the most prominent contemporary reviews were mixed, and while there was little or no unalloyed praise, reviewers touched upon a number of the intellectual and creative concerns Steinbeck himself had dealt with or built upon during the novel's writing, so the critical responses should not have taken him completely by surprise. The loudest scream appeared in the *New York Times*. On 1 October 1933, Virginia Barney called *To a God Unknown* a "curious hodge-podge of vague moods and irrelevant meanings" and a "symbolical novel conceived in mysticism and dedicated to the soil," which "attempts too much" and "achieves too little" and hence fails to cohere." A reviewer for the 18 October 1933 issue of *The Nation* found that *To a God Unknown* "reads like a novelized version of a Robinson Jeffers poem, and its setting is what may be known to tourists of the future as the 'Robinson Jeffers country.'" Having put Steinbeck in his place, so to speak, the reviewer judged the novel to be "pitifully thin and shadowy." A writer in the *Christian Century* on 20 September 1933 considered the novel "a modern appendix to *The Golden Bough*." Another critic, appraising the book for the 28 October 1933 issue of *Saturday Review of Literature*, claimed *To a God Unknown* "is full of . . . worship of the sun, the land, nature, the sexual act. And yet . . . it is almost without religious feeling." Nevertheless, it painted "a fairly interesting and (apparently) accurate picture of the region and the life of the times." Margaret Cheney Dawson, writing in *New York Herald Tribune Books* on 24 September 1933, called it a "strange and mightily obsessed book" that would appeal only to readers "who are capable of yielding themselves completely to the huge embrace of earth-mysticism." If you are of that persuasion, Dawson continued, and are "unconcerned with good or evil, solace or punishment, error or reason," then Steinbeck's novel "is the purest expression of it that I have ever encountered."

Even though there is a level of fair assessment in these contemporary critiques, Steinbeck bridled at the novel being called mystical. Understandably, then, when Wilbur Needham reviewed the book positively in the *Los Angeles Times*, Steinbeck thanked him for not branding it mystical: "all the devils . . . and all the mysticism and all the religious symbology in the world are children of the generalized unconscious. Can it be that most . . . critics . . . are sublimely unconscious of the investigations and experiments in human psychology which are marshalling not only a new knowledge of man but a new conception of realities? You may judge then my relief on finding that you did know what I was trying to do, understood the foundation and found it valid in literature."[25]

Good, bad, or indifferent, mythical or mystical, reviews didn't help move the book. Publisher Ballou printed 1,498 copies, of which 598 were bound and sold (at $2 each)—not enough copies sold to recoup the small advance he had paid Steinbeck.[26] Within a year Ballou, who Steinbeck considered a "fine" and "sensitive" man but too gentlemanly to fight New

York publishing battles, remaindered both *The Pastures of Heaven* and *To a God Unknown* and eventually rejected Steinbeck's *Tortilla Flat* manuscript as unsuitable. For a year or so Steinbeck was back in a familiar situation: he was writing under stressful circumstances (both his parents were seriously ill) and he was trying not to worry about publication. In Steinbeck's darkest moments, overwhelmed by constant sickroom duties and filial responsibilities, he resolved to fight against a gut-level feeling that he would never have the strength or time to write again.[27] His despair was temporary, although arguably, the time John (with Carol's frequent help) spent caring first for his mother (who died in February 1934), then for his father (who died in May 1935), probably did as much as anything else to end Steinbeck's interest in heroic, larger-than-life literary characters. Frequent interruptions to clean his mother's bedpans and wash loads of soiled sheets and later to witness his father's decline into senility refocused Steinbeck's attention on common life, on the realm of "clerks" who, when they broke through reality at all, broke into a far more circumscribed, even dubious, kind of heroism than Henry Morgan's or Joseph Wayne's. Steinbeck had already struck that chord in *Pastures,* but it would be with *In Dubious Battle, Of Mice and Men,* and *The Grapes of Wrath* that a gritty style and uncompromising vision of beleagured humans caught in overwhelming circumstances would carry his "new conception of realities" to yet another stage of achievement.

In 1934 Steinbeck signed with Covici-Friede, a small, progressive New York firm which would not only publish the rejected *Tortilla Flat* (it became a best-seller and won the Commonwealth Club's Gold Medal as the best California novel of 1935) but would also reissue both *The Pastures of Heaven* and *To a God Unknown* that year as well, followed by *In Dubious Battle* and *Of Mice and Men* over the next two years. (As I note in the following chapter in *Steinbeck's Typewriter,* when the Covici-Friede firm went bankrupt in mid-1938, Pascal Covici was hired as a senior editor by The Viking Press, which became Steinbeck's publisher for the rest of his life.) In April 1934, by the time Steinbeck thanked Wilbur Needham for his prescient review in the *Los Angeles Times,* he was at the threshold of becoming not only the accomplished writer he had started out to be seven years earlier but a relatively popular one as well. If the remainder of Steinbeck's career after *Tortilla Flat* can be seen as an anguished dance with fame, he had here arrived at a transitional moment when his sense of himself as a writer was still driven by the private pleasures of his art. "A couple of years ago," he confessed in August 1933, "I realized that I was not the material of which great artists are made and that I was rather glad I wasn't. And since then I have been happier simply to do the work and to take the reward at the end of every day that is given for a day of honest work" (*SLL*, 87). His belief in writing as a working process and his candor regarding his own talent still strikes a resonant chord, for Steinbeck rarely gave himself airs as a writer.

To a God Unknown is by general consensus not considered a great novel, but because it occupies a significant place in Steinbeck's career, it deserves serious consideration. Memorable among Steinbeck's productions as much for its quirky qualities as for its unusual characterizations and its prophetic vision of environmental crisis and ecological piety (perhaps Joseph Wayne will come to be recognized as an eco-hero), *To a God Unknown* may have taught John Steinbeck more about crafting long fiction than anything else he worked on during his apprentice period. Even though he was not the first to bring the muse into his California country, this novel, which nevertheless announced the presence of a "new eye in the west," laid the foundation for his later writing achievements.

Notes

[1] John Steinbeck and Webster Street, "The Green Lady" novel typescript, 15, Department of Special Collections, Stanford University Library, Stanford (*SCSU*, 142). The unpublished typescript, written in 1929 (hereafter cited as "GL"), is solely Steinbeck's work. Webster Street's original play ("The Green Lady," which predated the novel version) is discussed in this chapter.

[2] Elaine Steinbeck, foreword to *Cannery Row*, by John Steinbeck (London: Mandarin Books, 1995), 1. Steinbeck's statement to Murphy, written in February 1957, is published in *Your Only Weapon Is Your Work: A Letter by John Steinbeck to Dennis Murphy*, ed. Robert DeMott (San Jose, CA: Steinbeck Research Center, 1985), 3-4. A selective digest of Steinbeck's comments on writing, culled from a variety of primary autobiographical sources, is available in a pamphlet-length publication, *John Steinbeck on Writing*, ed. Tetsumaro Hayashi, Steinbeck Essay Series, no. 2 (Muncie, IN: Steinbeck Research Institute/ Ball State University, 1988).

[3] John Steinbeck, *To a God Unknown* (New York: Penguin Books, 1995), 54 (hereafter cited as *TGU*). Parenthetical page numbers refer to Penguin's Twentieth-Century Classics series edition of *To a God Unknown*, the text and

pagination of which is identical to the first edition (New York: Robert O. Ballou, 1933) and to the first edition, second issue (New York: Covici Friede, 1935). This chapter of *Steinbeck's Typewriter* on *To a God Unknown* refers to the Penguin Books paperback edition of Steinbeck's novel that is itself introduced by the original version of this essay. However, in this current version I have added full documentation and relevant informational and referential footnotes absent in the commercial edition's introduction. The text of this chapter, too, dispenses with some elementary biographical material that appeared in the original introduction and otherwise expands and augments key aspects of my original discussion.

[4] Howard Levant, *The Novels of John Steinbeck: A Critical Study* (Columbia: University of Missouri Press, 1974), 27; Warren French, *John Steinbeck's Fiction Revisited* (New York: Twayne Publishers, 1994), 42.

[5] John Steinbeck to George Albee, letter, May 1932, George S. Albee Papers, Bancroft Library, University of California, Berkeley.

[6] John Steinbeck to Robert Ballou, letter, 11 and 12 September [1933], Harry Ransom Humanities Research Center, University of Texas, Austin. Mahlon Blaine's striking jacket cover featuring the bearded Joseph Wayne as a mountain range can be observed in a photograph in the sale catalogue of Harry Valentine's now-dispersed collection, *John Steinbeck: A Collection of Books and Manuscripts* (Santa Barbara, CA: Bradford Morrow, Bookseller, 1980), 14.

[7] Webster Street, "The Green Lady" play typescript, [1927-1928], Department of Special Collections, Stanford University, Stanford (*SCSU*, 142). Hereafter page numbers are incorporated in the text of my essay. For more on the ur-texts of *To a God Unknown*, in addition to Benson's coverage (*TAJS*, 139-62), see especially Richard Astro's pioneering treatment (based on information provided directly from Street) in *John Steinbeck and Edward F. Ricketts: The Shaping of a Novelist* (Minneapolis: University of Minnesota Press, 1973), 81-84; and Carlton A. Sheffield's eyewitness account in *Steinbeck: The Good Companion* (Portola Valley, CA: American Lives Endowment, 1983), 145-48. Sheffield's extremely scarce (and typographically marred) photocopied book contains the complete transcription of Steinbeck's *God Unknown* journal (189-96), which Sheffield had earlier allowed Nelson Valjean to reproduce in *John Steinbeck: The Errant Knight* (San Francisco: Chronicle Books, 1975), 120-24. Benson draws on selections of the journal in *The True Adventures of John Steinbeck*.

[8] Webster F. Street, "Remembering John Steinbeck," interview by Martha Heasley Cox, *San Jose Studies* 1 (November 1975): 111.

[9] John Steinbeck to Robert Cathcart, letter, 14 April 1928, Department of Special Collections, Stanford University Library, Stanford (*SCSU*, 13).

[10] John Steinbeck to Katherine Beswick, letter, 22 May 1929, Department of Special Collections, Stanford University Library, Stanford (*SCSU*, 9).

[11] Compare this entry from the typescript with its counterpart in *To a God Unknown*, the opening paragraph of chapter 2: "After a time of wandering, Joseph came to the long valley called Nuestra Senora, and there he recorded his homestead. Nuestra Senora, the long valley of Our Lady in central California, was green and gold and yellow and blue when Joseph came into it. The level floor was deep in wild oats and canary mustard flowers. The river San Francisquito flowed noisily in its bouldered bed through a cave made by its lit-

tle narrow forest. Two flanks of the coast range held the valley of Nuestra Senora close, on one side guarding it against the sea, and on the other against the blasting winds of the great Salinas Valley. At the far southern end a pass opened in the hills to let out the river, and near this pass lay the church and the little town of Our Lady. The huts of Indians clustered about the mud walls of the church, and although the church was often vacant now and its saints were worn and part of its tile roof lay in a shattered heap on the ground, and although the bells were broken, the Mexican Indians still lived near about and held their festivals, danced La Jota on the packed earth and slept in the sun" (*TGU*, 4).

[12] John Steinbeck to Amassa Miller, letter, 10 March 1930, Department of Special Collections, Stanford University Library, Stanford (*SCSU*, 24). In late March Steinbeck told Miller that when his father read the manuscript he "was quite disgusted at the end. . . ." for he "expected Andy to recover and live happily ever after. . . . The American people demand miracles in their literature" (*TAJS*, 173).

[13] John Steinbeck to George Albee, letter, [1931], George S. Albee Papers, Bancroft Library, University of California, Berkeley. Steinbeck and Albee eventually had a falling out, but before that, throughout the early thirties, some of Steinbeck's meatiest literary correspondence was directed at Albee and reads like a monologue on craft and technique. Twenty letters written between 1931 and 1934 are printed in *Steinbeck: A Life in Letters*, though in many instances the published versions are severely edited. One letter in particular, written in the spring of 1931, runs sixty lines in length and covers nearly three handwritten pages. Printed, it is reduced to sixteen lines of text (*SLL*, 37). An excised portion speaks to Steinbeck's project in his Unknown God novel, a movement away from polite civilized values: "In America, people deny the covered passages of their minds until they eliminate them. If the sub stream gets too powerful there are liquors to stem and dam them. Americans do not like to be reminded that they have other characteristics than those 'tested and approved' by the American Magazine. They deny ferociously the most obnoxious truths about themselves . . .," including the myth of "the drive of our people to civilization."

[14] See Joseph Fontenrose, *John Steinbeck: An Introduction and Intepretation* (New York: Barnes and Noble, 1963), 15-19.

[15] John Steinbeck to Robert O. Ballou, letter, 27 February [1934], Harry Ransom Humanities Research Center, Austin. On Steinbeck's myth-rooted sensibility and his refutation of mysticism, see my "Toward a Redefinition of *To a God Unknown*," *University of Windsor Review* 8 (Spring 1973): 34-53. In a letter to me, written on 12 April 1972, Joseph Campbell recalled that he and Steinbeck "often discussed the relationship of mythic . . . symbolic forms." When Steinbeck read to him the passage in chapter 9 where Joseph Wayne helps Elizabeth climb into the great oak tree near his house, Campbell claimed that Steinbeck's comment on his own scene was "'strange religiousness.'"

[16] In an intriguing examination of Steinbeck's complex religiosity in *To a God Unknown*, Dennis Prindle claims that "religious tradition and patriarchal authority only seem to yield to a complete identification with an unmediated experience of nature. In fact, in his self-created nature worship Joseph is reading nature as though it were culture, shaping its neutral facticity to the form of

his own desire." See "The Pretexts of Romance: Steinbeck's Allegorical Naturalism from *Cup of Gold* to *Tortilla Flat*," in *The Steinbeck Question*, ed. Donald R. Noble (Troy, NY: Whitston Publishing, 1993), 31-32.

17 Stephen and Robin Larsen, *A Fire in the Mind: The Life of Joseph Campbell* (New York: Doubleday, 1991), 166 (herefter cited as *FM*). Campbell later confided in his 1932 Monterey journal, "John has a fine, deep, living quality about his work which ought to ring the bell, I think—if his work is ever discovered." In reconstructing Campbell's formative sojourn in the Monterey-Carmel area in the early thirties, his complicated relationship with John Steinbeck, his romantic attachment for Carol Steinbeck (not mentioned by Benson in *True Adventures of John Steinbeck*), and his memorable friendship with Ed Ricketts, the Larsens rely heavily on Campbell's revealing private journals, letters, and an unpublished novel, as well as an audiotape interview made in 1986 with Pauline Pearson of the Steinbeck Library in Salinas. See chapters 8 to 10 of the Larsens' book: "The Road to Monterey (1931-32)," "The Conspiracy Against Venus (1932)," and "The Grampus Adventure (1932)." Jay Parini's milder version of the affair appears in *John Steinbeck: A Biography* (New York: Henry Holt, 1995), 121-25. That there was cross-inspiration between Campbell and Steinbeck is evident in the following accounts. In March 1932, when Steinbeck received multiple contracts from Robert Ballou for *The Pastures of Heaven* and two later manuscripts (including *To a God Unknown*), he told George Albee: "All of this sounds impossible to me of course. Nothing so nice has ever happened to me" (*SLL*, 62). Witnessing Steinbeck's success Campbell confided in his journal: "My enthusiasms were whetted last week when John Steinbeck received a nice contract for his novel, and two additional contracts for his *next* two novels—sight unseen—this pitches me into a great enthusiasm for the art of words. And I think I'd better get again to *my* job" (*FM*, 169).

18 *The Anxiety of Influence: A Theory of Poetry* (New York: Oxford University Press, 1973), 96. Sounding something like a frontier version of Bloom, in *Archetype West: The Pacific Coast as a Literary Region* (Berkeley, CA: Oyez, 1976), 83-91, William Everson (formerly Brother Antonius) traced out a line of responsiveness among western American writers to the region's primal condition, its originary presence. One of his main exemplars of this creative force of Dionysian "charisma" is Robinson Jeffers (Everson's poetical father), from whose work he thought Steinbeck's *To a God Unknown* was "clearly derived." For Everson, however, Steinbeck never achieved the "apotheosis" of the pure archetype but remained too refined, because of the "imposition of aesthetic distance and the cultivation of a marmoreal style." Although he lacked direct "evidence," Lawrence Clark Powell was intuitively right in claiming "that Steinbeck was influenced by Jeffers." More patient than Everson, Powell links both writers as shared possessors of Monterey County's "double landscape." See "*To a God Unknown*," chap. 19 in his collection of essays, *California Classics: The Creative Literature of the Golden State* (Los Angeles: Ward Ritchie Press, 1971; reprint, Santa Barbara, CA: Capra Press, 1982), 225-29.

19 Robinson Jeffers, "Roan Stallion," in *The Selected Poetry of Robinson Jeffers* (New York: Random House, 1938), 149. See Robert J. Brophy's *Robinson Jeffers: Myth, Ritual, and Symbol in His Narrative Poems* (Cleveland, OH: Case Western Reserve University Press, 1973; reprint, with corrections and

additions, Hamden, CT: Archon Books, 1976) for a comprehensive view of the poetry's mythic dimensions. Many of Brophy's findings are applicable to Steinbeck's text as well.

[20] Ricketts's previously unpublished essays are in Joel Hedgpeth's handy collection, *The Outer Shores, Part 2: Breaking Through* (Eureka, CA: Mad River Press, 1978), 69-89. Ricketts also found this "deep thing" in *To a God Unknown*.

[21] John Steinbeck to Robert O. Ballou, letter, [early 1933], Harry Ransom Humanities Research Center, Austin. Only a very small portion of this important letter was originally published in 1984 (*SR*, 60).

[22] Joseph Fontenrose, *John Steinbeck*, 18-19; Lawrence Clark Powell, *California Classics*, 225-26.

[23] Louis Owens, *John Steinbeck's Re-Vision of America* (Athens: University of Georgia Press, 1985), 27. In his discussion of *To a God Unknown*, Owens provides a lucid summation of the chief responses to the religiosity of the novel's ending and positions himself in the pro-Joseph camp. Brian Railsback, in *Parallel Expeditions: Charles Darwin and the Art of John Steinbeck* (Moscow: University of Idaho Press, 1995), 113, situates the novel in a Darwinian perspective and finds Joseph to have "miscalculated" his place in the landscape.

[24] *The Long Valley* ledger book, Steinbeck Research Center, San Jose State University, San Jose. An abbreviated section of the notebook entry is printed in Benson (*TAJS*, 264). On the issue of (ir)resolution, David Wyatt claims: "Steinbeck's narrative allows for either interpretation. His interest lies less in the object than in the experience of belief, and seen in this way, the book presents Joseph's conviction of the continuity between the human and the natural as generous and enabling. . . . the question of whether man projects nature or nature man is kept precariously open." See "Steinbeck's Lost Gardens," chap. 6 of *The Fall Into Eden: Landscape and Imagination in California* (New York: Cambridge University Press, 1986), 133-34.

[25] John Steinbeck to Wilbur Needham, letter, 4 April 1934, reproduced in Martha Heasley Cox, "John Steinbeck," in *Dictionary of Literary Biography: Documentary Series, An Illustrated Guide*, vol. 2, ed. Margaret Van Antwert (Detroit: Gale Research, 1982), 285. That Steinbeck discerned a condescending attitude among eastern reviewers of his novel is evident in an undated letter he wrote to Frank Whitbeck: "you may imagine my gratification when . . . Mr. Needham dealt kindly with me and that in the face of eastern slaps due to a small advertising fund." See Harry Valentine's *John Steinbeck: A Collection of Books and Manuscripts*, 13. When fellow Californian Harry Thornton Moore reviewed *To a God Unknown* in his essay, "The American Novel To-Day," for *The London Mercury*, 31 (March 1935): 465, he refrained from calling the book mystical and instead heaped praise on it as a "powerful, earthy story" with "some of the finest prose yet written in America." The novel, Moore trumpeted, "gives promise of a career that will have to be measured ultimately by the careers of the great European and British authors of the day—Mann and Lawrence and Proust and Joyce." Four years later, however, in *The Novels of John Steinbeck* (Chicago: Normandie House, 1939), 23-33, the first book ever written on Steinbeck, Moore not only couldn't resist branding *God* as "mystical" but had tempered considerably his chauvanistic estimate of the work.

[26] See Adrian H. Goldstone and John R. Payne, *John Steinbeck: A Bibliographical Catalogue of the Adrian H. Goldstone Collection* (Austin: Humanities Research Center, 1974), 26. Outside of Thomas Fensch's often superficial rendition of the Steinbeck-Covici friendship (*S&C*), little has been written on Steinbeck's professional and commercial relations with the publishing industry before and after his arrival at Viking Press in 1938. Neither are there any studies of the influence of the marketplace or the book trade on Steinbeck's writing habits or modes of production (the degree, for instance, to which the estimated pre-arranged word length of his novels—stipulated in his contracts—influenced the form and style of his texts). Nor, I should add, are there any treatments of his works by way of contemporary cultural and theoretical approaches such as one finds in studies of the history of the book. See C. Deirdre Phelps, "Market Studies and Book History in American Literature," *Review* 12 (1990): 273-301, for a useful survey.

[27] Jay Parini, *John Steinbeck: A Biography*, 135.

"This Book Is My Life": Creating *The Grapes of Wrath*

"A book must be a life that lives all of itself."
—John Steinbeck to Elizabeth Otis and Pascal Covici (1938)

"I have to get into the work dream. And it *is* a dream—almost an unconscious state when one feels the story all over one's body. . . ."
—John Steinbeck, *The Wayward Bus* journal (1946) (Courtesy of the Pierpont Morgan Library, New York City)

"The story ends only in fiction and I have made sure that it never ends in my fiction."
—John Steinbeck to Dorothea Lange (1965)

1

While contemporary theories of authorship as a mechanistic, language-driven function have challenged, deconstructed, or even in some quarters displaced the romantic conception of the writer as an originating genius, there is still much to be said for the more or less traditional scriptive view, especially when it is modified to reflect personal contingencies, contextual dynamics, and narratalogical exigencies. Despite its participation in language's slippery domain, its nonteleological posture toward "what is," and its attempt to valorize compassion and understanding, there is nothing slickly detached or antiseptic about John Steinbeck's acknowledged masterpiece. Far from being distanced or erased by the constitutive presence of language or by the cumulative power of social determinants, Steinbeck was thoroughly implicated in the scene of writing and in his book's dimensions, discourses, strategies, and rhetorical audacities. "This book is my life. . . . When it is done, then will be the time for another life. But, not until it is done," he admitted in the

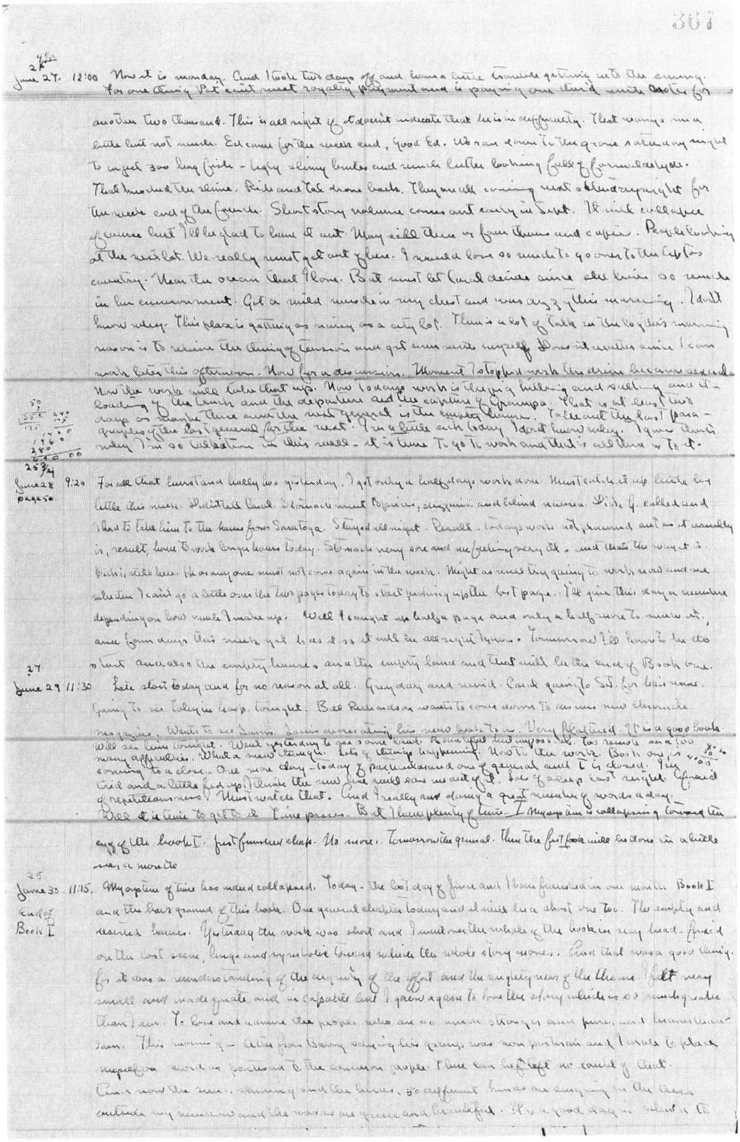

Four daily ledger entries covering 27-30 June 1938, from the autograph manuscript of Steinbeck's *Grapes of Wrath* journal, posthumously published in 1989 as *Working Days*. The journal, recently unsealed, was thought to be lost, and was not available when *Working Days* was being readied for publication.
Courtesy of the Pierpont Morgan Library, New York City.

novel's daily journal (*WD*, 77). To touch his book *The Grapes of Wrath* (and its companion piece, *Working Days*) is not only to experience the novel embedded in a demystified writing process, but it is to touch more of Steinbeck the man than has generally been thought possible: "The whole physical basis of the novel is discipline of the writer, of his material, of the language" (*WD*, 26).

For its author, writing out of the intense presence of his whole self (the body links experience and language), *The Grapes of Wrath* became a deeply engaging, utterly consuming novel. Though neither a transparent autobiographical confession nor a willful demonstration of unbridled egoism, *Grapes* was nonetheless acutely personal and arose as much from Steinbeck's physical desire to interpret the cataclysmic migrant farm worker situation in California in the mid-1930s, about which he rehearsed a number of different written versions, as from the psychic wound which was brought on by a particular moment of that experience in Visalia, California, in early 1938.[1] That is to say, as a novel, *The Grapes of Wrath* functions in a variety of coincident and contingent ways, not the least of them an explicit distress call to a segment of the American populace to halt social injustice before it might be too late to do anything about it. Steinbeck's "narrative enacts its own kind of oppression, and, by arousing in its readers a desire to fight this sense of inevitability, it works strategically to arouse us toward action to change the status quo."[2] In this sense, then, *Grapes* is a harrowing cry from the heart, but it is equally a cry of its own occasion, a dazzling demonstration of textual performance and devotional intelligence: "What some people find in religion a writer may find in his craft . . . a kind of breaking through to glory," Steinbeck recalled in 1965 (*CJS*, 95).

In the phalanx theory, worked out so energetically with biologist Edward F. Ricketts in the early to mid 1930s, Steinbeck proposed that the artist figure comes forward at the proper moment when he is needed to express a group's most important or pressing needs: "The writer sets down the desire of his own time, the action of the people toward attaining that desire, the obstacles to attainment and the struggle to overcome the obstacles."[3] Paradoxically, though, while the artist is *constructed* by social necessity and the conjunctive pressures of history and geography, he *expresses* himself not only according to the degree of felt life he invests in his work but also according to the inventive capacities of his own individual vision, imagination, technique, and style. The key point, however—modified by Steinbeck's later ruminations on the politics and aesthetics of storytelling—was to break through the old monolithic, totalizing conventions of ignorance and oppression by building living structures in language that invite active audience "participation" through emotional identification and psychological investment.[4] Chapter 23 of *The Grapes of Wrath*, which is devoted to the migrants' amusements, opens with a prominently foregrounded vignette: "And it came about in the camps along the roads, on the ditch banks beside the streams, under the sycamores, that the story teller grew into being, so that the people gathered in the low firelight to hear the gifted ones. And they listened while the tales were told, and their participation made the stories great."[5] The passage—which ends with the haunting account of the Army's campaign against Apache leader Geronimo in 1885-86 and narrates the parables of the murdered brave and the dead cock pheasant—functions as an elaborate trope for the key social themes of *Grapes*, including tyranny of surveillance, arrogance of power, and willful destruction of people and resources. The whole oral performance, at once realistically (re)presented and textually (re)flexive, also mirrors in miniature Steinbeck's methodology regarding his writerly situation: the storyteller is positioned not above his auditors but at their level so that they can key into his narrational experience and thereby lend it power and meaning. "Gifted" in this narratological context, then, refers to Steinbeck's mediating presence and his embedded—and sometimes unavoidably self-conflicted—role in the complex, shifting, indeterminate relationship among people, events, things, and words.[6]

Though Steinbeck told George Albee in 1933 that he believed art "is the property of the phalanx, not of the individual" (*SLL*, 80), six years later he came to see the bitterly ironic implications of that particular aspect of idealism. Given its spectacular commercial success, *The Grapes of Wrath* can be said not only to have simultaneously arisen from its time and transcended it but to have simultaneously created and fulfilled its group function. But as a result, the book took on a life of its own and, theoretically anyway, passed out of Steinbeck's possession, into the realm of public commodity: "*Grapes* got really out of hand, became a public hysteria and I became a public domain" (*WD*, 105). In an abstract sense, then, *Grapes* no longer belonged to Steinbeck at all but to an army of anonymous readers. If this satisfied the theoretical destiny of phalanx art, it did little to explain the pragmatism of the moment. In fact, Steinbeck eventually resented the reductive implications of an exchange that, instead of expunging him from the public gaze, could produce a monstrous, distorted "straw man," a "fictitious so-and so . . . out there in the public eye" (*CJS*, 18-19). Which is perhaps why he emphasized throughout his writing life that whatever portion of individual glory was possible resided primarily at home in the daily writing exercise itself, the gratifying renewal of the pen's contact with paper: "Work is the only good thing" (*WD*, 39).

Nevertheless, the pressure of working through nearly four years of the research, writing, publication, reception, and aftermath of this novel (all of which can be said to comprise its "creation") changed Steinbeck so profoundly that he became a different kind of artist after *The Grapes of Wrath*. But the breakthrough and transformation, notoriety and glory, and the critical backlash were still in the future when, on 18 June 1938, three weeks or so after starting the final version of *Grapes*, thirty-six-year-old Steinbeck—head full of lament—sang a doleful tune as he tried to negotiate with—or perhaps propitiate—the elements of his calling: "If I could do this book properly it would be one of the really fine books and a truly American book. But I am assailed with my own ignorance and inability. I'll just have to work from a background of these. Honesty. If I can keep an honesty it is all I can expect of my poor brain—never temper a word to a reader's prejudice, but bend it like putty for his understanding. If I can do that it will be all my lack of genius can produce. For no one else knows my lack of ability the way I do. I am pushing against it all the time" (*WD*, 29-30). Steinbeck did not shamelessly court posterity—he was mostly too self-deprecating, too candid, for that—and so his use of "American" here is not to be interpreted as the result of either egomania or jingoism; rather it indicates his desire to participate in a larger cultural conversation regarding America's tradition of revolutionary texts, particularly those which dismantle or subvert naive positivism.

But pushing against limits and unsettling boundaries was Steinbeck's forte. His first novel, *Cup of Gold* (1929), a historical romance based on the life of the seventeenth-century Welsh buccaneer Henry Morgan, gave no indication that Steinbeck would eventually be capable of producing a graphic novel with the startling magnitude, compassion, and power of *The Grapes of Wrath.* What transpired in the ten years between those books is as arresting an example of directed artistic growth as we have in American letters, for in the nine volumes of prose (mostly fiction) that Steinbeck produced in that decade, he simply became better and better—which is to say, more inventive, responsive, and focused—as a writer. His achievement is especially moving because he did not think of himself as naturally blessed with talent and rarely believed he had ever "arrived" as a writer: "I was not made for success. I find myself with a growing reputation. In many ways it is a terrible thing. . . . Among other things I feel that I have put something over. That this little success of mine is cheating" (*WD,* [1]). The guilt over his success, the provisionality of his authorial situation, the tenuousness of his hold over his own pen, so to speak, indicates the degree to which his gaze was often directed toward critiquing his own performance. John Steinbeck was his own harshest critic.

As *Working Days* reveals, Steinbeck's self-accusations were constant during *Grapes*'s composition, and yet ironically it not only turned out to be a "fine" book but is also generally considered to be the greatest of his seventeen novels. Like other rough-hewn products of the American literary imagination—Stowe's *Uncle Tom's Cabin,* Twain's *Adventures of Huckleberry Finn,* Kesey's *One Flew Over the Cuckoo's Nest,* and Walker's *The Color Purple* (four "flawed" novels that also humanize America's downtrodden by exposing intolerable social ills)—*The Grapes of Wrath* has a hybrid, home-grown quality: part naturalistic epic, part jeremiad, part captivity narrative, part road novel, part anthropological text, part conversion tale, part transcendental gospel. For some readers this combination has proved too unstable to be workable. Others, however, understand that Steinbeck's aggressive mixture of native philosophy, phalanx theory, New Deal politics, blue-collar radicalism, working-class characters, folk wisdom, and homespun literary form—all set to a jazzy, rhythmic style, bold, improvisational form, and nervy, raw dialogue—give the novel its idiosyncratic, inventive "American" qualities, its fusion of experience and discourse, realism and artfulness, specificity and universality, populism and antinomianism.[7] Even the novel's title, taken from Julia Ward Howe's "Battle Hymn of the Republic," was clearly in the subversive American grain: "It is a march and this book is a kind of march . . . in our own revolutionary tradition," Steinbeck announced on 10 September 1938 to Elizabeth Otis, his literary agent and confidante (*SLL*, 171).

After its composition from late May through late October 1938, *The Grapes of Wrath* passed from the 751-page typescript prepared by his wife, Carol, to published novel in record time—four months. In March 1939, when Steinbeck received copies from one of three advance printings, he told Pascal Covici, his editor at The Viking Press, he was "immensely pleased with them" (*SLL*, 182). The novel's impressive physical and aesthetic appearance was the result of its imposing size (619 pages) and Elmer Hader's striking dust jacket illustration of the Joads looking out on a lush California valley. And partly obeying Steinbeck's insistence that *The Grapes of Wrath* be "keyed into the American scene" (*SLL*, 174), Covici had Viking print the first page of the words and music from the "Battle Hymn" inside its front and rear covers in an attempt (unsuccessfully, it turned out) to deflect accusations of Communism against the book and its author. In gratitude for their assistance, Steinbeck dedicated the novel to Carol and to Tom Collins, relief camp specialist.

Given his emotional commitment to the California migrant laborers' situation and his own sense of the treacherousness of contemporary cultural politics during the Depression, Steinbeck refused to write a book cynically calculated to court commercial success. "Funny how mean and little books become in the face of such tragedies," he confessed to Otis (*SLL*, 159). It was doubly ironic, then, that shortly after its official publication date, 14 April 1939, spurred by the nearly ninety reviews (mostly positive) that appeared in newspapers, magazines, and literary journals between April and June, *The Grapes of Wrath* went to the top of best-seller lists for most of the year, selling 428,900 copies in hardcover at $2.75 each. *The Grapes of Wrath* won the 1940 Pulitzer Prize (Steinbeck gave the $1,000 prize to a Monterey friend and fellow writer Ritch Lovejoy). By 1941, when the Sun Dial Press issued a cloth reprint for a dollar, the publisher announced that over 543,000 copies of *Grapes* had already been sold. *Grapes* also eventually became the cornerstone of Steinbeck's 1962 Nobel Prize award and proved itself to be among the most enduring works of fiction by any American author. In spite of the flaws its critics perceive—factual gaffes, frequent sentimentality, flat characterizations, heavy-handed symbolism, and unconvincing dialogue—or perhaps because of them (common readers tend to embrace the book's mystic soul and are less troubled by its imperfect body)—*The Grapes of Wrath*, during the past fifty-six years, has sold more than fifteen million copies.[8]

True to Steinbeck's hope that "injustice cannot long exist in a nation aware," *Grapes* has, in short, emphatically entered both the American consciousness and the American conscience. *Grapes* has become a persistent presence, a cultural icon, and though this in itself has caused misrepresentations (some with well-deserved, intentionally hilarious results, as in "The Beaver of Wrath" chapter in Will Jacobs and Gerard Jones's *The Beaver Papers: The Story of the "Lost Season"*), it also has led a charmed life in other popular manifestations. Steinbeck sold the novel's film rights for $75,000 to producer Darryl F. Zanuck. Then Nunnally Johnson scripted a film version, directed by John Ford and released in 1940, which, though truncated, was nonetheless memorably paced, photographed, and acted, especially by Henry Fonda as Tom Joad, Jane Darwell as Ma Joad, and John Carradine as Jim Casy. (A "hard, straight picture . . . that looks and feels like a documentary film and . . . has a hard, truthful ring," Steinbeck reported after seeing its Hollywood preview [*SLL*, 195].) A few years ago, Frank Galati faithfully adapted the novel for his Chicago-based Steppenwolf Company, whose Broadway production, featuring Gary Sinise as Tom Joad, won a Tony Award as Best Play in 1990. Ike Sallas, the hero of Ken Kesey's latest novel, *Sailor Song* (1992), prizes the novel and places it among his collection of classic American books—"the essential heavies," he calls them. Singer Bruce Springsteen based the haunting title song of his 1995 album, *The Ghost of Tom Joad*, mostly on Ford's film version; novelist T. Coraghessan Boyle's latest fiction, *The Tortilla Curtain* (1995), pulls from *Grapes* for its epigraph. Such homage is obviously felt worldwide, for *The Grapes of Wrath* also has been translated into nearly thirty languages. It seems that Steinbeck's words continue, in critic Warren French's apt phrase, "the education of the heart."[9]

Steinbeck was an inordinately private person who recoiled at readers knowing what "went into the writing" of *Grapes* and disapproved of having his "crabbed hand exposed" (*SLL*, 180). The dream of modernist effacement and ego-less texts, however, has given way in our time to legitimate curiosity about the person behind the work. Given current interest in biographical agency and issues of authentication, as well as in compositional practices and theories of inscription, the story of the novel's making (variously recorded and amplified during the past dozen years in Jackson Benson's *The True Adventures of John Steinbeck*, my annotated edition of Steinbeck's *Working Days*, and more derivatively in Jay Parini's *John Steinbeck: A Biography*) is not at all "unimportant" as Steinbeck claimed to Covici. Rather, not to promote too fine a self-rationalization, the creation of *Grapes* is an intriguing and dramatic event in itself, full of some of the same turns and straightaways, travails and triumphs, twists and counter-twists that characterize the Joad family's journey to the Promised Land. While Steinbeck's puritanical doubts about his ability to carry out the plan of his ambitious novel surface repeatedly in *Working Days* (and can be said to inscribe a highly anxious composition narrative in itself), he rarely questioned the risks involved in bringing his whole sensibility—the leverage of his entire heart, so to speak—to bear upon its writing.

Like another populist manifesto of the American spirit, Whitman's *Leaves of Grass*, Steinbeck's novel had a complicated, tumultuous growth. *The Grapes of Wrath* was the product of Steinbeck's increasing immersion in the "Matter of the Migrants," which required a zigzag walk before he discovered the proper means of doing the topic justice. In one way or another, from August 1936, when Steinbeck told Louis Paul he had discovered a subject "like nothing in the world" (*SLL*, 129), through October 1939, when he resolved privately to put behind him "that part of my life that made the *Grapes*" (*WD*, 106), the migrant issue, which had wounded him deeply, was the central obsession for this obsessive writer: "the greatness of the human lies in the fact that he never attains his desire. His desire keeps bounding ahead of his attainment and his search is endless" ("Interview," 860-61).

The Grapes of Wrath's lineage, the overlapping path of its search, unfolds this way: first, Steinbeck produced a seven-part series of newspaper articles, "The Harvest Gypsies," then he worked on an unfinished novel, "The Oklahomans," and a completed, but destroyed, satire, "L'Affaire Lettuceberg," and finally—in a five-month stretch in 1938—he wrote *The Grapes of Wrath* itself. Each version shared at least a fixed core of elements: on one side, the entrenched power, wealth, authority, and consequent tyranny of California's industrialized agricultural system (symbolized by Associated Farmers, Inc.), which produced flagrant violations of the Dust Bowl migrants' civil and human rights and ensured their continuing peonage, their loss of dignity, through threats, reprisals, and violence; on the other side, the powerlessness, poverty, victimization, and fear of the nomadic American migrants whose willingness to work, desire to retain their dignity, and wish to settle land of their own were kept alive by their innate resilience and resourcefulness and by the democratic benefits of the government sanitary camps. From the moment he entered the fray, Steinbeck had no doubt that the presence of the migrants would change the fabric of California life and even liberalize its politics (*CJS*, 12), though he had little foresight about what his own role in that change would be (or, for that matter, what changes would be wrought in him). His purpose was avowedly humanitarian and partisan; he wanted to be an effective advocate, but he did not want to appear "presumptuous" (*TAJS*, 347): "Every effort I can bring to bear is and has been at the call of the common working people to the end that they may eat what they raise, use what they produce, and in every way and in completeness share in the works of their hands and their heads," he declared unequivocally to *San Francisco News* columnist John Barry on 30 June 1938 (*WD*, 152).

2

The Grapes of Wrath's communal vision was forged in the fire of Steinbeck's own labor, but the flames were fanned by numerous people. Few major American novels are more indebted to the generosity of others than *Grapes* is, especially Carol Steinbeck and Tom Collins, both of whom had significant impact on Steinbeck's work. Carol Henning Steinbeck, his outgoing first wife (they married in 1930), was far more politically radical than John, and she actively supported members of Northern California's local fugitive agricultural labor movement before he did.[10] Carol was an energetic, talented person in her own right, who agreed to relinquish a career in favor of helping to manage his. Their partnership and marriage was smoother and more egalitarian in the struggling years of Steinbeck's career; with the enormous success—and pressures—brought first by the runaway best-seller *Of Mice and Men* (1937) and then by *The Grapes of Wrath*, their situation became more tenuous, volatile, and even hostile. Carol Steinbeck was an extremely strong-willed, demonstrative person, and she was often frustrated, resentful, unpredictable, and sometimes jealous; her husband, inordinately shy, was frequently beleaguered, confused, selfish, and demanding. In the late 1930s, whenever he was writing daily, which was much of the time, Carol handled—not without resentment—most of the routine domestic duties. She also shielded her husband as much as possible from unwarranted disruptions and intrusions and oversaw some of the financial arrangements between Steinbeck and his literary agents, which became an increasingly large job, especially after the success of the novel and play versions of *Of Mice and Men* in 1937. "Carol does so much," Steinbeck admitted on 2 August 1938 (*WD*, 50).

Carol also served as his cultural envoy and stand-in. In January 1938, on a trip to New York City to attend one of the 207 performances of George S. Kaufman's long-running Broadway production of *Of Mice and Men*, she met with film maker Pare Lorentz, arranging between them his first visit to the Steinbeck's home in Los Gatos (ten miles south of San Jose) to discuss a joint Steinbeck/Lorentz movie version of *In Dubious Battle* (which was never made) and for a private showing of *The Plow That Broke the Plains* (1936) and *The River* (1937). These pioneering documentary films, made by Lorentz for President Franklin D. Roosevelt's New Deal-inspired Resettlement Administration (forerunner of the Farm Security Administration), dealt with human displacement and natural erosion caused by the Dust Bowl and the Mississippi Valley floods—themes close to Steinbeck's heart. After their initial meeting, Lorentz became an extremely important figure in the novelist's life, providing everything from practical advice on politics to spirited artistic cheerleading.

Carol left her stamp on *The Grapes of Wrath* in many ways. Her time was "too valuable to do purely stenographic work," Steinbeck told Otis (*SLL*, 171). She typed the manuscript, which in itself was a formidable task, because her husband could cram fifty-five or more lines of his spidery hand on a single page of his out-sized ledger book. She began typing from the early part of the holograph manuscript while her husband was still writing its latter sections, and she sometimes smoothed and edited the text as she went along, serving in the early stages as a rigorous critical commentator, whose acute judgments Steinbeck trusted completely. Moreover, Steinbeck had a "terrible time" with spelling and punctuation, he confessed to John C. Rice in 1939, "but since I have been married my wife copyreads all my work. She's wonderful—never misses a thing" (*CJS*, 16). (Understandably, however, after typing three hundred pages,

Carol told Elizabeth Otis she had lost "all sense of proportion" and felt unfit "to judge it at all," though she had no choice but to forge ahead.) In a brilliant and justly celebrated stroke, on 2 September, Carol chose the novel's title from Howe's "Battle Hymn of the Republic," perhaps inspired by her hearing of Lorentz's radio drama, *Ecce Homo!*, which ends with a martial version of Howe's song.[11] Steinbeck was impressed with the "looks of it—marvelous title. The book has being at last"; he considered it "Carol's best title so far" (*SLL*, 171). ("Tell Carol she is a whiz at picking titles and she has done it again with the new one," his drama agent Annie Laurie Williams exulted.) Her role as a facilitator is recorded permanently in one half of the novel's dedication: "To CAROL who willed it." On 23 February 1939, Steinbeck told Pascal Covici that he had given Carol the autograph manuscript of *The Grapes of Wrath*: "You see I feel that this is Carol's book" (*SLL*, 180).[12]

Eventually, Carol Steinbeck's brittle efficiency, managerial brusqueness, and violent mood swings seemed to become increasingly prominent. She too was exhausted by the novel's completion and at her wit's end over its histrionic reception: "The telephone never stops ringing, telegrams all the time, fifty to seventy-five letters a day all wanting something. People who won't take no for an answer sending books to be signed. . . . Something has to be worked out or I am finished writing. I went south to work and I came back to find Carol just about hysterical. She had been pushed beyond endurance," Steinbeck told Otis on 22 June 1939 (*SLL*, 185). His willful involvement with a much younger woman, a Hollywood singer named Gwyndolyn Conger, whom he met in mid-1939, and who quickly came to represent everything Steinbeck felt romantically lacking in Carol, signaled the beginning of the end of their marriage. They separated rancorously in April 1941 and divorced two years later.

The second part of the novel's dedication—"To TOM who lived it"—refers to Thomas Collins, the novelist's chief source, guide, discussant, and chronicler of accurate migrant information. Collins not only put Steinbeck in touch with people like the fictional Joads and Jim Casy, but himself served as Steinbeck's real-life prototype for Jim Rawley, the fictional manager of the "Weedpatch" government camp. That camp, an accurate rendering of Collins's Arvin camp, became an oasis of relief for the harried Joads, and is featured from chapters 22 to 26 of *The Grapes of Wrath*. Steinbeck portrayed Collins with photographic

THIS SIDE OF CARD IS FOR ADDRESS
SARATOGA
SEP 6
7 AM
1938
JEFFERSON
Elizabeth Otis
McIntosh & Otis, Inc.
18 E. 41st St.,
New York,
N.Y.

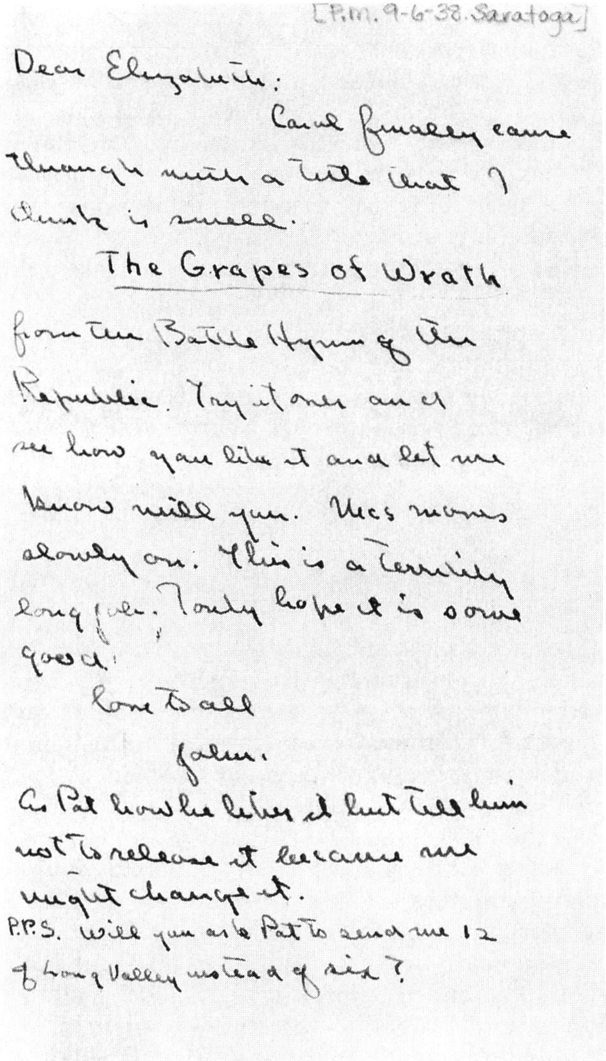

[P.M. 9-6-38. Saratoga]

Dear Elizabeth:

Carol finally came through with a title that I think is swell.

The Grapes of Wrath

from the Battle Hymn of the Republic. Try it over and see how you like it and let me know will you. Mss moves slowly on. This is a terribly long job. I only hope it is some good.

Love to all

John.

Ask Pat how he likes it but tell him not to release it because we might change it.

P.P.S. Will you ask Pat to send me 12 of Long Valley instead of six?

Steinbeck's postcard to his agent, Elizabeth Otis, with news that Carol Steinbeck had named the novel in progress. In *Working Days* on Saturday, 3 September 1938, Steinbeck wrote: "Carol got the title last night '*The Grapes of Wrath.*' I think that is a wonderful title. Must query Elizabeth, but will use it any way until I am forbidden. The looks of it—marvelous title. The book has being at last" (65).

Courtesy of Department of Special Collections, Stanford University Libraries, Stanford, CA.

accuracy in chapter 22: "A little man dressed all in white stood behind [Ma Joad]—a man with a thin, brown, lined face and merry eyes. He was as lean as a picket. His white clean clothes were frayed at the seams."[13] Steinbeck also caught Collins's effective interpersonal technique in having Jim Rawley wear frayed clothes and in winning over Ma Joad by the simple request for a cup of her coffee: "She looked for motive on his face, and found nothing but friendliness. Then she looked at the frayed seams on his white coat, and she was reassured" (*GOW*, 416).

An intrepid, resourceful, idealistic, and exceptionally compassionate man, Collins was the manager of a model Region IX Farm Security Administration camp, located in Kern County at the southern end of California's Central Valley. The twenty-acre Arvin Sanitary Camp was one of several proposed demonstration tent camps intended to provide humane, clean, democratic—but temporary—living conditions for ninety-six families at a time from the growing army of migrant workers entering California from the lower Middle West's Dust Bowl region. (More than two dozen camps were planned in 1935 by the Resettlement Administration; by 1940, with New Deal budgets slashed by conservatives in Congress, only fifteen were actually completed or under construction.) Collins possessed a genius for camp administration—first at Marysville, then at Arvin—and was respected throughout California. Labor historian Anne Loftis calls Collins a "hands-on" administrator.[14] Collins had the right mix of fanaticism, vision, propriety, solicitousness, and tactfulness. Collins and Steinbeck, both relatively idealistic and progressive New Deal Democrats who regarded the Dust Bowl migrants as dispossessed Jeffersonian yeoman farmers (an anomaly in California), hit it off immediately in the summer of 1936, and Steinbeck later thanked Collins for providing him with "one of the very fine experiences" of his life. One of the many legends that grew up around *The Grapes of Wrath* claimed that Steinbeck traveled with a migrant family all the way from Oklahoma to California; that never happened, though he and Carol did follow Route 66 on a car trip home from Chicago to Los Gatos in 1937. Actually, beginning in late summer 1936, when the novelist went into the Central Valley on the first of several grueling research trips during the next two years to investigate field conditions, Tom Collins was his primary contact and companion.

Fortunately, Collins, an amateur ethnographer, was a punctual and voluminous report writer. His extensive run of "Camp Manager's Weekly Reports" are lively, colorful accounts of the workers' activities, events, diets, entertainments, sayings, beliefs, music, and observations. They were intended to showcase the migrants' folkways and preserve their cultural integrity; taken as a whole the reports provide what literary anthropologists, following Clifford Geertz, might consider a "thick description" of that conflicted time and place. Eventually the "Manager's Reports" provided Steinbeck with a ready "authentic" documentary supplement to his own researches—Steinbeck called Collins's reports a "magnificent collection" because "there is drama and immediacy in these things" (*TAJS*, 348). In a sense, then, both in person and in writing, Collins guided Steinbeck through the intricacies of the agricultural labor scene and put him in direct contact with the cultural matrix of the migrant families. When plans to publish Collins's weekly reports eventually fell through in 1937, he willingly permitted Steinbeck to incorporate "great gobs" of information into his own writing.[15] "Letter from Tom," Steinbeck noted on 24 June 1938. "He is so good. I need this stuff. It is exact and just the thing that will be used against me if I am wrong" (*WD*, 33). Thus Tom Collins not only contributed accurate details to the surface portrait of the migrants that helped Steinbeck cover his own flanks, but, as Benson avers, also provided a significant "spirit at the heart of the novel" (*TAJS*, 346).

In 1939, at Steinbeck's recommendation, Collins worked as a lucratively paid technical advisor to John Ford's Twentieth Century-Fox production of *The Grapes of Wrath* ("Tom will howl his head off if they get out of hand," Steinbeck told Elizabeth Otis.) And later—probably spurred by the success of both novel and film—Collins himself (under the pseudonym of Windsor Drake) wrote an autobiographical/fictional memoir, to which Steinbeck, who appears as a character, added a foreword: "Windsor and I traveled together, sat in the ditches with the migrant workers, lived and ate with them. We heard a thousand miseries and a thousand jokes. We ate fried dough and sow belly, worked with the sick and the hungry, listened to complaints and little triumphs" (*Sheaves*, 213). The book, very stiffly written and only thinly fictionalized, was accepted but never reached print because the publisher reneged on the deal. By that time Collins's sympathy with Steinbeck's project had waned.

Publication of *The Grapes of Wrath* drastically changed Collins's standing in the migrant camps by calling into question his own complicity, which he somewhat melodramatically considered a "death sentence . . . written by John Steinbeck" (*Sheaves*, 232). After that, Collins resigned from the FSA, and he and Steinbeck passed out of each other's lives.

Clearly, whatever the toll in personal relationships, Steinbeck had a knack for associating himself with gifted, far-sighted, generous people; they in turn abetted the context of *The Grapes of Wrath*. George West, chief editorial writer for the progressive Scripps-Howard paper, *San Francisco News*, instigated Steinbeck's initial investigations of the migrant labor situation. Frederick R. Soule, the enlightened Regional Information Advisor at the San Francisco office of the Farm Security Administration, and his assistant Helen Horn (later, as Helen Hosmer, she directed the Simon Lubin Society) provided statistics and documents for his *News* reports, and otherwise opened official doors for Steinbeck that might have stayed closed. Soule's colleague, Eric H. Thomsen, Regional Director in Charge of Management at the FSA office in San Francisco, personally escorted Steinbeck to the Central Valley and introduced him to Tom Collins at the Arvin Camp for the first time in 1936. Indeed, as Jackson Benson quickly recognized, the federal government, eager for some positive coverage of its fledgling camp program, underwrote, in a convoluted, unintentional, and ultimately ironic way, part of Steinbeck's research and smoothed the path of his first major written account of the deplorable California agricultural situation.[16]

3

Not counting the scotched plans to edit and publish Tom Collins's reports, an abandoned play laid in "a squatter's camp in Kern County," or a warm-up essay called "Dubious Battle in California" in *The Nation* to "give a mild idea" of the civil war brewing under his "nose," Steinbeck's first lengthy excursion into the migrants' problems was published in the liberal, pro-labor, pro-New Deal *San Francisco News*. "The Harvest Gypsies" formed the foundation of Steinbeck's concern for a long time to come, raised issues and initiated forces, gave him a working vocabulary with which to understand current events, and furthered his position as a reliable interpreter of the labor scene. This stage resulted from the notoriety caused by his recently published strike novel, *In Dubious Battle* (1936), after which Steinbeck found—often against his will—that he was fast becoming considered a spokesman for the contemporary agricultural labor situation in a state that was primarily pro-management. This was a profound irony, because while *In Dubious Battle* exposed the capitalist dynamics of corporate farming, it was consciously nonteleological in its positioning and consequently took no side for or against labor, preferring instead to see the fruit strike as a symbol of "man's eternal, bitter warfare with himself" (*SLL*, 98).

At George West's invitation, Steinbeck produced "The Harvest Gypsies." These articles, peppered with Dorothea Lange's graphic photographs of migrants, appeared from 5 to 12 October 1936. Steinbeck's gritty reports detailed the plan of California's feudal agricultural labor industry. The pieces introduced the antagonists, underscored the anachronistic rift between the Okie agrarian past and the mechanized California present, explained the economic background and insidious effects of the labor issue, examined the deplorable migrant living conditions, and exposed the unconscionable practices of the interlocking conglomerate of corporation farms. (These elements remained central to the core and texture of *The Grapes of Wrath*.) Primarily, though, Steinbeck's eye was on the "nomadic, poverty-stricken harvesters," the "150,000 homeless migrants" who were "gypsies by force of circumstance," as he announced in his opening piece: "And so they move, frantically, with starvation close behind them. And in this series of articles we shall try to see how they live and what kind of people they are, what their living standard is, what is done for them, and what their problems and needs are. For while California has been successful in its use of migrant labor, it is gradually building a human structure which will certainly change the state, and may, if handled with the inhumanity and stupidity that have characterized the past, destroy the present system of agricultural economics."[17]

Although Steinbeck later admitted he was taken "over completely, heart and soul" by the "fine, brave people," in "The Harvest Gypsies" he maintained a measured style to promote understanding of and intelligent solutions for California's migrant worker issues. Steinbeck's articles are full of case studies and chilling factual statistics he had gleaned from official Resettlement Administration (including reports by Tom Collins), National Labor Board, and State Relief Administration documents, and an unsettling catalog of human woes (illness, incapacitation, persecution, death) observed from close contact with field workers he had met. Although he erroneously predicted that agriculture's dependence on foreign-born workers would wane and that the new work force would be made up of white Americans, Steinbeck's investigation for the most part rang true. In the spirit of advocacy journalism, Steinbeck concluded with prophetic recommendations for alleviating the conflict with federal aid and local support; this in turn would create subsistence farms, establish a migratory labor board, encourage unionization, and punish terrorism. When they were published in 1936 and again when they were reprinted in 1938 as a 25-cent pamphlet, *Their Blood is Strong,* by the nonprofit Simon J. Lubin Society (which sold ten thousand copies in four printings), Steinbeck's articles solidified his credibility—both in and out of the migrant camps—as a serious commentator in a league with Dorothea Lange's husband, Paul Taylor, and Carey McWilliams, two other influential, respected investigators.[18]

Steinbeck understood that the migrants wouldn't disappear, even though official California hoped they would. He also knew that the subject he had tied into reached further than he had imagined and was beginning to present itself as a possible novel. Consequently, Steinbeck built on his *News* pieces and on at least one more month-long field trip with Tom Collins in October and November of 1937. In Steinbeck's old panel truck (a pie delivery wagon in its former life), they probably started from Gridley, where Collins was managing a new camp, but then roamed California from Stockton to Needles, wherever migrants were gathered to work (*TAJS*, 362). His purpose was to gather more research for his next version, the "big" book of fiction which had apparently been on his mind for most of that year and which Steinbeck and Collins had obviously discussed. (In an undated letter to Collins, written probably in spring 1937, he said, "You know of course my plans for the long novel dealing with the migrant" [*WD*, lii].) A letter to Elizabeth Otis, written on 27 January 1937, indicates he had been wrestling with this version since the previous winter: "The new book has struck a bad snag. . . . The subject is so huge it scares me to death." Several months later, in an interview on 4 November 1937, in the *Los Gatos Mail-News*, Steinbeck publicly claimed for the first time that he had started a book whose topic was the Dust Bowl refugees, the "Oklahomans." Though he was "reluctant to discuss the characters and plot," he said it was "one third complete and will be about 1000 pages in length."[19] Given his comment to Otis in January and the fact that Steinbeck traveled a good deal that year (including a trip with Carol to the Soviet Union), three hundred pages of completed manuscript may have been wishful thinking on his part or it may have represented the total number of pages of Collins's reports and his own research notes (which have never been found, though he had claimed in September 1936 that his "material drawer" was "chuck full" [*TAJS*, 348]) that he had accumulated during the previous year. If nothing else, the interview announced his proprietary attention to the material, about which Steinbeck was known to have been protective—and as Tom Collins and photographer Horace Bristol later learned—even secretive to paranoiac degrees.

In a second interview two months later, on 8 January 1938, with journalist Louis Walther in the *San Jose Mercury-Herald*, Steinbeck apparently had not progressed much, if at all. After hitting several "snags," he was working on a "rather long novel" allegedly called "The Oklahomans," which was "still a long way from finished." Steinbeck, generally guarded with interviewers, revealed enough to Walther to indicate his novel's focus was the salutary, irrepressible character of the "southern dust bowl immigrants" who, he believed, would profoundly alter the tenor of life in California. "Their coming here now is going to change things almost as much as did the coming of the first American settlers." Furthermore, "The Californian doesn't know what he does want. The Oklahoman knows just exactly what he wants. He wants a piece of land. And he goes after it and gets it" (*CJS*, 11-12). In *The Grapes of Wrath*, Steinbeck did not relinquish his land-hunger theme or his belief that the migrants formed a specific phalanx group within the large national mass movement of the 1930s, but he certainly dropped his somewhat imperious and naive tone for a more tragic one.

As nearly as can be determined, between January and March 1938, Steinbeck quietly stopped work on this manuscript provisionally or conveniently named "The Oklahomans." Steinbeck never mentioned it again by name, the manuscript has never been found, and his boasts of three hundred completed pages aside, it is doubtful that he had actually written a substantial amount of it at all. In the first entry of *Working*

Days, on [7?] February 1938, he mentioned having written "ten pages" of an otherwise unidentified book: "You pages . . . are the dribble cap—you are the cloth to wipe up the vomit. Maybe I can get these fears and disgusts on you and then burn you up. Then maybe I won't be so haunted" (6). And six weeks later, on 23 March 1938, he again told Elizabeth Otis: "I've been writing on the novel but I've had to destroy it several times. I don't seem to know any more about writing a novel than I did ten years ago. You'd think I would learn. I suppose I could dash it off but I want this one to be a pretty good one. There's another difficulty too. I'm trying to write history while it is happening and I don't want to be wrong" (*SLL*, 162). These troubled comments in February and March 1938 have long been thought to refer to the beginnings of "L'Affaire Lettuceberg" (discussed below), but it is far more likely that they refer to his difficulties and dilemmas in writing one or more avatars of the "Oklahomans" book, the ur-*Grapes of Wrath*, which had, after more than a year and a couple of starts and stops, not yet found its proper impetus or creative urgency and in fact may have blown up in his face following his interview in the *San Jose Mercury-Herald*. But in mulling over, rehearsing, and living with the contestatory subject of this "long novel dealing with the migrant" for so long ("I've been three years on the material," he told critic Harry T. Moore in July), Steinbeck was staking his claim to that imaginative territory, repeatedly experimenting with and ruminating about a way to fictionalize material that was until then the stuff of contemporary "history" and his own newspaper reportage. The general chapters in *Grapes* would be especially influenced by his long rehearsal in this matrix of events.

Actually, the migrant situation had worsened and, along with it, Steinbeck's capacity for anger and his need for direct involvement had grown. The misery of the workers' condition was increasing in the winter of 1938, especially in Visalia and Nipomo, where thousands of families were marooned by floods. From Los Gatos, Steinbeck wrote Elizabeth Otis in February:

> I must go over into the interior valleys. There are about five thousand families starving to death over there, not just hungry but actually starving. The government is trying to feed them and get medical attention to them with the fascist group of utilities and banks and huge growers sabatoging the thing all along the line. . . . In one tent there were twenty people quarantined for smallpox and two of the women are to have babies in

> that tent this week. I've tied into the thing from the first and I must get down there and see it and see if I can't do something to help knock these murderers on the heads. . . . They think that if these people are allowed to live in camps with proper sanitary facilities, they will organize and that is the bugbear of the large landowner and the corporation farmer. The states and counties will give them nothing because they are outsiders. But the crops of any part of this state could not be harvested without these outsiders. I'm pretty mad about it. (*SLL*, 158)

In late February and early March 1938, Steinbeck witnessed these deplorable conditions firsthand at Visalia where, after three weeks of steady rain, "the water is a foot deep in the tents and the children are up on the beds and there is no food and no fire, and the county has taken off all the nurses because 'the problem is so great that we can't do anything about it.' So they do nothing," he again informed Otis, on 7 March 1938 (*SLL*, 161). In the company of Tom Collins, *Life* photographer Horace Bristol, and other FSA personnel, Steinbeck worked day and night for nearly two weeks, sometimes dropping in the mud from exhaustion, to help relieve the people's misery, though of course no aid seemed adequate (*Sheaves*, 221-22). Steinbeck was supposed to be writing an article with Bristol for *Life* magazine, but what he encountered was so devastating, he told Otis, that he was utterly transfixed by the "staggering" conditions; the "suffering" was so great that commercial reporting would only trivialize the moment: "I'm sorry but I simply can't make money on these people. . . . The suffering is too great for me to cash in on it (*SLL*, 161).[20] During that stretch Steinbeck must have realized that the issue was not as simple as portraying the "naive directness" of the migrants' desire for land (*CJS*, 12). Indeed, the cauldron of his own soul was beginning to boil with anger, frustration, and impotence (*Sheaves*, 225). Apparently neither the "Oklahomans" version—whatever that was—nor the proposed magazine article could adequately redress the injustices he had recently witnessed. "When I wrote *The Grapes of Wrath*," he declared in a 1952 Voice of America radio interview, "I was filled . . . with certain angers . . . at people who were doing injustices to other people" (*WD*, xxxiii).

As a novelist, Steinbeck often experienced a delayed reaction to piercing events. Perhaps as early as February—but certainly no later than early April ("New book goes very fast but I am afraid it is pretty lousy. I don't care much," he told Otis on 26 April 1938 [*SCSU*, 33])—through approximately mid-May 1938, Steinbeck worked at the third stage of his effort, "L'Affaire Lettuceberg." With this abortive—but necessary—sidetrack venture, Steinbeck's migrant subject matter took its most drastic turn, inspired by an ugly event in Salinas, California, his hometown. Earlier, in September 1936, Steinbeck had encountered the vicious clash between workers and growers in a lettuce strike—"there are riots in Salinas and killings in the streets of that dear little town where I was born," he told novelist George Albee (*SLL*, 132). The strike was smashed with "fascist" terrorism, including gas bombings, shootings, and strict lockouts; recollections of the workers' defeat and the systematic violation of their civil rights festered in Steinbeck for more than a year. "I am treasonable enough not to believe in the liberty of a man or a group to exploit, torment, or slaughter men or groups. I believe in the despotism of human life and happiness against the liberty of money and possessions," he railed in a 1937 statement for the League of American Writers.[21]

Perhaps as early as the first week of February 1938, and no later than the first week of April, galvanized by reports of the worsening conditions in Visalia and Nipomo, he felt the urgent need to do something direct in retaliation. John Steinbeck never became what committed activists would consider fully radicalized (his writings stemmed more from his own feelings and humane sensibility than from the persuasiveness of the national or international left's economic and social ideas), but by putting his pen to the service of this cause, he was stepping as close to being a firebrand as he ever would. He launched into "L'Affaire," a vituperative satire aimed at attacking the leading citizens of Salinas, a cabal of organizers called "the committee of seven" who foment the army (a thousand strong) of armed vigilantes recruited from the common populace of Salinas—"clerks, and service station operators, and small shopkeepers and generally dopes" (*LTE*, 7-8). "L'Affaire Lettuceberg" was a detour from his main concern for the migrant workers, already recorded in "The Harvest Gypsies" and adumbrated in the "Oklahoman" rehearsals. In fact, "L'Affaire" wasn't "literary" at all but a "vulgar" tract concocted to do a specific job. Sometime in early May 1938, Steinbeck, who had already written approximately sixty thousand words (and was aiming for ten thousand more), confessed to Annie Laurie Williams: "I'll have the first draft of this book done in about two weeks. . . . And it is a vicious book, a mean book. I don't know whether it will be any good at all. It might well be very lousy but it has a lot of poison in it that I had to get out of my system and this is a good way to do it" (*WD*, xxxix).

Shortly after that prediction, however, Steinbeck wrote again—probably in mid-May—to Otis and to Covici (who had already announced the publication of "L'Affaire") to inform them that he would not be delivering the manuscript they expected:

> This is going to be a hard letter to write . . . this book is finished and it is a bad book and I must get rid of it. It can't be printed. It is bad because it isn't honest. Oh! these incidents all happened but—I'm not telling as much of the truth about them as I know. In satire you have to restrict the picture and I just can't do satire. . . . I know, you could sell possibly 30,000 copies. I know that a great many people would think they liked the book. I myself have built up a hole-proof argument on how and why I liked it. I can't beat the argument but I don't like the book. And I would be doing Pat a greater injury in letting him print it than I would by destroying it. Not once in the writing of it have I felt the curious warm pleasure that comes when work is going well. My whole work drive has been aimed at making people understand each other and then I deliberately write this book the aim of which is to cause hatred through partial understanding. My father would have called it a smart-alec book. It was full of tricks to make people ridiculous. If I can't do better I have slipped badly. And that I won't admit, yet. . . . I had forgotten that I hadn't learned to write books, that I will never learn to write them. A book must be a life that lives all of itself and this one doesn't do that. . . . This one is an experiment in trickery and trickery in a book is treachery. (*WD*, xl-xli)[22]

Urged on by Carol, who hated "L'Affaire," Steinbeck made the right move. On 24 May 1938, Annie Laurie Williams, speaking for the staff at McIntosh and Otis, replied: "I admire you for having the courage of your convictions and know you would feel better if you could have heard what Elizabeth and Pat both said when they read your letter . . . [W]e all admire you more than ever for sticking by your instincts about your work" (*WD*, lv).

4

Steinbeck rebounded immediately and hit the ground running. Traditionally, he did not work weekends or holidays, so he probably took off Memorial Day weekend, which means that—judging from the fact that he wrote "turtle episode" or the third chapter (*WD*, 20) on Tuesday, 31 May, and calculating backwards from there at two thousand words per day—he probably began *The Grapes of Wrath* (as yet untitled) on Wednesday, 25 May, and certainly no later than Thursday, 26 May. His conscience squared, his integrity restored, Steinbeck quickly embarked on the longest sustained writing job of his career. Ridding himself of poison by passing through a "bad" book proved beneficial, he told Otis on Wednesday, 1 June 1938: "It is a nice thing to be working and believing in my work again. I hope I can keep the drive . . . I only feel whole and well when it is this way" (*SLL*, 167). Naturally, his partisanship for the workers and his sense of indignation at California's labor situation carried over, but they were given a more articulate and dramatic shape.

From the moment when Steinbeck struck the first lines of the new novel to paper—"To the red country and part of the gray country of Oklahoma, the last rains came gently, and ~~it~~ they did not cut the scarred earth. The plows crossed and recrossed the rivulet ~~cuts~~ marks."[23]—through the winter of 1939, when the last of the corrections and editorial details were negotiated—"I meant, Pat, to print *all all all* the verses of the Battle Hymn. They're all pertinent and they're all exciting. And the music if you can," he chastised (*SLL*, 175)—*The Grapes of Wrath* was a task which fully commanded Steinbeck's artistic energy and attention. Everything he had written earlier—from his 1936 *Nation* article through "Starvation Under the Orange Trees," an impassioned April 1938 essay that functioned as the epilogue to *Their Blood Is Strong*, and even "Breakfast," a poignant short story/sketch included in *The Long Valley* (1938)—became grist for his final attempt. "For the first time I am working on a book that is not limited and that will take every bit of experience and thought and feeling that I have," he claimed on 11 June 1938 (*WD*, 26).

From his numerous field travels with Collins and from countless hours of talking to migrant people, working beside them, listening to them, and sharing their problems, Steinbeck summoned the concrete details of human form, language, and

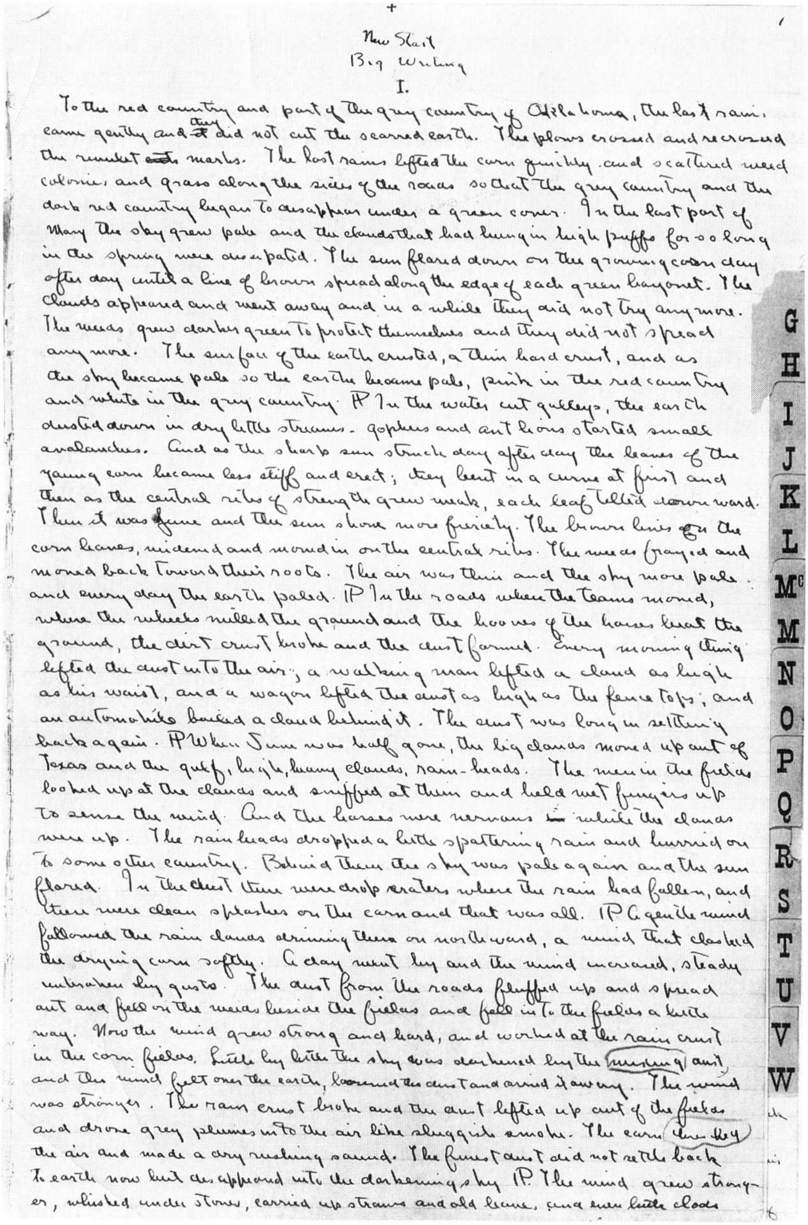

New Start
Big Writing

I.

To the red country and part of the grey country of Oklahoma, the last rains came gently and they did not cut the scarred earth. The plows crossed and recrossed the rivulet marks. The last rains lifted the corn quickly and scattered weed colonies and grass along the sides of the roads so that the grey country and the dark red country began to disappear under a green cover. In the last part of May the sky grew pale and the clouds that had hung in high puffs for so long in the spring were dissipated. The sun flared down on the growing corn day after day until a line of brown spread along the edge of each green bayonet. The clouds appeared and went away and in a while they did not try any more. The weeds grew darker green to protect themselves and they did not spread any more. The surface of the earth crusted, a thin hard crust, and as the sky became pale so the earth became pale, pink in the red country and white in the grey country. ¶ In the water cut gulleys, the earth dusted down in dry little streams. Gophers and ant lions started small avalanches. And as the sharp sun struck day after day the leaves of the young corn became less stiff and erect; they bent in a curve at first and then as the central ribs of strength grew weak, each leaf tilted downward. Then it was June and the sun shone more fiercely. The brown lines on the corn leaves widened and moved in on the central ribs. The weeds frayed and moved back toward their roots. The air was thin and the sky more pale and every day the earth paled. ¶ In the roads where the teams moved, where the wheels milled the ground and the hooves of the horses beat the ground, the dirt crust broke and the dust formed. Every moving thing lifted the dust into the air; a walking man lifted a cloud as high as his waist, and a wagon lifted the dust as high as the fence tops; and an automobile boiled a cloud behind it. The dust was long in settling back again. ¶ When June was half gone, the big clouds moved up out of Texas and the gulf, high, heavy clouds, rain-heads. The men in the fields looked up at the clouds and sniffed at them and held wet fingers up to sense the wind. And the horses were nervous while the clouds were up. The rain heads dropped a little spattering rain and hurried on to some other country. Behind them the sky was pale again and the sun flared. In the dust there were drop craters where the rain had fallen, and there were clean splashes on the corn and that was all. ¶ A gentle wind followed the rain clouds driving them on northward, a wind that clashed the drying corn softly. A day went by and the wind increased, steady unbroken by gusts. The dust from the roads fluffed up and spread out and fell on the weeds beside the fields and fell into the fields a little way. Now the wind grew strong and hard, and worked at the rain crust in the corn fields. Little by little the sky was darkened by the mixing dust, and the wind felt over the earth, loosened the dust and carried it away. The wind was stronger. The rain crust broke and the dust lifted up out of the fields and drove grey plumes into the air like sluggish smoke. The corn threshed the air and made a dry rushing sound. The finest dust did not settle back to earth now but disappeared into the darkening sky. ¶ The wind grew stronger, whisked under stones, carried up straws and old leaves, and even little clods

First page of *The Grapes of Wrath* manuscript; Steinbeck began his "New Start" by promising to make his handwriting larger and more legible.
Courtesy of the University of Virginia Library, Charlottesville, VA.

landscape that promote artistic verisimilitude, as well as the subtler, imaginative nuances of dialect, idiosyncratic tics, habits, and gestures that animate fictional characterization and would make his "people . . . intensely alive the whole time" (*WD*, 40).[24] From the outset in creating the Joad family to occupy the narrative chapters of *The Grapes of Wrath,* Steinbeck endowed his novel with a specific human context, a felt emotional quality, and a spacious dramatic dimension his earlier versions lacked: "Begin the detailed description of the family I am to live with. Must take time in the description, detail, detail, looks, clothes, gestures. . . . We have to know these people. Know their looks and their nature," he reminded himself on 17 June (*WD*, 29). By marshalling precise journalistic details Steinbeck established a recognizable texture of facticity and a sense of the specificity of the Joad's world. Then, on top of that strata, by deliberately conceiving the Joads as "an over-essence of people," Steinbeck elevated the entire (hi)story of the migrant struggle into a symbolic realm and joined the mythic westering journey with his latently heroic characters, according to this key notation on 30 June: "Yesterday . . . I went over the whole of the book in my head—fixed on the last scene, huge and symbolic, toward which the whole story moves. And that was a good thing, for it was a reunderstanding of the dignity of the effort and the mightyness of the theme. I feel very small and inadequate and incapable but I grew again to love the story which is so much greater than I am. To love and admire the people who are so much stronger and purer and braver than I am" (*WD*, 36). His transformation of Rose of Sharon from "silly pregnant" teenager to mysterious madonna figure in the novel's final scene was not only long prepared for in his imagination but became, in a sense, the novel's alpha and omega, at once its point of departure and its finale.

It is a critical commonplace that many American authors, often with little in the way of a shared novelistic tradition to emulate, or finding that established fictional models don't suit their sensibilities, forge their own way by synthesizing their personal vision and experience with a variety of cultural forms and literary styles. Steinbeck was no exception, no stranger to the dialogue between what Emerson once called originality and quotation. To execute *The Grapes of Wrath* Steinbeck drew on the jump-cut technique of John Dos Passos's *USA* trilogy (1937), the narrative tempo of Pare Lorentz's radio drama *Ecce Homo!*, and the sequential quality of Lorentz's films *The Plow that Broke the Plains* and *The River*, the stark visual effects of Dorothea Lange's photographs of Dust Bowl Oklahoma and California migrant life, the timbre of the Greek epics, the rhythms of the King James Bible, the refrains of American folk music, and the biological impetus of his and Edward F. Ricketts's ecological phalanx, or group-man, theory. As the functioning artist of the phalanx, Steinbeck negotiated these multiple resources, especially Old and New Testament themes, parallels, analogies, allusions, and inversions into his own holistic structure, his own architecture of accommodation. No single thread, no single echo from prior texts, no affinity or parallel with a single style, form, art, discourse, or genre will alone explain the heteroglossic design of *The Grapes of Wrath.* Malcolm Cowley's claim that a "whole literature is summarized in this book and much of it is carried to a new level of excellence," is especially pertinent and underscores the width and breadth of Steinbeck's taste and the capacious dimensionality of his novel.[25]

If Steinbeck's precursors were disparate and polymorphous and if they influenced him as he pushed back at them in return, his conception of the novel's structure was quite a bit more uniform. The epic scale and technical plan of *Grapes* apparently crystallized between 15 May and 25 May of 1938. During that fertile transitional moment the organizational design of the novel established itself securely in Steinbeck's mind. Unlike William Faulkner, say, Steinbeck was not an elite literary practitioner or formal innovator, but he still achieved in *Grapes* a compelling combination of commensurate style, visual realism, and rambunctious, symphonic form that was at once accessible and experimental, documentarian and fictive, expository and lyrical. He anticipated almost precisely the novel's length and the amount of time it would take to complete it. He apparently did not work from a formal outline or notes (at least no written versions have ever turned up); rather, he sketched out the novel in his head in aggregate first (he appears to have assembled a nearly complete list of potential topics for his intercalary, or general, chapters by the time he started writing), followed by a brief planning session each day or every few days if he happened to be working on a long chapter, such as the 20th.[26] On 18 August, he noted: "Now away from the daily life and into the book. I read a couple of chapters to company last night and could see the whole thing clearly. Also it doesn't sound bad. Today is going to take a long time. I have to get on the line of my family again. The outline of today will carry over some days. Must get it straight, must get it clear and straight" (*WD*, 58). Sticking to his outline became increasingly important, because this chapter, continually disrupted by intrusions, took him from 18 August to 3 September to complete. When it was finished, Steinbeck scrawled at the bottom of manuscript page 109, "long son of a bitch too."

On 6 July 1938, Steinbeck confided to Harry T. Moore that he was employing what was for him a "new method" of fictional technique that purposefully combined a suitably elastic form and elevated style to express the far-reaching tragedy of the migrant drama.[27] Influenced by Tolstoy's construction in *War and Peace*—which Steinbeck told Merle Danford a few months later was his favorite "literary creation" (*CJS*, 23)—he devised for *The Grapes of Wrath* a contrapuntal structure, alternating short lyrical chapters of exposition and background pertinent to the migrants as a group (chapters 1, 3, 5, 7, 9, 11, 12, 14, 15, 17, 19, 21, 23, 25, 27, 29) with the long narrative chapters of the Joad family's dramatic exodus to California (chapters 2, 4, 6, 8, 10, 13, 16, 18, 20, 22, 24, 26, 28, 30). Steinbeck structured his novel by juxtaposition. His "particular" chapters are the slow-paced and lengthy narratives that embody traditional characterization and advance the dramatic plot, while his jazzy, rapid-fire "interchapters" work at another level of (re)cognition by expressing an atemporal, universal, synoptic, contextual view of the migrant condition. In a sense, then, fiction and its prefictive antecedents march together; textuality and its historical matrix exist side by side. As Steinbeck composed chapters 5 and 6, for instance, he reminded himself that for maximum participatory effect, "I want the reader to be able to keep [the general and particular chapters] separate in his mind" (*WD*, 23-24). In fact, his "general" or intecalary chapters ("pace changers," Steinbeck called them) were expressly designed to "hit the reader below the belt. With the rhythms and symbols of poetry one can get into a reader—open him up and while he is open introduce things on a intellectual level which he would not or could not receive unless he were opened up," Steinbeck revealed to Columbia University undergraduate Herbert Sturz fourteen years later.[28]

The Grapes of Wrath is an engaged novel with many complex voices and impassioned emphases. Except for *Grapes*' unflinching treatment of the Depression's climatic, social, and economic conditions, and those nonteleologically inspired interchapters that serve to contain the speaker's moral outrage and halt the slide of his characters' emotions toward sentimentality, there is nothing cynically distanced about it, nothing coolly modernist, in the way we have come to understand the elite literary implications of that term in the past eighty years. (*The Grapes of Wrath* is in some ways an old-fashioned novel, even down to its curious avoidance of scenes of human sexuality.) It is not narrated from the first-person point of view, yet the language has a consistently catchy eyewitness quality about it; and the vivid biblical, empirical, poetical, cinematic, and folk styles Steinbeck employs demonstrate the tonal and visual acuity of his ear and eye. Passages like this one, written on 22 September 1938, come from a place far deeper than the intellect alone, come, rather, from the visceral center of the writer's being, where his whole body is brought to bear on his text:

> There is a crime here that goes beyond denunciation. There is a sorrow here that weeping cannot symbolize. There is a failure here that topples all our success. The fertile earth, the straight tree arrows, the sturdy trunks, and the ripe fruit. And children dying of pellagra must die because a profit cannot be taken from an orange. . . . and in the eyes of the people there is the failure; and in the eyes of the hungry there is a growing wrath. In the souls of the people the grapes of wrath are filling and growing heavy, growing heavy for the vintage. (*GOW*, 477)

The tempo of this passage—one of the most striking in the novel—indicates the importance of musical and harmonic analogies to the text. Steinbeck told Merle Armitage on 17 February 1939 that in "composition, in movement, in tone and in scope," *The Grapes of Wrath* was "symphonic."[29] Steinbeck's covenant was with his own radical sense of the fiction-making process, not with a well-made linear formula. Indeed his fusion of intimate narrative and panoramic editorial chapters enforces a dialogic concert. Chapters, styles, and voices all speak to each other, set up resonances, send echoes back and forth—point and counterpoint, strophe and antistrophe—as in a huge symphony of language whose total tonal and spatial impression far surpasses the sum of its discrete and sometimes dissonant parts. It should come as no surprise that, almost religiously, Steinbeck listened to classical music either before or during his writing sessions. Tchaikovsky's ballet *The Swan Lake,* Stravinsky's "very fine" *Symphony of Psalms,* and Beethoven's symphonies and sonatas created a mood conducive to writing and established a rhythm for the day's work. For instance, on 21 June, in preparation for writing chapter 9, the short interchapter about the migrants deciding what, if anything, of their belongings they can take west, Steinbeck played *Swan Lake*, "because there too is the loss of a loved thing of the past" (*WD*, 31). And when he didn't have the record player going, he learned to content himself with the chug and whir of the washing machine.

Steinbeck's novel belongs to that vital class of fictions whose shape issues not from an ideal blueprint of aesthetic or ideological propriety, but from the generative urgency of its author's experience in history ("It *had* to be written," Stanley Kunitz said in the *Wilson Library Bulletin* in 1939). Steinbeck's awareness of and involvement in the plight of hundreds of thousands of Dust Bowl migrants in the latter half of the 1930s created his obsessive urge to tell their story honestly but also movingly:

> Boileau said that kings, Gods, and Heroes only were fit subjects for literature. The writer can only write about what he admires. Present day kings aren't very inspiring, the gods are on vacation and about the only heroes left are the scientists and the poor. . . . But the poor are still in the open. When they make a struggle it is an heroic struggle with starvation, death, or imprisonment the penalty if they lose. The writer sets down the desire of his own time, the action of the people toward attaining that desire, the obstacles to attainment and the struggle to overcome the obstacles. ("Interview," 861-62)

Steinbeck's sense of himself as mediator in that struggle, an agent of its inscription, surfaces often. "This must be a good book," he wrote on 10 June 1938. "It simply must. I haven't any choice. It must be far and away the best thing I have ever attempted—slow but sure, piling detail on detail until a picture and an experience emerge. Until the whole throbbing thing emerges" (*WD*, 25). Making his audience see and feel that living picture was the paramount concern. "I am not writing a satisfying story," he claimed to Pascal Covici on 16 January 1939: "I've done my damndest to rip a reader's nerves to rags, I don't want him satisfied. . . . I tried to write this book the way lives are being lived not the way books are written. . . . Throughout I've tried to make the reader participate in the actuality, what he takes from it will be scaled entirely on his own depth or hollowness. There are five layers in this book, a reader will find as many as he can and he won't find more than he has in himself" (*SLL*, 178-79). Steinbeck's participatory aesthetic, based on a circle of complicity which linked "the trinity" of writer, text, and reader to ensure maximum affective impact, helps explain the book's runaway popularity—each reader had a stake in it, each reader feels somehow that the book belongs to him or her. Reading *Grapes* is not a passive activity; indeed, though it is not a linguistically challenging text, making sense of the novel, completing the arc of subjectivity, nonetheless becomes the reader's task. On 7 June 1938, as Steinbeck completed chapter 5, for instance, he kept his eye steadily on his kinesthetic target: "Today's work is the overtone of the tractors, the men who run them, the men they displace, the sound of them, the smell of them. I've got to get this over. Got to because this one's tone is very important—this is the eviction sound and the tonal reason for movement. Must do it well" (*WD*, 23).

Steinbeck conceived his novel on simultaneous levels of existence, ranging from socio-economic/historic determinism to transcendent spirituality. Louis Owens succinctly explains how biblical parallels illuminate four of Steinbeck's layers: "On one level it is the story of a family's struggle for survival in the Promised Land. . . . On another level it is the story of a people's struggle, the migrants'. On a third level it is the story of a nation, America. On still another level, through . . . the allusions to Christ and those to the Israelites and Exodus, it becomes the story of mankind's quest for profound comprehension of his committment to his fellow man and to the earth he inhabits."[30] Thus Steinbeck pushed back the normative boundaries of traditional mimetic fiction and redefined the proletarian form, so that *Grapes* is a great deal more than simply a protest statement: "Organized, militant action is not at the center of Steinbeck's program for apocalyptic change. His concern is with consciousness. That is where the most meaningful revolution must occur."[31]

Like most significant American novels, *The Grapes of Wrath* does not offer codified social solutions or directly solve the persistent power struggles of race, class, and gender, but leads us deeper and deeper into complexities those issues raise. Even though it privileges a particular section of the white American migrant labor scene (Steinbeck ignores the problems of non-white migrant workers—Filipinos, Chinese, Japanese, and Mexicans—who made up a large percentage of California's agricultural labor force, according to Carey McWilliams's 1939 study *Factories in the Field*), his book—if the testimony of the late Cesar Chavez and others is any indication—still speaks to the larger experience of human disenfranchisement, still looks toward an authentic human ecology, still anticipates an ethos of individual and communal conversion. In this sense it is both a hermeneutical and heuristic text. At every level *The Grapes of Wrath* enacts the process of its author's belief and embodies the shape of his faith and devotional posture, as in this ringing synthesis from chapter 14:

> The last clear definite function of man—muscles aching to work, minds aching to create beyond the single need—this is man. To build a wall, to build a house, a dam, and in the wall and house and dam to put something of Manself, and to Manself take back something of the wall, the house, the dam; to take hard muscles from the lifting, to take the clear lines and form from conceiving. For man, unlike any other thing organic or inorganic in the universe, grows beyond his work, walks up the stairs of his concepts, emerges ahead of his accomplishments. (*GOW*, 204)

5

John Steinbeck lived to write. Despite its difficulty and his own pervasive sense of inadequacy, he believed writing could be redemptive, transformative work: "The pen feels good to my hand. Comfortable and comforting. What an extension of self is this pen. Once it is in my hand like a wand, I stop being the confused, turgid ugly and gross person. I am no longer the me I know" (*TAJS*, 291). William Howarth rightly claims that "Steinbeck attached a totemic significance to his writing habits."[32] Each weekday, generally between 10 A.M. and noon he brewed a pot of "ranch" coffee (clarified with a raw egg and sweetened with canned milk) and sequestered himself in the 8' x 8' work room of the small frame house he and Carol built in 1936 on Greenwood Lane in Los Gatos (they named it "Arroyo del Ajo"—"Garlic Gulch"): "Just big enough for a bed and a desk and a gun rack and a little book case. I like to sleep in the room I work in," he confided to George Albee (*SLL*, 133). In his study, or some days out on their porch deck (with its excellent view of the Santa Clara Valley) or in their guest cottage next to the house, he warmed up punctually with letters to Otis or Covici and an all-important entry in his working journal to give him "the opening use of words every day" (*WD*, 38), on his way to generating the all-important "work energy" and sometimes trance-like creative zone where he could picture vividly in his head the characters, scenes, and events. Thus, in composing two books at once—the novel and the diary—Steinbeck created a disciplined working rhythm and what he called a "unity feeling"—a sense of continuity and habitation with his material that made "it easy and fun to work" (*WD*, 27). "Let the damn book go three hundred thousand words if it wants to. This is my life. Why should I want to finish my own life? The confidence is on me again. I can feel it. It's stopping work that does the damage," he admitted on 7 July 1938 (*WD*, 39).

Ideally, for a few hours each day, the world Steinbeck created took precedence over the one in which he lived. Because, for a writer like Steinbeck, both worlds can be considered "real," at times during 1938 Steinbeck didn't know where one began and the other left off; walking back into the domestic world from the world of imagination and language was not always a smooth shift for him (or for Carol). "This book is my sole responsibility and I must stick to it and nothing more," he reminded himself on 26 September (*WD*, 77). His work demanded his attention so fully that he finally refused to dissipate his energy in extra-literary pursuits: "I won't do any of these public things. Can't. It isn't my nature and I won't be stampeded. And so the stand must be made and I must keep out of politics," he promised himself, though he continually worried about the oppression of migrant workers in California and news of Nazi/Fascist advances in Eastern Europe (*WD*, 73), which, though scarcely mentioned directly in the novel (see *GOW*, 447), was one of those latent signifiers that contributed to the book's edginess, to its sense of impending doom at the margins of consciousness and discourse, and to its pressurized language.

But as the summer wore on, the ceremonial aspect of writing turned to drudgery, and emerging ahead of his accomplishments seemed an insurmountable task, because, besides losing the "threads" that tied Steinbeck to his characters, he was low on patience and had lost his sense of humor. "Was ever a book written under greater difficulty?" (*WD*, 63), he whined. Nearly every day brought unsolicited requests for his name, his money, and his time, including unscheduled visitors, unanticipated disruptions and reversals. Domestic and conjugal relations with Carol were often strained (Steinbeck apparently remained mostly celibate when he was deeply immersed in his writing [*WD*, 34]). Houseguests trooped to Los Gatos all summer, including his sisters, Beth Ainsworth and Mary Dekker, and longtime friends Carlton Sheffield, George and Gail Mors, Ed Ricketts, Ritch and Tal Lovejoy, plus new celebrity acquaintances Wallace Ford and Broderick Crawford (stars of the recently closed New York Drama Critics Circle-award winning play, *Of Mice and Men*), Charlie Chaplin, and Pare Lorentz.

As if that weren't enough to erode the novelist's composure, the Steinbeck's tiny house on Greenwood Lane was besieged with the noise of neighborhood building and boisterous activity, which nearly drove them to distraction. By midsummer, hoping for permanent sanctuary, they decided to buy the secluded Biddle Ranch, a forty-seven-acre spread on Brush Road atop the Santa Cruz Mountains well above Los Gatos. Even though it was the most "beautiful" location they had seen (*WD*, 42), its original homestead was in disrepair, so besides buying the land they also would have to build a new house, and that too became a source of added distractions. The Steinbecks didn't move there until November 1938, a month after the novel was finished (final typing of the manuscript and corrections of the typescript and galley proofs took place at the Biddle Ranch from November 1938 to early February 1939), but preparations for its purchase ate a great deal of Steinbeck's time and energy from mid-July onward.

August proved the most embattled period. Early in the month—on the 3d—Steinbeck noted in his journal: "There are now four things or five rather to write through—throat, bankruptcy, Pare, ranch, and the book. If I get this book done it will be remarkable" (*WD*, 51). His litany of woes included Carol's tonsil operation, which incapacitated her; the bankruptcy of Steinbeck's publisher, Covici-Friede, which threatened the end of their current income and posed an uncertain publishing future for the novel he was writing; Pare Lorentz's arrangements for making a film version of *In Dubious Battle*; the purchase of the Biddle Ranch, which Carol also wanted badly and Steinbeck felt additionally compelled to buy for her (they argued over the pressure this caused); and the book itself, still untitled (and therefore without "being"), which seemed more recalcitrant than ever. By mid-August, roughly halfway through the novel,

THE COMPANY WILL APPRECIATE SUGGESTIONS FROM ITS PATRONS CONCERNING ITS SERVICE 1204

CLASS OF SERVICE

This is a full-rate Telegram or Cablegram unless its deferred character is indicated by a suitable symbol above or preceding the address.

WESTERN UNION

R. B. WHITE PRESIDENT — NEWCOMB CARLTON CHAIRMAN OF THE BOARD — J. C. WILLEVER FIRST VICE-PRESIDENT

SYMBOLS

DL = Day Letter
NM = Night Message
NL = Night Letter
LC = Deferred Cable
NLT = Cable Night Letter
Ship Radiogram

The filing time shown in the date line on telegrams and day letters is STANDARD TIME at point of origin. Time of receipt is STANDARD TIME at point of destination.

Received at

22 F NEW YORK NYJULY 19 1938

JOHN STEINBECK GREENWOOD ROAD

LOS GATOS CALIFORNIA

PAT SUDDENLY UNDER SEVERE FINANCIAL PRESSURE FROM PRINTER
REORGANIZATION INEVETABLE AFTER THURSDAYS MEETING WITH PRINTERS
HAVE BEEN IN CONFERENCE WITH PAT ALL AFTERNOON BE FORWARNED
BUT NOT ALARMED YOUR INTERESTS AS WELL PROTECTED AS POSSIBLE
WILL WIRE IMPORTANT DEVELOPMENTS...ELICABETS...430PM

Western Union telegram to Steinbeck from his agent, Elizabeth Otis, 19 July 1938, concerning inevitable financial collapse of his publisher Covici-Friede. The next day Steinbeck wrote in his journal, *Working Days*: "Well last night a wire that Pat is in trouble. I've been expecting it. I'm so sorry for him. Our two thousand dollars, our year's royalties, are pretty important to us but we're eating and working and that's more than we have any right to expect" (46). When Covici was hired later that summer by The Viking Press as a senior editor, he took his chief author, Steinbeck, with him to his new firm.

Courtesy of Steinbeck Research Center, San Jose State University, San Jose, CA.

Steinbeck took stock of his situation: Viking Press had bought his contract (for $15,000), hired Pat Covici as a senior editor as part of the deal, and planned a first printing of fifteen thousand copies for Steinbeck's collection of short stories, *The Long Valley*; a string of famous houseguests had either just departed or were about to arrive; and he and Carol had closed on the Biddle property for $10,500.

On 16 August, in the middle of what he called a "Bad Lazy Time," he lamented: "Demoralization complete and seemingly unbeatable. So many things happening that I can't not be interested. . . . All this is more excitement than our whole lives put together. All crowded into a month. My many weaknesses are beginning to show their heads. I simply must get this thing out of my system. I'm not a writer. I've been fooling myself and other people. . . . This success will ruin me as sure as hell. It probably won't last and that will be all right" (*WD*, 56). Four days later, on 20 August, Lorentz, the newly appointed director of the United States Film Service, arrived for the weekend. His visit broke Steinbeck's depression and logjam. They discussed further a full-length movie of *In Dubious Battle*, then rushed off to visit Chaplin at Pebble Beach, where they stayed up all night, drinking and talking about the state of America.[33] Though their film project would soon fall through, Steinbeck was encouraged by Lorentz's optimism about the country at large and his prescience in predicting his "monumental" book would be one of "the greatest novels of the age." Steinbeck doggedly kept up his daily stint (he aimed for two thousand words at each sitting, some days managing as few as eight hundred, some days, when the juices were flowing, as many as twenty-two hundred) through what Carol called the "interminable details and minor crises" of August and September (*WD*, 17-18).

That Steinbeck lost only four or five working days during that entire stretch points up just how deeply he augmented his talent with discipline, determination, and plain hard work. Where his characters use tools to elevate work to a dignified level—a "clear definite function"—Steinbeck turned to his pen. For Steinbeck, writing was also a means of textual habitation, a way of living in the world he created. He wrote books methodically the way other people built walls, houses, dams, which is to say, word by word, sentence by sentence, paragraph by paragraph. His act of composing was also an act of validation and self-creation, a way of fulfilling his emotional and psychological dream of belonging, by being "at home," by living in the architectural spaces he created. In fact, this creative, interior, or *architextual* level of engagement is the elusive and heretofore unacknowledged fifth layer of Steinbeck's novel.

Although Steinbeck liked to imagine that he could efface his own presence in *The Grapes of Wrath* (*SLL*, 180-81), the fact remains that it is a very personal book, rooted in his own compulsions and conditioned by his own contemporary experiences. Indeed, though Steinbeck later denied it, aspects of his life bore directly on manuscript decisions. During his planning session on 13 July, admittedly confused by the increasing lure of owning the Biddle Ranch—"I want that ranch" (*WD*, 42)—he decided to write chapter 14, the general on Manself which became one of the most important theoretical chapters and perhaps the most significant summation of organismal philosophy Steinbeck had yet written. The first half includes the paean to the universal human capacity for creation. The second half expresses the core of Steinbeck's mature phalanx theory, the creation of an aggregate, dynamic "We" from distinct, myriad selves (*GOW*, 206). The summary quality of this chapter suggests that he intended to use it later as a kind of climactic crescendo (achieved now by chapter 25).

Instead Steinbeck inserted it at the mid-point of the novel for several reasons: its dithyrambic tone and heightened language reawakened his flagging interest; its optimistic, theoretical bias restored focus and clarity to the narrative line; its extolment of creativity, based on humanity's willingness to "suffer and die for a concept" (*GOW*, 205), provided an immediate reminder that his own compositional process could be endured for the sake of the cause he espoused; and its concern for families who had lost their land and homes may have partly assuaged his guilt, if not his sense of irony, as he was about to make the biggest property purchase of his life, one that threatened to cut him off from the larger social field. In a sense, then, in working out the "clear lines" in this much-heralded chapter, Steinbeck not only "put something" of himself into the creation but managed to "take back something" as well—a "form from conceiving." Furthermore, the "plodding" pace of Steinbeck's writing schedule informed the slow, "crawling" movement of the Joads' journey, while the harried beat of his own life gave the proper "feel" and tone to his beleaguered characters. Their unsavory weaknesses and vanities, their naivety, their outlandishness, their struggle for survival, their resistance, their unsuspecting heroism are in part Steinbeck's as well. Culturally conditioned or not, romantically inspired or not, if *The Grapes of Wrath* praises the honorableness of labor and ratifies the obsessive quest for a home, it is because the author himself felt these essentials called into being the most committed, the most empathetic, the most resourceful qualities of the human psyche—"qualities" from which a "new system" will grow ("Interview," 862).

In early October, goaded often by Carol's rebukes, Steinbeck roused himself from another bout of "foolishness" and "self indulgence" to mount the final drive—"Now there can be no lost days and no lost time. Straight through to the finish now without loss. . . . Shall gather all my will together and go on" (*WD*, 81). Like a gift, the last five chapters of the novel came to him so abundantly that Steinbeck had more material than he could use (the death of Rose of Sharon's infant was to be caused by measles). On Wednesday, 5 October, and again on Friday, 7 October, he planned chapter 26:

> And my story is coming better. I see it better. Ma's crossing with the clerk, and then Tom's going out—meeting Casy, trying to move the men in the camp. Arrest and beating. Return in secret. Move. Cotton—flood. And the end—Tom comes back. Stolen things. Must go. Be Around. Birth. And the rising waters. And the starving man. And the end. What more? (*WD*, 82-83)

> This leisurelyness must go on although the tempo gets faster the details must be as slow. Today the hiding of Tom and the scene with his mother. The cut in wages. Tom has to go. Getting together. The drop to starvation level of the wages. The trapped quality. Must get it in—Difficulty of getting clean. No soap. No money to buy soap. Then peaches. The rush of workers and the fight for the peaches. Fight to get them. Must get this all in. There's so damned much in this book already. I must keep it coming. (*WD*, 84)

Now the full force of Steinbeck's experience at Visalia eight months earlier came into play, prompting his metamorphosis from right-minded competency to inspired vision. There is more than the agency of language at work here, more than an impersonal channeling of historical forces. What Steinbeck had witnessed in that "heartbreaking" sea of mud and debris called forth every ounce of his moral indignation, social anger, and empathy, which in turn profoundly effected his novel's climax. Steinbeck's internal bruise, his "ache . . . inside" (*Sheaves*, 226) opened the floodgates of his affection, created *The Grapes of Wrath*'s compelling justification, provided its haunting spiritual urgency, and rooted it in the deepest wellsprings of democratic fellow-feeling. In the same way that rain floods the novel's concluding chapters, so the memory of Steinbeck's cataclysmic experience at Visalia, colored by guilt, futility, and impotency, pervades the ending of the book; its ominous emotional climate is charged by a terrible beauty symbolized by Rose of Sharon's gratuitous act of sharing her breast with a starving stranger. "It must be an accident, it must be a stranger, and it must be quick," Steinbeck instructed Covici. "To build this stranger into the structure of the book would be to warp the whole meaning of the book. The fact that the Joads don't know him, don't care about him, have no ties to him—that is the emphasis. The giving of the breast has no more sentiment than the giving of a piece of bread" (*SLL*, 178). This prophetic final tableau scene—often comdemned and misunderstood, but for that no less subversively erotic, mysteriously indeterminate—refuses to fade from view; before the apocalypse occurs, before everything is lost in forgetfulness, Steinbeck suggests, *all* gestures must pass from self to world, from thought to word, from desperateness to acceptance, from participation to communion. Though it changed nothing directly in the hard world of California agribusiness, Rose of Sharon's act of converting wilderness to textuality was the perfect ending for his novel.[34]

Steinbeck's deep participation at Visalia also empowered his transformation of Tom Joad, the slowly awakening disciple of Jim Casy. Tom's acceptance of the crucified preacher's gospel of social action occurs just as the deluge is about to begin: "Wherever they's a fight so hungry people can eat, I'll be there. Wherever they's a cop beatin' up a guy, I'll be there. If Casy knowed, why, I'll be in the way guys yell when they're mad an'—I'll be in the way kids laugh when they're hungry an' they know supper's ready. An' when our folks eat the stuff they raise an' live in the houses they build—why, I'll be there. See? God, I'm talkin' like Casy. Comes of thinkin' about him so much. Seems like I can see him sometimes" (*GOW*, 572).

In one of those uncanny transferences possible in moments of extreme exhaustion or receptivity, Steinbeck believed that his fictive alter ego not only floated above *The Grapes of Wrath*'s "last pages . . . like a spirit," but he imagined that Tom Joad actually entered the novelist's work space, the private chamber of his room: "'Tom! Tom! Tom!' I know. It wasn't him. Yes, I think I can go on now. In fact, I feel stronger. Much stronger. Funny where the energy comes from. Now to work, only now it isn't work any more," he recorded in his journal on 20 October (*WD*, 91). With that breakthrough—at once a visitation and a benediction, a presence and an absence—Steinbeck arrived at the intersection of novel and journal, that luminous vector, that fifth layer of involvement where writer and text not only merge but interpenetrate. He entered fully the architecture of his own novel and, however briefly, lived in its fictive space, its scene of writing, where, like Tom Joad, Steinbeck discovered it was no longer necessary to lead people toward a distant new Eden or another illusory Promised Land; rather, the most heroic and honest action was simply to learn to be present, to inhabit the "wherever" fully and at once.[35]

The terms of his complex investment fulfilled, Steinbeck, stretched to the edge, needed only a few more days to finish his novel. Around noon on Wednesday, 26 October 1938, Steinbeck, "so dizzy" he could "hardly see the page" (*WD*, 93), completed the last 775 words of the novel; at the bottom of the 165th and concluding manuscript page, Steinbeck, whose writing was normally miniscule, scrawled in letters an inch-and-a-half high, END#. It should have been cause for wild celebrating, but between bouts of bone-weary tiredness and nervous exhaustion, Steinbeck felt only numbness and perhaps some of the mysterious satisfaction that comes from having transformed the weight of his whole life, his entire body, into the new book, though at that moment he had no idea how debilitating that would prove to be. Though the worst was yet to come, the multiple streams of subjective experience, ameliorism, graphic realism, biblical themes, symbolic forms, and textual authentication gathered in *The Grapes of Wrath* to create the "truly American book" Steinbeck had planned. "Finished this day," his final journal entry concluded simply, "and I hope to God it's good" (*WD*, 93).

6

In 1963 Steinbeck told Caskie Stinnett: "I wrote *The Grapes of Wrath* in one hundred days, but many years of preparation

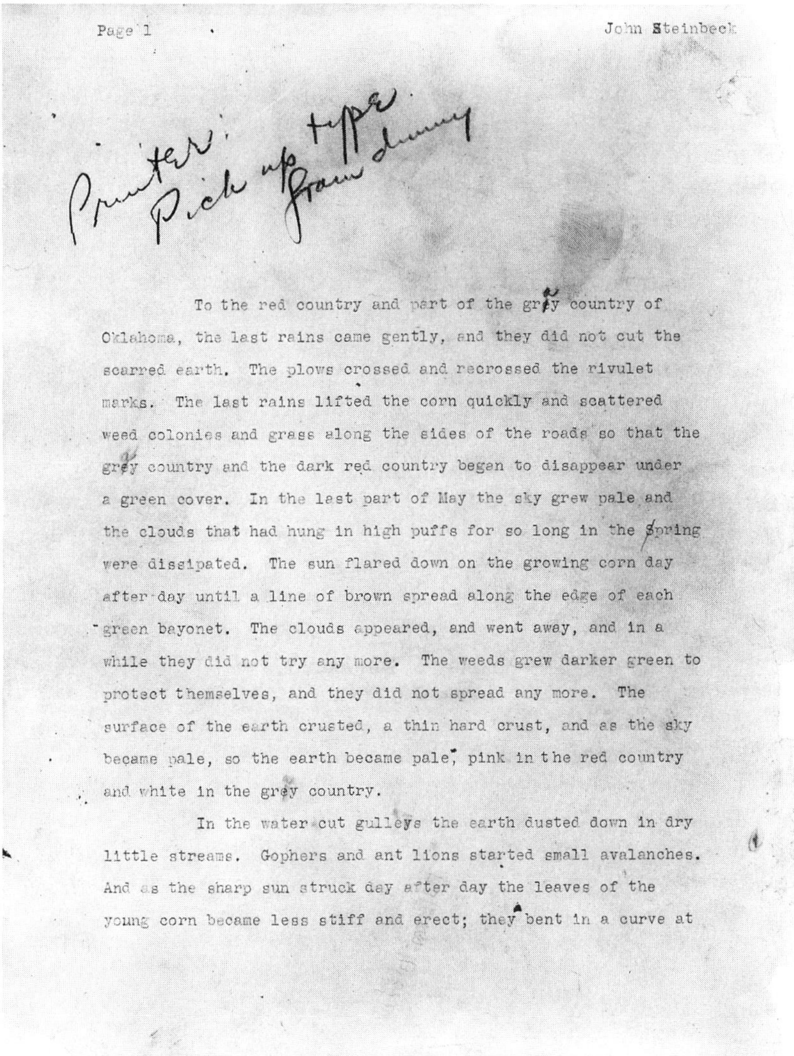

Page 1 John Steinbeck

Printer: Pick up type from dummy

To the red country and part of the grey country of Oklahoma, the last rains came gently, and they did not cut the scarred earth. The plows crossed and recrossed the rivulet marks. The last rains lifted the corn quickly and scattered weed colonies and grass along the sides of the roads so that the grey country and the dark red country began to disappear under a green cover. In the last part of May the sky grew pale and the clouds that had hung in high puffs for so long in the Spring were dissipated. The sun flared down on the growing corn day after day until a line of brown spread along the edge of each green bayonet. The clouds appeared, and went away, and in a while they did not try any more. The weeds grew darker green to protect themselves, and they did not spread any more. The surface of the earth crusted, a thin hard crust, and as the sky became pale, so the earth became pale, pink in the red country and white in the grey country.

In the water-cut gulleys the earth dusted down in dry little streams. Gophers and ant lions started small avalanches. And as the sharp sun struck day after day the leaves of the young corn became less stiff and erect; they bent in a curve at

First page of Carol Steinbeck's typescript of *The Grapes of Wrath*.
Courtesy of the Library of Congress, Washington, DC.

preceded it. I take a hell of a long time to get started. The actual writing is the last process" (*CJS*, 87-88). Though Steinbeck made ninety-nine entries in his daily journal and actually wrote the novel in ninety-three sittings, it was his way of saying that *The Grapes of Wrath* was an intuited whole that embodied the form of his devotion. The entire 200,000 word manuscript took up 165 handwritten pages (plus one smaller sheet) of a 12" x 18" lined ledger book. When he was hot, Steinbeck wrote fast, paying little or no attention to proper spelling, punctuation, or paragraphing. On top of that his script was so small he was capable of cramming over 1300 words on a single oversized ledger sheet (page 156 of the manuscript is the equivalent of four pages of Viking Press text). In short, the novel was written with remarkably preordained motion and directed passion; the relative cleanness and clarity of the holograph manuscript is awesome. To British scholar Roy S. Simmonds it displays a "phenomenal" unity of purpose and an example of "spontaneous prose" long before Jack Kerouac wrote *On the Road*.[36]

Page after page went essentially unmodified from autograph manuscript to typescript to published novel. Ironically, though Steinbeck severely doubted his own artistic ability and in fact wavered sometimes in regard to such niceties as chapter divisions (he originally conceived the novel in three major books), in writing this novel he was creating with the full resiliency and resourcefulness of his imagination. His ability and endurance to execute a work of its magnitude places him among the premiere creative talents of his time. Although he told Tom Cameron in July 1939, "I'm not even a finished writer yet. I haven't learned my craft" (*CJS*, 20), from the vantage point of history, his *Grapes of Wrath* venture stands as one of those happy occasions when a writer simply wrote better than he thought he could.

In fact, Steinbeck had completely lost sight of the novel's effectiveness and had little grasp on its potential popularity, so he warned Covici and Viking Press against a large first printing. Viking ignored him and spent $10,000 on publicity and printed an initial run of fifty thousand copies. After recuperating in San Francisco, the Steinbecks moved to their new Brush Road mountain home. It was still under construction, so they camped a while in the old homestead, where Carol finished the huge typescript and together they made "routine" final corrections. After Covici had read four hundred pages of the typescript on a visit to Los Gatos in late October (*WD*, 91), he badgered Steinbeck, who gave in and sent the first two chapters to him on 29 November. The whole of Carol's cleanly typed—but occasionally improperly transcribed—copy, which was actually only the second draft of the book (*SLL*, 171), was sent to his New York agents on 7 December 1938, roughly six months after Steinbeck had started. (An announcement about the novel had appeared in *Publishers Weekly* on 31 December 1938.) Elizabeth Otis visited Los Gatos in late December to smooth out some of Steinbeck's rough language, such as the dozen or so instances of "fuck," "shit," "screw," and "fat ass" that were the chief offenders. They reached a workable compromise: Steinbeck agreed to change only those words "which Carol and Elizabeth said stopped the reader's mind," otherwise "those readers who are insulted by normal events or language mean nothing to me," he told Covici on 3 January 1939 (*SLL*, 175). The novel's enthusiastic reception at Viking was partly spoiled by the wrangling that ensued over the controversial Rose of Sharon ending, which the firm wanted Steinbeck to change, not only to make it more "integral" to the plot, but also because it seemed larcenously close to de Maupassant's tale, "Iddyle" (1884). On 16 January 1939, Steinbeck fired back:

> I am sorry but I cannot change that ending. . . . The giving of the breast has no more sentiment than the giving of a piece of bread. I'm sorry if that doesn't get over. It will maybe. I've been on this design and balance for a long time and I think I know how I want it. And if I'm wrong, I'm alone in my wrongness. As for the Maupassant story, I've never read it but I can't see that it makes much difference. There are no new stories and I wouldn't like them if there were. The incident of the earth mother feeding by the breast is older than literature. You know that I have never been touchy about changes, but I have too many thousands of hours on this book, every incident has been too carefully chosen and its weight judged and fitted. The balance is there. (*SLL*, 178)

The entire postwriting flurry, including answering the persistent marginal queries on the typescript posed by a copy editor (whose initials were DZ) and later proofreading the galleys and fending off Viking's requests for public appearances, struck the novelist, by then suffering from sciatica and tonsillitis, as anticlimactic: "Do you really think we've lost a single reader by refusing to do the usual things? By not speaking at luncheons do you think I've lost sales? I don't. And if it were true I'd rather lose that kind of readers" (*SLL*, 181).

While Steinbeck had lost interest, plenty of other people had not, however. *The Grapes of Wrath* was widely and favorably reviewed and its fidelity to fact, its level and degree of social realism, discussed and debated in the popular press when it was first published. It has been praised by the left as a triumph of proletarian writing, nominated by critics and reviewers alike as "The Great American Novel," given historical vindication by Eleanor Roosevelt and by Senator Robert M. La Follette's inquiries into California's tyrannical farm labor conditions, and validated by Carey McWilliams, whose own great work, *Factories in the Fields*, is the classic contemporary sociological counterpart to Steinbeck's novel. But *The Grapes of Wrath* also has been attacked by elitist scholars as sentimental, unconvincing, and inartistic, banned repeatedly by school boards and libraries for its rebellious theme and frank language, and denounced by right-wing ministers, corporate farmers, and politicians as Communist-inspired, immoral, degrading, warped, and untruthful. The Associated Farmers mounted a smear campaign to discredit the book and its author, who often felt his life was in danger (*SLL*, 187). Rebuttals, designed to whitewash the Okie situation, such as *Of Human Kindness*, written by Steinbeck's Los Gatos neighbor, Ruth Comfort Mitchell, had no lasting impact whatsoever.[37]

Since then, in spite of Steinbeck's warning that its "structure is very carefully worked out. . . . Just read it, don't count it," *The Grapes of Wrath* has been steadily scrutinized, studied, interrogated, dissected, and analyzed by literary critics, scholars, historians, and creative writers.[38] It is no exaggeration to say that, during the past half century, few American novels have attracted such passionate attacks and equally passionate defenses. It seems hard to believe that critics read the same novel. Philip Rahv's complaint in the *Partisan Review* (Spring 1939) that "the novel is far too didactic and long-winded" and "fails on the test of craftsmanship" should be weighed against Charles Angoff's assessment in the *North American Review* (Summer 1939) that it is "momentous, monumental, and memorable" and an example of "the highest art." This dialectic still characterizes the novel's critical reception. In a 1989 speech, critic Leslie Fiedler attacked the novel as "maudlin, sentimental, and overblown"; a month later, in a review of the fiftieth anniversary edition, novelist William Kennedy praised it for standing "tall . . . a mighty, mighty book."[39]

If the past fifty-six years have witnessed precious little consensus about the exact nature of the novel's achievement ("We have been slow to read this novel well," Robert Con Davis claims), at least contemporary analysts are inclined to treat the book as a legitimate work of fiction, to be approached from a variety of the usual practical and aesthetic angles and also increasingly from theoretical angles rather than as a reductive propagandistic tract. No matter which lens *Grapes* is viewed through, however, the book's textual and narratological richness, its many strands of representation, discourse, action, language, and characterization (as well as its intertextual relatedness with *Working Days*) continues to repay enormous dividends—in John Ditsky's words "the Joads are still in motion, and their vehicle with them." Certain academic theories to the contrary, reading remains a subjective act, and perhaps the only sure thing about *The Grapes of Wrath* is its capacity to elicit powerful audience responses. Even Harold Bloom, never known to be a fan of Steinbeck's writings, concedes that "there are no canonical standards worthy of human respect that could exclude *The Grapes of Wrath* from a serious reader's esteem. . . . wisdom compels one to be grateful for the novel's continued existence."[40] Such of course was Steinbeck's hope throughout: "Almost prayerful that this book is some good," he confided (*WD*, 88).

As a result of shifting political emphases, the enlightened recommendations of the La Follette Committee (that the National Labor Relations Act include farm workers), the effects of loosened labor laws (California's discriminatory "anti-migrant" law, established in 1901, was struck down by the Supreme Court in 1941 in a decision which *The Grapes of Wrath* helped create), the creation of compulsory military service, and the inevitable recruitment of migrant families into defense plant and shipyard jobs caused by the booming economy of World War II that signaled the beginning of their successful assimilation (California growers soon complained of an acute shortage of seasonal labor), the particular set of epochal conditions that crystallized Steinbeck's awareness in the first place passed from his view.[41] Like other momentous American novels that embody the bitter, often tragic, transition from one way of life to another, *The Grapes of Wrath* possessed, among its other attributes, a certain indisputable timeliness. That sense of timing situates *The Grapes of*

Wrath among a variety of remarkably memorable and innovative works which arose from the same historical nexus and were published at roughly the same time: in fiction, John Dos Passos's *U.S.A.* trilogy (1937) and Richard Wright's *Native Son* (1940); in documentary photos with texts, Dorothea Lange and Paul Schuster Taylor's *An American Exodus: A Record of Human Erosion* (1939) and James Agee and Walker Evans's *Let Us Now Praise Famous Men* (1941); in personal history and sociology, Louis Adamic's *My America* (1938) and Carey McWilliams's *Factories in the Field* (1939). In concert with these and other texts that attempted to document, capture, or interpret "America" as a contested physical and metaphysical place, *The Grapes of Wrath*'s appearance helped change the literary and cultural geography of the United States.

It also changed Steinbeck permanently. Many "have speculated," Jackson Benson writes, "about what happened to change Steinbeck after *The Grapes of Wrath*. One answer is that what happened was the writing of the novel itself" (*TAJS*, 392). The effects of writing 260,000 words in a single year "finished" him, Steinbeck told Lawrence Clark Powell on 24 January 1939. After his long siege with the "Matter of the Migrants" ("I don't know whether there is anything left of me," he confided in October 1939), his "will to death" was so "strengthened" that by the end of the decade he was sick of writing fiction (*WD*, 106). It was a decision many critics and reviewers held against him for the rest of his life; they wanted him to write *The Grapes of Wrath* over and over again, which he refused to do, intent as he was on reclaiming his own life. "The process of writing a book is the process of outgrowing it," he told Herbert Sturz. "Disciplinary criticism comes too late. You aren't going to write that one again anyway. When you start another—the horizons have receded and you are just as cold and frightened as you were with the first one" ("Statement," 92).

The unabated sales, the frenzied public clamor, and the vicious personal attacks on Steinbeck over *The Grapes of Wrath* confirmed his worst fears about the fruits of success. "A writer, anyway, is just one step above a buffoon—an entertainer," he revealed in July 1939. "If the public makes him think he is really somebody it destroys him. He pontificates and that's the end of him" (*CJS*, 20). All of the hullaballoo proved an uncanny prophecy he had penned several years earlier: "The *rewards* of work are so sickening to me that I do more with the greatest reluctance" (*TAJS*, 331). The pressures pushed the tensions between the Steinbecks to the breaking point, a situation exacerbated by his willful romance with Gwyn Conger, and his repeated absences in Hollywood and Mexico. Steinbeck did not quit writing as he had once threatened, but by the early 1940s, "finishing off a complete revolution" and having "worked the novel" as far as he could "take it" (*SLL*, 193-94), he was no longer content to be the man—or the writer—he had once been.

Steinbeck's change from phalanx spokesperson and social realist to fabulist and experimental metafictionist was not caused by a bankruptcy of talent, a change of venue, or a failure of honesty. Rather, it was the result of his arriving at the end of a consciously planned and committed design of work that included his labor trilogy—*In Dubious Battle, Of Mice and Men,* and *The Grapes of Wrath*—and the result of the backlash he experienced from the worst kind of "posterity"—an unprecedented and unanticipated success that caused a "nightmare" year of being vilified and lionized and an altogether repugnant "hysteria" (*SLL*, 187-89). "I have always wondered why no author has survived a best-seller," he told John Rice in a June 1939 interview. "Now I know. The publicity and fan-fare are just as bad as they would be for a boxer. One gets self-conscious and that's the end of one's writing" (*CJS*, 15). His new writing lacked the aggressive bite of his late 1930's fiction, but it had the virtue of being different and varied. After 1940 much of his important work centered on explorations of a new topic—the implications of individual choice for imaginative consciousness. A prophetic postmodernist, Steinbeck's deep subject in *Sea of Cortez* (1941), *Cannery Row* (1945), *East of Eden* (1952), *Sweet Thursday* (1954), *The Winter of Our Discontent* (1961), and *Journal of a Novel* (1969) was creativity itself, the phenomenological dance of the law of thought and the law of things, as other essays in *Steinbeck's Typewriter* attempt to show.

The Grapes of Wrath remains among the most wrenching fictional indictments of the myth of California as Promised Land and ruptures the prevalent American dream of westering. Ironically, as John Steinbeck composed this novel that tested a social group's capacity for survival in a hostile world, he was himself so thoroughly implicated in its creation that he became unraveled in the process. As a consequence, the particular angle of vision, the vital signature, the group dynamic, the moral indignation, that made his art exemplary and sought after in the first place by an enormous participatory audience could never be repeated with the same integrated force. Once his name became a "symbol," inseparably linked with the title of his most famous novel, once he became imprisoned in his own notoriety (*SLL*, 193), once he became convinced that the people destroy everything they admire (*CJS*, 18), Steinbeck could never quite fully escape the influence of his earlier life, but thankfully, it is tempting to say, neither can we. As native Kern Countian Gerald Haslam affirms, *Grapes* is still a novel that "stretches" the soul.[42] Wherever human beings dream of a dignified and free society in which they can harvest the fruits of their own labor, *The Grapes of Wrath*'s voices can still be heard. Every strong novel redefines our conception of the genre's dimensions, reorders our awareness of its possibilities. As a tale of dashed illusions, thwarted desires, unconscionable suffering, and betrayed promises—all strung on a gossamer thread of hope—*The Grapes of Wrath* not only added immeasurably to the Depression era's socially conscious art but, beyond that—for honesty, integrity, emotional urgency, sustained drama, and evocative power—has few peers in American fiction.

Notes

[1] Although Joseph Henry Jackson, in "Why Steinbeck Wrote *The Grapes of Wrath*," *Booklets for Bookmen*, no. 1 (New York: Limited Editions Club, 1940), 3, was among the first commentators to suggest the novel issued from Steinbeck's profound shock and "hurt," the view of Steinbeck as a wounded writer, a haunted writer, an emotionally hooked writer, has never been commonplace. His experience with the migrants at Visalia, discussed in greater depth below, suggests otherwise and opens the door, however slightly, to future reconsiderations of his generative authority. Moreover, *Working Days* may be seen as a mirror testimony to his emotional commitment, which is almost fetishistic in its insistence on rehearsing problems of enactment and signification. But while Steinbeck's journal reinforces the affective level of the novel, it also disrupts the novel's autonomy by allowing us to see behind the veil of its making.

[2] Stephen Railton, "Pilgrim's Politics: Steinbeck's Art of Conversion," in *New Essays on "The Grapes of Wrath,"* ed. David Wyatt (New York: Cambridge University Press, 1990), 32. Although he arrives at a different destination with a different set of coordinates, it is worth considering Nicholas Visser, who writes in "Audience and Closure in *The Grapes of Wrath*," *Studies in American Fiction* 22 (Spring 1994): 22, "Much of the novel's effect derives from giving the impression that it is engaged in revealing the hitherto unknown to

an audience socially and culturally distant from the novel's characters."

[3] "Steinbeck's Suggestions for an Interview with Joseph Henry Jackson," in *"The Grapes of Wrath": Text and Criticism*, ed. Peter Lisca (New York: Viking Press, 1972), 860 (hereafter cited as "Interview"). Steinbeck prepared this self-created set of questions and answers in early 1939 for Jackson's radio show, just prior to publication of *The Grapes of Wrath*. Steinbeck did not appear on the broadcast, though Jackson read the questions and answers for him.

[4] After three years of research and investigation, in June 1933, Steinbeck began writing enthusiastic letters to George Albee and Carlton Sheffield about his communal, group organism "theme," his theory of "larger units, which I have called phalanx" (*SLL*, 74-82). As with so much of the correspondence in *Steinbeck: A Life in Letters*, the letters to Albee and Sheffield are injudiciously edited. In his extremely revealing mid-1933 letter to Albee (printed in edited form in *SLL*, 79-82), this is one of several statements excised from the text: "this theory is religion and emotion and poetry and these three are bound to be true." (The original is among the George S. Albee Papers at the Bancroft Library, University of California, Berkeley.) After a couple of more years of research, Steinbeck attempted to codify his investigations on mass movements and group psychology and behavior in a two-page typed document called "Argument of Phalanx," written ca. 1935, and also to be found among the Albee Papers at Berkeley. "Argument of Phalanx" has never been published in its entirety, though sections of it appeared for the first time in Richard Astro's *John Steinbeck and Edward F. Ricketts: The Shaping of a Novelist* (Minneapolis: University of Minnesota Press, 1973), 64-65. See also Benson (*TAJS*, 268-69) and DeMott (*SR*, 130-31) for additional information, including news of another early fictional phalanx attempt by Steinbeck called "Case Study." The clearest fictional treatment of phalanx is in Steinbeck's *In Dubious Battle* (1936), where it is more discursive and insistent than in *The Grapes of Wrath*. By the time Steinbeck wrote the latter, more of the "religion and emotion and poetry" got into the mix, which is of course the point: dispassionate nonteleology hindered the creation of an affective dimension. In addition, *Grapes* shows the influence of Steinbeck's increased attention to the dynamic free play of reading and audience response. His belief in participation (a precursor to contemporary reader-response theory), which was itself a refinement to his phalanx ideas, became increasingly important as his career went on and balanced the earlier emphasis on constitutive aspects of the group's will to expression. In another unpublished document (this one housed at the Harry Ransom Humanities Research Center, Austin, TX), a self-created "Introduction by Pascal Covici" written in September 1942 (though not used to preface the first *Viking Portable Steinbeck* for which it was apparently intended), Steinbeck focused on the participatory effects of reading, for example in this opening paragraph, which may be read back as a gloss for his position in *The Grapes of Wrath*: "There are some books, some stories, some poems which one reads over and over again without knowing why one is drawn to them. And such stories need not have been critically appreciated—in fact many of them have not been. The critic's approach is and perhaps should be one of appraisal and evaluation. The reader if he likes a story feels largely a participation. The stories we go back to are those in which we have taken part. A man need not have a likeness of exact experience to love a story but he must have in him an emotional or intellectual tone which has

keyed into the story and made him part of it. No one has ever read *Treasure Island* or *Robinson Crusoe* objectively. The chief character in both cases are merely the skin and bones of the reader. The poetical satires of Gulliver have long been forgotten but the stories go on. The message or the teaching of a story almost invariably dies first while the participation persists. Perhaps the best balance of message and participation in all literature is the story of Jesus—for there step by step the mind is opened by association with the man and his suffering to the things he said." For additional insight, consult Louis Owens, "Participation and Education: the Narrative Structure," chap. 5 in *"The Grapes of Wrath": Trouble in the Promised Land* (Boston: Twayne Publishers, 1990), 28, who states: "It is this participation in the lives of the Joads that will capture the reader and carry him through the experience of a long novel, and it is only through this participation that the full emotional impact Steinbeck desired can be achieved."

[5] John Steinbeck, *The Grapes of Wrath* (New York: Penguin Books, 1992), 444 (hereafter cited as *GOW*). Parenthetical page numbers refer to Penguin's Twentieth-Century Classics series edition of *The Grapes of Wrath*, the text and pagination of which is identical to the first edition (New York: Viking Press, 1939). Like the previous chapter on *To a God Unknown*, this chapter of *Steinbeck's Typewriter* is an amplified and updated version of an Introduction I published with the 1992 Penguin edition and elsewhere.

[6] Marilyn Chandler, in "The Metaphysics of Style," which appeared in *"The Grapes of Wrath," A Special Issue*, ed. Susan Shillinglaw, *San Jose Studies* 16 (Winter 1990): 45, writes that "even the enterprise of storytelling becomes not a simple transmission of lore, but a complex act . . . like a complicated dance step, to interest us in action and words themselves and in the collective patterns of individual destinies about which there can be no universal and resounding conclusion." Regarding the province of discourse and speech and writing acts, see also Michael G. Barry, "Degrees of Mediation and Their Political Value in Steinbeck's *Grapes of Wrath*," in *The Steinbeck Question: New Essays in Criticism*, ed. Donald R. Noble (Troy, NY: Whitston Publishing, 1993), 108-24, for an illuminating assessment on a relatively neglected topic—the role of language and representation. Barry concludes that Steinbeck's "attitudes toward language . . . are part of a larger project, an admirable project, and one that rewards careful reading."

[7] Peter Lisca was one of the first commentators to treat *Grapes* seriously as a multiform fiction. His ground-breaking essay, "*The Grapes of Wrath* as Fiction," appeared in *PMLA* 72 (March 1957): 296-309. It is reprinted in the Viking Critical Edition of *"The Grapes of Wrath": Text and Criticism*, 729-47. (also to be included in the revised second edition by Lisca and Kevin Hearle forthcoming from Penguin in 1996). The essay formed the basis for his *"The Grapes of Wrath,"* chap. 9 of *The Wide World of John Steinbeck* (New Brunswick, NJ: Rutgers University Press, 1958), 144-77.

[8] In 1982 the *New York Times* claimed *Grapes* was the second-best-selling paperback novel in America. I arrived at the 15 million-plus figure this way: according to sales information provided in a March 1985 letter to me from William Strachan, a former senior editor at Viking Penguin, *Grapes* had sold over 14 million copies at that time; meantime, the novelist's widow, Elaine Steinbeck, informed me recently that during the past decade *Grapes* sold ap-

proximately 100,000 paperback copies each year. The novel's spectacular sales seem to have made it a particularly inviting target for critics, ever-vigilant to show Steinbeck as a fraud by exposing his weaknesses in execution or methodology. See especially Floyd C. Watkins, "Flat Wine from *The Grapes of Wrath,*" in *In Time and Place: Some Origins of American Fiction* (Athens: University of Georgia Press, 1977), 19-29, who, in the manner of Twain's attack on Cooper (but lacking the comic edge) castigates Steinbeck for writing about "Okies, a people he did not know." Watkins's unrelenting critique of the text's body, while instructive in regard to some factual particulars and misprisions, misses its spirit completely.

[9] Warren French, *John Steinbeck's Fiction Revisited* (New York: Twayne Publishers, 1994), 75. French first coined this much-quoted phrase over three decades ago in the first edition of *John Steinbeck* (New York: Twayne Publishers, 1961), 95. Feminist critic Mimi Reisel Gladstein illuminates the novel's "continuing and universal appeal" by striking a moving personal note in her essay, "*The Grapes of Wrath*: Steinbeck and the Eternal Immigrant," in *John Steinbeck: The Years of Greatness, 1936-1939,* ed. Tetsumaro Hayashi (Tuscaloosa: University of Alabama Press, 1993), 132-44. For a handy list of foreign language translations consult Robert B. Harmon, *"The Grapes of Wrath": A Fifty Year Bibliographic Survey* (San Jose, CA: Steinbeck Research Center/San Jose State University, 1989), 15-32.

[10] Contrary to popular belief, Steinbeck was never a Marxist or a member of the Communist party. According to his most thorough biographer, Steinbeck—essentially a New Deal Democrat—was not interested in imported doctrinaire political theories at this point of his career. See Jackson J. Benson, "The Background to the Composition of *The Grapes of Wrath,*" in *Critical Essays on Steinbeck's "The Grapes of Wrath,"* ed. John Ditsky (Boston: G.K. Hall, 1989), 52-53. Until Susan Shillinglaw completes her biography of Carol Steinbeck, Benson's *The True Adventures of John Steinbeck* is the most complete view of her life available. See also Jay Parini, *John Steinbeck: A Biography* (New York: Henry Holt, 1995), especially 187-88, 197-98, and 213 for some differences and antagonisms between Carol and John during this period.

[11] Pare Lorentz, interview by author, 27 December 1988, Armonk, NY. See also Pare Lorentz, *FDR's Moviemaker: Memoirs and Scripts* (Reno: University of Nevada Press, 1992), 121. Joseph Henry Jackson, "The Finest Book John Steinbeck Has Written," *New York Herald Tribune Books,* 16 April 1939, 3, was first to claim the impact of Lorentz's work, particularly "the effect of the sound track in . . . *The River* . . . stays with you, beats rhythmically in your mind long after you have put the book down." See also "Why Steinbeck Wrote *The Grapes of Wrath,*" 10-11. (Jackson's essay also was used as the introduction to the luxurious Limited Editions Club edition of *The Grapes of Wrath* illustrated by Thomas Hart Benton in 1940.) Steinbeck told Jackson in May 1939 that the influence of Lorentz was "strong" in chapter 12 of *The Grapes of Wrath*—"the chapter of the route where the towns are named" (*SR,* 142).

[12] In 1954 the manuscript was sold to Clifton Waller Barrett through book dealer John Howell of San Francisco. The manuscript is item 6239 in the John Steinbeck Collection, Clifton Waller Barrett Library, Manuscripts Division, Special Collections Department, University of Virginia Library, Charlottesville. The typescript was presented to the Library of Congress by lawyer

and book collector Frank J. Hogan in 1941. The typescript is item MMC-1713, Box 1, in the Manuscripts Division, Library of Congress, Washington, DC.

[13] John Steinbeck, in his foreword to *Bringing in the Sheaves*, by Windsor Drake [Thomas Collins], in Jackson J. Benson, "'To Tom Who Lived It': John Steinbeck and the Man from Weedpatch," *Journal of Modern Literature* 5 (April 1976): 211 (hereafter cited as *Sheaves*), recalled: "The first time I saw Windsor Drake it was evening, and it was raining. I drove into the migrant camp, the wheels of my car throwing muddy water. The lines of sodden, dripping tents stretched away from me in the darkness. Just standing under a roof, and sitting at a littered table was Windsor Drake, a little man in a damp, frayed white suit. The crowding people looked at him all the time. . . . He had a small moustache, his graying, black hair stood up on his head like the quills of a frightened porcupine, and his large, dark eyes, tired beyond sleepiness, the kind of tired that won't let you sleep even if you have the time and a bed." (Benson's indispensable article contains several photographs of Collins taken by Dorothea Lange at Arvin in 1936.) Unlike the portrait of Collins/Drake/Rawley, the equation between other historical human beings and fictional characters is blurred and conjectural. As nearly as can be determined, most of the major characters that came eventually to populate *The Grapes of Wrath* were probably composite creations of historical antecedents. See Benson, "Background to the Composition," 52-53, and *TAJS*, 341-42. It is, however, possible that Steinbeck got the Joad name directly from the British philosopher C.E.M. Joad, author of the 1936 treatise *Guide to Philosophy* (*SR*, 61), a book once owned by Ed Ricketts and part of his library at Pacific Biological Laboratories. Steinbeck's novel, chapter 14 especially, echoes Cyril Joad's creative progressivism.

[14] Anne Loftis, "Steinbeck and the Federal Migrant Camps," *San Jose Studies* 16 (Winter 1990): 80. Loftis's essay, which draws on Benson's "'To Tom Who Lived It'" but adds much new information, is a pertinent account of the California federal camp program and offers a balanced view of the program's strengths and drawbacks.

[15] Initially, after having drawn on Collins's weekly reports in his nonfictional "The Harvest Gypsies," Steinbeck was so impressed with their substance that he offered to help prepare them for publication by acting—in his words—as an "editor" or "synchronizer" (*TAJS*, 348). Steinbeck presented some of Collins's material to Pascal Covici, whose publishing firm, Covici-Friede, was a socially conscious house. Covici, however, found the camp reports too "sectional" for wide commercial interest and turned them down, though at Steinbeck's insistence, his agents, McIntosh and Otis, kept circulating Collins's documents to one or more other publishers, though again, by the end of 1937 nothing came of it (*WD*, lii-liii). Had the Collins/Steinbeck collaboration succeeded, one can only speculate that *The Grapes of Wrath* might have been a far different book, for Steinbeck might not have wanted to incorporate material in his novel that had already been published in extended form elsewhere. After 1937, his renewed attraction to and dependence on Collins's sociological documents were due both to their intrinsic excellence and to their underground status.

[16] Benson, "'To Tom Who Lived It,'" 184. For a completely different agenda on Steinbeck's involvement with the migrants and for an intriguing but

often extreme and biased comparison of Dorothea Lange's process of photographing them (positive and above-board) with Steinbeck's process of fictionalizing them in *The Grapes of Wrath* (negative and underhanded), see Carol Schloss, in *In Visible Light: Photography and the American Writer: 1840-1940* (New York: Oxford University Press, 1987), 228, who concludes, rather cavalierly, that: "For whatever personal reason, when writing Steinbeck needed to obliterate his ego, to become the 'not me.' He wanted to stand in the dark, behind the headlights, and look around. . . . For his search violated everything that his adversaries in the central California valleys had violated by their vigilante activities. . . . By entering and looking, he turned the experiences of the unwitting poor into private capital; by his stealth, he robbed them of the self-presentation that allows people to encounter each other as equals, and by taking, he destroyed their gifts." A more positive, historically informed view of *The Grapes of Wrath*'s relatedness to its political and artistic times is available in the fourth volume of Kevin Starr's study, *Americans and the California Dream*. See *Endangered Dreams: The Great Depression in California* (New York: Oxford University Press, 1996), especially chap. 9, "Documenting the Crisis: *Annus Mirabilis* 1939," 246-271.

[17] *The Harvest Gypsies: On the Road to "the [sic] Grapes of Wrath,"* ed. Charles Wollenberg (Berkeley, CA: Heyday Books, 1988), 19. According to Tom Collins, in a weekly report ending 10 October 1936, residents of the Arvin Sanitary Camp responded positively to Steinbeck's articles but were dismayed by the editorial title. Steinbeck apologized in a letter printed in the 20 October 1936 edition of *San Francisco News*, in which he claimed that the "title was used ironically, since it is ironical that a huge group of workers should, through the injustice and bad planning of our agricultural system, be forced into a gypsy life. Certainly I had no intention of insulting a people who are insulted beyond endurance." Collins's "Camp Manager's Weekly Report: Arvin Migratory Labor Camp" and similar documents are housed at the San Francisco branch of the National Archives in San Bruno, CA; photocopies are available at the Steinbeck Research Center, San Jose State University. See also Benson, "'To Tom Who Lived It,'" 180-81; and Loftis, "Steinbeck and the Federal Migrant Camps," 82, 89.

[18] The text of *Their Blood Is Strong*, which includes an additional entry, "Epilogue: Spring 1938," is reprinted in Warren French's *A Companion to "The Grapes of Wrath"* (New York: Viking Press, 1963), 53-92.

[19] Dorothy Steel, "Oklahomans' Topic of Steinbeck," *Los Gatos Mail-News*, 4 November 1937, p. 1. Susan Shillinglaw, "Local Newspapers Report on 'The Oklahomans,'" *Steinbeck Newsletter* 2 (Fall 1988): 4, notes an "unconvincing" tone and sanitized political view (emphasizing the migrants' upward social mobility) that emerges in this interview and in the next one with Louis Walther. She wonders if Steinbeck wasn't making a "bid for hometown favor at a time when he feared reprisal from the Associated Farmers and law enforcement officers." To make things more confusing—or interesting—Joseph Henry Jackson, "John Steinbeck, A Portrait" *Saturday Review of Literature*, 25 September 1937, 18, claimed Steinbeck was working on "three related longer novels" during 1937.

[20] After Visalia, Steinbeck pulled back from Bristol, preferring instead to throw his efforts into his own fictional version, which he was beginning to

conceive in tragic terms and which he knew would require his undivided attention. This led to hard feelings on the photographer's part, who, out of a self-confessed naivety, seems not to have understood Steinbeck's prior involvement with the migrants and the fact that Steinbeck had been searching all along for a fitting way to write about the experience (not an untoward plan for a man who by that time had published six novels). Furthermore, Bristol also undervalued the symbolic—almost allegorical—dimension Visalia came to have for Steinbeck, especially regarding the flood conditions and Bristol's photograph of the madonna-like young woman breast feeding her infant, the original of which Steinbeck transformed so memorably in the final episode of *Grapes*, but which he also problematized in ways Bristol, who accused him of "sensationalizing" that moment, could not understand or accept (*WD*, lv-lvi). Bristol's Visalia photographs, with some captions from *The Grapes of Wrath*, turned up in *Life*, 5 June 1939, 66-67, and again in *Life*, 19 February 1940, 10-11, in order to prove the authenticity of John Ford's cinematic version of the novel. See also Horace Bristol's "Documenting *The Grapes of Wrath*," *The Californians*, January/February 1988, 40-47, which includes his striking portrait of the breast-feeding woman. The shape of Bristol's career is displayed in an exhibition catalog, *Stories from Life: The Photography of Horace Bristol* (Athens: University of Georgia Museum of Art, 1995). For a different, more suspect, view of Steinbeck's motives (guilt, not compassion) concerning Bristol and the meaning of the Visalia experience and for a discussion of Steinbeck's affinities with photography and journalism, see William Howarth, "The Mother of Literature: Journalism and *The Grapes of Wrath*," in Wyatt's *New Essays on "The Grapes of Wrath,"* 71-99.

21 John Steinbeck, letter in *Writers Take Sides: Letters about the War in Spain from 418 American Authors* (New York: League of American Writers, 1938), 57. The Salinas lettuce strike extended from 4 September to 3 November 1936 and was especially violent. (It is still considered the Salinas Valley's worst agriculture strike.) Less certain is whether Steinbeck actually went to Salinas to investigate events for himself or whether he viewed the battle from a distance, either from Los Gatos, or from the site(s) of his field research. The strike was a nationally covered event, so plenty of information was available in newspapers (none note Steinbeck's presence), especially the *San Francisco Chronicle*, which Steinbeck undoubtedly followed. Brad Leithauser, in his introduction to *The Grapes of Wrath* (London: Everyman's Library, 1993), xii, picks up this thread of anger and outrage when he speaks of the relevance of Steinbeck's "rage" to the novel's effectiveness.

22 The full text of Steinbeck's letter is printed in Lewis Gannett's introduction to the revised edition of *The Portable Steinbeck* (New York: Viking Press, 1946), xxi-xxiii.

23 ["The Grapes of Wrath"], autograph manuscript, 1938, 1. Pagination refers to Steinbeck's handwritten numerals at the top right or top lefthand side of each page, not to the numbers printed on each ledger page. To be precise, Steinbeck's first words on the paper were "New Start" superposed over "Big Writing." This referred to his new start after "L'Affaire" and the fact that Carol made him promise to write in larger and more legible script to make her typing job easier. By writing in larger script, however, he felt he might be in danger of sacrificing compression and emotional intensity.

[24] Making his book lively required that Steinbeck utilize his sources emphatically. He returned frequently for inspiration and material to Collins's reports. For instance, in a section called "Bits of Migrant Wisdom," noted in "Kern Migratory Labor Camp Report for week ending 2 May 1936," Collins records a heated discussion with two women about how best to cut down on the extravagant use of toilet paper. Steinbeck saw the humor in the account of "the great toilet paper scandal" (*WD*, 71) and employed some of the original material on 13 September for chapter 22 of *Grapes*, "'Hardly put a roll out 'fore it's gone. . . . One lady says we oughta have a little bell that rings ever' time the roll turns oncet. Then we could count how many ever'body takes'" (431). See Benson, "'To Tom Who Lives it,'" 174-79, 187-90, for more examples of the kind of detailed material and observations Collins incorporated in his reports. Martha Heasley Cox, "Fact into Fiction in *The Grapes of Wrath*: The Weedpatch and Arvin Camps," in *John Steinbeck: East and West*, eds. Tetsumaro Hayashi, Yasuo Hashiguchi, and Richard F. Peterson, Steinbeck Monograph Series, no. 8 (Muncie, IN: John Steinbeck Society of America/Ball State University, 1978), 18-19, offers some parallels not developed in Benson.

[25] *Think Back on Us . . . A Contemporary Chronicle of the 1930's*, ed. Henry Dan Piper (Carbondale: Southern Illinois University Press, 1967), 350. In the same vein, Peter Lisca, *The Wide World of John Steinbeck*, 164, says, "No other American novel has succeeded in forging and making instrumental so many prose styles." In their pioneering Bakhtinian study, "Dialogic Structure and Levels of Discourse in Steinbeck's *The Grapes of Wrath*," *Arizona Quarterly* 45 (Winter 1989): 77, Louis Owens and Hector Torres assert that "Steinbeck shows no interest in substituting one 'monologic' voice for another. Instead . . . he creates a text in which no single voice speaks with final authority: the endings of neither the Joad chapters, nor the interchapters, nor the novel as a whole can be taken as final narrative closures. Rather, these endings foreground Steinbeck's complex view of the subject and subjects of his novel and the complex levels of discourse contained within it."

[26] Steinbeck's autograph manuscript and his published novel both have thirty chapters in exactly the same sequence, though the former begins with an alternating system of roman and cardinal numerals (to indicate general and narrative chapters respectively), then shifts to cardinal numbers at manuscript page 29. Uniform numbering of chapters 1-30 first took place on the typescript and may have been Carol's suggestion. That which became chapter 20 in the typescript and in the published novel was originally chapter 8 of book 2 of the autograph manuscript. Roy S. Simmonds, "The Original Manuscript," *San Jose Studies* 16 (Winter 1990): 131-32, brings some order to Steinbeck's "chaotic" numbering by providing a handy appendix that compares the text of the manuscript with Viking's first edition.

[27] Moore, working on *The Novels of John Steinbeck: A First Critical Study* (Chicago: Normandie House, 1939), had written Steinbeck for "information for a critique of some kind" (*WD*, 38).

[28] Letter, 10 February 1953, [1]. Herbert Sturz kindly provided me with a photocopy of Steinbeck's autograph original before donating it to the Rare Book Room of the B. Davis Schwartz Library of Long Island University at Greenvale, New York. The letter was published in the *New York Times* on 6 August 1990 and again in Phyllis T. Dircks, "Steinbeck's Statement on the Inner

Chapters of *The Grapes of Wrath,*" *Steinbeck Quarterly* 24 (Summer-Fall 1991): 91-92 (hereafter cited as "Statement").

[29] Quoted in my essay, "'Working Days and Hours': Steinbeck's Writing of *The Grapes of Wrath,*" *Studies in American Fiction* 18 (Spring 1990): 14. In early 1939, Steinbeck claimed "Edgar Varese the modern composer wants to do—'a work of great scope'—based on one of my books. I wrote him that I thought *Grapes* might be a theme for a symphony. . . . He is the first person who has recognized that I used the mathematics of musical composition in writing" (*LTE*, 11). *The Grapes of Wrath*'s affinities with documentary photography and its iconic dimensions have attracted numerous commentators, but the novel's equally significant musical influences remain relatively unexplored. The beginning place for further investigation is with John Ditsky, "The Late John Steinbeck: Dissonance in the Post-*Grapes* Era," *San Jose Studies* 18 (Winter 1992): 20-32.

[30] Louis Owens, *"The Grapes of Wrath": Trouble in the Promised Land,* 45. Scholarship on Steinbeck's use of the Bible in *The Grapes of Wrath* is understandably extensive. Six of the most prominent and frequently cited essays from the 1950s and 1960s—by Martin Schockley, Eric W. Carlson, George De Schweinitz, H. Kelly Crockett, Charles Dougherty, and Gerald Cannon—are handily gathered in *A Casebook on "The Grapes of Wrath,"* ed. Agnes McNeill Donohue (New York: Thomas Y. Crowell, 1968), 90-122. For a convenient review, consult John H. Timmerman, "John Steinbeck's Use of the Bible: A Descriptive Bibliography of the Critical Tradition," *Steinbeck Quarterly* 21 (Winter-Spring 1988): 24-39. Tamara Rombold, "Biblical Inversion in *The Grapes of Wrath,*" *College Literature* 14 (Spring 1987): 146-66, skillfully negotiates Steinbeck's problematized text, which rejects "the agency of God and . . . traditional Christianity," yet "clearly uses the very Bible of the organized religion it rejects."

[31] Stephen Railton, "Pilgrim's Progress: Steinbeck's Art of Conversion," in Wyatt's *New Essays on "The Grapes of Wrath,"* 34. See also Warren French, in "From Naturalism to the Drama of Consciousness—The Education of the Heart in *The Grapes of Wrath,*" chap. 6 in the second edition of his *John Steinbeck* (Boston: G.K. Hall, 1975), 92, who writes that the novel enacts "the awakening of man's consciousness that coincides with the awakening of . . . conscience."

[32] "The Mother of Literature: Journalism and *The Grapes of Wrath,*" in Wyatt's *New Essays on "The Grapes of Wrath,"* 84.

[33] Part of Steinbeck's cryptic entry for 23 August 1938 reads: "Pare came over the weekend. Big time. Carol sprained her ankle q.t. Went down to the peninsula with Pare and spent the night at Chaplin's place. Talked all night" (*WD*, 59). Lorentz, *FDR's Moviemaker*, 117-19, recalls the excursion to Chaplin's house in more vivid style and provides details that indicate pressure from writing the novel made relations between the Steinbecks not just tense but bordering on callous.

[34] Martha Heasley Cox, "The Conclusion of *The Grapes of Wrath*: Steinbeck's Conception and Execution," *San Jose Studies* 1 (November 1975): 73-81, was the first to examine the novel's ending in light of Steinbeck's stated intentions in the as-yet-unpublished "Diary of a Book" (later titled *Working Days*). She also provides a review of the scholarly conversation on the ending

up to that point. Steinbeck's deft layering of biblical allusions in the final barn scene is demonstrated by J. Paul Hunter, "Steinbeck's Wine of Affirmation in *The Grapes of Wrath*," in Lisca's *"The Grapes of Wrath": Text and Criticism*, 813, who notes that in the "fusion" of Old Testament deluge, New Testament stable, and contemporary ritual, "the novel's mythic background, ideological progression, and modern setting are brought together; Mt. Ararat, Bethlehem, and California are collapsed into a single unit of time, and life is affirmed in a massive symbol of regeneration." See also Owens, *"The Grapes of Wrath": Trouble in the Promised Land*, 72-73, for a view of how "the biological, transcendental, and Christian threads of the novel come together" here.

35 In his introduction to *New Essays on "The Grapes of Wrath,"* 21, David Wyatt notes the conclusion's "open-ended way": Steinbeck's "subtle rhetoric generalizes the project into the problem of learning to live in existential time." Sylvia J. Cook arrives at a similar destination in "Steinbeck's Poor in Prosperity and Adversity," in *The Steinbeck Question*, 141, when she shows how Steinbeck's text keeps open "the enduring conflicts" rather than closing them off in pat resolution.

36 "The Original Manuscript," 129. In one instance Steinbeck inserted an unnumbered sheet between pages 87 and 88 of the manuscript. This contained three short bridge passages to explain Noah Joad's abandonment at the Colorado River (totalling approximately five hundred words). There is also a very ungainly passage of 159 words, originally intended to be part of chapter 21 of the novel, which one of the Steinbecks wisely cancelled when proofreading the typescript (the passage appears on page 110 of the autograph manuscript and, in its cancelled form, on page 462 of the typescript of *The Grapes of Wrath*):

> Once the Germans in their hordes came to the rich margin of Rome; and they came timidly, saying 'we have been driven, give us land.' And the Romans armed the frontier and built forts against the hordes of need/ .xxxxxxxxxxxxxxxxxxxxxxxxxxxxxxx And the legions patrolled the borders, cased in metal, armed with the best steel. And the barbarians came, naked, across the border, humbly, humbly. They received the swords in their breasts and marched on; and their dead bore down the swords and the barbarians marched on and took the land. And they were driven by their need, and they conquored [sic] with their need. In battle the women fought in the line, and the yellow-haired children lay in the grass with knives to hamstring the legionaries, to snick through the hamstrings of the horses. But the legions had no needs, no wills, no force. And the best trained, best armed troops in the world went down before the hordes of need.

Not in the manuscript or the typescript but in the galleys of the Viking Press text, a passage of 82 words was later added to chapter 26 and one of 228 words designed for effective pacing was added to chapter 30. Otherwise, the emendations are neither major nor substantive—often just changes in syntax, punctuation, paragraphing, spelling, and names (the family that shares the flooding boxcar with the Joads at novel's end were called the Hamills in manuscript, but Steinbeck changed that to the Wainwrights in Carol's typescript). Volume 2 of the Library of America's Steinbeck project (1996), features Gila Bercovitch's carefully corrected text of *Grapes* based on a collation of John's manuscript, Carol's typescript, and Viking's galley sheets.

[37] See Susan Shillinglaw, "California Answers *The Grapes of Wrath*," in *John Steinbeck: The Years of Greatness*, 145-64, for a detailed study of anti-*Grapes*/anti-Steinbeck efforts by the Associated Farmers, the California Citizens Association, and individual reactionary writers. Carey McWilliams, in "California Pastoral," *Antioch Review* 2 (March 1942), 103-21, further "verified the general picture of conditions in the state as set forth in *The Grapes of Wrath* and *Factories in the Field*." McWilliams's important article is reprinted in Donohue's *A Casebook on "The Grapes of Wrath,"* 332-51, and in Lisca's *"The Grapes of Wrath": Text and Criticism*, 657-79. See also Martin Shockley's indispensable study, "The Reception of *The Grapes of Wrath* in Oklahoma," *American Literature* 15 (January 1944): 351-61, which is conveniently reprinted in French's *A Companion to "The Grapes of Wrath,"* 117-29; Donohue's *A Casebook on "The Grapes of Wrath,"* 52-62; and Lisca's *"The Grapes of Wrath": Text and Criticism*, 680-91. Shockley's essay is a compendium of outraged and outrageous contemporary responses by all segments of Oklahoma's community of readers.

[38] Steinbeck's "A Letter on Criticism," first published in *The Colorado Quarterly* in 1955, is reprinted in *Steinbeck and His Critics: A Record of Twenty-Five Years*, eds. E. W. Tedlock and C. V. Wicker (Albuquerque: University of New Mexico Press, 1957), 53. To put the critical history of the novel in perspective, see John Ditsky, "Introduction," *Critical Essays on Steinbeck's "The Grapes of Wrath,"* 1-21, for the most exhaustive and reliable survey since Peter Lisca's "Editor's Introduction: The Pattern of Criticism," in *"The Grapes of Wrath": Text and Criticism* 695-707. Ditsky updated his overview in "*The Grapes of Wrath*, at 50: The Critical Perspective," *San Jose Studies* 16 (Winter 1990): 46-53. In addition to Lisca's and Ditsky's books, there are now seven other compilations of essays on *Grapes*, all with different introductory bearings: Warren French, ed., *A Companion to "The Grapes of Wrath"* (1963); Agnes McNeil Donohue., ed., *A Casebook on "The Grapes of Wrath"* (1968); Robert Con Davis, ed., *Twentieth Century Interpretations of "The Grapes of Wrath": A Collection of Critical Essays* (Englewood Cliffs, NJ: Prentice-Hall, 1982); Harold Bloom, ed., *John Steinbeck's "The Grapes of Wrath"* (New York: Chelsea House, 1988); Tetsumaro Hayashi, ed., *Steinbeck's "The Grapes of Wrath": Essays in Criticism*, Steinbeck Essay Series, no. 3 (Muncie, IN: John Steinbeck Research Institute/Ball State University, 1990); Susan Shillinglaw, ed., special issue of *San Jose Studies* (1990); and David Wyatt, ed., *New Essays on "The Grapes of Wrath"* (1990). Anthologies by Davis, Donohue, Lisca, and Ditsky all contain one or more original pieces among the standard reprints (several of the most durable essays appear in more than one book); contributions in Shillinglaw's and Wyatt's collections are original.

[39] The contemporary reviews by Rahv and Angoff are available in John Ditsky's *Critical Essays on Steinbeck's "The Grapes of Wrath,"* 30-31, 33-35. *John Steinbeck: The Contemporary Reviews*, eds. Joseph McElrath, Jesse Crissler, and Susan Shillinglaw, is forthcoming from Cambridge University

Press in 1996 and will contain a large section on *The Grapes of Wrath.* Otherwise see Ray Lewis White, "*The Grapes of Wrath* and the Critics of 1939," *Resources for American Literary Study* 13 (Autumn 1983): 134-63, for a compilation of 108 annotated contemporary reviews. Harmon, *Fifty Year Bibliographic Survey*, 37-152, lists 844 reviews and scholarly articles on *Grapes*. Leslie Fiedler's critique is in "Looking Back After 50 Years," *San Jose Studies* 16 (Winter 1990): 55; William Kennedy's laudatory assessment appears in "'My Work is No Good,'" *The New York Times Book Review*, 9 April 1989, 44-45.

[40] See Robert Con Davis, "Introduction," *Twentieth Century Interpretations of "The Grapes of Wrath,"* 11; John Ditsky, "Introduction," *Critical Essays on Steinbeck's "The Grapes of Wrath,"* 15; and Harold Bloom, "Introduction," *John Steinbeck's "The Grapes of Wrath,"* 5.

[41] Information in this paragraph is gleaned from Philip Brooks, "Notes on Rare Books," *New York Times Book Review*, 1 February 1942, 22; Walter J. Stein, *California and the Dust Bowl Migrants* (Westport: Greenwood Press, 1973), 279-81; James N. Gregory, *American Exodus: The Dust Bowl Migration and the Okie Culture in California* (New York: Oxford University Press, 1989), 172-73; Dan Morgan, *Rising in the West: The True Story of an "Okie" Family From the Great Depression Through the Reagan Years* (New York: Knopf, 1992); and from Dick Meister and Anne Loftis, *A Long Time Coming: The Struggle to Unionize America's Farm Workers* (New York: Macmillan, 1977), passim.

[42] *The Other California: The Great Central Valley in Life and Letters* (Santa Barbara, CA: Capra Press, 1990), 97. See also Michael Pearson, "A Strip Angled against the Pacific: Steinbeck's California," chap. 6 of his *Imagined Places: Journeys into Literary America* (Jackson: University Press of Mississippi, 1991): 240-50, who establishes through contemporary personal encounters with Mexican-American farm workers in the Salinas Valley the validity of Steinbeck's labor view in *The Grapes of Wrath.*

"One Book To A Man": Charting a Bibliographical Preface to *East of Eden*

"In order to arrive at this effect—do you follow me?—I invent the character of a novelist, whom I make my central figure; and the subject of the book, if you must have one, is just that very struggle between what reality offers him and what he himself desires to make of it."

—André Gide, *The Counterfeitors*
(Trans. Dorothy Bussy)

"Writing is a very silly business at best. . . . And the greatest foolishness . . . lies in the fact that to do it at all, the writer must believe that what he is doing is the most important thing in the world. And he must hold to this illusion even when he knows it is not true. If he does not, the work is not worth even what it might otherwise have been."

—John Steinbeck, *Journal of a Novel* (1969)

1

Although *The Grapes of Wrath* is almost universally acknowledged as John Steinbeck's masterpiece, he always considered *East of Eden* to be his "big" book, for which he felt all the others were merely "practice," as he told several of his friends and confidantes in the three years prior to its writing in 1951. His stake in the book was enormous for a number of reasons, not the least of them because it represented a dramatic change in his fictional method. "I've been practicing for a book for 35 years and this is it," he told John O'Hara in 1949. "I don't see how it can be popular because I am inventing method and form and tone and context. And of course I am scared of it. It's a cold lonely profession and this is the coldest and loneliest because this is all I can do, and when it is done I've either done it or I never had it to do" (*SLL*, 360).

In doing "it," Steinbeck abandoned the "modern fashionable method" (*JN*, 43), the reigning mode of critical realism, with its emphasis on verisimilitude, seamless unity, and exact resemblances. "I don't think the lovers of Hemingway will love this book" (*JN*, 29). Instead, in the manner of Fielding's *Tom Jones*, Melville's *Moby-Dick*, and Gide's *The Counterfeitors* (three works Steinbeck explicitly praised), he created an open, reflexive form that allowed for autobiographical intrusion and personal, editorial digressions. "There will be no plot in the true sense of the word," he told the *Salinas Californian* in 1948. "It will be entirely different from my previous work" (*CJS*, 50). The work of writing and the text itself became a locus of renewal for Steinbeck, a clean sweep of his stylized past, and a moment for reinvention and authorial self-fashioning: "I think perhaps it is the only book I have ever written. I think there is only one book to a man" (*JN*, 5). Such reimaginings meant drastic narratological changes, including the use of alternating, even disruptive, points of view. Judging from such recent novels as Toni Morrison's *The Bluest Eye* (1973) and Tobias Wolff's *The Barracks Thief* (1984), to name two powerful and critically acclaimed examples, our age is far more comfortable with technical maneuvers that mix first- and third-person perspectives.

But this is now and that was then: from the outset, Steinbeck feared critics might not agree with his new departure (when The Viking Press published *East of Eden* in September 1952, it was ninety thousand words shorter than his capacious original; to this day, few have read the initial draft, with its haunting salutariness, its continuous paternal addresses on reality and illusion to the novelist's young sons, Thom and John, and its intersubjective modality). In a humorous, self-deprecating response to a *Saturday Review* inquiry in the summer of 1952 (not published until 27 February 1954), Steinbeck predicted the reviews of *Eden* in "advance":

> *The New Yorker* . . . will never forgive me for not being Proust. God! If I could only write in French and have a bad translation I would get a good review there. Monastic *Time* will turn out the pin-striped monks who will intone, "IT IS A GOOD BOOK BUT IT FAILS." . . . *The Chicago Tribune* will have confused me with England to my benefit and the Hearst papers will spell my name Steinberg and review my latest volume of cartoons. And last—the intense young men with receding hairlines who are too smart to do a daily

> Piece—they will save (I think they call them interpretations) for a book. They will find me *passe*. (8)[1]

A few of Steinbeck's judgments proved true for that time and that place. In *The New Yorker*, high-toned Anthony West said, "Mr. Steinbeck has written a precise equivalent of those nineteenth-century melodramas in which the villains could always be recognized because they waxed their moustaches" (125). *Time*'s reviewer, true to form, claimed Steinbeck had "done some of his best writing in *East of Eden*. . . . But whether as a novel about pioneers in a new country or just as men and women working out their private, earthly fates, *East of Eden* is too blundering and ill-defined to make its story point" (110). For the Hearst chain, which Steinbeck long considered his enemy, Clark Kinnaird's thumbnail impression of *Eden*, syndicated in the "Parade of Books" section in the Sunday pictorial weekly magazine of such papers as the *Chicago Herald American* and the *Pittsburgh Sun Telegraph*, was typical: "While it is a major achievement for Steinbeck . . . and one with more popular appeal than any recent work of his, it suffers by comparison with Hemingway's latest [*The Old Man and the Sea*]." The Hearst papers were silent on one topic, however, because no one discovered that their recently deceased founder, William Randolph Hearst (1863-1951), was the subject of Steinbeck's scathing criticism in chapter 34 of *Eden* ("When this man died the nation rang with praise and, just beneath, with gladness that he was dead").

However sweet revenge was, sweeter yet must have been Steinbeck's considerate treatment at the hands of some contemporaries. For example, even the *Chicago Tribune* reviewer, Paul Engle, admired *Eden* "for the sweep and range of its conception and the variety of its human qualities" (3). On the front page of the *New York Herald Tribune Book Review*, Joseph Wood Krutch hailed the novel, prophesying that the "merits of so ambitious and absorbing a book are sure to be widely and hotly debated" (1). In *Saturday Review*, Harvey Curtis Webster began "Out of the new-born Sun," by stating that, while "*East of Eden* isn't a great novel according to the strict conventions of formal purity so widely accepted today . . . it will take almost equal quantities of pride and stupidity to deny that it is one of the best novels of the past ten years and the best book John Steinbeck has written since *The Grapes of Wrath*" (11). Webster's praise was reinforced by the magazine's cover illustration. An out-sized Steinbeck (shown from the neck up) appears foregrounded against rolling agricultural fields; as the writer gazes out under a furrowed brow, he seems to transcend the natural landscape from which he drew inspiration.

And yet despite these prominent hurrahs, Steinbeck's *Saturday Review* predictions can be regarded as fairly accurate gauges to the mixed critical and scholarly reaction during most of the past four decades. Indeed, *East of Eden* as a kind of "magnificent failure," or what Warren French in 1961 called a "patchwork leviathan" (152), is a persistent refrain in this critical literature. In fact, Steinbeck's huge novel proved so vexing to some of his contemporaries that one writer, Mark Schorer, who boldly praised *Eden* as Steinbeck's "best" novel in his *New York Times Book Review* front-page review, "A Dark and Violent Steinbeck Novel," later completely reversed his opinion and regretted ever having published the review at all. (Ironically, Schorer had written "Technique as Discovery," the groundbreaking essay on modern literary process in 1948.) In his 1952 review for *New Republic*, Arthur Mizener, taking a direct cue from Edmund Wilson's notoriously influential 1949 *New Republic* critique-turned book, *The Boys in the Back Room* (1941), claimed:

> There is evidence even in *East of Eden* of what is quite clear from Steinbeck's earlier work, that so long as he sticks to animals and children and to situations he can see and to some purpose from the point of view of his almost biological feeling for the continuity of life he can release his considerable talent and sensitivity which are naturally his. . . . Let us hope that some day he will go back to the Long Valley he really knows and maybe even find Jody Tifin [*sic*] there. (23)

Mizener, who seems not to have read the novel very carefully, would later denounce the propriety of Steinbeck's Nobel Prize award with a *New York Times* essay, "Does a Moral Vision of the Thirties Deserve a Nobel Prize?" Meantime, the "basic premise" of R. W. B. Lewis's "John Steinbeck: The Fitful Daemon" (1959) was the "badness of *East of Eden*," which he pronounced "a literary disaster" (123, 132). Here, too, is a significant irony—another example of giving with one hand while taking away with the other. In this essay, Lewis, famous for his earlier book, *The American Adam: Innocence, Tragedy, and Tradition in the Nineteenth Century* (1955), devalued Steinbeck's version

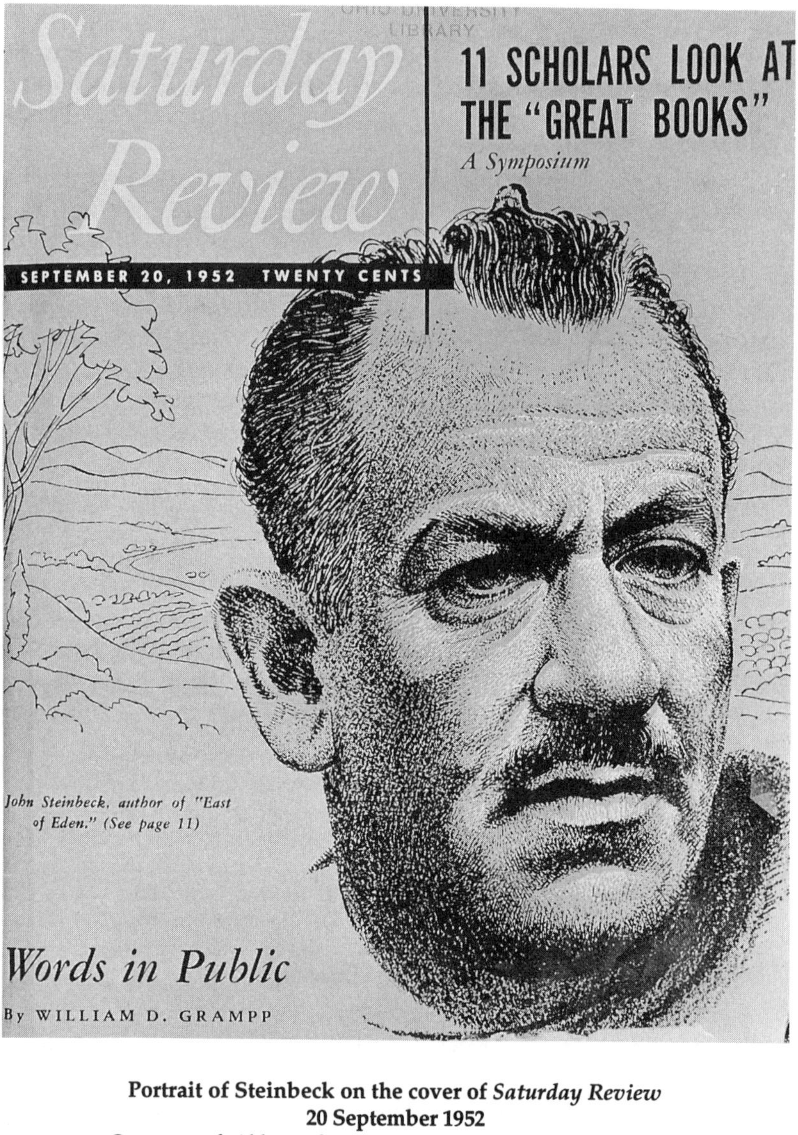

Portrait of Steinbeck on the cover of *Saturday Review*
20 September 1952
Courtesy of Alden Library, Ohio University, Athens. OH.

of the Adamic mythos in *Eden*. Lewis's comments about the "contemporary situation" of American fiction in the epilogue of *American Adam* (he mentions *The Great Gatsby*, "The Bear," *Invisible Man, The Catcher in the Rye,* and *The Adventures of Augie March* as examples of the Adamic tradition "in a comic or tragic perspective by . . . novelists who have escaped . . . the arrested development of innocence and the premature old age of an absorption with sin"), might have provided a natural framework for his later discussion of the fifty-year-old Steinbeck's *East of Eden*, but Lewis's 1959 essay signified no such continuity, and one is left wondering why and how the rules of the game always seem to change when Steinbeck comes up to bat. "Critics . . .," Steinbeck once told his editor, Pascal Covici, in 1949, "are building their own structures which have little reference to mine" (*TAJS*, 650).

Schorer's vacillation and Mizener's and Lewis's out-right disapproval seem in retrospect not only to sum up the reactions of privileged establishment critics in general but also to have exerted an authoritarian presence, for Roger Sale's "Stubborn Steinbeck," a 1980 *New York Review of Books* essay-review (on Thomas Kiernan's woeful biography, *The Intricate Music*, and Penguin reprints of *The Wayward Bus* and *Eden*) proved that entrenched attitudes among literary sophisticates (based more on personal taste than the critic admits) die slow deaths. "Though there is a place called Steinbeck country," Sale says, "though there are 'ideas' we can now call Steinbeck's themes, he seems a writer without a source of strength. For years he thought he had a subject, a big book about the Salinas valley that only he could write. But all that came out of this was *East of Eden*, a bloated, pretentious, and uncertain book" (10).

In his introduction to *John Steinbeck* in Chelsea House's Modern Critical Views series (1987), Harold Bloom claimed, with characteristic hubris, that *Eden* does not even "bear rereading" (1). Karen Hopkins's succinct reaction still speaks directly to the issue of mandarin condescension: "There is something disturbing about the criticism of . . . *East of Eden*" (63). Her point is similar to complaints made forcefully by biographer Jackson J. Benson in essay after essay, and book after book, in his attempt not to gloss over Steinbeck's faults as a writer ("When he was good, he was very, very good, and when he was bad, he was terrible," he states in a recent collection of essays) but to show how Steinbeck's work—and that of some other western American writers—has been skewed to such a degree by many disdainful eastern reviewers that even the virtues of the prose, the excellent sense of story, for instance, are no longer laudable, having been lost in charges of sentimentalism, and other endless critical qualifications, reversals, and caveats.[2]

2

Overall, then, Steinbeck has been especially susceptible to the politics of literary fashion and to the overt and covert agendas of book reviewers and critics. Yet I say above "most of the past four decades" because many recent commentaries on the novel, beginning with John Ditsky's influential revisionist monograph, *Essays on "East of Eden"* (1977), and continuing in selected instances through Hopkins's spirited defense (1978), Martha Cox's presentation of "Steinbeck's Family Portraits: The Hamiltons," in a special *Eden* issue of *Steinbeck Quarterly* (1981), John Timmerman's detailed "Harvest of the Earth: *East of Eden*," chapter 8 of his informative *John Steinbeck's Fiction* (1986), and Roy S. Simmonds's keynote address, "'And Still the Box Is Not Full': Steinbeck's *East of Eden*," delivered at Steinbeck Festival XI, in Salinas, California, in August 1990 (printed in revised form in *San Jose Studies* in 1992)—all show evidence of taking seriously Steinbeck's opinion of the novel's "big" achievement and of weighing the importance his transformed artistic sensibility had upon *Eden*'s moment, method, and material. I do not intend to present the entire history of critical trends on *East of Eden* (good starting places are Richard Peterson's 1979 chapter in Tetsumaro Hayashi's *A Study Guide to John Steinbeck (Part II)*, Daniel Buerger's essay in the 1981 "Mapping *East of Eden*" issue of *Steinbeck Quarterly*, and Charles Etheridge's 1993 overview of changing attitudes toward Steinbeck's naturalism, in Donald Noble's *The Steinbeck Question*), however, it may prove instructive, as a prelude to the accompanying bibliographic guide, to mention that, like Schorer, one of our generation's leading Steinbeck critics also reconfigured his attitude toward *East of Eden*. This time, however, the change was efficacious, signifying that Steinbeck has become increasingly relevant rather than *passe*.

Steinbeck critic and Native American novelist Louis Owens's change of tune about *East of Eden* can be considered a trope for this current trend toward reevaluating Steinbeck's novel in a positive light and for considering the book—among many other possibilities, including its humanistic bent—as a postmodernist creation or metafictional construct. Owens's first book, *John Steinbeck's Re-Vision of America* (1985), took a derivative stance toward *East of Eden*, heavily dependent upon the 1950's ambivalence about Steinbeck in general and its hostility about *Eden* in particular. This rigorous, regulatory strain of formalist criticism, which emphasized wit, irony, dispassion, authorial effacement, and autonomous form, necessitated severe qualifications toward Steinbeck's work. This divided opinion characterized Peter Lisca's often grouchy New Critical appraisal of *East of Eden* in his otherwise valuable and pioneering *The Wide World of John Steinbeck* (1958), and it was also to be found in the accounts of *Eden* by Warren French (1961), Joseph Fontenrose (1963), and Howard Levant (1974), though the latter two found much to praise. Lisca condemned the book because he found that the elements of "greatness" which some critics had discerned "might have been brought to fulfillment in a subtle fusion of *East of Eden*'s imposing theme and its more credible human beings and events—a fusion which is not accomplished in the novel" (273-74). Two decades later, Lisca continued his attack in *John Steinbeck: Nature and Myth* (1978). In one of the sharpest indictments of the novel, Lisca pilloried the "pernicious influence" of the narrator's function: "The novel soon escapes from the narrator's control, just as *Moby Dick* gets away from Ishmael" (172). Like Lisca, Owens was unappreciative of the novel's experimental elements, denouncing Steinbeck for failing "unmistakably" (141) and having "lost his way" in the wilderness of conflicting structure and thought (155).

Owens's insistence in *Re-Vision* that *Eden* only can be analyzed as an objective product has changed drastically. This may be a result of the tolerant critical trends and shifting sensibilities that affect us all in the academy, not the least of them our revised notions of the nature of narrativity and literary representation. Just as the cover portrait of Steinbeck on the 20 September 1952 issue of *Saturday Review* (reproduced above) might once have been taken only as a statement of the novelist's autonomous genius and mimetic posture toward the Salinas Valley, so from our vantage point forty-five years later, the picture also can be read as a testimony not to authorial ennoblement or imaginative sovereignty but to authorial indeterminacy (it is possible to detect a questioning, hesitant look in Steinbeck's heavily shadowed face), the kind of natural give and take of text and context, on which Steinbeck's books erected themselves. In a larger way, the cover art can be interpreted as an icon of Steinbeck's post-World War II situation as a literary con man, a perpetrator of fictive illusion, a juggler of the "preposterous" in literature (*JN*, 168). Such transformations in the way we think about writing and the critical act have conditioned a greater willingness to embrace Steinbeck's own theoretical statements in the obvious places, such as *Steinbeck: A Life in Letters, Journal of a Novel*, and *Conversations with John Steinbeck*. But it also means looking at fugitive items such as his revealing appreciation of Gide's *The Counterfeitors*, in which he claimed, "*The Counterfeitors* is one of the greatest books that I have read. . . . Gide knew how to write, because his mind knew how to explore . . . Because he thought what he wanted to and gave form to his curiosities."[3]

Addressing the form of Steinbeck's curiosity in three overlapping essays (in 1989, 1990, and 1993), Louis Owens has focused his attention on *East of Eden* as a processive construct and a self-conscious fiction, aspects far more congenial to understanding the dynamics of Steinbeck's complicated effort in narrative form and characterization than the blueprint methods of earlier criticism. Indeed, in the first revisionist statement, "The Story of a Writing," Owens, echoing Steinbeck, self-consciously announced: "When I said, in my recent study of Steinbeck's fiction [*Re-vision*], that *East of Eden* fails 'unmistakably,' it seemed to me that it was so. Now I have bent close with a glass over the fine print of the novel and reread the footnotes, and I wonder if it is true" (60). Later, in "The Mirror and the Vamp," in James Barbour and Tom Quirk's *Writing the American Classics* (1990), Owens confesses, "*East of Eden* is a more subtle and complex construction than we are at first prepared to believe" (256). In *John Steinbeck's Fiction*, John Timmerman concurs: "Steinbeck possessed a far clearer perception of structural unity and of moral theme . . . than has been commonly assumed" (218).

Others feel that way too. In a 1970 essay in *The Fifties*, Pascal Covici, Jr., suspecting "that there has been a profound underrating of Steinbeck's importance," took up the enigma of *Eden*'s shifting fictional strategies as a source of its staying power, and suggested, "a careful look at just how narrative point-of-view is handled in *East of Eden* could carry one very far into the aesthetic and psychological problems of presenting a sense of freedom in art" (70-71). In his 1975 revision of *John Steinbeck*, Warren French, taking a clue from Lawrence William Jones's provocative, seminal study of fabular form, addressed *Eden* as a "cosmogony" (141). By considering Steinbeck's late fictions to be "dramas of consciousness," fluid texts that freely break down the boundaries of traditional narrative categories, French's influence is still being felt. In an especially valuable essay on *Eden*'s postmodernist qualities, Steven Mulder established the ways Steinbeck's novel not only anticipates but participates in metafictional discourse, the slippery transactions between domains of fictiveness and reality that define what might loosely be called the postmodernist "moment," the place where, in Roland Barthes's terms, "readers" become "writers" (116).

Besides intense interest in the poetics of Steinbeck's narrative processes and the intertextual relatedness of novel and journal, contemporary critics also have been engaging similarly pressing topics, including the controversial and conflicting role of women and minority characters in his novel (by Beatty, Bedford, Gladstein, Hayashi, Jain, Timmerman); the importance of the first manuscript version in understanding Steinbeck's presumed intentions and original scope (by Govoni, Nakayama, Simmonds); the mirroring of literal and symbolic landscapes and environment (by Owens, Turner); the examination of his myriad literary, linguistic, historical, cultural, and personal sources, borrowings, and parallels (by Fontenrose, Gribben, Kawata, Quinones, Yarmus); and the adaptations of his novel into cinematic forms (by Morsberger, Rathgeb). In the third version of his Twayne United States Authors Series book, *John Steinbeck's Fiction Revisited* (1994), Warren French revisions *Eden* yet again, this time finding that its difficulty resides in Steinbeck's uneasy juxtaposition of the Hamilton's "pastoral history" with the Trasks's "Gothic fantasy" (118).

In short, however, although recent analysis of *East of Eden* has become responsible and responsive, the definitive word on many topics is yet to be written. Even that fundamental staple of biographical interpretation—Steinbeck's unquestioned privileging of his maternal line, the Hamiltons—has obscured his debt to his other family, the paternal Steinbeck line, whose gruesome experiences, including rape and murder, in Jaffa in the 1850s throw some startling new light on *East of Eden*'s characters as I have shown in a 1993 *Steinbeck Newsletter* piece. Other new avenues are emerging as well: consider Jackson Benson's biography, *The True Adventures of John Steinbeck*, which claims *Eden* "seems destined to be read and remain a part of our literature for some time to come," yet its "unconscious" companion, *Journal of a Novel*, "may be" a "greater" book (691); and Nancy Zane's essay—the first of its kind—exclusively on the *Journal* as an independent "Romantic" text. Both of these positions call to mind Gide's enticing pronouncements, through his character Edouard, in the second part of *The Counterfeitors* (1927): "'My note-book contains, as it were, a running criticism of my novel. . . . Just think how interesting such a note-book kept by Dickens or Balzac would be; if we had the diary of the *Education Sentimentale* or *The Brothers Karamazof!*—the story of the work—of its gestation! How thrilling it would be . . . more interesting than the work itself.'"[4]

Indeed, the more so, because though it has been commonly believed that the only journal Steinbeck kept while writing *Eden* was eventually published as *Journal of a Novel*, the fact is that he kept two other private diaries during 1951: one is an oversized 10" x 16" ledger, *The Year 1951* (manufactured by National Blank Book Company); the other, which measures "8 x ll," is *The Standard Diary for 1951* (manufactured by Standard Diary Company).[5] In both books, the head of each page is stamped with the day's date, leaving plenty of lined space to be filled with words; but the running heads also include the total number of days elapsed in the year to that point and the number of days left to go in the year. This feature adds, I think, a flavor of temporality to authorship, providing Steinbeck with a constant reminder of daily horizons and diurnal reckonings to be dealt with. It seems fitting that in his entry for 30 March in *The Standard Diary for 1951*, Steinbeck, after attending the opening of Rodgers and Hammerstein's *The King and I* and drinking with novelist John O'Hara at Sardi's, found himself overtaken by a "curiously hopeless" feeling caused partly by "O'Hara's talk of emminence [sic]. . . . [a]lways this immortality talk makes me sad."

Considered together, then, the three journals reveal the degree of seriousness and commitment with which Steinbeck approached his new life with Elaine (his third wife) and how the writing of *East of Eden* became a prime symbol of that new phase. In his large red leather ledger, *The Year 1951*, Steinbeck noted on New Year's Day: "A really good life is pointing out ahead of me. All I have to do is be worth it to Elaine and Way

[Waverly Scott; Elaine's daughter] and the boys [his sons, Thom and John, who lived nearby with his ex-wife Gwyn]. . . . This year I must make a new start in writing but a very good new start. I want to do the Salinas Valley book this year and I want it to be good."

While the daily warm-up entries in *Journal of a Novel* provide a direct access to each day's composition of the novel and attempt, more or less, a pure focus on the book (though, in a sense, this was impossible, given everything happening in his life at the time), the other diaries (entered daily for irregular stretches) tend to reflect Steinbeck's private life, the world outside the novel, though in fact in these diaries, too, plenty of the novel's concerns slip in. So do some interesting revelations: for example, in *Journal of a Novel*, there is no mention of Steinbeck's reading of Genesis (the source of his title) until 11 June; but in his *Standard Diary for 1951*, he notes "reading the Bible—particularly the Cain Abel sequence" on 19 February, almost four months earlier.[6]

But to my mind, the remarkable thing about his compositional field is the clashing welter of events, the nexus of inner and outer worldly occurrences—domestic disruptions, plans for remodeling, visits from Pat Covici and Elizabeth Otis, dinner parties, requests for his time, guilt over the quality of his parenting, running battles with Gwyn, distressing dreams and sleepless nights—stresses that, against Steinbeck's wish not to give in to "personal feelings and emotions which can so easily taint a book" (*JN*, 44), probably entered the moment of *Eden*'s writing, not in a debilitating or overwhelming way but enough to become determining conditions that Steinbeck had not so much to master as to bargain with or negotiate. "Dear Gwyn," he wrote on 17 May 1951, "I don't know why I should be astonished that everything happens at once because it always does. I'm trying to keep up with my book, with future work and to plan for the summer. And my mind perhaps is not adequate for the task."[7] Furthermore, to see *East of Eden* embedded this way, in a kind of thick soup of circumstance, is to open the door to reconsiderations of Steinbeck as a writer and to lend greater credence to his belief, stated in 1958, that "a novelist is a kind of flypaper to which everything adheres" (*SLL*, 591-92). Most of all, it isn't too much to claim that, after more than four decades, the frontiers of critical exploration are just beginning to open. As John Ditsky, pathfinder in this wilderness, said in his Steinbeck

Monograph Series booklet, *Essays on "East of Eden,"* "A negative acknowledgement is also due: to the man's many detractors who condemn what they have rarely ever read, my thanks for leaving so much to be said" (vi).

The sane, judicious application of contemporary critical theory is another conspicuously neglected area in Steinbeck studies where much indeed is yet to be said. Outside of Karen Hopkins's energetic advocacy of *East of Eden* through the ideas of Roland Barthes, Jacques Derrida, and E. D. Hirsch, other poststructuralist critics are rarely invoked, though in fact understanding the thrust of theoretical discourse about such highly charged terms as *agency, subjectivity, history, gender, culture, desire,* and *representation,* to name a few key concepts, would be especially pertinent to *Eden,* a book which, at least in part, subverts normative fictional presentation and interrogates attributes of western humanism by offering an historiographic vision of American experience. In addition, our conception of Steinbeck's sense of authorship might have to be less exclusively focused on the traditional, recognizable genre of commercial fiction and more inclusively focused on the wider scene, including all his "writing" at any given moment—including letters, journal and diaries—all of which constitute variations of scriptive art themselves and, when allied to a novel such as *East of Eden,* comprise an extensive intertextual, compositional construct, and thus a whole new ground for examination and interpretation.

To complicate matters, Steinbeck's project, which turned radically from constructing phalanxes (as evinced, say, in *The Grapes of Wrath*) toward negotiating contexts of individualism in *East of Eden,* was influenced not only by personal traumas—his 1948 divorce from Gwyn, his second wife, and the death that same year of his soul mate Edward F. Ricketts—but also by the larger implications of American intellectual response to the Soviets during the Cold War and our entrance into the Korean conflict. The writer's desire to metaphorize the ironic quest for a unique American character defined outside imperialism is evident in his post-1948 correspondence, as well as in a number of anticommunist entries in *Journal of a Novel* and in a Voice of America broadcast Steinbeck made on 21 February 1951 "concerning art under dictatorship" (*JN,* 15). A two-page outline "for V.O.A." at the back of his unpublished *Standard Diary for 1951* reveals his thorough-going hatred for totalitarianism: "If an artist in any line does his work in good faith and later says he was wrong, he is a liar either in his good faith or in his recantation. An artist may be clumsy or inept but he is not wrong for all creation is the product of one man's brain working alone." Again, at the bottom of his first page of general comments, he wrote: "Art is a constant experiment; it must be. Every generation rejects the proceeding [sic] one and then accepts a part of it. But Totalitarianism forbids experiment." Far from being ancillary or superfluous, these valuations strike to the heart of Steinbeck's project during *Eden*'s composition and indeed to all of his post-1950 writings as well (including his unfortunate encouragement of America's Vietnam War policy in the 1960s).

In fact, such extraliterary elements are especially germane to all future contextual discussions of *East of Eden*, as David Wyatt suggests in his new historicist introduction to Penguin's Twentieth-Century Classic series reprint (xviii-ix), which situates Steinbeck amid the myriad conflicting gender, cultural, and historicizing forces of his time. The fact that Steinbeck bifurcated his own narrative points of view indicates a self-conscious interrogation of all forms of hegemony. Given Steinbeck's interest in the fictiveness of history and the performative nature of narrative consciousness, an analysis of Steinbeck's construction, or authoring, of himself (as both recorder and participant, subject and object) in that national drama of exceptionalism ought to be an especially engaging topic to pursue. In "its sense of fiction as belonging to a discourse that subsumes its author, *East of Eden* belongs less with the great books of modernism than the texts that would come after them," Wyatt avers. Further, *East of Eden* cries out for Bakhthinian discourse analysis, or a dialogic investigation, for *heteroglossia*, the linked multiplicity of social voices, is a key feature of Steinbeck's polyphonic text. In any case, while we have come far in our appreciation of *Eden*, its special qualities, its animating peculiarities and curiosities, will allow it to elude us unless we learn more about Steinbeck's conception of rhetoric, language, history, and referentiality. Louis Owens strikes a proper note when he concedes, in his 1993 essay, "Steinbeck's *East of Eden*," that the novel still "may be the most misunderstood of all Steinbeck's creations" (85).

Thirty years ago John Milton proclaimed to the Western History Association Conference in Oklahoma City that "*East of Eden* will one day be seen as a major western novel" (72). Indeed, despite (or perhaps because of) its rifts, swerves, ruptures, and dissonances, *Eden* has come increasingly to stand as an iconic Steinbeck text, though it might eventually prove to be central for reasons quite different than those promulgated three decades ago. Nearly everything has changed since 1964, and—in the aftermath of those cataclysmic influences on the way we conduct literary business—whether *Eden* will ever be considered a truly great novel or even the most representative Steinbeck text of his later years are questions unanswerable now. Some theorists would consider questions of transcendent greatness, of writerly genius and achievement, to be spurious categories and hence no longer part of the critical conversation, though for the sake of a healthy, on-going debate it seems to me that the question of origins, intentions, and selfhood can never be fully abandoned if we desire to gain a full—not just temporally conditioned—view of experience.

East of Eden, which has never been out of print, continues to gain respect: in 1992, Penguin Books kicked off the repackaging of all Steinbeck's books into its Twentieth-Century Classics series with *East of Eden*, introduced capably, as I have already noted, by David Wyatt. The Library of America, publisher of uniform editions of America's significant writers, has launched a multivolume Steinbeck project with *East of Eden* slated for the third volume. (Still needed, however, at least for serious scholars and Steinbeck afficianados, is a facsimile edition of the autograph manuscript, with its alternating sections of the daily journal and the unabridged text of the novel, or, at the very least, an edition of both novel and journal bound as one, as Steinbeck himself envisioned in 1965.)

Roy Simmonds may have been precipitous when he predicted in his keynote address in Salinas a few years ago that the critical and scholarly "limelight will slowly but surely shift from *The Grapes of Wrath* toward *East of Eden*," but there is no denying that in the past decade increasing critical interest in and sophisticated commentary on the latter has occured. Indeed, *Eden* has recently become a Steinbeck text of choice in discussions of American writing: besides Owens's piece in Barbour and Quirk's *Writing the American Classics*, see also Frederick Turner's *Spirit of Place*, David Wyatt's *The Fall into Eden*, and Ricardo Quinones's *The Changes of Cain*—all demonstrate *Eden*'s richness and resonant possibilities. As Jay Parini summarizes in his approving biography, *John Steinbeck*, "American literature would certainly be poorer without it" (365). Finally, after forty years of debate, what goes around, comes around. It turns out to be neither sinful nor shameful that, in Harvey Curtis Webster's prescient view (in his 1952 *Saturday Review* critique), Steinbeck "never learned or cared to learn the lesson of Henry James" (11).

3

Amid this abundance and promise of good things to come, however, it is easy to forget that a convenient bibliography of primary and secondary writings is always a needful and worthwhile thing, for it provides a chart of the journey, a map of the landscape, which is perhaps more necessary than ever in these times of critical slippage and scholarly insouciance. It is a lesson *Steinbeck Quarterly* and Steinbeck Monograph Series founder Tetsumaro Hayashi taught three decades ago when he published *John Steinbeck: A Concise Bibliography (1929-1965)* in 1967, the first of literally dozens of bibliographies and reference books on American and English writers he would produce during the following two decades for the durable Scarecrow Press of Metuchen, New Jersey. His comprehensive bibliography (the first of its kind) ushered in an era of change by serving notice that—to quote Lee in *East of Eden*—studying Steinbeck could no longer be a "simple" matter and might, in fact, prove to be "desperately complicated." (Prior to his retirement from Ball State University in Muncie, Indiana, in 1993, Hayashi had several times updated and revised his Steinbeck bibliography; his former doctoral student, Michael J. Meyer, will carry on the project with a new bibliography covering the 1980s and 1990s that Scarecrow, recently relocated to Lanham, Maryland, plans to publish in 1997).

In the sense that a useful bibliography can itself be a mode of pragmatic discourse and that it too is a kind of textual negotiation—both of its subject and of itself—I offer for the last time the following English language checklist to facilitate continued discussion and serious investigation of *East of Eden.* As with its predecessors, the latest version, appearing here in *Steinbeck's Typewriter* with substantially revised preface and updated checklist, is not exhaustive, but does attempt to cover the range and variety of writing on *East of Eden.* I have taken the liberty of modifying the traditional *Chicago Manual of Style* format by adding inclusive page numbers at the end of *all* relevant entries, not just to periodical listings, and by including, in addition to entries devoted solely to the novel, a sampling of important general essays (Jackson Benson's "John Steinbeck: Novelist as Scientist," John Ditsky's "Music from a Dark Cave," and his "Rowing from Eden: Closure in the Later Steinbeck Fiction," and John H. Timmerman's "John Steinbeck's Use of The Bible" are four examples) whose theoretical or practical bearings relate directly to the novel. These too are part of the evolving picture of *East of Eden*, in which, whether or not it proves to be an illusion, "everything is an index of everything else."

Notes

[1] Complete publishing information for quotations deriving from or pertaining to *East of Eden* is provided in the accompanying bibliographical checklist.

[2] See Benson's introduction to his excellent anthology, *The Short Novels of John Steinbeck: Critical Essays with a Checklist to Steinbeck Criticism* (Durham, NC: Duke University Press, 1990), 1-13. His approach regarding Steinbeck's treatment at the hands of "Eastern establishment critics" is developed further in "John Steinbeck: The Favorite Author We Love to Hate," in Donald R. Noble, ed., *The Steinbeck Question: New Essays in Criticism* (Troy, NY: Whitston Publishing, 1993), 8-22. *Washington Post* book editor Jonathan Yardley's attack on Steinbeck and his unreasonable evaluation of Steinbeck's writing is a current example of reviewer hostility. Yardley's review of the Library of America's first Steinbeck volume, *Novels and Stories 1932-1937*, is marred by his elitist agenda. His pronouncement, based on "purely literary terms" (which he is unable to fully define), that Steinbeck "simply does not belong" in the Library of America's publishing venture beside the work of Melville, Faulkner, and Dreiser, or for that matter, beside James Fenimore Cooper, Sarah Orne Jewett, and Sinclair Lewis, is utterly useless as meaningful criticism. See "Dregs of Wrath," *Washington Post Book World* 9 October 1994, 2.

[3] Steinbeck's one-paragraph statement, "Un Grand Romancier de Notre Temps," was published in a special *La Nouvelle Revue Francaise* issue, "Hommage à André Gide 1869-1951," in November 1951, n.p. (English translation by Professor Lois Vines, Department of French, Ohio University.)

[4] André Gide, *The Counterfeitors. With Journal of "The Counterfeitors,"* trans. Dorothy Bussy and Justin O'Brien (New York: Alfred A. Knopf, 1951), 174. See Steinbeck's 14 July 1965 (Bastille Day) letter to Elizabeth Otis: "When I was writing East of Eden, before each day's work as a kind of warm-up I kept a work diary but addressed to Pat. It is perhaps as complete a record of a book as has ever been done. But I had never seen it since I sent it off in handwriting. Pat and I often discussed publishing it either in conjunction with a complete and uncut E. of E. or by itself. Then Pat died and I wondered what would happen to it. Recently I wrote to Pascal Jr. and told him I would like to see it. He sent me a copy and I have just been reading it. And it is much better

than I remembered, a little repetitious and perhaps in some places too personal, but I think very interesting and book length. . . . Elaine has read it and she agrees. It is a fascinating account of the making of a book" (*SLL*, 824). This information hardly accords with what Steinbeck had told Associated Press reporter Hal Boyle four years earlier. Then Steinbeck claimed that he routinely threw away his writing ledgers because "'they don't seem awfully damn important to me'" (*CJS*, 77). But that might have been a deliberate lie on a couple of levels, for Steinbeck did actually "keep" at least the diaries and/or journals—he often referred to them by the hybrid term "day books"—that he wrote while he was composing most of his major fiction, though not all of the completed ledgers have been published. His *Grapes of Wrath* journal (*Working Days*), the first *complete*, daily, beginning-to-end compositional record he ever kept (earlier journals, such as those for *To a God Unknown*, *Of Mice and Men*, and *The Long Valley*, were sporadic and fragmentary), became a touchstone for such endeavors for the rest of his career. In his unpublished *Wayward Bus* journal (a complete work of approximately 30,000 words in itself and in many ways the most intriguing and revealing of all his record books), and in his *East of Eden* journal (*Journal of a Novel*), Steinbeck refers to his *Grapes* day book as a model disciplinary effort and as a reminder of the constancy and tyranny of his own creative struggles. He was always fascinated by the process of his books' making. A single volume gathering together all of Steinbeck's diaries and journals would be a welcome, desirable addition to his canon, and would indicate the degree to which his attention to process was central, not ancillary, to his conception of himself as a worker in words.

[5] With Elaine Steinbeck's approval both items (MA 4688 and MA 4689) have been removed from restricted status at the Pierpont Morgan Library; they are quoted with her permission and that of the Morgan Library.

[6] Another recently unsealed Morgan Library ledger—in this one Steinbeck warmed up daily before and during the composition of *The Wayard Bus*—indicates he had planned a fictional/dramatic work ("the old play novel form that I have tried so often") on the Cain-Abel theme of fraticide as early as 11 January 1946. His exploratory musings on a pre-*Wayward Bus* manuscript (never completed) that he hoped would be "a companion piece to *The Pearl*," instead throw light on *East of Eden* five years later: "For Cain killed much more than Abel. He was the creative—the positive element. Abel was negative [,] accepting [,] retiring. This in itself is a powerful defensive thing but it is not creative. It chooses avenues of escape. It will always retreat and draw into itself. Can my Abel analyze this? Can he judge himself clearly [?] Can he know what he is doing and be unable to help it—that is dramatically and without cant or humility of the more flamboyant kind [?]" (MA 4685, p. 9).

[7] Steinbeck's unpublished letter is part of an extensive collection of his correspondence to his second wife, housed at Bancroft Library, University of California, Berkeley.

1. PRIMARY WORKS

Note: The related manuscripts of John Steinbeck's *East of Eden*, housed at the Harry Ransom Humanities Research Center, University of Texas, Austin, are comprised of the 540-page holograph first draft manuscript, written in a 10 3/4 x 14 inch, lined ledger book (which also includes Steinbeck's concurrent daily commentary later excerpted as *Journal of a Novel*) and more than 900 pages of typescripts, including emendations, deletions, discards, and extensive revisions. Two collateral items—unpublished handwritten personal diaries for 1951—are held at the Pierpont Morgan Library, New York City.

A. TEXTS

"The Sons of Cyrus Trask." *Collier's* 12 July 1952, [14]-15, 38-41. (Prepublication excerpt from chapter 3, sections 1-4, and chapter 4, section 1, which differs significantly on many points from the novel's text; reprinted in British *Liliput* 31 [November-December 1952], 89-102.)

East of Eden. New York: Viking Press, 1952. (Published September 1952 in a limited, signed edition of 1,500 copies—750 for private distribution—in brown paperboard slipcase, and a trade edition of 112,621 copies with colored pictorial dust jacket; British edition published in London, November 1952 by William Heinemann.)

Chapter Thirty-Four From the Novel "East of Eden" By John Steinbeck. Bronxville, NY: Privately printed by Valenti Angelo, 1952. (Limited edition chapbook of 125 copies with variant titles.)

Journal of a Novel: The "East of Eden" Letters. New York: Viking Press, 1969. (Posthumous publication of Steinbeck's daily journal—29 January 1951 to 1 November 1951—addressed to his editor, Pascal Covici, during composition of the novel. Limited edition of 600 copies, in blue slipcase, specially bound with facsimiles of the original manuscript, and a trade edition in brown dust jacket; paperback edition available from Penguin Books.)

East of Eden. Introduction by David Wyatt. New York: Penguin Books, 1992. (Paperback reprint of first edition Viking Press text, with 23-page introduction; inaugural Steinbeck volume in Penguin's Twentieth-Century Classics series.)

B. CORRESPONDENCE, INTERVIEWS, AND RELATED DOCUMENTS

[Comments on *East of Eden* and on hand-carved box for Pascal Covici.] In Laura Z. Hobson, "Trade Winds," *Saturday Review* 30 August 1952, 4.

[Note on importance of *East of Eden* to his career.] In Bernard Kalb, "The Author," *Saturday Review* 20 September 1952, 11. ("Once . . . I read and wept over reviews. Then, one time I put the criticisms all together and found that they canceled each other out and left me non-existent. . . . I feel a little numb about this book. . . . I think everything else I have written has been, in a sense, practice for this. I'm fifty years old. If *East of Eden* isn't good, then I've been wasting my time. It has in it everything I have been able to learn about my art or craft or profession in all these years. Do you know, I want terribly for people to read it and to like it. I'll be miserable if they don't." This issue features Steinbeck on its cover.)

[Bilingual letter prefacing Greek translation of *East of Eden*.] Thessalonika: A. N. Suropoulis, [1953?]. ("To have my work published in Greece is at once a pleasing and frightening thing. . . . To the literature of the world, Greece is the mother. Perhaps this book is a wandering child come home to visit.")

[Excerpted letter predicting *East of Eden*'s reviews.] *Saturday Review* 27 February 1954, 8.

Steinbeck: A Life in Letters. Ed. Elaine Steinbeck and Robert Wallsten. New York: Viking Press, 1975, 417-40.

"John Steinbeck." Preface by Nathaniel Benchley. *Writers at Work. "The Paris Review" Interviews*. Fourth Series. Ed. George Plimpton. New York: Viking Press, 1976, 179-207. (Not a typical *Paris Review* interview on the "Art of Fiction," but a topical selection from *Journal of a Novel* and *Steinbeck: A Life in Letters*, arranged by George Plimpton and Frank Crowther.)

Steinbeck and Covici: The Story of a Friendship. By Thomas Fensch. Middlebury, VT: Paul S. Eriksson, 1979, 143-94. (Some repetition of entries in *Journal of a Novel* and letters in *Steinbeck: A Life in Letters* but valuable for Covici's correspondence and for corrected texts of some Steinbeck letters.)

Conversations with John Steinbeck. Ed. Thomas Fensch. Jackson: University Press of Mississippi, 1988, 49-63. (Reprinted brief interviews and informal talks with Steinbeck, conducted by various people from 1948 through 1955, entirely or in part about *East of Eden*.

2. SECONDARY WORKS

A. SELECTED CONTEMPORARY REVIEWS

Bloomfield, Paul. *Manchester Guardian* 5 December 1952, 4.

Brunn, Robert R. *Christian Science Monitor* 25 September 1952, 15.

Engle, Paul. *Chicago Sunday Tribune* 21 September 1952, 3.

Gurko, Leo. "Steinbeck's Later Fiction." *Nation* 20 September 1952, 235-36.

Hughes, Riley. *Catholic World* 176 (November 1952): 150-51.

"It Started in a Garden." *Time* 22 September 1952, 110.

Jackson, Joseph Henry. *San Francisco Chronicle* 21 September 1952, 20.

Kinnaird, Clark. *Chicago Herald American Sunday Pictorial Review* 28 September 1952, [8].

Krutch, Joseph Wood. "John Steinbeck's Dramatic Tale of Three Generations." *New York Herald Tribune Book Review* 21 September 1952, 1. Reprinted in *Steinbeck and His Critics: A Record of Twenty-Five Years*, eds. E. W. Tedlock and C. V. Wicker. Albuquerque: University of New Mexico Press, 1957, 302-05; and in *Dictionary of Literary Biography: Documentary Series, An Illustrated Guide*. Vol. 2, ed. Margaret A. Van Antwert. Detroit: Gale Research, 1982, 314-17.

"Larger Than Life." *Times Literary Supplement* 5 December 1952, 789.

Magny, Claude-Edmond. "Magny on Steinbeck." Trans. Louise Varese. *Perspectives USA* 5 (Fall 1953): 146-52.

Mizener, Arthur. "In the Land of Nod." *New Republic* 6 October 1952, 22-23.

Phillips, William. "Male-ism and Moralism: Hemingway and Steinbeck." *American Mercury* 75 (Autumn 1952): 93-98.

Pickrel, Paul. *Yale Review* 42 (Autumn 1952): viii-ix.
Prescott, Orville. *New York Times* 19 September 1952, 21.
Rolo, Charles. "The Peripatetic Reviewer." *Atlantic* 190 (October 1992): 94.
Schorer, Mark. "A Dark and Violent Steinbeck Novel." *New York Times Book Review* 21 September 1952, 1, 22.
Scott, J. D. "New Novels." *New Statesman and Nation* 44 (1952): 698-99.
Smith, Eleanor T. *Library Journal* 77 (August 1952): 1303.
Webster, Harvey Curtis. "Out of the New-born Sun." *Saturday Review* 20 September 1952, 11-12.
West, Anthony. "California Moonshine." *New Yorker* 20 September 1952, 121-22, 125.

B. BIBLIOGRAPHICAL RESOURCES

Beebe, Maurice, and Jackson R. Bryer. "Criticism of John Steinbeck: A Selected Checklist." *Modern Fiction Studies* 11 (Spring 1965): 95-96.
DeMott, Robert. "*East of Eden*": A Bibliographical Checklist." *Steinbeck Quarterly* 25 (Winter-Spring 1992): 14-28.
—. "Charting *East of Eden*": A Bibliographical Survey." In *After "The Grapes of Wrath": Essays on John Steinbeck in Honor of Tetsumaro Hayashi*, eds. Donald V. Coers, Paul D. Ruffin, and Robert J. DeMott. Athens: Ohio University Press, 1995, 148-71.
French, Warren. "John Steinbeck." *Sixteen Modern American Authors: A Survey of Research and Criticism*, ed. Jackson R. Bryer. New York: W. W. Norton, 1963, 383, 514, 517, 519, 526.
—. "John Steinbeck." *Sixteen Modern American Authors*. Vol. 2, *A Survey of Criticism Since 1972*, ed. Jackson R. Bryer. Durham, NC: Duke University Press, 1990, 607-09.
Goldstone, Adrian, and John R. Payne. *John Steinbeck: A Bibliographical Catalogue of the Adrian H. Goldstone Collection*. Austin, TX: Humanities Research Center, 1974, 75-78.
Gross, John, and Lee Richard Hayman, eds. *John Steinbeck: A Guide to the Collection of the Salinas Public Library*. Salinas, CA: Salinas Public Library, 1979, 45.
Harmon, Robert B. *The Collectible John Steinbeck: A Practical Guide*. Jefferson, NC: McFarland, 1986, 43-47.
—. *Steinbeck Editions: A Bibliographic Checklist*. San Jose, CA: Bibliographic Research Services, 1992, 12-15.
Hayashi, Tetsumaro. *John Steinbeck: A Concise Bibliography (1930-1965)*. Metuchen, NJ: Scarecrow Press, 1967, passim.
—. *A New Steinbeck Bibliography, 1929-1971*. Metuchen, NJ: Scarecrow Press, 1973, passim.
—. *A New Steinbeck Bibliography, 1971-1981*. Metuchen, NJ: Scarecrow Press, 1983, passim.
Morrow, Bradford. *John Steinbeck: A Collection of Books & Manuscripts Formed by Harry Valentine of Pacific Grove, California*. Santa Barbara, CA: Bradford Morrow, Bookseller, 1980, 55-57.
Parks, Robert. "John Steinbeck in the Pierpont Morgan Library." *Steinbeck Newsletter* 8 (Winter-Spring 1995): 19-21.

Payne, John R. "John Steinbeck in the Humanities Research Center, The University of Texas at Austin." *Steinbeck Quarterly* 11 (Summer-Fall 1978): 100-02. Reprinted in *A Handbook, for Steinbeck Collectors, Librarians, and Scholars*, ed. Tetsumaro Hayashi. Steinbeck Monograph Series, no. 11. Muncie, IN: John Steinbeck Society of America/Ball State University, 1981, 33-34.

Timmerman, John H. "John Steinbeck's Use of the Bible: A Descriptive Bibliography of the Critical Tradition." *Steinbeck Quarterly* 21 (Winter-Spring 1988): 24-39.

Todd, William B. *John Steinbeck: An Exhibition of American and Foreign Editions*. Austin: Humanities Research Center/University of Texas, 1963, 26-27.

Woodward, Robert H. *The Steinbeck Research Center at San Jose State University: A Descriptive Catalogue*. San Jose, CA: San Jose State University, 1985, 51-53.

C. BIOGRAPHY AND BACKGROUND

Astro, Richard. *John Steinbeck and Edward F. Ricketts: The Shaping of a Novelist*. Minneapolis: University of Minnesota Press, 1973, 193, 207-12.

Benson, Jackson J. *The True Adventures of John Steinbeck, Writer*. New York: Viking Press, 1984, 666-68, 700-03, 731-34.

—. *Looking for Steinbeck's Ghost*. Norman: University of Oklahoma Press, 1988, 11, 27, 95, 183, 195-96, 223-24.

Cox, Martha Heasley. "In Search of John Steinbeck: His People and His Land." *San Jose Studies* 1 (November 1975): 41, 45-47.

—. "Steinbeck's Family Portraits: The Hamiltons." In *Mapping "East of Eden,"* ed. Robert DeMott. Special issue of *Steinbeck Quarterly* 14 (Winter-Spring 1981): 23-32.

—. "John Steinbeck." *Dictionary of Literary Biography: Documentary Series, An Illustrated Guide*. Vol. 2, ed. Margaret A. Van Antwert. Detroit: Gale Research, 1982, 314-19.

DeMott, Robert. "Steinbeck's Other Family: New Light on *East of Eden*?" *Steinbeck Newsletter* 7 (Fall 1993): 1-3.

Kiernan, Thomas. *The Intricate Music: A Biography of John Steinbeck*. Boston: Little, Brown, 1979, 295-301.

Parini, Jay. *John Steinbeck: A Biography*. New York: Henry Holt, 1995, 347-69.

Pearson, Michael. "A Strip Angled against the Pacific: Steinbeck's California." *Imagined Places: Journeys into Literary America*. Photographs by John Lawrence and Joel Mednick. Jackson: University Press of Mississippi, 1991, 238-39.

D. CRITICAL ANALYSIS

Atkinson, Rebecca L. "Steinbeck's *East of Eden*." *Explicator* 48 (Spring 1990): 216-17.

Beatty, Sandra. "A Study of Female Characterization in Steinbeck's Fiction." *Steinbeck Quarterly* 8 (Spring 1975): 50-56. Reprinted in *Steinbeck's Women: Essays in Criticism*, ed. Tetsumaro Hayashi. Steinbeck Monograph Series, no. 9. Muncie, IN: John Steinbeck Society of America/ Ball State University, 1979, 1-6.

Bedford, Richard C. "Steinbeck's Uses of the Oriental." *Steinbeck Quarterly* 8 (Winter-Spring 1980): 5-19.

Benson, Jackson J. "John Steinbeck: Novelist as Scientist." *Steinbeck and the Sea*, eds. Richard Astro and Joel Hedgpeth. Corvallis: Oregon State University Sea Grant College Program (April 1975): 15-28. Reprinted in *Novel* 10 (Spring 1977): 248-64; and in *John Steinbeck*, ed. Harold Bloom. New York: Chelsea House, 1987, 103-23.

Brown, Joyce C. "Steinbeck's *East of Eden*." *Explicator* 38 (Fall 1979): 11-12.

Buerger, Daniel. "'History' and Fiction in *East of Eden* Criticism." In *Mapping "East of Eden,"* ed. Robert DeMott. Special issue of *Steinbeck Quarterly* 14 (Winter-Spring 1981): 6-14.

Burningham, Bradd. "Relation, Vision, and Tracking the Welsh Rats in *East of Eden* and *The Winter of Our Discontent*." *Steinbeck Quarterly* 15 (Summer-Fall 1982): 77-90.

Covici, Pascal, Jr. "From Commitment to Choice: Double Vision and the Problem of Vitality for John Steinbeck." In *The Fifties: Fiction, Poetry, Drama*, ed. Warren French. Deland, FL: Everett Edwards, 1970, 63-72.

DeMott, Robert. "The Interior Distances of John Steinbeck." *Steinbeck Quarterly* 12 (Summer-Fall 1979): 86-99.

—. Introduction. In *Mapping "East of Eden."* Special issue of *Steinbeck Quarterly* 14 (Winter-Spring 1981): 4-5.

—. "'Culling All Books': Steinbeck's Reading and *East of Eden*." In *Mapping "East of Eden."* Special issue of *Steinbeck Quarterly* 14 (Winter-Spring 1981): 72-83.

—. "Cathy Ames and Lady Godiva: A Contribution to *East of Eden*'s Background." *Steinbeck Quarterly* 14 (Summer-Fall 1981): 72-83.

—. "'A Great Black Book': *East of Eden* and *Gunn's New Family Physician*." *American Studies* 22 (Fall 1981): 41-57. Reprinted as "Steinbeck's *East of Eden* and Gunn's *New Family Physician*," *Book Club of California Quarterly News-Letter* 51 (Spring 1986): 31-48; and slightly altered as "Creative Reading/Creative Writing: The Presence of Dr. Gunn's *New Family Physician* in Steinbeck's *East of Eden*." In *Rediscovering Steinbeck: Revisionist Views of His Art, Politics and Intellect*, eds. Cliff Lewis and Carroll Britch. Lewiston, NY: Edwin Mellen Press, 1989, 35-57.

—. *Steinbeck's Reading: A Catalogue of Books Owned and Borrowed*. New York: Garland Publishing, 1984, xxxii-xliii.

—. "'Of Ink and Heart's Blood': Adventures in Reading *East of Eden*." *Connecticut Review* 14 (Spring 1992): 9-21.

Ditsky, John. "Music from a Dark Cave: Organic Form in Steinbeck's Fiction." *Journal of Narrative Technique* 1 (January 1971): 59-66.

—. *Essays on "East of Eden."* Steinbeck Monograph Series, no. 7. Muncie, IN: John Steinbeck Society of America/Ball State University, 1977.

—. "The 'East' in *East of Eden*." *John Steinbeck: East and West*, eds. Tetsumaro Hayashi, Yasuo Hashiguchi, and Richard F. Peterson. Steinbeck Monograph Series, no. 8. Muncie, IN: John Steinbeck Society of America/ Ball State University, 1978, 61-70.

—. *John Steinbeck Life, Work, And Criticism*. Fredericton, New Brunswick: York Press, 1985, 10-11, 21, 23, 25, 30.

—. "'I' in *Eden*: The Narrational Voice in Steinbeck." *Kyushu American Literature* 27 (September 1986): 57-69.
—. "Rowing from Eden: Closure in the Later Steinbeck Fiction." *North Dakota Quarterly* 60 (Summer 1992): 87-100.
Etheridge, Charles L. "Changing Attitudes Towards Steinbeck's Naturalism and the Changing Reputation of *East of Eden*: A Survey of Criticism Since 1974." In *The Steinbeck Question: New Essays in Criticism*, ed. Donald R. Noble. Troy, NY: Whitston Publishing, 1993, 250-59.
Everest, Beth, and Judy Wedeles. "The Neglected Rib: Women in *East of Eden*." *Steinbeck Quarterly* 21 (Winter-Spring 1988): 13-23.
Farrell, Keith. *John Steinbeck: The Voice of the Land.* New York: M. Evans and Company, 1986, 145-55.
Fontenrose, Joseph. *John Steinbeck: An Introduction and Interpretation.* New York: Barnes and Noble, 1963, 118-27.
French, Warren. *John Steinbeck.* New York: Twayne Publishers, 1961, 152-56.
—. *John Steinbeck.* Rev. ed. Boston: G. K. Hall, 1975, 141-52.
—. *John Steinbeck's Fiction Revisited.* New York: Twayne Publishers, 1994, 114-119.
Frohock, W. M. *The Novel of Violence in America.* 2d ed. Dallas: Southern Methodist University Press, 1957, 141-43.
Fuller, Edmund. *Man in Modern Fiction.* New York: Random House, 1958, 20-31.
Geismar, Maxwell. *American Moderns: From Rebellion to Conformity.* New York: Hill and Wang, 1958, 164-67.
Gladstein, Mimi Reisel. *The Indestructible Woman in Faulkner, Hemingway, and Steinbeck.* Ann Arbor, MI: UMI Research Press, 1986, 75-100. Partly reprinted as "Abra: The Indestructible Woman in *East of Eden*." In *John Steinbeck*, ed. Harold Bloom. New York: Chelsea House, 1987, 151-53.
—. "The Strong Female Principle of Good—or Evil: The Women of *East of Eden*." *Steinbeck Quarterly* 24 (Winter-Spring 1991): 30-40.
Govoni, Mark. "'Symbols for the Wordlessness': A Study of John Steinbeck's *East of Eden*." Ph.D. diss., Ohio University, 1978.
—. "'Symbols for the Wordlessness': The Original Manuscript of *East of Eden*." In *Mapping "East of Eden,"* ed. Robert DeMott. Special issue of *Steinbeck Quarterly* 14 (Winter-Spring 1981): 14-23.
Gribben, John. "Steinbeck's *East of Eden* and Milton's *Paradise Lost*: A Discussion of Timshel." In *Steinbeck's Literary Dimension: A Guide to Comparative Studies*, ed. Tetsumaro Hayashi. Metuchen, NJ: Scarecrow Press, 1973, 94-104.
Hayashi, Tetsumaro. "'The Chinese Servant' in *East of Eden*." *San Jose Studies* 18 (Winter 1992): 52-60.
Hopkins, Karen J. "Steinbeck's *East of Eden*: A Defense." In *Itinerary: Criticism. Essays on California Writers*, ed. Charles L. Crow. Bowling Green, OH: Bowling Green State University Press, 1978, 63-78.
Jain, Sunita. *Steinbeck's Concept of Man.* New Delhi, India: New Statesman Publishing, 1979, 82-92. Reprinted as "Steinbeck's Celebration of the Human Soul" in *Indian Response to Steinbeck: Essays Presented to Warren French*, ed. R. K. Sharma. Jaipur, India: Rachana Prakashan, 1984, 271-76.

Jones, Lawrence William. *John Steinbeck as Fabulist*, ed. Marston LaFrance. Steinbeck Monograph Series, no. 3. Muncie, IN: John Steinbeck Society of America/Ball State University, 1973, 25-28.

Kawata, Ikuko. "'*Timshel*': Steinbeck's Message through the Hebrew Original." In *John Steinbeck: Asian Perspectives*, eds. Kiyoshi Nakayama, Scott Pugh, and Shigeharu Yano. Osaka, Japan: Osaka Kyoiku Tosho, 1992, 73-87.

Levant, Howard. *The Novels of John Steinbeck: A Critical Study*. Columbia: University of Missouri Press, 1974, 234-58.

Lewis, Clifford. "John Steinbeck: Architect of the Unconscious." Ph.D. diss., University of Texas, 1972, 252-66.

Lewis, R. W. B. "John Steinbeck: The Fitful Daemon." In *The Young Rebel in American Literature*, ed. Carl Bode. London: Heinemann, 1959, 121-41. Reprinted in *Steinbeck: A Collection of Critical Essays*, ed. Robert Murray Davis. Englewood Cliffs, NJ: Prentice-Hall, 1972, 163-75.

Lisca, Peter. *The Wide World of John Steinbeck*. New Brunswick, NJ: Rutgers University Press, 1958, 261-75.

—. *John Steinbeck: Nature and Myth*. New York: Thomas W. Crowell, 1978, 161-78.

McCarthy, Paul. *John Steinbeck*. New York: Frederick Ungar, 1979, 116-24.

McDaniel, Barbara. "Alienation in *East of Eden*: The 'Chart of the Soul.'" In *Mapping "East of Eden."* ed. Robert DeMott. Special issue of *Steinbeck Quarterly* 14 (Winter-Spring 1981): 32-39.

Marks, Lester. *Thematic Design in The Novels of John Steinbeck*. The Hague: Mouton, 1969, 114-31. Reprinted as "*East of Eden*: 'Thou Mayest.'" *Steinbeck Quarterly* 4 (Winter 1971): 3-18.

Martin, Stoddard. *California Writers: Jack London, John Steinbeck, The Tough Guys*. London: Macmillan, 1983, 110-17.

Milton, John R. "The Novel in the American West." In *Western Writing*, ed. Gerald W. Haslam. Albuquerque: University of New Mexico Press, 1974, 72.

Morsberger, Robert F. "Steinbeck's Happy Hookers." *Steinbeck Quarterly* 9 (Summer-Fall 1976), 110-13. Reprinted in *Steinbeck's Women: Essays in Criticism*, ed. Tetsumaro Hayashi. Steinbeck Monograph Series, no. 9. Muncie, IN: John Steinbeck Society of America/Ball State University, 1979, 43-46.

Mulder, Steve. "The Reader's Story: *East of Eden* as Postmodernist Metafiction." *Steinbeck Quarterly* 25 (Summer-Fall 1992): 109-18.

Nakayama, Kiyoshi. "Steinbeck's Creative Development of an Ending: *East of Eden*." In *John Steinbeck: Asian Perspectives*, eds. Kiyoshi Nakayama, Scott Pugh, and Shigeharu Yano. Osaka, Japan: Osaka Kyoiku Tosho, 1992, 193-98.

Owens, Louis. *John Steinbeck's Re-Vision of America*. Athens: University of Georgia Press, 1985, 140-55.

—. "The Story of a Writing: Narrative Structure in *East of Eden*." In *Rediscovering Steinbeck: Revisionist Views of His Art, Politics and Intellect*, eds. Cliff Lewis and Carrol Britch. Lewiston, NY: Edwin Mellen Press, 1989, 60-76.

—. "The Mirror and the Vamp: Invention, Reflection, and Bad, Bad Cathy Trask in *East of Eden*." In *Writing the American Classics*, eds. James Barbour and Tom Quirk. Chapel Hill: University of North Carolina Press, 1990, 235-57.

—. "A Garden of My Land: Landscape and Dreamscape in John Steinbeck's Fiction." *Steinbeck Quarterly* 23 (Summer-Fall 1990): 78-88.

—. "Steinbeck's *East of Eden* (1952)." In *A New Study Guide to Steinbeck's Major Works, With Critical Explications*, ed. Tetsumaro Hayashi. Metuchen, NJ: Scarecrow Press, 1993, 66-89.

Peterson, Richard. "*East of Eden*." In *A Study Guide to Steinbeck, Part II*, ed. Tetsumaro Hayashi. Metuchen, NJ: Scarecrow Press, 1979, 63-86.

Pratt, John Clark. *John Steinbeck*. Grand Rapids, MI: William B. Eerdmans, 1970, 24-32.

Quinones, Ricardo J. "The New American Cain: *East of Eden* and Other Works of Post-World War II America." In *The Changes of Cain: Violence and the Lost Brother in Cain and Abel Literature*. Princeton: Princeton University Press, 1991, 134-44.

Sale, Roger. "Stubborn Steinbeck." *The New York Review of Books* 20 March 1980, 10-12.

Satyanarayana, M. R. *John Steinbeck: A Study of the Theme of Compassion*. Hyderabad, India: Osmania University Press, 1977, 112-24.

Shimomura, Noburo. *A Study of John Steinbeck: Mysticism in His Novels*. Tokyo: Hokuseido, 1982, 152-85.

Simmonds, Roy S. *Steinbeck's Literary Achievement*. Steinbeck Monograph Series, no. 6. Muncie, IN: John Steinbeck Society of America/Ball State University, 1976, passim.

—. "Cathy Ames and Rhoda Penmark: Two Child Monsters." *Mississippi Quarterly* 39 (Spring 1986): 91-101. Reprinted in *Steinbeck's Literary Dimension: A Guide to Comparative Studies, Series II*, ed. Tetsumaro Hayashi. Metuchen, NJ: Scarecrow Press, 1991, 102-13.

—. "'And Still the Box Is Not Full': Steinbeck's *East of Eden*." *San Jose Studies* 18 (Fall 1992): 56-71.

Sreenivasan, K. "*East of Eden*: Steinbeck's Testament of Faith." In *John Steinbeck: A Study of His Novels*. Trivandrum, India: College Book House, 1980, 144-58. Reprinted in *Indian Response to Steinbeck: Essays Presented to Warren French*, ed. R. K. Sharma. Jaipur, India; Rachana Prakashan, 1984, 258-70.

Timmerman, John. *John Steinbeck's Fiction: The Aesthetics of the Road Taken*. Norman: University of Oklahoma Press, 1986, 210-47.

Turner, Frederick. "The Valley of the World: John Steinbeck's *East of Eden*." In *Spirit of Place: The Making of an American Landscape*. San Francisco: Sierra Club, 1989, 249-82.

Watt, F. W. *Steinbeck*. New York: Grove Press, 1992, 93-99.

Wyatt, David. "Steinbeck's Lost Gardens." In *The Fall Into Eden: Landscape and Imagination in California*. New York: Cambridge University Press, 1986, 131-32.

Yano, Shigeharu. *The Current of Steinbeck's World*. Tokyo: Seibido, 1978, 148-64.

Zane, Nancy. "The Romantic Impulse in Steinbeck's *Journal of a Novel: The 'East of Eden' Letters*." In *Steinbeck's Posthumous Work: Essays in Criticism*, eds. Tetsumaro Hayashi and Thomas J. Moore. Steinbeck Monograph Series, no. 14. Muncie, IN: John Steinbeck Society of America/ Ball State University, 1989, 1-12.

E. ON THE FILM VERSION

Kazan, Elia. *Elia Kazan: A Life*. New York: Alfred A. Knopf, 1988, 534-39.

Levin, Bruce, ed. *James Dean in Mendocino: The Filming of "East of Eden."* Mendocino, CA: Pacific Transcriptions, 1995.

Millichap, Joseph. *Steinbeck and Film*. New York: Frederick Ungar, 1983, 137-52.

Morsberger, Robert E. "*East of Eden* on Film." *Steinbeck Quarterly* 25 (Winter-Spring 1992): 28-42.

Pearson, Pauline, and Mary Jean S. Gamble. *"East of Eden" Film Notes*. Salinas, CA: John Steinbeck Library, 1987.

Rathgeb, Douglas. "Kazan as Auteur: The Undiscovered *East of Eden*." *Literature/Film Quarterly* 16 (1988): 31-38.

—. "The Four Faces of Cal Trask: Steinbeck's Troubled Hero and James Dean." *Steinbeck Newsletter* 6 (Winter 1993): 8-9.

PART THREE: INTERIOR DIMENSIONS

". . . to break through the mind tide and submerge deep in the creative zone."

—John Steinbeck, *The Wayward Bus* journal (1946) (Courtesy of the Pierpont Morgan Library, New York City)

"A writer must so rearrange reality so that it will seem reasonably real to the reader. There's a sentence for you—reasonably real to the reader. The difficulty with most stories lies in the fact that they don't seem real to the writer. That's where it must start. A thing's happening doesn't make it seem real; sometimes quite the opposite."

—John Steinbeck, in an excised portion of *Travels with Charley* (1962) (Courtesy of the Pierpont Morgan Library, New York City)

"I don't know when I became aware, writing these essays, that I was writing about myself."

—Terry Caesar, *Conspiring with Forms: Life in Academic Texts* (1992)

"The Girl of the Air":
A Speculative Essay on Steinbeck's Love Poems

"*Creation*. To create the legend in which I could fit the key which would open her soul."
—Henry Miller, *Sexus* (1949)

"He simply manufactured the woman he wanted, rather like that enlightened knight in the Welsh tale who made a wife entirely out of flowers. Sometimes the building process went on for quite a long time, and when it was completed everyone . . . was quite confused."
—John Steinbeck, "About Ed Ricketts" (1951)

1

Next to the tumultuous shapings and seizings of the romantic imagination—those magical and buoyant moments when we fall in love, or when we enter the luminous presence of a great fictive work (which is, I think, another kind of erotic tantalization both for reader and writer)—there are few more exciting events in the otherwise uneventful life of the literary scholar than actually discovering or at least becoming aware of previously unknown writings by a favorite author, especially when such a discovery points to a dimension of that writer's life not revealed in the assembled archives and published records of his or her career. Thankfully, there will always be lacunae in a writer's life waiting to be filled, and lost or misplaced texts waiting to be brought to light. The thought of such possibilities, such adventures, should gladden us all.

In John Steinbeck's case this is especially valid, for the past fifteen years have been quite generous in turning up primary documents that illuminate otherwise shadowy, even secret, areas of his work and life. James Robertson's unearthing of Steinbeck's *Zapata, the Little Tiger*, the original narrative from which Steinbeck and Elia Kazan eventually fashioned the 1952 film *Viva Zapata!* is a good example, and points up the impressive care with which Steinbeck approached his historical research. (Both versions of *Zapata* were published in one volume by Penguin in 1993.) Now part of Stanford University's outstanding collection, ample files of Steinbeck's letters to Katherine Beswick (*SCSU*, 1-13) have been augmented by his letters to Margaret Gemmell; both archives illuminate the early period of his life and work that might otherwise have been less well-documented, especially regarding Steinbeck's first three books—*Cup of Gold, The Pastures of Heaven,* and *To a God Unknown.* The opening in the late 1980s of the Annie Laurie Williams collection at Columbia University's Butler Library, which includes more than two hundred pieces of correspondence between Steinbeck and his drama agent at McIntosh and Otis, was especially propitious to me in preparing *Working Days.* The recent unsealing of several important Steinbeck notebooks (regarding the composition of *The Wayward Bus* and *East of Eden*) at New York City's Pierpont Morgan Library promises to have a similarly positive effect on future scholarship.

Because I was involved in its purchase, I recall with pleasure San Jose State University's acquisition of Steinbeck's correspondence to Wanda Van Brunt, the former Mrs. Mark Marvin, whose husband was one of the production managers of Steinbeck's 1941 filmscript, *The Forgotten Village.* Written over eleven months, from September 1948 to August 1949, these thirty-one letters, purchased in October of 1985 by San Jose's Steinbeck Research Center, add particulars to one of the bleakest eras of the novelist's life, when, reeling from personal setbacks, including an impending divorce, he retreated to his family's Eleventh Street cottage in Pacific Grove, California, to lick his wounds. These letters are all the more intriguing because Van Brunt's name is nowhere mentioned in Steinbeck biographies or letter publications, though she was one of several people responsible for his emotional rescue during his soul's dark night.[1]

If the mark of an important writer is the capacity to keep surprising us with wilderness areas, then I believe Steinbeck qualifies. Whenever we think we have safely arrived at a consensus about him, fresh evidence turns up that causes us to view his life and/or his career anew. John Ditsky stated it succinctly in his keynote speech, with which he opened Steinbeck Festival IX in Salinas in 1988: "Once we have piled up enough data about the 'linear' [chronological] Steinbeck . . . we can begin the effort to see him *whole*—whatever that may prove to mean for his future reputation."[2] As with all of Ditsky's insights in establishing "a more appropriate"—which is to say, more contemporary—"perspective" on Steinbeck, I believe these are sound words we can all live by; they echo my sentiments precisely. But first we need to possess more of the facts, which is why—to quote Ditsky's speech again—in order to judge Steinbeck "by intellect and not by hearsay; by reading instead of rumor," I encourage investigation among Steinbeck's abundant unpublished archives and resources, encouragement that I hope the following circuitous excursion into an uncharted area of Steinbeck's career will validate.

2

Over a decade ago, in that antedeluvian age before Jackson Benson's monumental biography of Steinbeck appeared, I had just turned in the completed manuscript of *Steinbeck's Reading* to Garland Publishing Company and I was beginning the earliest forays into editing *Working Days*, a diary stretching intermittently from February 1938 through January 1941, which Steinbeck kept during and after his writing of *The Grapes of Wrath*. The autograph manuscript of the ledger had not yet been unsealed at the Pierpont Morgan Library (and for my purposes did not exist), so I was working with the less perfect but more readable typed manuscript, housed at the Harry Ransom Humanities Research Center at the University of Texas in Austin.

Through the palest, most muted of allusions in one later entry, I intuited some clandestine activity by Steinbeck, some subterfuge carried on without the knowledge of Carol Henning Steinbeck, his resourceful, talented, straight-speaking wife of the 1930s, who had, perhaps more than anyone else, facilitated Steinbeck's maturation from the jejune literary style of the Donn Byrne-inspired *Cup of Gold* to the unflinching critical temperament of *In Dubious Battle, Of Mice and Men,* and *The Grapes of Wrath* (the latter, as if to underscore the irony of personal history, is dedicated "To CAROL Who Willed It"). Steinbeck's veiled journal reference to "the other"—was it a person, or some secret writing?—intrigued me and piqued my curiosity, especially when I eventually discovered that the encoded writing—the text beneath the text, so to speak—was a suite of love poems produced secretly for Gwendolyn Conger (additional

Carol Steinbeck photographed in 1941 at the Steinbeck's Brush Road home, Los Gatos.
Courtesy of John Steinbeck Library, Salinas, CA.

specifics about the poems' composition appear in section 5 below). After protracted machinations, Gwyn (I adopt her preferred spelling for the rest of my essay) would become Steinbeck's lover and, from 1943 to 1948, his second wife and mother of his only children (after their divorce they remained antagonistic toward each other). But well before that, to protect their anonymity, they concocted elaborate smoke screens and cryptic communiques, addressed through Steinbeck's boyhood friend, Max Wagner, their go-between in Hollywood. "Will you also tell the secretary," Steinbeck wrote Wagner in late December 1940, "that the heat is on the mail a little bit and some other arrangements will have to be worked out. Fix that at the next meeting of the club" (*SLL*, 220). A few months later, in another letter to Wagner, he said, "I'll phone the secretary Monday from Monterey" (*SLL*, 224).

Meanwhile, Benson's monumental biography appeared. His indispensable narrative of the disastrous John-Carol-Gwyn relationship added much to the one-sided account in *Steinbeck: A Life in Letters* and filled in many gaps in my own emerging structure of the triangle. Benson's emphasis on Steinbeck's propensity to idealize Gwyn out of all proportion to her character coincided with my own intuitions in the matter (*TAJS*, 402-05, 494-96, 618-22). But unless you read Benson's book very closely you might have missed two of the sources for his characterization: "Only by reading his love letters and the dozens of love poems addressed to her can one comprehend the extent of his adoration" (*TAJS*, 620). I had already examined the thick bundle of more than 120 of Steinbeck's detailed, lovelorn, and frequently sad (because often unrequited and unanswered) letters to Gwyn at the Bancroft Library at the University of California, Berkeley, but it wasn't until much later that Benson informed me in a private conversation at one of the annual Salinas Steinbeck Festivals that he had only "glanced at" the poems (which were then still owned by a very-much-alive Gwyn) during one of his interviews with her in Palm Springs in the early 1970s. So, until I quoted them selectively in "Aftermath," the final bridging commentary in my edition of Steinbeck's *Working Days* (102-03), the poems had not been in general circulation, and had never appeared in any form, even in previous biographies on Steinbeck.[3]

The original manuscript containing the twenty-five poems is handwritten in a small pocket-size notebook. When

Gwyn died in 1975 the booklet was purchased by Richard Schwartz, owner of Stage House II Book and Art Gallery in Boulder, Colorado (where Gwyn had been living). In turn, at the direction of John and Gwyn's children—brothers Thom Steinbeck and John Steinbeck IV—Schwartz sold it, as part of a large archive of Gwyn's holdings, to the Jenkins Rare Book Company of Austin, Texas; John Jenkins retained much of the archive but sold the poetry manuscript to Black Sun Books of New York City. From Black Sun it was purchased in 1979 for $16,500 by Edwin and Anne-Marie Schmitz, recognized Steinbeck devotees, collectors, and owners of the Book Nest in Los Altos Hills, California. In 1981 the Schmitzes donated the notebook to the Steinbeck Library in Salinas, with the provision that it be sealed.

While their precaution put the autograph manuscript out of circulation, the tale doesn't end there. Enter Terry G. Halladay, one-time literature manager of Jenkins Rare Books, who knew a good thing when he saw it. Drawing on the Gwyn Steinbeck collection in 1977 *before* it was broken up and sold, Halladay transcribed nearly a dozen seven-inch reel-to-reel audio tapes, recorded in 1971, containing Gwyn Conger Steinbeck's memoirs. In 1979 Halladay used the archive to produce his now-valuable MA thesis, "'The Closest Witness,'" which concludes with Halladay's complete transcription of Steinbeck's love poems.[4]

Written for Gwyn Conger, practically under the nose of Carol Steinbeck (which explains the concealable pocket-sized notebook), the poems were generated out of the adulterous longing and nostalgic "ache" (Poem 4) of Steinbeck's wayward heart, as a means of bridging the distance between the lonely Launcelot in Los Gatos and his Guinevere in Hollywood. In the tradition of medieval love lyrics, Poem 1 functions as an address to his beloved (Gwyn's name is nowhere mentioned in the suite) and as an invocation to the eternal woman, a fantastic and impossible-to-attain combination of goddess and muse. She is the imagined fulfillment of his transcendent "longing for a home," a chord that reverberates like a dove's cry throughout the sequence:

I will speak to you always
    young, milk-skinned
Smelling of a sweetness that has
    no simile;
Smell of warm, young, clean skin,
Smell of the unknown house
And a dear home.

I will address you always
Although your name change
And your sister sit
In the seat you made warm. ("CW," 301)

With apologies to Steinbeck, I call his collection "The Girl of the Air," a convenient working title that comes from the major image of the fifteenth poem of his suite, the longest and in many ways the most revealing and resonant of the lot. If Steinbeck scholars and readers wish to find a source for his courtly propensity to be enamored of the goddess archetype, to create seemingly reductive portraits of women in his fiction, and to idealize/idolize Gwyn, they need look no further than this startling confession of a vision that occurred in his sixteenth year:

Once in an empty year
I, working in a field, hoeing weeds
With a sharp hoe that flashed
In and out of the soft earth,
Painted in the air a girl and kept
her there
Floating beside me to look at
to wonder at
As I worked in the hot sun.
And she, made of air and mind
became eternal
And all girls since have shared her,
Have been a little piece of her. . . . ("CW," 315)

His beloved, invested with the sustaining qualities of this "eternal" visionary woman, "red haired and lovely / White breasted with hard lusting nipples," has "taken the place of the air girl / Who floated beside me." Furthermore, the fatalism of Steinbeck's erotic gaze, his "howling love," and his transference of desire is linked so deeply to his aggressive imagination that, he writes, "You cannot save yourself from being / The girl of the air" ("CW," 317). In this fetishistic leap toward a self that is "me more than I am I," in this self-consuming formulation of libidinous attraction, Steinbeck crossed the line into a potentially tragic realm. "I love you beyond words, beyond containing," he wrote Gwyn early in their relationship. "Remember that always when the distance seems so great and the time so long."[5] With such heightened, fanciful expectations of the female as eroticized, eternalized "Other," what normalcy could follow?

Publicity photograph of Gwyn Conger, ca. 1939. Inscribed "To my darling dancing partner John, here's hoping you tap your way to the tops" from "Bette Grable Conger."

Courtesy of the Steinbeck Research Center, San Jose State University, San Jose, CA.

3

The time seems right, then, to put some solid footing under "The Girl of the Air." I suspect that, fifty-five years later, these poems still provide an occasion for stimulating our curiosity and bridging our distances—sufficient reason, though they cannot be called "great" art—for sharing Steinbeck's erotic text. Gwyn was of that opinion too: "He gave me a small notebook containing twenty or so love poems which he wrote me. They are love poems, granted, but the world is being denied them and I think that is a shame. John had a poetical mind. I am not saying the poems are comparable to William Blake or John Donne or even James Joyce, but they are beautiful and poignant, and frankly, they could be directed by any man to any woman he is in love with. They are not personalized as such, and I believe strongly that the world should know that he wrote these things" ("CW," 275-76).

As with many suites, or serial poems, these are not lyrically even or logically coherent, but they do adhere in voice and subject to an inner, alogical romantic urgency, a quality of passionate emotional promise balanced with despair at the lovers' separation. After having made love, the speaker "must forget nothing." In Poem 11 the sensualist of memory merges past and present ecstacies, inscribed in the text through a metonymic device:

> Once long ago the music played
> And I remember only a foot and ankle
> A foot dressed in a white slipper
> And silk cords crisscrossing on the ankle
> No dress, no girl, no face,
> Only a pretty foot dressed in white
> What beauty must have been there
> To remember it.
> And my heart winces a little
> remembering. ("CW," 311)

Despite many flat, prosaic lines and naive notions of lovers' complaints, Steinbeck often achieves a chimeric presence where his words of love and his love of words conjoin. Benson's comment applies here: "For Steinbeck, romantic love was part of the magic, the myth, and the emotional intensity that was also literature" (*TAJS*, 621). Throughout the entire sequence Steinbeck's subject is the woman as sexual presence as well as textual articulation. Few other places in Steinbeck's work show the evocative signification of the pen as phallic instrument and its medium—ink—as spermatic.[6] For instance, in Poem 5, he writes:

I said I would make a song for you
And not a dirge, but a song of fullness
And fulfillment.
My body is angry for your lack
And there is a death in every night
And little birth in the morning
    of loneliness. ("CW," 305)

Perhaps, then, amid this transport of narcissism, we might almost believe all over again—as I am convinced Steinbeck did—that "being in love," with its lusty guises and star-crossed shapes, is the key to life, the efficacious spur that propels the heart from hiding, grants the courage to defy reason, tradition, and common sense, encourages lovers to create impossible expectations, and motivates people to turn their backs on the past, and in so doing—for all its folly and its glory—to refashion themselves as individuals and artists, even if that refashioning is accomplished solely in language. "Some living thing has been born of us / Which can of, and in itself sustain itself. . . ." he says in Poem 14. "This we create, project, draw back / And the whole is good and beautiful and kind" ("CW," 314). Such passionate investment, such rebellious bonding, is first and foremost an act of imagination. Amid unrealistic expectations and potentially reductive beliefs, Steinbeck produced this testament of faith in Poem 23, which measures perhaps better than anything else the depth of his commitment to Gwyn and the lengths to which he would go to follow his illicit desire:

Whatever path time may clear for me on the
    mountain
Know this—that it will bend and curve and climb
Because of you. And going back and forth
I shall take the curves you contrived—
When I have forgotten the anguish of clearing
Still the path will curve, and I will make
Such turnings as the path prescribes. ("CW," 325)

Again in Poem 24, Steinbeck's words ("printed deep in you") create a climactic eternal present, a sexually charged, mystical penetration of lover/writer and beloved/reader: "I will speak to you always / I will speak to you out of all mouths . . . / Even when you have forgotten" ("CW," 326). Even in the grip of desire and longing Steinbeck could not abandon his belief in language, the power of the text, not just to approximate experience but in fact to become experience. The poems comprise a text written as much with as from the lovers' expressive bodies. Eroticizing language was nothing less than a transgression of boundaries.

Indeed, given such corporeality, such prurience of word and deed, this essay might as easily have been called "Of Lust and (Wo)Men" or "The Pheromones of Wrath," because in a very real sense what I speak of is a prototypical human fable of chemical attraction, a Steinbeckian parable of the fall from innocent, tender bonding to bitter, violent denunciation, and the subsequent slow birth of self-wisdom. "If I were to think of it in astrological terms," Gwyn recalled, "John was a Pisces and I a Scorpio. Scorpios and Pisces make great lovers, but they don't stay married very long" ("CW," 277). It is an old human drama—probably the oldest of all—but one the mystical, chivalric (and perhaps repressed) Steinbeck had never acted in before. Between a settled but romantically thin existence of domestic attachment and financial security with Carol and an exciting life of uncertain, "impossible future" (*SLL*, 240) but passionate feeling with Gwyn, Steinbeck vacillated miserably in late 1940 and early 1941. "My nerves cracked to pieces and I told Carol the whole thing, told her how deeply involved I was and how little was left," he explained to Mavis McIntosh on 16 April 1941. "She said she wanted what was left and was going to fight. So there we are. All in the open, all above board. I'm staying with Carol as I must. I don't know what Gwen will do nor does she. Just as badly tied there as ever—worse if anything. . . . Anyway, Carol won the outside and G the inside and I don't seem able to get put back together again" (*SLL*, 227).

Steinbeck as Humpty-Dumpty—his head was in one place, his heart in another. A few weeks after the embarrassing confrontation in April 1941 between Carol and Gwyn (both claimed to be pregnant; both later recanted) at the Steinbecks' recently purchased Eardley Street house in Pacific Grove, the victor—Gwyn—finally walked off with the spoils and the matter was settled, more or less. "I have probably done a brutal and horrible thing," Steinbeck confessed to McIntosh after setting Carol and Gwyn at odds over him. "I suppose I have outraged every social law and every rule," he continued. "I've even searched myself for guilt in the matter of Gwen and I cannot find any. I would do the same thing again and I do not feel guilty. But I do feel very very badly about Carol's hurt. Just as surely I know that she now has a chance to be a person and perhaps a happy person where with me she had none."[7] The heart inflamed is indeed unrepentant, its dispensations implacable.

While this exercise in inside biography is, then, both a footnote to Benson's *True Adventures* and an elaboration on the last section of *Working Days*, it is, perhaps most of all, a kind of cautionary tale which can and does apply everywhere the human heart seeks the fulfillment it cannot or should not have. Less than a year after his letter to McIntosh quoted above, Steinbeck sent his attorney and financial adviser, Webster Street, his wish list: "I want about ten acres near the ocean and near Monterey and I want a shabby comfortable house and room for animals, maybe a horse, and some dogs and I want some babies. Maybe I can't ever get that but it's what I want. And I'm pretty sure it's what Gwyn wants too" (*SLL*, 240). It turned out that Steinbeck really did not know what Gwyn wanted (she rebelled at being an "incubator" for him and not being able to maintain her professional musical career ["CW," 259]). The only thing worse than not getting what you want, Oscar Wilde reminds us in *Lady Windemere's Fan*, is getting what you want. "I think we were star-crossed from the start," Gwyn recollected. "There were beautiful moments, but I don't think I was the woman for him" ("CW," 280). But here I am rushing ahead of myself, and will only say now that, in his writings of the early 1950s, including *Burning Bright*, *East of Eden*, and *Sweet Thursday*, Steinbeck eventually found recompense—even mild revenge—for getting his heart broken.

4

Nineteen thirty-nine was a watershed year for Steinbeck. I put it mildly when I say that it was an exceptionally difficult one. It had been a trying winter, physically speaking. He was laid up or impaired for weeks on end with dental problems, tonsilitis, varicose veins, and severe sciatica—part of it, along with sheer mental exhaustion, the ironic fruit of his sedentary vocation. For five months the previous year—from late May through late October 1938—Steinbeck hunched daily over the outsize ledger book at the desk of his tiny, cramped workroom in his Greenwood Lane house in Los Gatos, where he parceled out his two thousand word allotment on what would become—though he wasn't then convinced—his most magnificent achievement,

The Grapes of Wrath. Here, for example, is a representative journal entry, written 20 October 1938, a week or so before finishing his novel: "A late start. After last night it is no wonder. My nerves blew out like a fuse and today I feel weak and powerless. I wish it hadn't happened until I was through. Guess I better not press my luck. Just write today until I am tired and not force it. . . . I hope the close isn't controlled by my weariness" (*WD*, 91). A tired, harried man, stressed all the time by a thousand demands on his time and attention, Steinbeck finished *The Grapes of Wrath* in a depleted, entropic state, a fragile psychic and physical condition not unlike advanced aging or a thorough-going "collapse" (*SLL*, 179). The cumulative strain of physical impairment and mental exhaustion took an enormous toll in the late fall of that year and the winter of the next.

But in some ways, the spring and summer of 1939 were even worse. With the incredible success of *The Grapes of Wrath* (published officially on 14 April 1939), Steinbeck got what he thought he wanted, though when success as a novelist arrived full-blown at his doorstep, it shook him so deeply he needed to run from it, escaping, if at all possible, into anonymity. First he fled to Chicago where he interned with Pare Lorentz, who was filming *The Fight for Life*. Later he was in and out of Hollywood where ostensibly he consulted on the filmscripts of *Of Mice and Men* and *The Grapes of Wrath*, but where, in June 1939, he met Gwyn Conger, a beautiful, twenty-year-old singer and aspiring actress who was then working in the chorus line at CBS Studios and doing bit-part work in an Irene Dunne movie, *Theodora Goes Wild*, as well as "moonlighting" nights as a singer at Brittingham's cafe ("CW," 33-34). That fall—with Carol along—Steinbeck took an automobile trip north to Seattle and to Vancouver, British Columbia, to visit musician John Cage and his wife Xenia. (Steinbeck planned to write some musical pieces with Cage, though he apparently never followed up on them.) The following spring—again with Carol in tow as a cook for the crew—Steinbeck sailed for six weeks aboard the *Western Flyer* on a collecting trip he organized with Ed Ricketts that would result in the collaborative book of travel and research, *Sea of Cortez*. Finally, he went back and forth to Mexico several times in 1940 and 1941 during the making of his film, *The Forgotten Village*, directed by Herbert Kline.

During some of these sojourns, particularly to Hollywood, Carol was left at their new house, a fairly isolated mountaintop ranch on Brush Road in Los Gatos. It fell on her shoulders to answer mail (sometimes fifty to seventy-five letters a day) and requests from strangers wanting their copies of *The Grapes of Wrath* signed, to fend off an incessant stream of uninvited telephone callers and visitors, to manage their increasingly complex financial arrangements with agents McIntosh and Otis, and otherwise to keep a lid on an explosive situation, not an easy task for a person who was herself volatile, independent, moody, and restless and who considered herself deserving of more honorable treatment.

The steady, unrelenting sale of *Grapes* between March and December of 1939 brought unprecedented fame, notoriety, and financial success to the Steinbecks, exceeding their wildest dreams. But it also tested their collective resistance and brought personal chaos, domestic discord, and intense unhappiness to husband and wife, whose marriage had already been cracking under earlier strains. "Something has to be worked out or I am finished writing," the novelist complained to Elizabeth Otis on 22 June 1939. "I went south to work and I came back to find Carol just about hysterical. She had just been pushed beyond endurance" (*SLL*, 185). Carol, Steinbeck told Otis a month later, is "pretty shell shocked too. . . . My nerves are just about worn out. . . . My leg is still painful but gradually receding . . . Amazing how it shot my nerves though. Several times I've felt as if I were going over the edge" (*LTE*, 17-18).

In mid-October, roughly a year after he had finished writing *The Grapes of Wrath*, while still wrestling with his paralysis and gauging the nearness of the precipice, Steinbeck also was entertaining the need to alter the direction of his life. Here is a revealing entry from *Working Days*, written on 16 October 1939, which is, I think, both a summary and a prophecy. Note especially the blight already tainting the rose of success:

> It is one year less ten days that I finished the first draft of the *Grapes*. Then we came up here to the ranch and then my leg went bad and I had ten months of monstrous pain. . . . This is a year without writing (except for little jobs —mechanical fixings). The longest time I've been in many years without writing. The time has come now for orientation. What has happened and what it has done to me. In the first place the *Grapes* got really out of hand, became a public hysteria and I became a public domain. I've fought that consistently but I don't know how successfully. Second, we are rich as riches go. We have money enough to keep us for

> many years. We have this pleasant ranch which is everything one could desire. It lacks only the ocean to be perfect. We have comfort and beauty around us and these things I never expected. Couldn't possibly have expected. . . . Now I am battered with uncertainties. That part of my life that made the *Grapes* is over. . . . I have to go to new sources and find new roots. . . . I don't know whether there is anything left of me. I know that some of my forces are gone. . . . My will to death is strengthened. In a sense, my work is done because there wasn't much to me in the beginning. But my mind ranges and ranges and searches. . . . I must work alone. That is necessary. I must think alone. (*WD*, 105-07)

If it changed sharply the literary landscape of the United States, *The Grapes of Wrath* altered Steinbeck just as drastically, because it made him vulnerable to sweeping internal changes. As he told Carlton Sheffield on 13 November 1939, "I must make a new start. I've worked the novel . . . as far as I can take it. I never did think much of it—a clumsy vehicle at best. And I don't know the form of the new but I know there is a new thing which will be adequate and shaped by the new thinking. Anyway, there is a picture of my confusion. How's yours?" (*SLL*, 194). Amid his intellectual and emotional confusion, Steinbeck was clear about two things. He was sick of being constrained; what he wanted above all else, he told Sheffield, were "freedom from respectability" and "freedom from the necessity of being consistent" (*SLL*, 193). Fed up with the prison house of his career, and already emotionally captivated by Gwyn, Steinbeck's life in the next two years became a vicious circle; the more celebrated he became, the more resentful he turned toward Carol (and she toward him), whose brittle efficiency, brusque managerial style, and violent mood swings only depressed him further. Suddenly, everything associated with his public fame and private success—especially his marriage—had become a repugnant "nightmare" to him.

In withdrawing from Carol, Steinbeck threw himself into a variety of writing projects, hoping to resurrect the discipline necessary to become productive again, even though several of his new jobs were collaborations, a situation he never fully liked. He turned his back on the "clumsy" novel (between 1939 and 1945 he published eight books, only half of them fiction). Instead, he tried his hand at a whole new range of genres, including comic drama, documentary film, scientific prose, travel writing, and poetry. As part of his complete revolution Steinbeck deliberately cast off the straitjacket of novelist and took up the dashing coat of the man of letters. "Do you realize that the thing which seemed to be happening is happening," he lamented to Otis on 21 April 1940. "I'm so busy being a writer that I have not time to write anything" (*LTE*, 25). Ultimately, his new garment proved to be an imperfect fit, but the experimental writing of this period—from late 1939 through 1942—situated him at the threshold of a new consciousness, an arena of endeavor that he believed more truly honored his own sense of liberated sexual and psychological transformation. "I must have got from my father (a man who never lived fully until it came his time to die) a feeling that I should so live and think and act that I could admire myself, that I could feel that I was just and good and decent. I tried that for a long time. There is no better way of cutting oneself off. Now I don't admire myself at all and I know I have been unjust and not good nor decent and far from being a bad thing it makes me feel very much related to people and to things."[8] After 1941, Steinbeck's writing centered on sustained explorations of new subjective topics—the dimensions of individual choice, romantic/domestic relationships, and imaginative consciousness. Ironically, if these new topics all contained excessive potential for sentimentality and partial portraiture, they also contained enormous possibilities for technical experimentation—for instance the kind of freedom to be found in parables and fables. It was a risk Steinbeck was willing to take to prevent being "cut off."

His new writing, especially his love poems and, in an odd way, *Sea of Cortez*, too, allowed Steinbeck to trade his role as social documentarian for that of private expressionist, because both works required an enormous amount of personal emotional "energy." Working on *Sea of Cortez* in 1941 was a "life saver," he told McIntosh, not only, we can surmise, because it gave him steady, two thousand-words-a-day work that helped him manage his panic, his emotional "horrors" over the strained emotional situation with Carol, from whom he was separated, but also because it was a book in which Carol's voice had been silenced and all meaningful presence of her as a member of the *Western Flyer*'s crew had been expunged. It seems almost too symbolically pat, but conversely, the suite of poems was full of Gwyn's presence as a lover and the sense of her bodily difference from the erased Carol. Steinbeck's willingness to reclaim aspects of the indulgent sensibility he felt he had abdicated during his career with Carol probably had more to do with changes in his domestic, psychological, and emotional situation (which fostered a personal interest in poetical allegory) rather than with such causes as his alleged decline in artistic ability or his move from native California to adopted New York, charges so often leveled in Steinbeck criticism that they have become by now useless cliches.

So, on that fateful night in June 1939, Steinbeck—physically ill, crippled from sciatica, severely depressed, drinking too much for his own good while he hid out from publicity at the Aloha Apartments off Hollywood's Sunset Boulevard—was visited by a stunning, sexy, red-haired showgirl. When Gwyn, a self-confessed "half-assed Florence Nightingale," brought him, at his friend Max Wagner's instigation, homemade chicken soup (which he hated) and tender ministrations (which he loved), the pheromones began to fly, a door opened in Steinbeck's heart, and he took the first step through. When he did, a whole structure of pastness began to crumble and a new future rose like a seductive promise to take its place. ("Gwen is as generous as Carol is not," he later said; "Gwyn can run a hospitable house where I am welcome," while Carol's efforts were seen as un-welcome and "doleful"). A year later, the poems themselves, like the mysterious condition of "home" they long to create, became the proof and the test of his knightly devotion; when his long-distance courting began to pick up steam, the secret text of his private notebook became a meeting point for reality and imagination, present and future, despair and desire, as in Poem 3:

> We will sit down together, my love,
> Red haired and lonely.
> And for a little while the winds
> Will go around. And the house chinks
> Will be tight: I will feel safe and warm
> In your strong weakness and you
>   in my weak strength,
> I will be young in your youth, and you
> Thinking I have seen future,
> Will feel a future more secure
> Against the winds.
> We will be wrong, my love, both wrong
> But our wrongness will be right and I
> Truly will be young who has never been young;
> And you secure who are balanced
> In uncertainty. ("CW," 303)

When their affair finally got rolling, Steinbeck was clearly more and more deeply slain by Gwyn, as she was by him. Like Petrarch, "Love caught him naked with his shaft." Much as Charles Smithson, the hero of John Fowles's *The French Lieutenant's Woman*, who, when he saw the mysterious, fascinating Sarah Woodruff for the first time was lost forever, so Steinbeck was lost. By "lost," of course, I mean that overwhelming intuitive awareness that a large part of his compartmentalized earlier life—his professional respectability and station, his ten-year long marriage to Carol based on discipline, sacrifice, and commitment, his sense of home and being in the world, perhaps even his sense of himself as a dutiful son—was revealed to be false, or at least wanting in the kind of passionate emotion and potential for sexual fulfillment he had spent his whole life seeking in the hidden, perhaps traitorous, recesses of his heart. "I get so dreadfully homesick I can't stand it and then realize that it's not for any home I ever had," he confessed to Webster Street in December 1940 (*SLL*, 218). It took Steinbeck four years to walk all the way over the threshold (after two years of separation, Carol and John divorced on 18 March 1943; eleven days later he married Gwyn in New Orleans [*SLL*, 251; *TAJS*, 515]), but once through Steinbeck emerged a different man and, I think, a different kind of writer. "What happened between us that night was pure chemistry. . . . What occurred that night cannot be recorded. . . . Whatever I was able to provide was something he needed," Gwyn later recalled in her memoir ("CW," 36, 37). Except for the part about not being able to record their passions, Steinbeck agreed; in Poem 7, he wrote:

> Somewhere in the long seeking
> There has been a finding, a chemistry
> Out of two combinations of elements. . . .
> Atom finding orbit with atom
> Chest close fit with breast
> Lingham in yoni. Some pattern
> Sought and found in a moment
> And lost again.
> . . . the rarity of such chemistries. . . .
> The glory of synchronization of
>   ductless glands. ("CW," 307)

The last line, surely one of the most horrid ever penned, nevertheless offers a key to understanding the poet's motive.

During the next eighteen months, as the relationship proceeded off again, on again, Steinbeck was deeply hooked, investing nearly everything in his imaginative creation of "Earth Woman" Gwyn ("CW," 39) that he felt Carol lacked. Carol, Benson states, "was flesh and blood. Gwyn was an ideal" (*TAJS*, 620). In Poem 10, Steinbeck wrote:

> This thing is good, to be taken and loved
> Although it crisp and die in our hands
> This thing is good although it wound us
> You and I—I who created you
> You who created me. ("CW," 310)

Beyond simply idealizing Gwyn, Steinbeck believed that their love was a separate entity, with an identity of its own: "I want you to keep the thing we have warm and inviolate and waiting—the person who is neither I nor you but us."[9] Even admitting his avowed, ironically prophetic risk of failure (a refrain in the suite), such desire was a shaky, ethereal foundation on which to construct a new life; such deep nostalgia for a shared, but unspecified, emotional "home" we have all probably experienced ourselves, just as we all probably come to realize such habitations exist mostly in the penumbra of longing and mostly at the expense of someone else's integrity. On the other hand, nothing ventured, nothing gained. In other words, if Richard Wilbur's catchy line, "love calls us to the things of the world," is true, then Steinbeck had no choice but to follow his bliss, even if it was toward a future "smothered in uncertainties" ("CW," 321). He could not refuse the siren call because it must have seemed his destiny, an incomparable gift he had been waiting for much of his life. Answering the call created a dramatic breakthrough with its own set of demands and required new codes of behavior, and even a new language to replace the old conventions, as Steinbeck intimates in Poem 25:

> When you have forgotten, girl of air,
> I will continue to demand one constancy
> And it is nameless, wordless as dry grief.
> But you will know it, recognize it
> Obey it, and your throat will thicken
> With it as mine does, and you,
> will be constant
> Even when you have forgotten. ("CW," 327)

Compared to the "mannish" Carol ("CW," 48), Gwyn was "all woman, every bit woman," Steinbeck later crowed to McIntosh (*WD*, 99). But then, he had no idea what he was really in for, a point Mildred Lyman understood quite well when she later claimed he had "very peculiar ideas of women" in those days.[10]

5

When the majority of Steinbeck's readers, including the most seasoned and knowledgeable students of his work, think of the dimensions of his literary career, they invariably base their assessment on his achievements in three genres: his novels and short fiction; his dramas and screenplays; and his nonfictional prose. In this summary of familiar modes, poetry is conspicuously absent. My guess is that Steinbeck is rarely thought of as a poet outside of some notable elevated passages in his fiction; the emotionally engaged, densely symbolic, nakedly dithyrambic intercalary sections of *The Grapes of Wrath* or, in a more muted vein, the sure, quiet, lyrical touches of "The Chrysanthemums" and *The Red Pony*. Furthermore, even for the informed follower of his career, Steinbeck is considered a poet (better yet a "versifier") only in connection with his college juvenilia, his occasional bawdy verses, such as the "Ballad of Quid Pro Quo" and others (excerpted by Carlton Sheffield in his introduction to *Letters to Elizabeth*) or the controversial homoerotic poems by "Amnesia Glasscock," still frequently and erroneously attributed to Steinbeck, though in fact they were written by Carol. And yet as a child and teenager growing up in Salinas, then during Professor William Herbert Carruth's class on Versification (English 35) at Stanford University, which Steinbeck took in spring 1923 (one of only 6 A's he received in college), and on through the late stages of his career, Steinbeck not only read a great deal of poetry, but he did in fact write it.

Not all his poems have been preserved, because for him—and this is an important qualification—poetry was a type of private utterance, a kind of personal exercise akin to his journal keeping and intended, as he once said of Robinson Jeffers's intentions (in "Apology for Bad Dreams"), to "exorcise" demons from the household (*SLL*, 608). Steinbeck seems to have indulged in poetry for various reasons, including his abiding love of words, his use of poetry as therapy when he was temporarily blocked in his attempts to write fiction ("For poetry is the mathematics of writing and closely kin to music," he counseled Robert Wallsten [*SLL*, 661]), and in the present case, his desire to express and validate passionate personal feelings such as "the ache of loneliness" and the mystical belief that a woman's love, like a sacred grail, brings the quester salvation found nowhere else. In critic Mimi Reisel Gladstein's terms, Gwyn becomes yet another avatar of the "indestructible woman," prominent in so much of his fiction.[11] In Poem 20, Steinbeck writes, "If this venomous race survive / You and your symbol only can save it" ("CW," 322), emphatic lines that reach back to Ma Joad and Rose of Sharon in *The Grapes of Wrath* and forward to Juana, Mordeen, Abra Bacon, and Suzy in *The Pearl, Burning Bright, East of Eden,* and *Sweet Thursday,* respectively.

"Please tell Gwyn that I am making a song for her and I have never made a song for anyone else," Steinbeck informed his confidant Max Wagner on 23 November 1940. "I love you both. And protect her a little, please. For she is dear to me" (*SLL,* 217). This statement helps answer my initial query about Steinbeck's shadow writing. The external reference to the poems' composition, plus some internal ones from the songs themselves—"I said I would make a song for you" (Poem 5), which I quoted earlier; "red leaves under the mountain frost" (Poem 6), which accurately renders autumn conditions in the Santa Cruz Mountains; "the colored bird who is life and death" (Poem 9), which describes the totemic, mummified birds (each in its own wooden coffin) Steinbeck picked up from a medicine woman in Mexico earlier in the year when he was working on *The Forgotten Village*—help locate the poems in time and place. They also identify the oblique references to "the other" as Steinbeck's code word both for Gwyn and for the suite of poems he was writing for her—at least at the beginning—right under Carol's otherwise watchful eye. Further, they also help explain the frequent tone of paranoia and arcane allusion one encounters in his entries in the post-*Grapes of Wrath* section of *Working Days* and in *Steinbeck: A Life in Letters,* though once we realize he is alluding to Gwyn in Hollywood, his subterfuge becomes clear.

He began to write the suite of poems for Gwyn at his Biddle Ranch home in Los Gatos between late September and late November 1940, between trips back and forth to Mexico and Hollywood for the filming and editing of *The Forgotten Village.* Here is Steinbeck talking to himself on 12 December 1940; once again, note the prophetic tone, the need to whistle in the dark:

> Back from Mexico again and this time I'm through there I hope. And back from Hollywood again and definitely not through there. I try to stay relaxed about that. It isn't possible to be more than it is, and I know that. What a fiasco that would be. And I like it and will continue. It seems the best thing to do and surely the pleasantest in many ways, but there are stomach

> pains in it too. How will it end—tragically, I imagine, but that is part of it too. I won't even run from that. (*WD*, 122)

He didn't run from "that" but instead continued making the song, courting the woman, braving if not tragedy, then melodrama, all the while adding to the poem sequence through the late winter and spring of 1941, while Carol was restoring her health and sanity in Hawaii for six weeks (*SLL*, 224-25). Meantime, as soon as Carol was taken care of, beginning sometime in February 1941, Steinbeck began secretly staying with Gwyn—"hiding out," he later called it—at his sister Esther's beach cottage amid a pine woods in Pacific Grove (the cabin is now part of the Asilomar Conference grounds) as he worked on the manuscript of *Sea of Cortez* (*SLL*, 278; *WD*, 125-26). In their first extended dalliance together they settled into a delicious, gratifying daily routine. Imagery from that time suffuses the late poems: "grey waves of bending grass / Under a hillside wind" and crashing "surf on the beaten beach" (Poem 24) become the backdrop for the ebb and flow of the lovers' mystical flights and languid cessations.[12]

In the manner of two of Steinbeck's favorite models—J. M. Synge's translation of Petrach's *Sonnets to Laura* and E. P. Mathers's translation of *Black Marigolds*, both of which were capable of moving him to tears—these secret poems also have a fragile sadness, a transcendent, almost mystical strain, and a resonance of lament that haunts the whole suite. But Gwyn was not the angelic Laura, unapproachable and chaste, so the thrust of these poems also celebrates the senses and testifies to the power of human sexuality, mutual intimacy, physical attraction, and—perhaps above all else—the dignity and transport of earthy love-making, "stallion's squeal" and "mare nibbling" (Poem 22). In the late 1930s John and Carol's relationship was often celibate. If the cryptic entries in *Working Days* and Gwyn's recollections of her candid confrontation with Carol at the Eardley Street house in April of 1941 can be believed ("CW," 47), Steinbeck did not mix intercourse and writing during his marriage; apparently he and Carol occupied separate entrances and beds, both at the Greenwood Lane house and later at the Biddle Ranch.[13] Beginning in 1938, their separateness may have become habitual, and while this is partly salacious conjecture, it does help explain that when Steinbeck made love to Gwyn the first time (according to Gwyn's memoir, this took place in Oceanside in the summer of

Judith Diem's oil painting of a composed John Steinbeck at work on *Sea of Cortez*, winter of 1940-41.
It is one of the few portraits of Steinbeck painted from life.
Courtesy of the Steinbeck Research Center, San Jose State University, San Jose, CA.

One of Ellwood Graham's preliminary charcoal sketches for an oil portrait of Steinbeck. The sketches were made at Graham's Pebble Beech studio in the winter of 1940-41 as Steinbeck worked on *Sea of Cortez*. "John, who was divorcing his wife Carol, was in a turmoil," Graham said.

Courtesy of the Steinbeck Research Center, San Jose State University, San Jose, CA.

1940), "the glory of synchronization of ductless glands" (Poem 7) quickly obliterated most traces of his marital faithfulness and constancy. The explicit recollection in Poem 8 of sexual pleasure and the praise of Gwyn's bountiful physical attributes, especially her hair and vagina, symbols of her sublime power and appeal, comprise nothing less than a holy spell, a magic, almost religious, incantation—"Oh! Red and gold and black"—which, the blissful lover concludes, "has been God in many times to many men. / And still is God" ("CW," 308).

As Steinbeck later confided to McIntosh, Gwyn's "affectionate" feminine presence transformed his entire life and made his "sloppy and sentimental . . . indulgences"—the risk that his work would "suffer"—seem a worthwhile gamble (though many observers thought it was one he lost). "The house is easy and it has been so long since I have lived in an easy house. My work has jumped in amount and I don't have to fight it. My sex life is prodigious and I take strength rather than depletion from it. This is all selfish. It has to be placed against my cruelty in cutting Carol off. And maybe she will never recover from it. But from what [?] She wasn't happy with me, she never was easy nor relaxed."[14] Is it any wonder, then, that Carol failed to regain her husband? Against Steinbeck's holy distortion and Gwyn's fleshly magic she didn't have a mortal's chance of success. If Carol's side of the story has been a long time coming to light (it is being written by Susan Shillinglaw), at least she can be credited with the most realistic assessment of her husband's behavior and subsequent actions. There is no other way to say this and still honor Carol's salty tongue: "He left me for a better piece of ass," she is reported to have said in 1948.[15]

6

If 1939 was a trying year for Steinbeck, 1948 was a tragedy. His two soul mates left him—in May, Ed Ricketts was killed in an auto/train crash ("When Ed died, a drastic change came about in John and our marriage" ["CW," 273]); shortly after that, showing very little compassion or sense of timing, Gwyn told him she wanted a divorce ("As much as I loved John, I couldn't live with him. . . . I was wrong for him" ["CW," 230]). The combined force of these two blows—especially the latter, about which there was a great deal more rancor, deceitfulness, and subterfuge on Gwyn's part than she makes it appear in her own memoir

(*TAJS*, 616-22)—nearly destroyed Steinbeck. Though she later retracted her concocted confession, Gwyn stunned Steinbeck by taunting him with the news that she had illicit affairs during their marriage.[16] Realizing he had endured—and in part ignored—three years of "consistent treachery," Steinbeck confessed to Wanda Van Brunt on 16 January 1949, "I can't take that kind of pain."

John Steinbeck's obsessive urge to make a goddess of Gwyn, then accuse her of being a monster when she failed to live up to his impossible standards, does not automatically absolve Gwyn of her share of provocation and blame (she later called their marriage "tragic" but generally whitewashed her own role ["CW," 277]). Nevertheless, the lingering endurance and persistence of their affair suggests that it was the most intense romantic relationship either had ever had ("I certainly was never in love again the way I was in love with John Steinbeck," she confessed ["CW," 263]). Though it wounded everyone involved, there is no denying that it remained a constant touchstone of his personal and literary experience for more than a decade. Steinbeck was fond of repeating the story of how Ed Ricketts, very much like Lleu Llaw Gyffes, "that enlightened knight in the Welsh tale" of *The Mabinogian*, "manufactured" the woman he wanted. But the fact was that, like Math, who conjured a woman "entirely out of flowers" *for* Lleu in the medieval epic, Steinbeck was projecting on Ricketts his own propensity to build "his own woman" and create "her from the ground up."[17] "I am afraid I built a person who wasn't there," he admitted to Pascal Covici in December 1948. "When one's whole pattern of thinking proves untrue it seems to cause a seismic shock." Jackson Benson's appraisal seems particularly apt: "The sadness of Steinbeck's plight was that he had brought a literary inspired passion to his writing, and it drove him to success, but when he brought it to his life, it nearly dstroyed him. There was further irony in the circumstance that one of the major themes of his writing had been the destructiveness of myth when it is used as a pattern for living" (*TAJS*, 621-22).

And yet, by creating other literary patterns Steinbeck mitigated the errant mythology of the moment and managed to compensate for his volcanic experiences. "Gwyn once told me she could do anything and I would come crawling back. At the time I was very much in love with her but even then I told her not to depend on it," he explained to Covici on 1 November

1948. "A woman holds a dreadful power over a man who is in love with her but she should realize that the quality and force of his love is the index of his potential contempt and hatred" (*SLL*, 338). Steinbeck accomplished his therapy by confronting his demons head on: he reprised the darkest aspect of his marriage to Gwyn (especially the issue of legitimate parenthood) in the eerie play-novella *Burning Bright*, and he continued to exorcise his memory of her in his chilling portrait of the evil, conscienceless "monster," Cathy Ames, who, in *East of Eden*, knowingly tortures her husband, Adam, with the news that their son Cal is not his. But perhaps it wasn't really until his next book, the slap-dash comedy, *Sweet Thursday*, that one of his characters—ironically or perhaps fittingly a woman—struck the summary note on the subject of Girls of the Air: "When a man falls in love it's ninety to one he falls for the dame that's worst for him." It was an evaluation many of Steinbeck's friends and family members already knew about his past (*TAJS*, 621). And with that intentionally humorous, self-deprecating remark, Steinbeck began to draw to a close a bittersweet chapter in his emotional life that began fifteen years earlier.

Notes

[1] Steinbeck may have had a brief fling with Wanda. On an otherwise bleak trip to New York City in late April 1949, both for business and to see his sons, Steinbeck also visited Wanda. On the flight home he wrote two notes to her: the first, postmarked 5 May, says, "I was very happy and you were my happiness"; the second, also postmarked that day, says, "I remember every minute and love all of them. And don't think your present is not deeply, deeply appreciated. Good night darling." Both are signed "J." More importantly, in the overall picture of that year, Steinbeck thanked her for her "help and encouragement" when his "flag was down" (courtesy of the Steinbeck Research Center). For more on these letters, see Dana Rubin, "SJS buys 31 Steinbeck letters," *San Jose Mercury News*, 26 October 1985, 1B, 2B, and Carol Ryan, "University buys Steinbeck's 'dark night' letters, "*Salinas Californian*, 26 October 1985, 1, 12. Stanford University Library's Department of Special Collections has also actively increased its superb holdings of Steinbeck letters, including a recently acquired archive of forty-eight letters (only one of which appears in *Steinbeck: A Life in Letters*) written between 1954 and 1964 to Leslie Brady, an American diplomat in Paris, Moscow, and Washington, who had helped with Steinbeck's *Figaro* publications and later helped arrange Steinbeck's cultural visit with Edward Albee to the Soviet Union. See Margaret J. Kimball, "Stanford's Steinbeck Collection Recent Acquisitions," *Steinbeck Newsletter* 6

(Summer, 1993): 10-11. For more on the rich holdings in the Columbia and the Pierpont Morgan archives, see Bernard R. Crystal, "John Steinbeck Letters and Manuscripts in the Columbia University Libraries," *Steinbeck Newsletter* 6 (Winter 1993): 14-17; and Robert Parks, "John Steinbeck in the Pierpont Morgan Library," *Steinbeck Newsletter* 8 (Winter-Spring 1995): 19-21. Though somewhat outdated, a useful overview of various Steinbeck collections is available in Tetsumaro Hayashi's *A Handbook for Steinbeck Collectors, Librarians, and Scholars*, Steinbeck Monograph Series, no. 11 (Muncie, IN: John Steinbeck Society of America/Ball State University, 1981).

[2] John Ditsky, "John Steinbeck—Yesterday, Today, and Tomorrow," *Steinbeck Quarterly* 23 (Winter-Spring 1990): 12. Ditsky continues: "We have a long way to go toward finally understanding the thinking of John Steinbeck, and also toward extricating it at last from the critical thicket where it is difficult to tell it from that of Ed Ricketts. I believe that we are nearly at the day in which there will be . . . a lot more of reading him straight and direct—from his book, and with imagination" (15). Allowing for variations in methodology, point of view, and theoretical biases, similarly refreshing attitudes about (re)reading Steinbeck are to be found in the continuing work of Jackson J. Benson and in these recent studies: Brian Railsback's *Parallel Expeditions: Charles Darwin and the Art of John Steinbeck* (Moscow: University of Idaho Press, 1995); Charlotte Hadella's *"Of Mice and Men": A Kinship of Powerlessness* (New York: Twayne, 1995); and Roy S. Simmonds's *John Steinbeck: The War Years, 1939-1945* (Lewisburg, PA: Bucknell University Press, 1996).

[3] Regrettably, only about twenty of Steinbeck's letters to Gwyn (many simply excerpted from longer missives) are represented in *Steinbeck: A Life in Letters*. Steinbeck's letters and his poems to Gwyn are not mentioned in Nelson Valjean's *John Steinbeck: The Errant Knight* (San Francisco: Chronicle Books, 1975), in Thomas Kiernan's *The Intricate Music: A Biography of John Steinbeck* (Boston: Little, Brown 1979), or in Jay Parini's *John Steinbeck: A Biography* (New York: Henry Holt, 1995). Jackson Benson's account of his interview with Gwyn, the substance of which he passed on to me that day in Salinas, later appeared in "Gwyn and Kate: Two Women in His Life," chap. 6 of his *Looking for Steinbeck's Ghost* (Norman: University of Oklahoma Press, 1988), 95-104. Benson's book is a savvy autobiographical "collection" recounting his fifteen-year odyssey in producing *The True Adventures of John Steinbeck*.

[4] My information about the location of Steinbeck's poetry manuscript comes from several sources: a Black Sun Books Catalogue; a brief note by Kiyoshi Nakayama, "Steinbeck's Love Poems," in *The John Steinbeck Society of Japan Newsletter* 7 (May 1984): 13; a letter written to me on 17 August 1984, by Mary Jean S. Gamble, Steinbeck Librarian, John Steinbeck Library, Salinas, CA; a telephone conversation with Steinbeck's eldest son, Thom Steinbeck, on 3 October 1985; and the introduction by Terry Grant Halladay to "'The Closest Witness': The Autobiographical Reminiscences of Gwyndolyn Conger Steinbeck," (master's thesis, Stephen F. Austin University, 1979), 6-19 (hereafter cited as "CW"). The bulk of this 330-page work is a rendering of Gwyn's unfinished and frequently interrupted oral reminiscences and interviews, recorded with Douglas Brown between March and May 1971. Halladay edited the jumbled, contradictory, and often sordid (but always revealing) material into a relatively coherent narrative and added appropriate introductory statements,

annotations, and notes. The thesis is available on demand from University Microfilms, 300 N. Zeeb Road, Ann Arbor, MI 48106 (order number 1313147). Recently, I learned that Thom Steinbeck and the late John Steinbeck IV had once planned to publish a separate edition of their father's poems to their mother. Catalogue Four (1990) of MacDonnell's Rare Books (Austin, TX) lists for sale (at $250): "*Love Poems to Gwyn Conger Steinbeck.* Austin, 1978. Unpublished typescript. 27pp. A collection of twenty-five poems with mock-up of title page and colophon, prepared for private publication for members of the Steinbeck family, but apparently never published" (entry 453).

[5] John Steinbeck to Gwyn Conger, n.d. [ca. 1940-41], Bancroft Library, University of California, Berkeley.

[6] It seems instructive that a decade later, speaking of "creative juices," Steinbeck linked semen and ink: "The joy thing in me has two outlets: one a fine charge of love toward the incredibly desirable body and sweetness of woman, and second—mostly both—the paper and pencil or pen. . . . They are . . . but the trigger into joy—the shout of beauty—the cacajada of the pure bliss of creation" (*JN*, 10). Some intriguing psychobiographical implications of Steinbeck's sexual/textual transference are noted in Kenneth Lynn's review of the 50th Anniversary Edition of *The Grapes of Wrath* and *Working Days* in *The American Spectator* (August 1989): 41-42. Writing as a site of erotic energy is an area of Steinbeck studies that deserves more sustained critical investigation. John Ditsky, however, has made some strong beginnings: see "Rowing from Eden: Closure in the Later Steinbeck Fiction," *North Dakota Quarterly* 60 (Summer 1992): 97-99; and especially his provocative lecture, "'Your Own Mind Coming Out in the Garden': Steinbeck's Elusive Woman," in *John Steinbeck: The Years of Greatness, 1936-1939*, ed. Tetsumaro Hayashi (Tuscaloosa: University of Alabama Press, 1993), 16-19. In the latter, Ditsky's summation—"ultimately Steinbeck's elusive and remarkable Woman is the work herself"—provides a salient gloss on the nature of Steinbeck's love poems to Gwyn: the poems became the woman; the woman became the poems. See also Peter Brooks, *Body Work: Objects of Desire in Modern Narrative* (Cambridge: Harvard University Press, 1993), 6, who finds suggestive interpretative possibilities in all literary works when "the text itself represents the body, and the body the text. . . ."

[7] John Steinbeck to Mavis McIntosh, n.d. [May 1941], Clifton Waller Barrett Library, Special Collections Department, University of Virginia Library, Charlottesville. This is one of thirteen candid, no-holds barred letters to his agent and confidante that Steinbeck wrote between May and September 1941. Most are undated, except for occasional indications of the day of the week.

[8] John Steinbeck to Mavis McIntosh, Sunday, n.d. [May-September 1941], Clifton Waller Barrett Library, Special Collections Department, University of Virginia Library, Charlottesville.

[9] John Steinbeck to Gwyn Conger, n.d. [ca. 1940-41], Bancroft Library, University of California, Berkeley.

[10] Mildred Lyman to Annie Laurie Williams, [7? February 1949], Rare Book and Manuscript Library, Columbia University, New York.

[11] Mimi Reisel Gladstein, *The Indestructible Woman in Faulkner, Hemingway, and Steinbeck* (Ann Arbor, MI: UMI Research Press, 1986), 75-100. Professor Gladstein's approving overview of the major women in Steinbeck's fiction

needs to be read against her most recent account, "Missing Women: The Inexplicable Disparity Between Women in Steinbeck's Life and Those in His Fiction," in Donald R. Noble, ed., *The Steinbeck Question: New Essays in Criticism* (Troy, NY: Whitston Publishing, 1993), 84-107. Paradoxically, Steinbeck's poeticizing of Gwyn falls in both camps: he mythologizes her, but he also places her squarely in his work; that is, given the erotic terms inscribed in the poems, Steinbeck's fetishization of Gwyn both emancipates and enslaves her.

12 A couple of very different oil portraits of Steinbeck showing him at work on *Sea of Cortez* were painted during the winter of 1940-41. The portraits, which reflect aspects of his exterior and interior life, suggest that both views are needed in assessing the truth of Steinbeck's situation. Steinbeck seemed, at least on the surface anyway, calm, peaceful, and fully focused—the way Judith Diem depicted him in her colorful portrait, suggesting, once again, how, despite personal crises, Steinbeck could always find a degree of serenity in the process of composition, when he entered, for a few hours each day, the world of his writing. "The work flows easily and is fun," he said at his sister's cabin on 29 January 1941, the second day of writing *Sea of Cortez* (*WD*, 125-26). And yet, there was still plenty of turmoil, anger, and uproar in his life that winter. On the following day, agonizing over Carol's "unhappiness" (she was alone in Los Gatos) and lonely for Gwyn's company (she was in Hollywood), Steinbeck noted, "I am ill—ill in the mind. My head is a grey cloud. . . . I'm bludgeoned and feel beaten" (*WD*, 127). Diem's husband at the time, former WPA muralist and abstract artist Ellwood Graham, captured that conflicted and pained emotional condition in a series of preliminary charcoal sketches and a final oil painting of Steinbeck. Diem's portrait was recently purchased by the Steinbeck Research Center at San Jose State University, which also owns one of Graham's charcoal studies. See Bonnie Gartshore, "Portrait of Steinbeck to be Unveiled Today," *Monterey County Herald Go!* 23 February-1 March 1995, 6. Graham's oil painting, which Steinbeck had commissioned, was owned by film director John Huston. For more on Graham's painting and his reminiscences about Steinbeck, see Ted M. Taylor, "Painting Out Loud," *Monterey County Herald Coast Weekly* 23 February 1995, 14-15. In describing the reproductions of paintings pinned to the walls on the interior of Doc's Western Biological Laboratory in chapter 5 of *Cannery Row*, Steinbeck included one by Graham. Besides the charcoal sketch reproduced here in *Steinbeck's Typewriter*, another preliminary sketch appears on the dust jacket and as the frontispiece of the cloth edition (long out of print) of Richard Astro and Tetsumaro Hayashi's *Steinbeck: The Man and His Work* (Corvallis: Oregon State University Press, 1971). Graham's sketch was dropped entirely when the book was published in a paperback format.

13 In *John Steinbeck: A Biography*, Jay Parini adds an intriguing twist to the cumulative account of John and Carol's marriage and one, if true, that might help explain the extreme tension in their relationship during *The Grapes of Wrath* period. Parini claims that, when Carol got accidentally pregnant in late 1938, "Steinbeck panicked, insisting that she get an abortion." She developed a uterine infection that required a hysterectomy, a devastating blow to a woman "who wanted a child very badly" (227). Parini, the first biographer to publicize this event, based his account on Joseph Campbell's comments, quoted by Stephen and Robin Larsen in *A Fire in the Mind: The Life of*

Joseph Campbell (New York: Doubleday, 1991), 211. To that Parini added the testimony of one Allison Harley, a friend of Carol's (Harley's name turns up nowhere else in the biographical literature on Steinbeck). Interestingly, Gwyn, who could dish dirt with the best of them, and claims to have gotten an earful (in their April 1941 confrontation at the Eardley Street house) from Carol about Carol and John's three-year abstention from sexual intercourse, never mentions Carol's abortion in her memoir, though Gwyn claims she had one herself, having gotten "knocked up" the very first time she made love to Steinbeck in 1940 ("CW," 46-48). Recently, Sparky Enea, one of the crew members on the *Western Flyer*, offered his recollections of the sexual intrigues surrounding John, Carol, and Gwyn. See his boozy memoir, as told to Audry Lynch, *With Steinbeck in the Sea of Cortez* (Los Osos, CA: Sand River Press, 1991), 4, 66-67.

[14] John Steinbeck to Mavis McIntosh, n.d. Thursday [May-September 1941], Clifton Waller Barrett Library, Special Collections Department, University of Virginia Library, Charlottesville.

[15] Note on a private conversation with Carol Steinbeck, Harry Ransom Humanities Research Center, University of Texas, Austin.

[16] See Benson, *Looking for Steinbeck's Ghost*, 172, for the consequences of this startling evidence. In *John Steinbeck* Parini does not mention Gwyn's heartlessness but does provide corroboration from eyewitnesses for Gwyn's untrustworthiness and jealousy. In assessing what went wrong between them, Parini continues: "the substantial age difference . . . must have been an impediment to mutual understanding. Neither partner entered the marriage with a clear view of the other. It was a classic case of misheard cues, and mistaken assumptions" (326). The tale of Steinbeck's bitter crash and demoralization, his violent moods and fierce, uncompromising misogyny, and his sense of betrayal and rejection, as well as the slow struggle toward recovery with Elaine, his third wife, is told admirably in Benson's biography, *The True Adventures of John Steinbeck*, and recapitulated in somewhat sketchier terms in Parini's book.

[17] John Steinbeck, *The Log from the "Sea of Cortez"* (New York: Viking Press, 1951), li.

"Of Ink and Heart's Blood": Adventures in Reading Steinbeck

"There will be many things in this story which may not be exactly and objectively true. They seem to me true because I remember them."
—John Steinbeck, opening pages of "The Salinas Valley" (1951)

"A work of art that enters us to feed the soul offers to initiate in us the process of the gifted self which some antecedent gift initiated in the poet. Reading the work, *we* feel gifted for a while, and to the degree that we are able, we respond by creating new work (not art, perhaps, but with the artist's work at hand we suddenly find we can make sense of our own experience)."
—Lewis Hyde, *The Gift: Imagination and the Erotic Life of Property* (1983)

"Literature is . . . exactly what criticism must strive to become."
—G. Douglas Atkins, *Estranging the Familiar: Toward a Revitalized Critical Writing* (1992)

1

Several years ago, halfway through my stint as the visiting director of San Jose State University's Steinbeck Research Center, I found an Associated Press news clipping dated 24 April 1969 that stopped me in my tracks: "Steinbeck Book Saves U.S. Newsman." During the Vietnam War, the life of Jack Russell, a National Broadcasting Company newsman, was saved when a grenade fragment embedded itself in the paperback copy he was carrying of John Steinbeck's book of World War II battle reports, *Once There Was a War*. I was taken by the startling unpredictability of the event and the catch-22 quality of a man being rescued from annihilation by a book about annihilation. I imagined that embattled Steinbeck (who had died five months earlier in December 1968 amid unresolved tensions stemming from his controversial support of American troops in Vietnam, his publicized friendship with President Lyndon Johnson, and his own private pessimism about the feasibility of the war) would have appreciated the irony.

What happened to Jack Russell had happened to me too: Steinbeck had saved our lives. Steinbeck's book had literally saved Russell's skin that day in a rice paddy eighteen miles south of Saigon, and without upstaging or trivializing Russell's dire predicament, I can say that on another level, a little less than five years before that day in Southeast Asia, Steinbeck's fiction—*East of Eden* in particular—saved my skin too. His books didn't protect me from mortal harm, but they did alter me considerably by giving me a sense of purpose and motivation at a moment in my early twenties when, as a floundering undergraduate at a New England college, I had almost no direction at all. My life took a marked turn after my first exposure to Steinbeck's writing. I gained a second chance, which is one way of defining a writer's gifted appeal and power, one way of saying grace to what Steinbeck himself called the "sacred" and authentically "magic" property of books.

Through a combination of persistence, lucky breaks, and the good will of generous people, I finally left New England eight months after college, quit my deadend job as a clerk in a liquor store, and turned my back on the temptation of going into business with my father (or with one of my other entrepreneurial relatives). One slick winter night, newly married, my wife and I fled our families and headed to Ohio, first to Cleveland and Kent for graduate school, then, in 1969, to Athens where I got a job teaching American literature to Ohio University students, many of whom were not so different in their youthful anxieties, political unrest, and academic uncertainties than I had been a few years earlier. A circle seemed to have closed: from the moment the critically neglected Steinbeck (the establishment already considered him officially "dead," several years before his actual demise in late 1968) redeemed my ragtag intellectual life by providing access to a literary world I could enter with a depth and intensity I didn't know I had, his writing became a significant presence to me. More than that, precisely because his writing has always somehow existed on the edges of fashionable discourse in an area resolutely apart from the traditional mainstream, it is doubly appealing to me. Sometimes the reading that matters most is visceral rather than cerebral, and comes as a surprise rather than being planned; such reading manages to move us in unaccountable ways toward an end we didn't imagine it was possible to see, much less reach.

This essay, then, is really a confession, because as I conjure up my first reading of *East of Eden*, for example, it had a slightly sinful quality, as though I had looked in a window and witnessed something unexpected or lurid pass between strangers, or as though I had stolen some precious object which I hardly knew what to do with once I had it in the palm of my hand. Far from being a reflection of reality—though of course it is that—the act of reading can be a reality all its own, which then becomes part of the ineluctable fabric of memory, like "something that happened to me," as Steinbeck once said of his own reading. This testimony is a homage to a lifesaving experience I consider a gift and a celebration of the fortuitous entrance of an altering presence into my life, an unexpected offering I could not refuse to accept. I see now that among the books I have loved excessively during my life, *East of Eden* is another gifted presence, another touchstone of value and meaning around which some related personal events have clustered.

2

One autumn afternoon in 1964, I was sitting alone in the third-floor walkup apartment in Worcester, Massachusetts, that I shared with my exotic Nebraska-born roommate, the first "Westerner" I had ever known. (I was born and raised in Connecticut, fifty miles from New York City, and had never been west of the Hudson River, which is a gentle way of saying that my notions about the West were distorted: I was sure all Californians surfed and drove "Woodies" and all Montanans bucked broncos, drank whiskey straight, and rode their horses to town to fetch the weekly mail.) I was drinking a Carling Black Label beer and rummaging around in a volume of the *Norton Anthology of English Literature*, trying to get a handle on some ideas for a required senior year thesis, but I kept getting distracted by the brilliant leaves of a few oaks and maples, which blinked like neon signs in the preternatural light of an unexpected October snow squall visible through the sooty windows of our living room. My concentration span for such research was about ninety seconds, so I knew I was going to be in for a rough year.

I was becoming so panicky that I began to think about changing my major from English to something more practical (one that wouldn't require writing a thesis), but that stymied me too, because not only had I already switched once (I started college as a biology major but had bailed out to save myself the certain humiliation of flunking a year-long course in organic chemistry), I also couldn't think of anything socially acceptable or practical that I actually enjoyed doing. Any pursuit requiring chemistry, physics, or mathematics was out because I didn't have a clue about what made them tick. Besides, I would probably hate working regular hours and being at the beck and call of a beauracratic type.

A vocation at once independent and glamorous was what I craved. I vaguely thought I would like to have been a metal sculptor, but my college didn't have a program in sculpting, so instead I fantasized about quitting school to try out with one of the semiprofessional hockey teams in Providence or in New Haven (I played ice hockey in high school and in college), to move to California to become a surf bum (The Beach Boys were at the height of their fame then; "Little Surfer Girl," or "Surfin' Safari," I think, was playing frequently on the radio), or better yet, to turn my back entirely on civilization and become a fishing guide in Montana or Wyoming, where I would lead people on horseback for weeks at a time into limitless expanses of wilderness to fish for trout as long as their arms.

Our dingy urban apartment was located a few miles from the small, men-only Catholic college that had informed a half dozen of us at the end of our junior year the previous spring that we would no longer be allowed to live on campus because we could not be expected to act like "civilized gentlemen." We were considered such disruptive influences on the intellectual and social life of that monastic institution that it was considered in the best interest of the student body that our dormitory privileges be revoked. At once proud and embarrassed, we cared and did not care. After I swallowed my guilt and got up the nerve to tell my parents (who were, as usual, extremely understanding), the expulsion was actually thrilling and set us apart from our staid classmates, who nevertheless frequently traveled from their dorms to our places, to eat homemade meals, to drink beer, to dance with the women who came over from the local colleges on Saturday nights, and to be at ease in a way the artificial environment of the college would not allow, with its clubby, formal talk of the New Testament, Aristotle, St. Thomas Aquinas, and T. S. Eliot, its curfew hours and tight restrictions, and especially its ironclad belief in the constitution of the "good life," as though a blueprint existed that ensured success for what my professors and coaches called the "whole man," that elusive, nostalgic paradigm of Renaissance humanistic perfection.

Far from being a whole man, Catholic or otherwise, or even grasping what the concept meant, I found my academic and mental life in pieces. Away from my enormous Italian family, with its interlacing web of grandparents, uncles, aunts, and cousins, its raucous family meals, and shared news of each day's events, I had little sense of intellectual community or worldly home, scant sense of belonging any place solid in the outside world. I felt as aimless as those aberrant snowflakes whirling through the afternoon air, ringing their changes on my windows before melting, as though they had never existed at all. The sheer bulk of the *Norton Anthology* open in front of me (I often used it to block the front wheel of my car so it wouldn't roll into the street) became so intimidating that I nearly wept in despair. I loved to read, which is why I had switched to English in the first place, but wading through those endless fields of tiny print sown by long-dead writers seemed to me as pointless as cutting the grass on all the graveyards in New England: it would kill me. Clearly, my ass was in a sling; I needed a new direction, something that would rescue me from myself, restore some promise to my future, and justify all the hard-earned money my working parents had provided for my thus-far disastrous education.

My college was a bastion of conservatism, its English department a hothouse of New Criticism. Biography was anathema and any form of populism heresy. Metaphysical poetry was the ideal. Except for Wordsworth, who was fairly tame, expressive, no-holds-barred romanticism was scorned; John Donne was in; Walt Whitman was out. Hemingway was considered a bad joke—too autobiographical; so was D. H. Lawrence, whose brain, we were told, was between his legs. James Joyce's *The Portrait of the Artist as a Young Man* was a model book: just the right emotional content crystallized in epiphanies, just the right seriousness of intellectual matter, just the right concept of experimental language and form combined with dispassionate impersonal narration. (It was, I recall, the only work of literature that turned up regularly on the reading lists for classes in English, philosophy, and religion. It seemed that there was no getting away from Stephen Dedalus, his Aquinian aesthetic, his pursuit of wholeness, harmony and radiance.)

The Chairman of this Intellectual Combine conducted himself with the imperious mien and condescending manner of a British don. (From the moment in my sophomore year when I told him he should read Ian Fleming's James Bond series because they were "fun," he considered me an unregenerate, backsliding n'er-do-well; nothing I ever did afterward in my graduate or professional life erased that first impression.) That man, unfortunately for me, taught the bulk of the English courses. Even worse, he believed that stuffed-shirt T. S. Eliot was the twentieth-century's reigning cultural god, *The Waste Land* and "Tradition and the Individual Talent" its secular bibles. His passwords were *irony, classicism, aesthetic distance, ambiguity, well-wrought form,* not one of which was a living concept to me, but remained for a long time arcane notations, mysterious hieroglyphics, not unlike the secret lingo of a private club designed, I imagined, to keep foreigners like me out. (I kept banging at the door, though, in that blind, frontal way most Italian-Americans know, figuring eventually, perhaps, my good intentions—I really did want to learn—would pay dividends with Professor High-And-Mighty, but I never received a grade higher than C+ from him in two years of trying.)

But sometimes even the unwashed get lucky: I had the incredible fortune to know John Burke and Mike O'Shea, two new young faculty members who had some different ideas, different tastes than the rest of the pack. A week or so earlier, probably because he was exasperated by my continual whining, O'Shea, the younger of the two, had suggested I read John Steinbeck, a California writer whose name I had only vaguely recollected ever hearing before. "You might like *Tortilla Flat,*" he said. "It's about a bunch of *paisanos* who raise hell all the time and have trouble fitting in with society. Steinbeck wrote about underdogs, and he got kicked out of college so often he never finished." Immediately, I was intrigued, though as usual I couldn't gauge the note—much less the degree—of irony in his voice. John Burke, who had done his graduate work not in the tweedy East but at a state university in the Southwest, in what I imagined was still the wild and wooly frontier, seconded the idea, and suggested that I try reading *Of Mice and Men.* Both men warned me, however, that Steinbeck had fallen out of fashion in academic circles, and that since the stunning success of *The Grapes of Wrath* twenty-five years earlier, he had never again lived up to his "promise." As a quick fix for my temporary thesis problems, however, Steinbeck would be just the ticket to salvage my woeful undergraduate career. (Neither man dreamed I would eventually go to graduate school, much less turn my blundering encounter with Steinbeck into an abiding interest. I realize now, however, that there was a certain symmetry in the pairing of a marginalized student with a marginalized writer, a way of suggesting that we get what we deserve in this life, whether we expect it or not.)

I hadn't read enough criticism of American literature to know whether their verdict was true or not, but in my desperate state I guessed that any living writer—has-been or not—would be a better project than trooping through the Norton mausoleum again. So that Sunday in October 1964, undeterred by my ignorance and with snow swirling as much through my head as it was outside, I drove to the college library on my way to hockey practice, and hunted through the stacks until I reached "Steinbeck, John." I grabbed the first book my eye lit upon; it was *Travels with Charley*, at that time his most recent work. I read the first fifteen pages or so and I was hooked. Steinbeck's voice was alive, he seemed to be speaking directly to me; in his description of Hurricane Donna, he was the first writer I'd ever encountered who wrote of a contemporary event I had lived through as well, for a few years earlier, Donna had swept up past the eastern end of Long Island, roared across Long Island Sound, and came slashing into the shore area of southwestern Connecticut where I lived. Forget Pope's Twickenham, Dickens's London, Joyce's Dublin, Eliot's Thames—none of which I had ever laid eyes on—here was something close to home, something I could get my teeth into. Silently, I gave thanks to the two new professors for sending me this gift.

3

I became a man with a mission. During the next couple of days, cheered on by my roommate and my other n'er-do-well exile friends, I skipped my religion and philosophy classes and devoured everything by Steinbeck I could get my hands on. There was no order to my reading, just a headlong, willy-nilly immersion in his words, his characters, and his landscapes. I read *The Long Valley*, then *The Winter of Our Discontent*; I read *The Pas-*

tures of Heaven, then *The Wayward Bus*. If I was shocked by the fact that my exotic, high-plains roommate turned out to be more of a suburbanite than I was (he wore mostly Brooks Brothers clothes, never a cowboy hat or boots), imagine my consternation over Steinbeck's descriptions of California landscapes. In my part of New England, particularly Connecticut, water was taken for granted because it was everywhere. I could drive a few minutes to Long Island Sound to swim, sail a boat, or cast a lead jig for blue fish; I could walk to Hailey's Pond or to Wood's Pond to fish for bass and pickerel in the summer and to play hockey in the winter. Lush, alder-banked streams, creeks, and rivers, all clean and cool enough to support a trout population (not all hatchery-reared fish either; some were brilliantly colored natives) ran all year round. Water was in our blood, in the air around us, part of the way we viewed the world. What we couldn't drink, swim or fish in, boat or skate on came back at us the rest of the time as rain, humidity or snow; water, in one form or another, simply defined our existence, colored our lives from one sharply defined season to the next.

My first inkling that conditions might actually be different in California came when I hit this passage in "Flight," one of the powerful stories in Steinbeck's collection *The Long Valley*: "Below him lay a deep canyon exactly like the last, waterless and desolate. There was no flat, no oak trees, not even heavy brush in the bottom of it. And on the other side a sharp ridge stood up, thinly brushed with starving sage, littered with broken granite. Strewn over the hill there were giant outcroppings, and on the top the granite teeth stood out against the sky,"[1] This sounded more like hell than heaven, more like a nether land than nirvana. My cherished view of California as a balmy tropical paradise took a sharp turn; further beatings came in rapid succession when I encountered the drought in *To a God Unknown*, the ominous fog (a condition I believed indigenous to New England) which hangs like a lid over Elisa Allen in "The Chrysanthemums," the brutality of the orchard strike in *In Dubious Battle*, and Lennie Small's sacrificial murder in *Of Mice and Men*. (Where, I asked myself, did the concept of the "whole" man with its ethically upright posture, its yearning toward radiance, harmony, and goodness, fit into these novels? I wished some of my professors had leavened their Aquinas with Steinbeck.) Clearly, California was another country; apparently, as a friend of mine said, they did things differently there. (Years later, when I set foot in California for the first time, my reading of Steinbeck, which by then had become extensive, helped ease but did not eliminate my sense of culture shock. I could never shake the feeling that I was in a foreign country, and I began to sense that Steinbeck's paranoia was accurate when he said that actions that were tolerated elsewhere in the United States were probably crimes in California.)

But such rude awakenings aside, Steinbeck's unpretentiousness, his accessibility, struck me as thoroughly refreshing. I loved the way his weird, crazy characters, like The Seer in *To a God Unknown*, never quite fit into a blueprint and the way his serious ones too, like Doc Burton in *In Dubious Battle*, always probed the axis of reality with their questionings. They were just the opposite of the ethereal protagonists I was reading about in my class on British fiction. For the first time in my life literature seemed recognizably "real." Steinbeck's characters reminded me of members of my own kin: the kindness of Billy Buck, the obsessiveness of Joseph Wayne, the chicanery of Danny, the hunger of Peter Randall, the frustration of Elisa Allen. In Steinbeck's family portraits I recognized all the positive gestures as well as the grotesqueries, willful rationalizations, and psychological quirks because they were my own, or belonged to members of my own blood—this aunt, that uncle, those cousins; the more I read, the more I began to think of his work in terms of similarities rather than differences only, in terms of a family beyond the family I already possessed.[2]

I admit there were enormous holes in my reading, periods of Steinbeck's career I skipped over, either out of ignorance, nonchalance, or gaps in the library's holdings (inter-library loan was an idea whose time had not come to me yet). Reading critically was generally foreign to me anyway because I had little sense of a novel being anything but a gratuitous arrangement of words on paper, a kind of labyrinthian museum of language I could browse in until I found a shiny sculpture here, a bright painting there to arrest my attention and perhaps even give some cause for pleasure. Reading as the appropriation of a life in art was unknown to me: that reading could lead to reflection, meditation, or even salvation was suspect to me. Indeed, while preparing to write this essay I picked off my shelves the worn, faded Bantam Books editions of *The Pastures of Heaven* and *In Dubious Battle* I bought that fall: full of ink underlinings —sometimes whole pages of them—as though I couldn't distinguish what parts of a scene were more important than others; when I did make comments in the margins there was nothing reflective or analytical about the annotations, just paraphrases of the plot, to remind myself, I guess, what was happening without having to reread previous pages in case I fell asleep, which of course I often did. It kills me to quote that bastard Eliot, but maybe he was right: I was one of those readers who had the experience but missed the intellectual meaning. Still, except for a set of uniformly bound Penguin Greek and Roman classics which I read for a freshman Western Civilization course, those Bantam and Compass Steinbeck paperbacks were the first texts I labored over, monk-like, with pen in hand.

Anyway, I knew that I liked Steinbeck's range, but his books were all so different I despaired of ever finding a uniform pattern in them to write about. I was just savvy enough about prevailing critical theory to know I needed to find some order to structure my thesis coherently. I owed Professor O'Sheu at least that much since, probably against his better judgment, he had agreed to direct my project. Many weeks later, in the middle of those ongoing ruminations, as I sat in my apartment wishing my daydreams about life in California hadn't been so severely disrupted and still holding out hope that Montana was as beautiful and soul-satisfying as Steinbeck claimed it was for him in *Travels with Charley*, I picked up *East of Eden*. Once I got past the come-hither Bantam cover, which featured a sexy bare-shouldered, full-bodied woman in an alluring peasant outfit, I was on my way to having an epiphany all my own.

4

East of Eden is a huge, sprawling book; it requires an enormous investment of time and psychological commitment to read. Dickens's *Bleak House* was the only other fat novel I had ever read, and I knew what a daunting experience that had been, but I promised myself I would slug through anyway. Personal, autobiographical, chatty, loose, and digressive, *East of Eden* was unlike anything I had read before and, so in its way, continued the assault on my preconceptions. Like the puck at a hockey match, the book seemed to fly in several directions at once: the plot moved back and forth between the Trasks and the Hamiltons; the chapters alternated between dramatic narrative and editorial philosophy. Except for my two personal favorites—Tom Hamilton and Cal Trask, whose morbidity appealed to the depressive side of my nature—I needed a scoreboard to keep all of the other "Cain and Abel" characters straight. I could not say that I understood the rationale of *Eden*'s alternating points of view or even very much liked or recognized its flat portrait of my native Connecticut in the early part of the novel (the Trask farm seemed unconvincing; Edwards the whoremaster rang no bells in my memory). I was astonished, however, when the door swung open on the X-rated parts featuring Cathy Trask and her poor victims because I did not think it was legal to say such things in a modern book. I was impressed, though, at the unflinching honesty and candor with which Steinbeck treated those scenes, which of course diminished their titillating salaciousness and made me feel I was being addressed as a serious adult, a situation the college's priestly censors rarely felt obligated to acknowledge.

I was equally impressed with the way Steinbeck used Genesis (4:1-16) as a touchstone for the action, characterization, and the title of his novel. His wasn't the kind of formal biblical exegesis my religion professors espoused and about which I had been quizzed and tested into dumb submission like a typical catechism student, but something more inventive and certainly closer to my own loose requirements for a simple belief in freedom of choice. Furthermore, Steinbeck's statement in chapter 19 that the "church and the whorehouse arrived in the Far West simultaneously" and that they were a different facet of the same thing" (*EE*, 217) was at once one of the most startling and most familiar things I'd ever read, because it was not at all unlike the kind of shocking but ultimately pragmatic and profound statements my mother's loquacious brother was capable of making, while driving toward some fishing outing or, more outrageous yet, while seated around the dinner table at my grandmother's house. I was always predisposed to listen to a person who speaks directly, so just as my uncle was capable of grabbing my attention with his assertiveness, I was immediately and equally engaged by *East of Eden*'s personal narrator who made the book, studded with personal commentary and offhand remarks, seem like a guided tour of a heaven and hell that seemed more and more like the neighborhood I had grown up in. Just the brusque tone and gritty lingo I needed, I told myself, to balance my rarefied Catholic education.

My field of vision was expanding in other ways too, because it was literally my first realization that a novelist had the right to condense, rearrange, or heighten selective elements in his fiction. It began to dawn on me that, like glimpsing the bottom of a fast-moving river, there was a marvelous but shadowy process to be apprehended in the world of fiction, and even more so, that there was some shaping power at work in Steinbeck's novels, though I am positive I did not have the language yet to articulate that impression. I felt something more than mere journalistic realism was taking place, though, as in the scene in chapter 17, when the narrator begins to change his mind about whether murderous Cathy Trask is a human "monster."

Or, on a more upbeat note, this moment in chapter 23 when Steinbeck appears as a character in his own novel and recalls going on a fishing trip with his uncle, Tom Hamilton:

> We started before the sun came up and drove in the rig straight toward Fremont's Peak, and as we neared the mountains the stars would pale out and the light would rise to blacken the mountains. I can remember riding and pressing my ear and cheek against Tom's coat. And I can remember that his arm would rest lightly over my shoulders and his hand pat my arm occasionally. Finally we would pull up under an oak tree and take the horse out of the shafts, water him at the stream side, and halter him to the back of the rig. (*EE*, 281)

If at first the aridity of the flinty Hamilton family farm near King City, California, shocked my water-soaked new England sensibility, here was a lovely reminiscence which entered a note of balance, hopefulness, and "gallantry," as Steinbeck himself said. This passage, which I reread several times, brought a small measure of consolation when I learned that Tom eventually killed himself. I think I felt that by rereading it I could keep him alive somehow, which is probably the reason I tried not to think too long and hard about the fact that, like him, my uncle and I also tied our own trout flies. Was exotic California so different from puritan Connecticut after all, I wondered?

More than that, in *East of Eden* Steinbeck seemed generous, even forgiving, in temperament. Here was a writer, I mused, in whose imagination the most striking opposites could reside undiminished, and one who embraced the society of outcasts, the renegade screwups of this world, of which I was a card-carrying member. Cal Trask and I seemed to be cousins under the skin: we were well-meaning, intent, even passionate with a kind of groping hunger, but we were also self-righteous, quick to be wounded, brooding, and at least a couple of steps out of sync with the world around us. We lived in the land of Nod, always, it seemed, just outside of Eden. When I read the final deathbed scene, where the dying Adam Trask at last blesses his wayward son Cal with the word "*Timshel!*" ("Thou Mayest!"), thereby empowering his free will, I was moved to tears, as I had been one earlier time when I read Whitman's "When Lilacs Last in the Dooryard Bloom'd." Embarrassed by my own sentimentality, I went into my bedroom of our apartment and closed its door because I didn't want my roommate—a Dean's List economics major headed for law school—to see me weeping. Though I knew nothing at all about John Steinbeck's personality, his private habits, or his family, in the enclosure of my room I felt reassured by the fact that he was alive somewhere in the world and that this book had the undeniable capacity to move my soul. "*Timshel!* yourself," I thought.

Such affective awareness, however, wasn't enough for my senior thesis, which hung over me with the same implacable weight as Salinas Valley fog. I eventually wrote a stupid derivative paper on the biologist as hero in selected novels, which allowed me to unite my equally abortive careers as a former biology major and a current English major. But the thesis was a terrible botch, and after graduation, I burned all the copies out of disgust and embarrassment. I had no original ideas that could stand up to the bright light of critical scholarship. Almost all my analysis had been conditioned primarily by Joseph Fontenrose's *John Steinbeck: An Introduction and Interpretation*, a wonderful, lucid book whose ideas and spirit I mangled beyond recognition. I also had help from F. W. Watt's quirky *Steinbeck* and Peter Lisca's encyclopedic, and in most cases very informative, *The Wide World of John Steinbeck*. These were three of the six books then available on Steinbeck and, of those, only Fontenrose's gave any sense of the pleasure one might receive from reading Steinbeck. The library didn't have Harry Moore's *The Novels of John Steinbeck* or Warren French's *John Steinbeck*, and of course I was too beleaguered to fill out the forms to order them on loan; E. W. Tedlock and C. V. Wicker's *Steinbeck and His Critics*, which the library did have, was printed in type so small and dense that I kept falling asleep over the closely reasoned critical essays, though now and again some of Steinbeck's own statements on writing or his salvos against critics stayed with me, such as this one, which I typed up and attached to my reading lamp: "Please believe me when I say I have nothing against the scholarly or critical approach. It does seem to me to have very little to do with the writing or reading of books."[3]

While they helped me form my views on the biologist hero, none of these critical books, I remember, were very laudatory about *East of Eden*. In fact, Peter Lisca really torpedoed the novel, finding it an unsuccessful hodgepodge of form, full of scrambled syntax and awkward expression, a failure of language, intention, and execution. In those cold marble halls of New Criticism, it seemed, there was no room for a reader's personal response or for an emphasis on process rather than product. Lisca's analysis of *East of Eden* struck me as chilling and preemptive. It reminded me of the literary judgments the chairman of my department leveled at minor works of literature (which I think he considered almost everything ever written by an American) or, closer to home, judgments he leveled at the compositions and research papers I handed in—the kind of cutting dismissals that, with a few swipes of the tongue or the pen, made me doubt the validity and integrity of my own opinion. I wondered how a man who published very little himself could be so cocksure when it came to lambasting others. (I vowed then and there that if I ever became a teacher I would treat my students' work with more respect than he had shown mine.)

Nevertheless, compared to the starchy diet of British novels I was then trying to digest, reading *East of Eden*, flaws and all, had a very liberating effect. That book helped me identify the quality of Steinbeck's work I most admired—his sense of story, family history, and oral tradition, all elements very much out of fashion in that time and place because they eschewed ambiguity and aesthetic distance and so were suspected of being *sentimental*, that most grievous of critical sins. For me, though, who couldn't distinguish one type of ambiguity from the next or irony from a villanelle, and who hailed from a long line of sentimentalists capable of breaking into tears at the drop of a hat, Steinbeck's familiar tone was not only convincing but downright reassuring. It was just what I needed then because it seemed completely honest, trustworthy, and believable. His world in *East of Eden* touched mine in numerous recognizable places. His literary voice was the first one I ever encountered that spoke *to* me and not at me. It was a conversational voice—

there is no other way to explain it—a patient, instructive voice weaving those many oral facets together, directing his words toward me in such a way that I felt comforted, not abused, and reassured, not undercut, by the world's warring opposites: "Humans are caught—in their lives, in their thoughts, in their hungers and ambitions, in their avarice and cruelty, and in their kindness and generosity—in a net of good and evil. I think that this is the only story we have and that it occurs on all levels of feeling and intelligence," he proclaims in chapter 34 of *East of Eden. Amen!* I scribbled in the margin of my book.

Deeper than that, though, *East of Eden* was the first book that gave me a handle on symbolic experiences, the first to make personal journeys, choices, and continuities seem like palpable endeavors. In a strangely unexpected way, I suppose, Steinbeck continued the work my uncle had already started; corny as it sounds, *East of Eden* gave me a sense that life was a journey through and around a series of alternative choices, and it also prepared me for a world in which the heroic beauty of Samuel Hamilton and the diabolical brutality of Cathy Ames could exist side by side. I wasn't Stephen Dedalus traveling the road out of Dublin to forge in the smithy of my soul the consciousness of my race; I just wanted to learn how to live among its daily contradictions and maybe catch a few big trout along the way. I didn't want to reject all aspects of orthodoxy, of patriarchy (my feelings toward my chairman, New Criticism, and the Catholic Church aside); like most Italian-Americans, I simply wanted to choose the elements of continuity that were meaningful to me, even if they were nominally conflicting ones, and somehow manage to pass them on intact (though at that time I didn't know to whom).

Steinbeck's authorial tone, his assessments on the universality of good and evil, the dance of opposites in the world's body, the mythology of each person's inevitable fall from grace and potential resurrection, and perhaps most of all his emphasis—so different in this talky novel from his omniscient earlier ones—on the necessity of individual creativity, all seemed to me wonderful and honorable, earned and realistic, which is why I was willing to listen. His narrative voice didn't claim the past was such a transcendentally elevated time that we should give up the ghost because we could never live there again; his voice told how the past was different in degree, not in kind, from the present and how it was another part of a universal, unbroken emotional process we all participated in, as though we each stepped at different places into a river that flowed just outside our doors, somewhere around, say Norwalk, Connecticut, Livingston, Montana, or Salinas, California. *East of Eden*, I decided, was a book that schooled the motions of the heart.

Which is why I think those hard-nosed critics had missed the point. Accusations of sentimentality, ponderousness, loose and baggy form seemed beside the point. In this moment of desperate metaphysics I resort to metaphors to illuminate the metaphor: reading *East of Eden* was like riding with my garrulous Uncle Tony in his old De Soto coupe. We were headed out before dawn to go trout fishing on the Norwalk, the Saugatuck, or the Aspetuck, one of those rivers that seemed to have its headwaters in a past known to him but which now cut through a transformed geography, a world become more suburban than rural, which I would have to learn to navigate with my own compass, even if it meant leaving it altogether and seeing it only in my mind's eye. The attitude, the posture, my uncle taught was to regard the present not as irrevocably diminished and played out but as being full of its own kind of promise and bounty. Nostalgia, I think he felt, was the ability to be at home everywhere and at once, without condemning one place for another. More than that, reading *East of Eden* was for me like riding with someone who was just familiar enough not to be terrifying and just unknown enough to be exciting, and who ultimately roused in me a sense of adventure, a heartbeat of inspiration, a horizon of possibilities, where I might, with a little luck or perseverance, carve my own niche, be in and of the place I chose to inhabit, the place where words and deeds, history and personality, heart and mind flow together.

First, though, as my uncle would say, you need the wood to carve, and as his regal car sashayed up Route 7 the headlights picked out this landmark or that, distorting them in such a way that those once-accustomed objects (Orem's Diner, Old Man Abbott's house, Hurlbutt's Orchard, the Revolutionary War cannon in North Wilton) seemed utterly new and beckoning, invested now—just as dawn was about to spark up the eastern horizon—with the charged, knee-knocking anticipation of the trout fishing venture itself, but more than that, I realize now, with the inseparably humorous and even at times tragic pronouncements and recollections of my uncle, whose gruff voice and elaborate, digressive stories (of himself, of our family, of the people we knew or were bonded with) weren't so much tendentious or pontifical as they were philosophical, wise, and knowing, full of the gravity of experience, the weight and palpability of a life observed with attention, all of which, I think, were delivered to me with much love. Even as my uncle told his stories of good and evil, delivered his heart-felt sermons, or drew his cynical, shameless, prurient, or sappy conclusions about human folly and glory, he knew I would screw things up; he expected it was my right to do so even before I knew I would. But again, like Steinbeck in *East of Eden*, despite his occasional tyrannical fierceness, he was mostly patient, forbearing, generous; he would have to have been, because he handed over to me anyway that bittersweet emotional landscape, that convoluted watershed geography of southwestern Connecticut, trout and all. It was a precious gift, the more so because it could not be bought, sold, refused, or denied but only savored in the memory, lighted up in images, transmitted in the imperfectness of words. "Sometimes," as Steinbeck says in chapter 13 of *East of Eden*, "a kind of glory lights up the mind of man. It happens to nearly everyone" (*EE*, 131).

5

So while I left it out of my pathetic undergraduate thesis —there is no biologist hero in it—*East of Eden* affected me in an odd but profound way, and for all the years afterward when I thought of Steinbeck as a writer, *East of Eden* was always the first book that came to mind, even before *Tortilla Flat, Of Mice and Men, The Red Pony,* or *The Grapes of Wrath.* The mark of an intriguing novel, much like a fine trout stream, it seems to me now, is its capacity to surprise us on each subsequent reading by revealing greater depths, successive unfoldings, new flashes of color, motion, and brilliance without ever giving up its true meaning, if in fact a novel—or a river—can ever be said to have one true meaning. *East of Eden* continues to impress me as such a wonder book, because it is a landscape of incandescent words, a torrent of mutable meanings. I have read it countless times, both in its enormous original version and in its shorter, 691-page published form. I have taught it often—and successfully, I think—to college students in Ohio and in California (who rank it among their preferred Steinbeck titles). I have repeatedly bent close over *Journal of a Novel,* Steinbeck's posthumously published record of its making, so I know something of the excruciating process that brought the novel into being. I also know that Steinbeck's mentoring tone, that sagacious voice and demeanor, was part of his original thematic and structural intent: the first draft of the novel (initially called "The Salinas Valley") is addressed directly to his two young sons and represents a way for a divorced father to pass on, like a gift, what he knows of his world to his children. And my research has delivered many of the lurid ins and outs of Steinbeck's private marital, domestic, and familial history that inform the book and surround it with a net of intentions, psychological ramifications, and interventions more complex than I think sometimes I wanted to know. (After my own divorce in 1980, the novel—and this tangled era of Steinbeck's life expressed in it—took on yet another level of importance to me and became a mirror for my own upheaval, reflecting the convoluted relationship with my ex-wife and my desire to establish a lasting legacy for my daughter.) Always I have found something new in its pages to fuel my obsession or to assail my sensibility.

A dozen years after college, when the dream of becoming an outdoor guide in Montana had been supplanted by a career as a literature teacher (which I suspect is another kind of fishing guide), I spent a good part of a December week holed up in a hermetically sealed, windowless room of the cathedral-like Humanities Research Center in Austin, Texas. It was 80 degrees and brilliantly sunny outside. I was about as far from Ohio's snowy wastes as I could reasonably get and I had plenty of urge to play hooky and walk around Austin, but good researcher that I had become in those years since college and graduate school, I instead hunched over the original manuscript and typescript of *East of Eden*. I owed my resolve to Ohio University, which had given me a grant to begin my exploration of Steinbeck's far-flung manuscripts, housed at archives in Texas, New York, and California, for a proposed book on Steinbeck's literary influences (eventually published as *Steinbeck's Reading*, 1984); but more than that, I felt I owed staying put to Steinbeck, because I wanted to honor his herculean effort, his brave intention, his artistic experiment. And in a way I felt uncannily sure he was about to deliver something to me, there among those cascading leaves of white paper.

Among the hundreds of canceled typescript pages I studied, I found some material that I selfishly wished Steinbeck hadn't cut from his novel, because it would have been part of my initial reading in 1964 and would have given me an even clearer sense of his purpose and achievement, his conscious reaction against the prevailing literary modes and practices of the era. The first snippet is a section which originally introduced chapter 8 (which now begins, "I believe there are monsters born in the world to human parents"). Steinbeck penned this on 28 March 1951 (two full months into his nine-month writing stint); it was the opening paragraph of that day's writing about Cathy, the villainous "heroine." The gist of this section is that Steinbeck descried the modernist, New Critical tendency to favor what he called "the writerless book." He continued: "For all the arts are nothing but the long and hard and passionate search for true things. Art may have guess or conjecture but deliberate untruth has never and will never be permitted. Thus when the writer thought he had eliminated himself from his story he was falling into error. Himself chose the story, and he chose the details and picked out the words, and arranged the sequences. The writer was in every line."[4]

Steinbeck of course was in every line of his book, a fact that disturbed and unnerved his formalist critics. (I learned over the years that Steinbeck is a writer in whom the unresolvable issues of "academic correctness," including complications of politics, gender, technique, and canon formation, still make many people skittish and resentful; like some members of the elite critical establishment or some of my former colleagues at San Jose State, they always want Steinbeck to be something other than what he is.) But generally, to our far more catholic sensibilities this late in the century, his textual intrusiveness was a bold prophetic stance, a precursor of certain fabular, postmodernist fictional strategies. Had it been published twenty years later or published in tandem with *Journal of a Novel,* as Steinbeck intended, *East of Eden,* I fantasized, might have had a warmer reception.

Conjecture aside, just how deeply he was rooted in *East of Eden* is signified in this second excision, a draft of the prologue which Steinbeck wrote in unabashed homage to Cervantes. It was another of those discoveries that stopped me in my tracks: "Reader—I have thought endlessly about my book which I now submit to you. It is compounded of ink and heart's blood—lighter than ink and darker than blood. Thousands of hours have gone into it to make it agreeable to your ear and sweet to your understanding." Here at last was that most elusive creature, the "whole man"; he turned out to be not a Platonic, Socratic, Aristotelian, Aquinian, or Eliotic philosopher, as my college teachers had desired, but a deeply flawed, personally divided, unorthodox, modern novelist, humble about his own shortcomings just as he was a little proud when he hoped we would be mindful of his scriptive achievements: "Sometimes I have felt that I held fire in my hands to spread a page with shining, but I have never been able to shake off clumsiness and ignorance and aching inability." The ethical posture, the moral stance, it turned out, was not an absolute blueprint for behavior, the way some of my college teachers believed, but something they rarely talked about: a way of being in the world, an acceptance and cultivation of the demanding, strenuous, obsessive habit of mind that makes writing—or teaching—possible, rewarding, and necessary, even if imperfect, frustrated, and conflicted.

Before everything is said, I go back to that scene in the bedroom of my college apartment a lifetime ago, where I retreated in what I see now was pure terror and dread from my roommate's cold critical stare. It was a failure of nerve born of ignorance, a youthful timorousness. Older now, I am not ashamed to confess that *East of Eden* still moves me as it moved me then, which is to say emotionally, irrationally, affectively, mythically, sublimely. It is a passionate book that calls forth passionate responses. In my first encounter with such a work, at a time when I saw all around me repeated examples of emotional abnegation among my teachers and peers, I could not help being fascinated by a writer who put so much of himself in his book—I mean as a person, as a character, and as a narrator.

It was, I see now, an act of courage or, better yet, an act of faith, like filling a blank page, teaching the blind to read, or casting a fly line in the dark. Steinbeck, I discovered, existed in the house of his fiction, in the fictive architectural space and language of his own making, the deepest investiture of his own imagining. "A man's writing is himself," he remarked in one of the nuggets I gleaned from *Steinbeck and His Critics* that had stuck in my head from my Assumption College days. I think I sensed that even in 1964: when I touched *East of Eden* for the first time, I seemed to have touched the man as well, though it was a long, long time and a rather circuitous journey before I could say why and how. When the heart's blood and the dark ink begin to flow, when an author hands us his gift, who among us can tell the writer from the written, who among us can refuse being moved or can dare say no to the dream of being saved?

Notes

[1] I bought a first printing of the Compass Books paperback edition of *The Long Valley* (1956) at a used book store in Worcester that fall. The quotation from "Flight" appears on page 69. The Compass editions duplicated Viking's cloth first editions—cover illustration, format, size, text, font, and pagination were the same. In a sense, the physical appearance of the book contributed to my mistaken, first impression opinions about California. The Compass reproduction of Elmer Hader's original dust jacket painting of a red pony gazing over a gently rolling, inviting California valley later clashed drastically with the stark, violent imagery of this passage from "Flight."

[2] A second printing of Pascal Covici's anthology, *The Steinbeck Pocket Book* (New York: Pocket Books, 1943) was another of the cheap paperbacks I acquired that year. My readerly response toward familial identity may have come in part from Covici's foreword, in which he claimed Steinbeck's characters were "entirely human: their beings contain the greed and love and hatred shared by all mankind—and like many of their fellow creatures they insist upon eating their daily bread and getting their glimpse of the moon" (viii).

[3] Steinbeck's "A Letter on Criticism" first appeared in the *Colorado Quarterly* in 1955, and then was reprinted in Tedlock and Wicker's *Steinbeck and His Critics: A Record of Twenty-Five Years* (Albuquerque: University of New Mexico Press, 1957), 52-53.

[4] Steinbeck's statement appears in the 540-page autograph manuscript of *East of Eden*, and in the 945-page typescript, but was cancelled from the published novel. This excised section and the Cervantes-inspired prologue quoted below are in a box of *East of Eden* "Dead Material" in the John Steinbeck Works collection at the Harry Ransom Humanities Research Center, University of Texas, Austin.

Steinbeck's Hermes typewriter
Gift of Thom Steinbeck to the Steinbeck Research Center,
San Jose State University, San Jose, CA.

Steinbeck's Typewriter: An Excursion in Suggestiveness

"I am not a great writer but I am a competent one. And I am an experimental one."

—John Steinbeck, *The Wayward Bus* journal (1946) (Courtesy of the Pierpont Morgan Library, New York City)

"It's quite a performance. I bet some of it is even true, and if it wasn't, it is now."

—John Steinbeck, encomium for Gypsy Rose Lee's memoir, *Gypsy* (1957)

1

In the autumn of 1969, Tetsumaro "Ted" Hayashi, editor of the newly launched *Steinbeck Quarterly*, wrote from Muncie, Indiana, inviting me to participate in a Steinbeck conference he was co-organizing with Richard Astro to be held at Oregon State University. Slated for April 1970, it would be only the second Steinbeck conference ever convened (the first, which both Ted and I attended, was a thirtieth anniversary celebration of *The Grapes of Wrath* organized by John Seelye a year earlier at the University of Connecticut). Fresh out of graduate school, I was trying to turn my dissertation on the creative process in Thoreau's major writings into a book. At the same time I was trying to suppress the growing realization that, except for being a well-intentioned and nominally intriguing topic, the dissertation was stiff and pedantic and would probably be a boring read. When the summons came from Hayashi, toward the end of my first quarter of full-time teaching at Ohio University, I put down Thoreau and picked up Steinbeck's just-published *Journal of a Novel: The "East of Eden" Letters*. Borrowing from Steinbeck's writing journal, as well as from some of my Thoreau-*cum* Georges Poulet/Gaston Bachelard-inspired theories, and armed with a recent reading of Richard Brautigan's avant-garde fiction and Allen Ginsberg's poetry and prose (part of my eventual title came from his essay on legalizing marijuana), I opened a rough-hewn hermeneutic path into *Sweet Thursday*, a novel I felt had taken undeservedly hard knocks from the formalist critics who held sway in academic circles during the 1950s and 1960s.

The result was "Steinbeck and the Creative Process: First Manifesto to End the Bringdown Against *Sweet Thursday*," a metacritical divagation temperamentally at home in that age of late 1960's unbridled iconoclasm and which—true to its era—raised more questions than it answered. The essay's tenuousness and irreverent tone—its breezy affectiveness and hip talk of *Sweet Thursday* being a parable of the artist, a "novel about the writing of a novel"—owes partly to the fact that I labored on it in the dead of an unusually cold Appalachian winter in a rented house that—my family and I learned too late—had a faulty furnace, a coal burner ineptly converted to burn fuel oil. Between dives into the cellar to coax the ancient beast back to life, I worked in the absentee owner's window-lined study laboriously writing and typing in woolen gloves and heavy clothes. Like Doc in the novel I was attending to, I couldn't sustain my concentration long enough to develop my argument in a more systematic manner, and so the essay became susceptible to its context, but was not wholly constructed by it. (The legitimacy of some poststructuralist beliefs aside, common sense tells us that such makings never are wholly unmixed but rise from a reciprocity of self and context, language and experience.) As a result, I was conscious of abandoning many pretenses of objectivity in allowing the essay to become a performative piece about a self-displaying text, a way of "using something to cover up something else," in Mack's definition of "substitution," which appears in chapter 9 of *Sweet Thursday*.[1]

There are few more excruciating events than rereading one's own early writing, but as I realize now (without, I hope, being narcissistic or vain), the informal voice and personal stance of "Steinbeck and the Creative Process" fit the conversational format and ebullient dialogue of the Corvallis conference, though since being printed in Astro and Hayashi's *Steinbeck: The Man and His Work*, its silences, rifts, and lacunae seem to have grown more blatant, rather than less so. It would be impossible to redress all its shortcomings—nor, at this late date, would I care to, for I believe that absences have a way of becoming part of the permanent record and that both objectivity and dispassion remain for me—in certain contexts, anyway—elusive and dubious goals. Yet I am grateful for another chance not only to elaborate a few old points about Steinbeck's controversial little book, *Sweet Thursday*, but also to resurrect a neglected public debate on its merits (a 1954 television broadcast), offer an important popular culture influence (Al Capp's *Li'l Abner* comic strip), and without, I hope, being too fanciful or precious, arrive at a new trope of relevancy (Steinbeck's portable typewriter) in the following circuitous, suggestive revisitation to this as-yet underrated fable of the life in art.

Revisiting the original site of this essay constitutes a renewed arc of connection initiated in the late 1960s when Ted Hayashi and I hit it off as graduate students at Kent State University and pooled our energies in getting his brainchild, the *Steinbeck Quarterly*, off the ground. It was there too I first encountered through the efforts of my mentor, Howard Vincent, charismatic Melville scholar (whose chief subject and favorite topic was the compositional process of "becoming" encoded in the self-referring nature of much American literature), the liberating possibility that critical discourse could be enhanced by personal engagement and energetic, appreciative intervention. In that this essay also circles toward a meeting many years later with Steinbeck's eldest son, Thom Steinbeck, from whom I received, temporarily at least, his father's favorite typewriter (which became a metaphor for a way of looking at the elder Steinbeck's creative drive), the landscape of this chapter inscribes an intersubjective ground, a moving geography of inner and outer voices, private and public presences, self and text. Returning to this place, I am reminded once again of Thoreau's exquisite pleasure in *Walden* of catching two fish at once.

2

From the outset, the conversation surrounding *Sweet Thursday* was heated and antagonistic, as the following account by Pascal Covici demonstrates. One evening in early August 1954, Covici, John Steinbeck's loyal friend and his editor at The Viking Press, turned on the television set at his brother-in-law's house in New Rochelle, New York, to watch a show called "The Author Meets the Critics." The topic that night was Steinbeck's *Sweet Thursday*, released in June by Viking, and already selling by the box load.[2] Steinbeck was living in Paris with his wife, Elaine, and his two sons, Thom and John IV, that summer and, among other projects, was working on a series of nonfiction pieces for the French weekly, *Figaro Litteraire*, so he could not appear on the program (*SLL*, 480). The critics, however, were represented by chief discussants Lewis Gannett and Joseph Bennett.

Gannett, the book critic for the venerable *New York Herald Tribune*, and a longtime friend and supporter of Steinbeck's (*SR*, 45; *S&C*, 117-18), took the affirmative position toward the novel. Bennett, a founding editor of the upstart *Hudson Review* (1948-), argued negatively. Bennett's "salubrious" opinion that *Sweet Thursday* was "dull, repetitious and phony" met with extreme resistance from Gannett and the other panelists, who defended the novel for its "delightful" wit and humor. The moderator, perhaps sympathetic to Bennett's plight, broadened the topic to include the overall importance of Steinbeck's contribution to contemporary American literature. According to Covici, Bennett allowed how Steinbeck only had managed to produce some "worthwhile" fiction when he was "angry," as in *In Dubious Battle* and in *The Grapes of Wrath*. Steinbeck, however, was not one of the truly significant American novelists, but was merely a commercially successful writer who had skillfully learned how to "appeal to the largest public" audience possible. Gannett took the long view, arguing that Steinbeck had earned his recent success by virtue of his initial obscurity, his long years of hard work, and his willingness to experiment with the novel genre. Apparently, his persuasiveness carried the day, for at the end of his correspondence, Covici reassured Steinbeck that Bennett's "harangues" were unconvincing and would do nothing to injure the novel's reputation: "the book keeps on selling!"

There is truth on each side of this debate, just as there is misapprehension and intolerance. Bennett's rigorous intellectualism and Covici's glib commercialism both represent passionate positions but reductive ones too, which impede understanding. Covici never was a consistently brilliant appreciator of fiction's technical properties. Despite Thomas Fensch's inflated claim that, artistically and psychologically, Covici repeatedly saved Steinbeck's neck (*S&C*, 81, 102), the fact remains that Covici may more likely have done Steinbeck a disservice during his career by pushing the marketable aspects of the novelist's work above all else. On the other hand, from the vantage point of the production of literary commodities, Steinbeck was a professional writer who supported his family and earned his living by his pen (though he often claimed he would have gone on writing anyway, even without payment), so being financially successful at his chosen vocation need not automatically qualify as cause for shame or as proof that he had coopted himself. Ironically, Bennett, quick to wave the avant-garde flag, seems to have missed the contemporaneity of *Sweet Thursday*, especially its artistic playfulness and self-reflexivity, its internalization of the American frontier theme, and its fabular dimensions. Steinbeck's text seems to have appeared too soon in our critical history to have been amply tolerated; in some ways, it belongs more comfortably to the 1990s than to the 1950s. At the very least, even though Bennett, Gannett, and Covici were unable to recognize it, Steinbeck exposed the American reading public to an early example of experimental metafiction, on the order of what Linda Hutcheon has called an "autorepresentational" text.[3]

Historically—as the Bennett-Gannett fiasco symbolizes—*Sweet Thursday*'s reputation has always been unsettled. Even though many newspaper and magazine reviews were extremely critical, the book sold prodigiously: one day alone—on 15 June 1954—Viking sold 2,000 copies; the following day, Covici predicted it would top 100,000 for the year. Unimpressed by such abundance, *Time*'s anonymous reviewer castigated *Sweet Thursday* as "a turkey with visibly Saroyanesque stuffings. But where Saroyan might have clothed the book's characters and incidents with comic reality, Steinbeck merely comic-strips them of all reality and even of much interest." In *The New Yorker*, Brendan Gill called the novel "labored." And in the *New York Times*, Carlos Baker judged *Sweet Thursday* as "gaily inconsequential," while Robert H. Boyle told *Commonweal* readers it was "a grade-B potboiler."[4]

A few contemporary notices, however, reached a moderately balanced assessment, leavening disapproval, bewilderment, or reservation with optimism. Milton Rugoff covered *Sweet Thursday* for the *New York Herald Tribune's Book Review*, situating it in the "ancient and honorable tradition" of "low comedy"; Steinbeck saves the book from corniness, he says, by the "up-bubbling notes of rowdy humor, and the occasional broad satiric thrusts." *Saturday Review*'s Harvey Curtis Webster announced that "Steinbeck can become as great an American writer as we've had in our century (I thought so when I read

'East of Eden'); at other times, it appears that he is a gifted writer who can never control his fiction sufficiently to write a first-rate book. 'Sweet Thursday' makes one feel betwixt and between." Hugh Holman, writing in *The New Republic*, struck a rarely heard revisionary note:

> I think we have been wrong about Steinbeck. We have let his social indignation, his verisimilitude of language, his interest in marine biology lead us to judge him as a naturalist. . . . Steinbeck is . . . a social critic . . . occasionally angry but more often delighted with the joys that life on its lowest levels presents. I think *Sweet Thursday* implicitly asks its readers to take its author on such terms. If these terms are less than we thought we had reason to hope for from *The Grapes of Wrath*, they are still worthy of respect.[5]

Despite Holman's prophetic warning, however, with few exceptions, scholarly opinion of *Sweet Thursday* is, Roy Simmonds claims, "unfavorable and at best lukewarm."[6] Almost everyone agrees that *Sweet Thursday* isn't among Steinbeck's premier efforts, but there has been so much disagreement over the locus of the book's apparent flaws, its numerous aporia (does it fail in technique, characterization, gender coding, philosophy, or tone?), that even that minority cadre, including—beside Holman and myself—Charles Metzger, Richard Astro, and Howard Levant, who have found the book worth attention, cannot agree on the basis of the attraction.[7]

Moreover, during the past seventeen years, since Simmonds surveyed the scene, serious interest in *Sweet Thursday* has been nearly nonexistent. Brian St. Pierre and David Wyatt say nothing of it in their books on the California aspects of Steinbeck's career, *John Steinbeck: The California Years* (1983) and *The Fall Into Eden* (1986), respectively. Paul McCarthy's monograph, *John Steinbeck* (1980), only mentions the novel a few times in passing, and even Jackson Benson's scrupulously detailed biography has little on *Thursday* itself, though it does provide a factual context for the book's background and its inception as a musical comedy in 1953 called "Bear Flag" (*TAJS*, 740-45). Louis Owens's 1985 thematic study of Steinbeck's western fiction perpetuates a line of objection to the novel which extends all the way from Joseph Bennett through Warren French, who, in 1961, condemned it as a "sell-out," and a "genuinely anti-intellectual" book, and on to Stoddard Martin, who says it "fails distressingly." Like them, Owens finds the novel contemptuous and dismisses it out of hand. His judgment is founded on his belief that the novel rejects "the most meaningful symbol in Steinbeck's fiction and Western culture: the Christian sacrifice," though it is hard to imagine how such a caveat can be considered a universally applicable norm for judging twentieth-century fiction. More intriguing—but no less caustic—is the recent political argument on male authority/female portrayal in *Sweet Thursday* raised by feminist critic Mimi Reisel Gladstein, who exposes Steinbeck's "time-worn sexist cliches."[8]

Amid such looming dissensus, John Timmerman went against the grain and created a turning point. He advanced a positive view of *Sweet Thursday* based squarely on Wylie Sypher's theory of comedy and offered a convincing analysis of the novel as a literary "farce." His assay was persuasive, because meantime, in a chapter written for Jackson Benson's collection, *The Short Novels of John Steinbeck,* Louis Owens apparently rethought *Sweet Thursday* and came to consider it "an investigation into the role of the artist as author." His tune has a suspiciously familiar ring to it but makes good reading anyway when paired with another chapter in Benson's anthology, Mimi Gladstein's considered attempt—partly gender-driven, partly formalistic—to explain *Sweet Thursday*'s "enjoyable" but manipulative enigmas. Even Warren French's latest take on *Thursday* shows leniency: "The novel cannot be quite so simply dismissed . . . because Steinbeck apparently thought that there was something of more than passing entertainment value in the work," he admits. In defending *Sweet Thursday,* Jay Parini has also weighed in on the side of Steinbeck, whom, he accurately claims, "was not always writing realistic fiction. . . . His imagination was puckish, and he worked by charm, incantation, invocation, and philosophical musing."[9]

So if the opinions of Bennett and Covici represent mutually exclusive positions on *Thursday,* then perhaps Gannett's synthesism is the one to recommend. Criticism, his view suggests, is an act of understanding, a tolerance for what actually exists in a work of fiction, rather than a lament for what it lacks. This perspectival stance jibed with Steinbeck's own theories on writerly texts and readerly participation at this juncture of his career. Steinbeck's announcement in "Critics, Critics, Burning Bright" that an "experiment which at first seems outrageous to the critic and the reader who have not been through the process of its development, may become interesting and valid when it is inspected a second and third time" is germane here in educating his readers.[10] Equally relevant is his "wish" in *East of Eden* "that when my reader has finished . . . he will have a sense of belonging" (*JN*, 61), by which he invited his reader to actively enter the process of fictionality.

Both of these strategies carried over to "Mack's Contribution," the original, 156-line introduction to *Sweet Thursday*.[11] The fictional Mack, upon reading some unflattering reviews of *Cannery Row*, claims to "'have laid out a lot of time on critics'" and wonders whether they all read the same book: "Some of them don't listen while they read, I guess," he states, because they are more interested in assigning handy catchwords to a work—"overambitious," "romantic," "naturalistic doggavation" —than in "understanding." In the truncated, forty-seven-line version which became *Sweet Thursday*'s published prologue, Mack's pointed suggestions about chapter headings, character descriptions, and loose-limbed hooptedoodle are laid out as matters of personal preference, not as punitive markers, and they are eventually incorporated in the novel to undercut aesthetic distance and to initiate the process of the audience's belonging.

Most importantly, Steinbeck is in on the con game, part of its web of decentered intrigue. *Sweet Thursday*'s affective and constitutive implications—its multiple layers of meaning, its "reality below reality" (*ST*, 134), its rambunctious tone, and its wilful blurring of historical reality/actual persons with invented scenarios/made-up actions—took precedence over traditional, directed representational means. In other words, marginalized characters in an earlier *roman-a-clef, Cannery Row,* discuss a novel they appeared in; its real-life author follows their advice in a fictional sequel in which they once again appear as dramatic participants. At this juncture, then, before looking more closely at *Sweet Thursday* in the next section, it is worth recalling Steinbeck's 1959 letter to film director Elia Kazan, for it summarizes his radical epistemological project of the postwar era: "Externality is a mirror that reflects back to our mind the world our mind has created of the raw materials. But a mirror is a piece of silvered glass. There is a back to it. If you scratch off the silvering, you can see through the mirror to the other worlds on the other side. I know that many people do not want to break through. I do, passionately, hungrily" (*SLL*, 625).

3

Although critics and literary historians don't agree on much else, nearly all concur that John Steinbeck staked out two major themes in his fictional career: the California experience, including the westering process and the ironic vision of Eden; and the phalanx, or group man, theory of social and familial organization. Just about everything Steinbeck wrote touches one or both of these compelling concepts: they run so deep in the first twenty years of his career that one or the other (or both) inform his conceptions of character, setting, plot, style, and theme. When allied with his nonteleological philosophy and omniscient narrative technique, these aspects became recognizable signatures of the Steinbeck novel from the early 1930s through the late 1940s. Steinbeck's harshest critics (Edmund Wilson and Arthur Mizener, for instance) expected Steinbeck to play some variation of this music over and over again, an expectation he refused to fulfill because of his periodic dissatisfaction with the "clumsy" novel form (*SLL*, 194) and his resolute belief in the importance of constant experimentation. "I will go ahead and do my own work in my own way," he emphasized to Covici (*TAJS*, 650).

But if Steinbeck's proletarian narratives have a social necessity and documentary integrity that urges us to think of them as whole cloth fabric, his late fictions can equally profit from being grouped as products of necessity and integrity too, though of an aesthetic order and literary sensibility removed from normative documentary realism. Steinbeck's shift radiates from a confession in his 8 June 1949 letter to novelist John O'Hara, in which he relinquishes his earlier mode: "I believe one thing powerfully—that the only creative thing our species has is the individual, lonely mind. . . . The group ungoverned by individual thinking is a horrible destructive principle" (*SLL*, 359). Following this breakthrough, Steinbeck composed four experiments between 1950 and 1954: the play-novella *Burning Bright*, the filmscript *Viva Zapata!*, the epic *East of Eden*, and the comic *Sweet Thursday*. While these intensely personal books still carry elements of the Eden mythos and phalanx organization, and while they also evince a moral quality which can be said to perform a social or cultural function, overall they comprise a different order of fictionality from their predecessors. By calling attention to their own literariness through allusions, language play, scriptable referentiality, and artful framing devices, they demonstrate Steinbeck's turn toward an incipient postmodernism, a condition of textual openness, of theoretical difference, where the act of writing in all its paradoxical manifestations becomes its own valid end in eroding and destabilizing traditional boundaries.[12] "If a writer likes to write," he claimed in "Critics, Critics, Burning Bright" in 1950,

> he will find satisfaction in endless experiment with his medium. He will improvise techniques, arrangements of scenes, rhythms of words, and rhythms of thought. He will constantly investigate and try combinations new to him, sometimes utilizing an old method for a new idea and vice versa. Some of his experiments will inevitably be unsuccessful but he must try them anyway if his interest be alive. This experimentation is not criminal . . . but it is necessary if the writer be not moribund. (*SAHC*, 47)

The result of Steinbeck's (r)evolution has been the source of much notorious and uncompromising critical reaction to his work after *Cannery Row*. However, the canonical critical ground rules of formalism don't always apply to the later Steinbeck, whose writing moved farther away from naturalism and closer toward fabulation, parable, and magical realism; with his new-found prerogative, Steinbeck veered from the documentary novel toward a self-revealing scriptive art. In light of this dramatic swerve, I propose that in his late career he discovered nothing less than a third major theme, which I call "The Creative." This set of values was motivated by autobiographical consciousness, individual choice, redemptive love, domestic themes, and, of course, artistic experimentation, all of which enabled Steinbeck to explore a new narratological world after 1950.

Sweet Thursday was consciously proposed as a tonal, thematic counterbalance to the "weight" of *East of Eden* (*SLL*, 472). It is a boisterous sequel to Steinbeck's more famous *Cannery Row*, which appeared nine years earlier (treating Monterey's prewar era). *Sweet Thursday* shares the same geographical location and many of the same characters as *Cannery Row* but takes up the post-World War II life of Doc (based on Steinbeck's soul mate, Edward F. Ricketts, who had died in an auto-train crash on Ocean View Avenue in May 1948). The novel emphasizes Doc's difficulties in reestablishing his Western Biological Laboratory on Monterey's Cannery Row, including his vicissitudes with a scholarly treatise and his rocky off-again, on-again relationship with a tough-talking, golden-hearted hooker-turned-waitress named Suzy. It also features the burlesque-like antics of the Row's Palace Flophouse denizens (Mack, Hazel, and others) and Fauna, the madam of the Bear Flag, who—playing Cupid for Doc and Suzy—want to ensure a happy romantic ending.

As this brief precis suggests, when approached from a rigidly analytical position, *Sweet Thursday* can be considered sentimental (like most other hookers at Fauna's Bear Flag brothel, Suzy's indelible goodness erases her stigma as a prostitute), reductive (Doc imagines he cannot be happy without a woman to complete his identity), slapstick (events and characterizations have a cartoon-like quality), and improbable (the plot hinges on coincidences and convenient superficialities). Such flaws—trumpeted as indisputable proof that "Steinbeck had lost the powers of self criticism"—have made the book an easy target for snipers, as Tedlock and Wicker noted in 1957 (*SAHC*, xxxviii-ix). But to arrive at the deeper significance of this fiction, questions of character motivation, realism, agency, and gender portrayal need to be willingly suspended here (and may even be beside the point). Rather, *Sweet Thursday* is important for what it reveals of Steinbeck's continuing aesthetic and philosophical changes and for his attitude toward the necessity of fictive experimentation in the unsettling wake of a postwar depletion, an enervating realism, that influenced all levels of the Row's socio-economic, philosophical, aesthetic, personal, and linguistic existence. Old ways of doing business no longer obtain for Doc, for inhabitants of the Row, or for the narrator and author (implied or otherwise): "Discontent," he writes, is "the lever of change" (*ST*, 21). *Sweet Thursday*, then, is Steinbeck's effort at accomplishing what "has not been done a million times before" (*ST*, 23) in American writing, a way to "make new rules about this and this," as he later said (*SLL*, 532).

Steinbeck understood the corrosive nature of discontent and disaffection. There was a span in his career, beginning in mid-1948, when he was cut adrift from accustomed moorings by the death of Ed Ricketts and by his divorce from Gwyn (his second wife and the mother of his two children). On and off for over a year, mired in his own enervation, misogyny, and self-pity, Steinbeck's self-identity as a writer seemed splintered, fragmented, even fraudulent (*TAJS*, 624). After *The Pearl* and *The Wayward Bus*, both published in 1947, this customarily resilient writer found it increasingly difficult to settle on his next project (the many versions of *Zapata*, for instance, the false starts on *East of Eden*, as well as the several unwritten plays he planned during this period). Steinbeck's personal disarray and emotional discontentedness, coupled with his awakening reaction to America's cold war intellectual climate, which called into question the currency of social(ist) visions, set him willy-nilly on a road toward an end he could not yet envision but whose allurements he apparently could not refuse. In the feverish and sometimes blind searches of that period he underwent deep readjustments toward many things, not the least of them his own fictive art, his belief that his next book, "Salinas Valley" (working title for *East of Eden*), would be very far removed from *Of Mice and Men* (*S&C*, 114; *TAJS*, 630). In his relationship with his third wife, Elaine, whom he met in May 1949 and married in December 1950, Steinbeck discovered healing powers in love and domestic attachment which in turn had a direct, exponential bearing on his work energy and anticipation (*SLL*, 397) and, by his own admission, may have saved him from suicide: "And what changes there have been. I did not expect to survive them and I don't think I would have. Every life force was shriveling. Work was non-existent. . . . The wounds were gangrenous and mostly I just didn't give a dam [sic]. Now two years later I have a new life and a direction. . . . I am doing work I like" (*JN*, 95).[13]

Eventually, as if to validate that recovery by repeating it, Steinbeck raised his own emotional and creative processes to the level of subject, at once self-generating and historically determined. Once Steinbeck entered that thorny realm he probably realized he knew it as well as anything else, which is perhaps why he considered *Sweet Thursday* "a little self indulgent" (*SLL*, 473). In writing Doc trying to write, Steinbeck turned out to be narrating nothing less than the symbolic story of his own emotional rescue and artistic refashioning. In the process Steinbeck did not "purposefully . . . destroy or deprecate Doc," as Peter Lisca maintained.[14] Instead Steinbeck replaced Doc with himself; in recasting his portrait of the artist, he did so in an entirely familiar scale. Indeed, the intersubjectivity of writer and persona, reality and projection, text and context, seems to have been such a point of intrigue to Steinbeck in his last phase that even the seemingly straightforward genre of autobiography was called into question: "Since after a passage of time I don't know what happened and what I made up, it would be nearer the truth to set both down. I'm sure this would include persons who never existed. . . . But surely the fictionizing and day dreaming and self-aggrandizement as well as the self-attacks are as much a part of reality as far as the writing is concerned as the facts are. And even the facts have a chameleon tendency after a passage of time" (*SLL*, 798).

That Steinbeck took so much pleasure in writing this blissful, ludic novel should not, I think, be held against him. As a person who labored with words day in and day out, year after year, he often spoke of his need for his task to be "fun." "There is a school of thought among writers which says that if you enjoy writing something it is automatically no good and should be thrown out. I can't agree with this," he told Elizabeth Otis, his agent and the dedicatee of *Sweet Thursday*, on 14 September 1953 (*SLL*, 472). If *Cannery Row* represented the way things were, he explained two months later, then *Sweet Thursday* became the way things "might have" been (474). The two propositions ("the one can be as true as the other") are necessary for a holistic view of the novelist's mind and for an understanding of what the spirit of Ed Ricketts meant to Steinbeck, who didn't "seem able to get over his death" (474).

Thus, only by embracing comedy and tragedy, realism and fabulation, the inarticulate "transcendental sadness" of *Cannery Row* and the "frabjous" expression of joy of *Sweet Thursday*, could Steinbeck lay to rest the ghost of Ed Ricketts, which, by this time, had become the ghost of Steinbeck himself. In giving himself to revisionary impulses, Steinbeck presented his new Doc not as an unapproachable mythic hero, a practitioner of rigorous nonteleology, or an enigmatic isolato, but as a man—like the newly renovated Steinbeck—who was once again connected to quotidian life, to the local human community, and to author and readers, by common links—the search for meaningfulness, the potentially saving grace of love, and the ongoing struggle of the creative consciousness toward articulation:

> For hours on end he sat at his desk with a yellow pad before him and his needle-sharp pencils lined up. Sometimes his wastebasket was full of crushed, scribbled pages, and at others not even a doodle went down. Then he would move to the aquarium and stare into it. And his voices howled and cried and moaned. "Write!" said his top voice, and "Search!" said his middle voice, and his lowest voice sighed, "Lonesome! Lonesome!" He did not go down without a struggle. He res-

> urrected old love affairs, he swam deep in music, he read the *Sorrows of Werther*; but the voices would not leave him. The beckoning yellow pages became his enemies. (*ST*, 58-59)

Though I still endorse the premise that *Sweet Thursday* is a novel about the creative process, because it foregrounds the struggle of individual consciousness in (and through) language, I am inclined to regard Steinbeck's attitude toward the key artist figure in a less totalizing way than I did twenty-five years ago—that is, less as a result of Doc's masterful, isolated genius (his figurate role in *Cannery Row*) than as a workaday, representative negotiator between public and private realms: "When trouble came to Doc," Steinbeck notes, "it was everybody's trouble" (*ST*, 58). In chapter 6, "The Creative Cross," Doc's tribulations in researching and writing his proposed scholarly essay, "Symptoms in Some Cephalopods Approximating Apoplexy" (*ST*, 32), mirror aspects of Steinbeck's preparatory stages in his own creative regime; Doc's prewriting jitters and inability to concentrate are colored as well by Steinbeck's wrenching artistic and personal upheavals of the late 1940s. ("Wouldn't it be interesting if Ed *was* us and that now there wasn't any such thing or that he created out of his own mind something that went away with him," Steinbeck wrote the Lovejoys right after Ricketts's death. "I've wondered a lot about that. How much was Ed and how much was me and which was which" [?] [*SLL*, 316].)

Embedded behind Steinbeck's comic treatment of Doc's trials of mind and heart in disciplining himself to enter the "creative zone," there is a felt psychological validity and emotional immediacy. Steinbeck's new artistry lay in striking a balance between the old desire for the sovereignty of the imagination and the new awareness of contextual facticity, the ineluctable intervention of quotidian demands. Writing, like so many other endeavors in life, Steinbeck shows, is less a condition of mastery than it is hard, sweaty work, full of isolation, pitfalls, contingencies, insecurities, and disruptions. In *Sweet Thursday* this pragmatic balance took the form of a comedic stance toward the artist's traditionally elitist position. (Writing to his friend James S. Pope about William Faulkner's *Paris Review* interview in 1956, Steinbeck said, "When those old writing boys get to talking about The Artist, meaning themselves, I want to leave the profession" [*SLL*, 529].) Steinbeck does not entertain the death of the author (that would erase his own reason for being), but he does give us a restrained view of Doc's performance, suggesting that success lies as much in the marshalling of conjunctive forces and ambient fortune as it does in the completion of the writing project. Paradoxically, even though Doc is freighted with Steinbeck's own self-projection and his own autobiographical angst, there is also a telling difference in ends, because the form Steinbeck adopts for *Sweet Thursday* takes on a life of its own, "gives form to its own curiosities," as he said of André Gide's *The Counterfeitors*, and so veers away from the kind of objective, autonomous document a practicing scientist would be expected to produce.

Revising, Steinbeck must have realized as he reread and reprocessed the Doc of *Cannery Row* and "About Ed Ricketts," was not so much a tidy allegory as it was a way of reentering a slippery emotional place which was no less a part of the makeup of "reality" than the physicality of his present moment. Thus "Sweet Thursday" functions as a double signifier, at once private and public utterance, reference and object, process and product, text and work. The name refers to a "magic kind of day" (*ST*, 122) when all manner of unanticipated, fissionable, random events occur on Cannery Row (to which Steinbeck devotes three contiguous, titled chapters—19, 20, 21—at the midpoint of his novel, and one—39—at the very end). Then, refracted, "Sweet Thursday" (a time, a place in the mind, a historical context) becomes, like Hawthorne's "Scarlet Letter" or Melville's "Moby Dick," the title of the book Steinbeck brings into being, which operates in turn as a textual looking glass that reflects, distorts, enlarges, and/or magnifies the implicit ethereality and quantum activities of the "magic day" by borrowing a sense of its own disruptive form from the carnival quality of life on the Row.

That inherent duality, that fluid interchangeability, which is encoded in the title, also functions as a symbol for Steinbeck's imaginative concerns. When Fauna tells Joe Elegant that, "'When a man says words he believes them, even if he thinks he is lying'" (*ST*, 134), she is suggesting that language (not only experience) *is* a reality and a seductive one at that. Philosophically and aesthetically, after 1949 Steinbeck wrote out of a belief in the preeminence of individual—rather than group—creativity, but he did so in such a way that his expressivism was also a critique of realism, and the issue of origination was open to authorial skepticism. The moral center he wrote toward in his late works was, like Cannery Row itself, not so much a sacred ground as it was a negotiable site of contingency, dissonance, and indeterminacy.

Not for nothing, then, Steinbeck names chapter 10 "There's a Hole in Reality Through Which We Can Look if We Wish," for in its pointed artificiality, in its intertextuality, his fiction partially dismantles (but does not completely explode) the authority implicit or embedded in traditional authorship and in narrative propriety, and demonstrates that in the random, seesaw poetic form of *Sweet Thursday*, Steinbeck was able to bring both the narrative plot and the process of reflexive commentary into a single work, which has the spontaneity of appearing to be made up on the spot, to undercut its own profound pretensions, and to deconstruct the rules and format of its own invention and ontology: "There are people who will say that this whole account is a lie, but a thing isn't necessarily a lie even if it didn't necessarily happen" (*ST*, 57). In such instances as various characters' use of malapropisms and in Mack's humorous use of Latin phrases and exalted language, *Sweet Thursday* interrogates the representational qualities of language (and class) at the same time it validates the fluctuating process by which such mysteries emerge without ever being fully concluded. That characters as diverse as Doc, Joe Elegant, the Bear Flag's cook, who is writing a Freudian novel called *The Pi Root of Oedipus*, and Fauna, who not only writes horoscopes but authors Suzy's conduct and manners ("'I should write a book. . . .' 'If She Could, I Could'" [*ST*, 143]) all wrestle with compositional acts and problems of inscription invites us to consider seriously Steinbeck's perception that the tangled wilderness of language (whether of speech, writing, sexuality, body gesture, or masquerade dress) is one of the few frontiers left to us in a discontented, decentered, demystified apocalyptic age. Writing, he reminds us, can be a noun as well as a verb.

4

To the degree that the divorced Steinbeck was often himself emotionally uncentered and therefore an absentee parent to his boys, his writing in *East of Eden* (the original manuscript was addressed explicitly to his sons) and in *Sweet Thursday* represent surrogate ways of being a father, alternate means of assuaging his guilt and easing their dislocation by making them participants in his fictional landscape.[15] While young boys could hardly be expected to read on their own, much less understand, the philosophical blockbuster *East of Eden* (Thom was eight, John IV was six when it appeared), the comparatively slim, elegant *Sweet Thursday* was another matter, for with it Steinbeck wrote a humorous book that not only profited from being read by or read aloud to children but also explained in a comedic and self-deprecating manner what it was that their father did every day with sharpened pencils, yellow notepads, dictaphone, and typewriter.

In enacting this mysterious concept of "work," *Sweet Thursday* gains its exaggerated propriety from self-conscious adaptations of fictive reality, including Steinbeck's own prior writings (*Tortilla Flat* and especially *Cannery Row* are echoed in this text) and from parallel, engendering artifices. As I have detailed in *Steinbeck's Reading* and recounted in the first essay of this book, Steinbeck often read to write. *Sweet Thursday* is no exception to the rule of quotation. In the populist echoes and in the literary parodies, mimicries, puns, wordplays, echoes, and allusions to the Bible, *The Little Flowers of Saint Francis*, the Welsh *Mabinogian*, Coleridge's "Kubla Khan," Lewis Carroll's "Jabberwocky" and "The Walrus and the Carpenter" from *Through the Looking Glass*, Robert Louis Stevenson's *Child's Garden of Verses*, to list but a few, *Thursday* is enriched by Steinbeck's eclectic browsing in favorite works. Perhaps more than anything else, however, Steinbeck's avowed reading of Al Capp's enormously popular, extremely inventive *Li'l Abner* comic strip, which he and his family followed assiduously in newspapers at home and abroad, propelled *Thursday* toward what new historicists might consider its contextual thickness and its immersion, even implication, in a cultural network and tonality.[16] "Yes, comic strips," he told Sydney Fields in 1955. "I read them avidly. Especially Li'l Abner. Al Capp is a great social satirist. Comic strips might be the real literature of our time. We'll never know what literature is until we're gone" (*CJS*, 59). New historicism and cultural materialism aside, what more natural way to find common ground between a stoic father and his rambunctious sons than by employing the familiar language and gestures of their milieu—comic books?

I have long been an advocate of Steinbeck's ephemeral writings. Far from being marginal documents, his introductions, prefaces, dust jacket blurbs, and testimonials effectively illuminate his own art. In 1953, the same year he was working on "Bear Flag," the musical precursor of *Sweet Thursday*, Steinbeck introduced Capp's book-length collection, *The World of Li'l Abner*. Steinbeck did not habitually provide encomia or introductions to the work of other writers, but when he did, it was for a strong reason. As with many of Steinbeck's lesser known or fugitive items, this six-page brief reveals much about his creative bearings, influences, and purposes. Beneath his jaunty, tongue-in-cheek tone there are numerous revelations which bear directly on *Sweet Thursday*'s zany style and technique. To state it simply, *Sweet Thursday* is Steinbeck's attempt at writing a literary comic book, his conscious attempt "to get into Capp's act."[17]

Steinbeck theorizes that Al Capp "may very possibly be the best writer in the world today . . . the best satirist since Laurence Sterne." From a patrician point of view Steinbeck's reasoning might not at first seem convincing, and yet, while his proofs reveal some very large leaps of faith, given Steinbeck's interest in pictorialism, his populist beliefs, and his aggressively non-academic disposition, this argument is not entirely fallacious either and should not be dismissed out of hand. Steinbeck asserts that, like Dante, who redefined the established traditions of literature in his time by writing in Italian rather than in Latin, Capp too is a pioneer, perhaps even a visionary. The literature of the future, he claims, might eventually depart from the "stuffy" adherence to "the written and printed word in poetry, drama, and the novel" and eventually include popular forms of cultural discourse such as the comic book, Capp's metier. Steinbeck asks:

> How in the hell do we know what literature is? Well, one of the . . . diagnostics of literature should be, it seems to me, that it is read, that it amuses, moves, instructs, changes and criticizes people. And who in the world does that more than Capp . . . ? Who knows what literature is? The literature of the Cro Magnon is painted on the walls of the caves of Altimira. Who knows but that the literature of the future will be projected on clouds? Our present argument that literature is the written and printed word . . . has no very eternal basis in fact. Such literature has not been with us very long, and there is nothing to indicate that it will continue. . . . If people don't read it, it just isn't going to be literature. (*WLA*, iv)

The key point of Steinbeck's prophetic thesis is less shocking to a reader in the mid-1990s—accustomed as we are to issues of contingency and indeterminacy caused by recent theoretical debates over the existence of a uniform canon, shared texts, and the autonomy of representation—than it was forty years ago. Indeed, in an age which has ushered in interactive media forms, including virtual reality and hypertexts, the comic book as a literary form appears now to be rather tame.

Nevertheless, in Capp's ability to "invent" an entire world in Dogpatch, to give it memorable characters, recognizable form, and unique spoken language, he created just that quality of aesthetic "participation" Steinbeck aimed for in all his fictions, in which the reader concretized the text and otherwise completed his or her own arc of subjective transaction. The unbridled license to make up in any way that fits the artist's or the medium's immediate, compulsive demands—not those of a critical blueprint—is what Capp and Steinbeck share. Indeed, Steinbeck's description of the key elements of the *Li'l Abner* strip can also be applied to *Sweet Thursday*: the latter's plot has a "fine crazy consistency" of (il)logic, it satirizes the "entrenched nonsense" of blind human striving, respectable middle-class life, and normal male/female courting rituals; it constructs an entire fictive world in the Palace Flophouse and its larger domain, Cannery Row itself (where like Capp's Dogpatch, realistic outside rules of aesthetics and morality don't necessarily apply); and it also contains suitably exaggerated situations (Capp's Sadie Hawkins Day parallels Steinbeck's accounts of the annual return of monarch butterflies to Pacific Grove and The Great Roque War), as well as characters whose names are distinctive, colorful, and unique (Steinbeck's Whitey No. 1, Whitey No. 2, and Jesus and Mary Rivas; Capp's Hairless Joe and Moonbeam McSwine, for example). Finally, in Hazel's absurd run for the United States presidency, we catch Steinbeck's echoes of Zoot Suit Yokum's improbable presidential nomination in 1944 (*WLA*, 47).

Moreover, in its optimistic, life-affirming treatment of the roller-coaster love affair between Doc and Suzy, Steinbeck playfully echoes not only his own affair with Elaine but also the courtship and marriage of the recalcitrant Li'l Abner and the bountiful Daisy Mae. There are numerous examples of passages, such as the one in chapter 16 in which Mack believes he can heal the psychosomatic diseases of rich women, that not only pay homage to Capp (there are echoes in Mack's proposal of Marryin' Sam's "perspectus" for expensive weddings) but which also underscore Steinbeck's own self-mimicing method, his application of Capp's satiric "tweak with equal pressure on all classes, all groups," and his appreciation for the "resounding prose" of Capp's folk dialogue. Mack boasts:

> first I'd hire me a deaf-and-dumb assistant. His job is to just set and listen and look worried. Then I'd get me a bottle of Epsom salts and I'd put in a pretty little screwcap thing and I'd call it Moondust. I'd charge about thirty dollars a teaspoonful, and you got to come to my office to get it. Then I'd invent me a machine you strap the dame in. It's all chrome and it lights colored lights every minute or so. It costs the dame twelve dollars a half-hour and it puts her through the motions she'd do over a scrub board. I'd cure them! And I'd make a fortune too. Of course they'd get sick right away again, so I'd have something else, like mixed sleeping pills and wake-up pills that keeps you right where you was when you started. (*ST*, 102-03)

Perhaps more than anything else, however, there is a scene that serves as a special synecdoche in language, execution, and purpose for Capp's influence. All *Sweet Thursday*'s chapters have parodic or incongruent titles, similar to Capp's boldfaced commentary and frame headings in his comic strip; the chapters themselves are short and easily comprehended, like cartoon strip panels, which is one of the features Mack called for in his prologue. In chapter 28, "Where Alfred the Sacred River Ran," Steinbeck lampoons Coleridge in his title, then describes the action of a wild party and Doc's reaction to it, in a way that can best be understood if we imagine ourselves to be reading a comic strip or cartoon, blissfully participating in its "preposterous" *architexture*. It is necessary to quote at length from the following scene, a masquerade on the theme of "Snow White and the Seven Dwarfs," to suggest the flavor and dimensions of Steinbeck's boundary-breaking recitation:

> A fog of unreality like a dream feeling was not in him but all around him. He went inside the Palace and saw the dwarfs and monsters and the preposterous Hazel all lighted by the flickering lanterns. None of it seemed the fabric of sweet reality. . . .
>
> Anyone untrained in tom-wallagers might well have been startled. . . . Eddie waltzed to the rumba music, his arms embracing an invisible partner. Wide Ida lay on the floor Indian wrestling with Whitey No. 2, at each try displaying acres of pink panties, while a wild conga line of dwarfs and animals milled about. . . .

> Mack and Doc were swept into the conga line. To Doc the room began to revolve slowly and then to rise and fall like the deck of a stately ship in a groundswell. The music roared and tinkled. Hazel beat out rhythm on the stove with his sword until Johnny, aiming carefully, got a bull's eye on Hazel. Hazel leaped in the air and came down on the oven door, scattering crushed ice all over the floor. One of the guests had got wedged in the grandfather clock. From the outside the Palace Flophouse seemed to swell and subside like rising bread. (*ST*, 196-97)

This festive *carnivalesque* passage, which occurs in what Mack calls a "veritable fairyland" (189), is one of Steinbeck's most pleasurable fictive moments. It revels in a sense of fancifulness, in a luxurious staging and fluid movement that joins sacred and profane experience in startling, memorable ways. Steinbeck's reversals of gender expectations and his conscious abdication of the "fabric of sweet reality" accounts for the bizarre, ridiculous swelling house, the instances of cross-dressing and masquerade impersonation, the unpredictable loops and digressions of the novel's structure, its abandonment of overtly linear or "literary" progression in favor of a quantum randomness, and its one-dimensional (but not necessarily simplistic) characterizations. All in all, this blissful carnival scene is an example of his belief that "technique should grow out of theme" (*SLL*, 521).

Furthermore, Steinbeck's postwar change of aesthetic sensibility made an enormous difference between his treatment of Doc, whose "transcendent sadness" and essential loneliness closed *Cannery Row*, and this portrayal, which ends with the partially incapacitated, but romantically redeemed, Doc riding off with Suzy (she is driving) into the sunset of a day that was "of purple and gold, the proud colors of the Salinas High School." Steinbeck continues, "A squadron of baby angels maneuvered at twelve hundred feet, holding a pink cloud on which the word J-O-Y flashed on and off. A seagull with a broken wing took off and flew straight up into the air, squawking, "Joy! Joy!" (268). It is a moment that lends *Sweet Thursday* the same quality Steinbeck found in *The World of Li'l Abner*: "such effective good nature that we seem to have thought of it ourselves" (*WLA*, ii). Love, considered both seriously and as a form of play, Steinbeck suggests, heals the split between language and life, self and world, parent and children, text and audience. Inevitably, Doc and Suzy's marriage is less significant as a smarmy act of denouement than it is as proof of Steinbeck's abiding sense of the "joy" of creative drives: *Sweet Thursday* is an erotic coupling of textuality and sexuality, the result of exquisite "satisfaction" that comes when "words and sentences" and "good and shared love" combine (*SAHC*, 309).

Recognizing the supremacy of writerly *jouissance*, of playful fictive invention, underscores that for the late Steinbeck authoring was not a thoroughly mimetic task, a representational rendering of shared social reality; rather, it was the creation of a reality all its own, a blissful reality in/of language that created its own set of interpretative valuations. The norms, values, and ground rules of this fictiveness changed from work to work, so that even to speak of the novelist's task of creating a world in *East of Eden* would not be to describe the same created world in *Sweet Thursday*, published only two years after *Eden* and also set in a remembered California. Far from being a tired failure because he abandoned critical realism after *The Grapes of Wrath*, Steinbeck was a prophetic postmodernist, a journeyer in the literary fun house, and a traveler in the land behind the mirror of art, a mirror which in *Sweet Thursday* had become nearly silverless, so that we see his hand at work, calling attention to the house he is building, insistently redeeming it from "mechanical convention" by "unmasking" the originating system.[18] Thus the old thinking, with its imposition of preordained critical hegemonies of harmony, unity, distance, and mimesis, for instance, simply won't work with a textual construct like *Sweet Thursday* or, for that matter, with much of what Steinbeck wrote in the last phase of his career. Authoring these texts, he authored himself anew and vice versa.

The perjorative *Time* magazine review, which I quoted earlier, was only partly—and unintentionally—correct in its assessment of *Sweet Thursday*. Indeed, Steinbeck did "comic-strip" his characters of reality, but that, I suggest, was his desire; far from being proof of his decline into an undifferentiated Saroyanesque landscape, his appropriation of Al Capp's free-form inventiveness, vivid technique, exaggerated scenarios, and "dreadful folk poetry" helped further in the novel what Steinbeck saw in *Li'l Abner*—a "hilarious picture of our ridiculous selves" (*WLA*, ii). Even that most significant of late Steinbeckian topics—the role of the artist—came in for its share of satire; rather than elevating it to a vaunted, culturally unassailable position, Steinbeck demystifies it by emphasizing the prewriting process, the elusive valences of language, and the necessity for human bonding, rather than the austere finished result (Doc has yet to write his essay as the book ends). In lifting the veil to expose the process of fictionalizing the fictionalizing process, Steinbeck saves *Sweet Thursday* from being masturbatory or egregiously narcissistic by its parodic tone and functionally inspired purpose. "Don't think of literary form," he advised famous humorist Fred Allen. "Let it get out as it wants to . . . The form will develop in the telling. Don't make the telling follow a form."[19] In seeking its own trajectory, *Sweet Thursday* turns out to be, on closer inspection, not an overstuffed turkey but more like that gull which presides over the conclusion—earthbound on occasion but still capable of some startling flights of fancy. Pascal Covici was correct—the novel sold with abandon—and while its commercial success justified Covici's smug faith in Steinbeck, just as it fueled Bennett's scorn, there is, as with all Steinbeck's late work, a mediating ground, an aesthetic/emotional context, a cultural current, a text behind the text, which provides an enabling evaluative presence.

5

"You fix the day and hour," Steinbeck says in *Sweet Thursday*, "by some incident that happened to yourself" (*ST*, 121). In the fall of 1984, midway in the second semester of my visiting appointment at San Jose State University as director of the Steinbeck Research Center, I called on Thom Steinbeck, the novelist's eldest son, in Carmel Highlands. I meant only to deliver a photocopied mock-up of *Your Only Weapon Is Your Work*, a limited edition pamphlet publication of a 1957 letter Steinbeck had written to Dennis Murphy, the son of a longtime Steinbeck family friend and himself author of a highly acclaimed novel, *The Sergeant* (which Steinbeck had directed first toward Elizabeth Otis, who in turn successfully placed it with Viking Press). The day, however, quickly turned into something more. We spent that afternoon lounging on the deck of his splendid rented house, taking in its views of sheltering pines, craggy bluffs, and beyond them the sparkle and flash of the Pacific Ocean north of Big Sur. For a transplanted easterner the locale provided a spectacular glimpse of a remnant of the old Pacific Coast frontier, the intimidating unpeopled landscape of Robinson Jeffers's poems and Steinbeck's "Flight," and, on a different scale, "the foreign and fancy purlieus" where, in *Sweet Thursday*, Whitey No. 1 peddled raffle tickets for the Palace Flophouse sale. For several hours Thom and I talked and drank wine—much wine, as I recall—which undoubtedly helped create the glow of camaraderie in that seemingly luminous time and place. We were contemporaries—a year apart in age—and our sense of having shared generational experiences and opinions seemed pronounced that afternoon. (Judging from followup correspondence, telephone calls, and subsequent meetings, I suspected he felt the same way.)

Of course, we spoke often of his father and I remember vividly how Thom talked in that specially tinged, blustery, offhand, wounded, and amazed way that children of the celebrated and famous have of communicating their conflicted sense of acceptance and estrangement, honor and renunciation, pride and embarrassment, validation and denial in their legacy. The afternoon was interrupted by at least two long-distance telephone calls from John IV, Thom's younger brother who was living in Colorado (their monthly phone bill was over $700), and while these hiatuses stopped the flow of our talk for a while, each time Thom came back he was fueled with new energy, new reminiscences that put his father in perspective, often circling around sharply etched memories of the elder Steinbeck sharpening hundreds of pencils each morning before sitting down to write, or tales of his father reading aloud to the brothers, trying to induce them to read on their own and exasperated at their short attention spans. While I was not actively seeking gossip, I admit I was not averse to such inside news, though I was also leery of its implications and the burden of complicity or degree of co-option it might create in the future.[20] But such knowledge is always double-edged and serves unanticipated ends: listening to stories of Thom's troubled childhood following his parent's divorce, which he did not try to whitewash or soften in any way, I glimpsed something of the cause of his father's paternal attachment to Dennis Murphy, who became, for a while anyway, a surrogate son and long-distance apprentice.

As much as anything else that afternoon I was painfully aware that even with firsthand information I was being offered in moments of spirited fellow-feeling, I could not know this man's father, this John Steinbeck, whom I had spent so many years studying, in anything but a partial way, refracted through the bias of my own sensibility, the lens of my own preoccupation. Perhaps, I thought, I really had failed the test of perspectival criticism after all and had fallen a long way from the level of a Lewis Gannett, or, in my own time, a Jackson Benson who had, more than anyone else I knew, given Steinbeck's life and career its most comprehensive treatment and fairest appraisal. And yet if such musings made Steinbeck less a monument, less a cultural icon to me, I wasn't sure that I was willing to trade places with my host either, who, with his brother, knew even more than I did about the sordid wages of rebellious excess and the unrelenting burden of shadows cast by the living and the dead.[21] Sometimes, I figured, it is better to be an everlasting outsider, inventing reasons for the reasons, rather than having to live under the legacy of parental obsessions and failed expectations. In any event, I had no difficulty imagining Steinbeck's sons as models for some aspects of Cal and Aron Trask in *East of Eden*.

In the course of that afternoon, though, in addition to regaling me with raucous tales and anecdotes, Thom trotted out Steinbeck family memorabilia, and we briefly entertained the possibility of purchasing some items for the Steinbeck Center at a later date. (A year later, following another visit with Thom, I bought a number of 8 mm home movies for the center, including rare footage of Steinbeck and Ricketts' Sea of Cortez collecting trip. By that time, trying to raise money to support their respective and sometimes overlapping careers as filmmakers and writers, Thom and John, following their mother's precedent, had already conducted the first of three public sales of memorabilia and correspondence in their father's estate.)[22] As I was about to leave for Los Gatos, Thom said he had something he wanted me to have. I told him I was representing the Research Center and could not accept a gift for myself, though I could and would—gladly—receive one on behalf of San Jose State. He agreed, then hauled out a 1950's vintage portable typewriter, which he opened for my inspection. Steinbeck had hauled it along in his GMC pickup/camper when he toured the United States collecting impressions that would become *Travels with Charley*.[23] It was a Swiss-made Hermes, aptly named for the messenger of the gods and himself a deity who, in a classically pragmatic way, embodied plural functions—god of invention, god of thievery, and god of roads and travel—in short, if I can be allowed to bend the metaphor to my own purpose, the god of process. "This was my father's," Thom said. "I want you to have it."

But only after reaching home that night did I notice the most intriguing part of the gift: on the back of the typewriter's machine-grey cover Steinbeck had scratched indelibly with a pin, or a knife, or maybe a nail, these words—"The Beast Within." I think that it was his way—part humorous, part deadly serious—of personalizing an otherwise somber-looking mechanical device, giving a name and an identity to one of those technological gadgets that the inventor side of him dearly loved and remained fascinated by throughout his life. In its ideal state the typewriter (and its kin) enabled the writer's imagination, processed his arc of reality, helped turn emergent material, whatever its source, into fictive form, and—not to put too purple a shade on this—gave shape, weight, palpability to experience in/of language: "The discipline of the written word punishes both stupidity and dishonesty," he told Pascal Covici, Jr. "A writer lives in awe of words for they can be cruel or kind, and they can change their meanings right in front of you" (*SLL*, 523). As a mediating trope, so to speak, for transmission of shifting words, the typewriter paradoxically distorts, transforms, and modifies in order to clarify and illumine; although it is not an "appendage," an "umbilical connection" like the more comfortable pencil Steinbeck often preferred and frequently extolled, it still operates in the same way as a focusing "tool" (*SLL*, 624), like his later use of the dictaphone, that tends outward as well as inward, facilitating (and in some cases creating) his view of the world. The important thing, however, is the process of looking and of immersion implied in writing—the pen(cil) or knife or nail or typewriter key scratch on the surface of a papery medium—that records what it means to have been alive in the magnificent constellation of inner and outer experience. "'After all,'" Doc says, "'I guess it doesn't matter whether you look down or up—as long as you look'" (*ST*, 271).

In my moment of obsessive identification, the diminutive machine came alive as a cumulative metaphor for the entire complex of Steinbeck's working life, an artifice situated on a horizon somewhere between individual expressivism and determined constructionism. On one hand, it represents process: the constant tyranny of being driven by beastly internal compulsions toward expression (*SLL*, 411) and the daily, obsessive financial need to write (*SLL*, 491-92), which made him frequently moody, cantankerous, selfish, aloof, and inward-looking in a way no doubt only those who lived in his life—his wives, children, and stepchild, for instance—could fully ascertain and in a perverse way were fully qualified to judge. On the other hand, the Hermes symbolizes product: the indescribable and fleeting moments of success when a work was published and—whether or not critically and/or commercially viable—then nominally at least put behind him as he went on restlessly, fearfully, to the next project:

> Once the words go down—you are alone and commited. It's as final as a plea in court from which there is no retracing. That's the lonely time. Nine tenths of a writer's life do not admit of any companion nor friend nor associate. And until one makes peace with loneliness and accepts it as part of the profession . . . until then there are times of dreadful dread. I am just as terrified of my next book as I was of my first. It doesn't get any easier. It gets harder and more heartbreaking and finally, it must be that one must accept the failure which is the end of every writer's life no matter what stir he may have made. In himself he must fail as Launcelot failed—for the Grail is not a cup. It's a promise that skips ahead—it's a carrot on a stick and it never fails to draw us on. So it is that I would greatly prefer to die in the middle of a sentence and so leave it as all life must be—unfinished. That's the law, the great law. Principles of notoriety or publicity or even public acceptance do not apply. (*SLL*, 859-60)

Aware of his limitations to the end, just as he bridled against them, Steinbeck believed that "to finish is sadness to a writer—a little death. He puts the last word down and it is done. But it isn't really done. The story goes on and leaves the writer behind, for no story is ever done" (*SLL*, 523). The unfinished story surfaces in unforeseen ways, even when we think it is done, including its intrusion into this fragmentary attempt at synthesis and integration, when Steinbeck rewrites Ed Ricketts by reimagining Doc as himself, when he revises Capp's art by reinventing the comic book for his children, when I revisit the scene of my revisionism, and all of us—fathers and sons, current spouses and ex-lovers, past mentors and abiding friends—drive, so to speak, toward La Jolla, where all things seem to resolve, momentarily anyway, into metaphoric simplicity and intuitive clarity: "This is the greatest mystery of the human mind—the inductive leap. Everything falls into place, irrelevancies relate, dissonance becomes harmony, and nonsense wears a crown of meaning. But the clarifying leap springs from the rich soil of confusion, and the leaper is not unfamiliar with pain" (*ST*, 28). It is a moment when the machinery, the inventions, the necessary metaphors and tropes of leaping and journeying that so fixed and fascinated Steinbeck during his career—the Joad's Hudson Super Six, the *Western Flyer*, The Word, Juan Chicoy's broken-down bus, Olive Hamilton's airplane ride, the telescope that Mack and the boys present Doc at the conclusion of *Sweet Thursday* (he needed a microscope), Steinbeck's Hermes typewriter, his truck camper Rocinante, the hieroglyphic *Timshel*, the surreal, topsy-turvy architecture of Al Capp's Dogpatch, and Pigasus, the winged pig, his chosen personal emblem (*SLL*, 295-96)—all begin moving evocatively in roughly the same direction to fuel the transforming "drama of magic and alchemy" by which Steinbeck entered fascinating worlds of resonant language and rich experience, where, because the old strictures no longer applied, he felt obliged to make "new rules" of artistic conduct, propriety, and deportment (*SLL*, 532).

John Steinbeck's gift—much underrated in the final phase of his career—was his ability to make each book a different kind of "life experience" (*JN*, 61) by sending back reports from all the creative venues he entered—whether it was the tidepool, the conflicted labyrinth of the heart, or human speech and language. Maybe, after all interpretative second-guessing and critical wish fulfillment subsides, after the process of reading and the nature of writing itself have been redefined yet again according to whatever the future theoretical fashion will be, then what has gone around will come around, and John Steinbeck will prove to have been on the right road all along, the rest of us dust swirls in the spokes of his wheels.

Notes

[1] John Steinbeck, *Sweet Thursday* (New York: Viking Press, 1954; reprint, New York: Penguin Books, 1986), 64 (hereafter cited as *ST*).

[2] Information in this and the following three paragraphs is taken from two typed letters by Pascal Covici to John Steinbeck, written on 16 June 1954, and on 9 August 1954, housed at Harry Ransom Humanities Research Center, University of Texas, Austin. None of Steinbeck's biographers mention this episode.

[3] Linda Hutcheon, *Narcissistic Narrative: The Metafictional Paradox* (1980, reprint, New York: Methuen, 1984), xii. See also Ross Chambers, who writes in *Story and Situation: Narrative Seduction and the Power of Fiction*

(Minneapolis: University of Minnesota Press, 1984), 25, how certain texts are "situationally self-referential" and manage to create a conduit of attention between text and reader.

[4] "Back to the Riffraff," *Time* 14 June 1954, 121; Brendan Gill, *New Yorker* 10 July 1954, 71; Carlos Baker, "After Lousy Wednesday," *New York Times Book Review* 13 June 1954, 4; and Robert H. Boyle, "Boozy Wisdom," *Commonweal* 9 July 1954, 351.

[5] Milton Rugoff, "Business as Usual, and Fun, Too, on John Steinbeck's Cannery Row," *New York Herald Tribune Books* 13 June 1954, 1; Harvey Curtis Webster, "'Cannery Row' Continued," *Saturday Review* 12 June 1953, 11; Hugh Holman, "A Narrow-guage Dickens," *New Republic* 7 June 1954, 20.

[6] Roy S. Simmonds, "Steinbeck's *Sweet Thursday*," in *A Study Guide to Steinbeck, Part II*, ed. Tetsumaro Hayashi (Metuchen, NJ: Scarecrow Press, 1979), 141. Simmond's chapter is the most complete overview of critical reactions to *Sweet Thursday*.

[7] See Charles Metzger, "Steinbeck's Version of the Pastoral," *Modern Fiction Studies* 6 (Summer, 1960): 115-24; Richard Astro, "Steinbeck's Bittersweet Thursday," *Steinbeck Quarterly* 4 (Spring, 1971): 36-47; and Howard Levant, *The Novels of John Steinbeck: A Critical Study* (Columbia: University of Missouri Press, 1974), 259-72. Metzger's and Astro's essays are reprinted in *The Short Novels of John Steinbeck*, ed. Jackson J. Benson (Durham, NC: Duke University Press, 1990), 184-95, 204-15.

[8] Warren French, *John Steinbeck* (New York: Twayne, 1961), 158; Stoddard Martin, *California Writers: Jack London, John Steinbeck, The Tough Guys* (London: Macmillan Press, 1983), 101; Louis Owens, *John Steinbeck's Re-Vision of America* (Athens: University of Georgia Press, 1985), 196; Mimi Reisel Gladstein, "Missing Women: The Inexplicable Disparity Between Women in Steinbeck's Life and Those in His Fiction," in *The Steinbeck Question: New Essays in Criticism*, ed. Donald R. Noble (Troy, NY: Whitston Publishing, 1993), 92.

[9] John H. Timmerman, *John Steinbeck's Fiction: Aesthetics of The Road Taken* (Norman: University of Oklahoma Press, 1986), 174-80; Louis Owens, "Critics and Common Denominators," in *The Short Novels of John Steinbeck*, 200; Mimi Reisel Gladstein, "Straining for Profundity: Steinbeck's *Burning Bright* and *Sweet Thursday*," in *The Short Novels of John Steinbeck*, 244, 248; Warren French, *John Steinbeck's Fiction Revisited* (New York: Twayne Publishers, 1994), 122; Jay Parini, *John Steinbeck: A Biography* (New York: Henry Holt, 1995), 377-78.

[10] Steinbeck's "Critics, Critics, Burning Bright," first published in *Saturday Review* on 11 November 1950, is reprinted in *Steinbeck and His Critics: A Record of Twenty-Five Years*, eds. E. W. Tedlock and C. V. Wicker (Albuquerque: University of New Mexico Press, 1957), 47 (hereafter cited as *SAHC*).

[11] "Mack's Contribution" appears in the original autograph manuscript, the typed manuscript, and the unrevised galley proofs of *Sweet Thursday*, housed at Harry Ransom Humanities Research Center, University of Texas, Austin. I quote from the galleys. See also Louis Owens, "Critics and Common Denominators," in *The Short Novels of John Steinbeck*, 203, who states that Steinbeck's unrevised introduction, "more directly than the published prologue . . . provides a more obvious indication of Steinbeck's attitude in writing *Sweet Thursday*. Frustrated by critics' repeated failures to penetrate the complex

layers of his previous works, and the resultant myopic dismissals by critics such as the reviewers for *Time*, Steinbeck recognized an opportunity to make his feelings known."

[12] Jay Clayton, *The Pleasures of Babel: Contemporary American Literature and Theory* (New York: Oxford University Press, 1993), 10-11. *Sweet Thursday* can profit immeasurably from the application of contemporary literary theory. Such terms as *carnivalesque* and *jouissance* that derive respectively from Mikhail Bakhtin, *Rabelais and His World*, trans. Helene Iswolsky (Cambridge: MIT Press, 1968), and Roland Barthes, *The Pleasure of the Text*, trans. Richard Miller (New York: Hill and Wang, 1975), inform my exploration of the novel later in this essay.

[13] In his red leather *Standard Diary for 1951*, an unpublished *East of Eden* ledger housed at New York's Pierpont Morgan Library, Steinbeck entered the following on 29 May 1951: "It was two years ago tonight I met Elaine. The day really changed my life. I am pretty sure I would not be alive now if I had not."

[14] Peter Lisca, *The Wide World of John Steinbeck* (New Brunswick, NJ: Rutgers University Press, 1958), 282.

[15] Two short stories from this era, "His Father" (*Reader's Digest* September 1949, 19-21), and "The Affair at 7, rue de M----" (*Harper's Bazaar*, April 1955, 112, 202, 213), are drawn directly from family life and feature the Steinbeck children as protagonists. Following his divorce from Gwyn, Steinbeck's correspondence with his sons (some of it now in private hands) reveals an abiding sense of love and concern for them that shows he worked much harder at being a responsible parent than some biographers have granted.

[16] See Hunter Cadzow, "New Historicism," in *The Johns Hopkins Guide to Literary Theory and Criticism*, eds. Michael Groden and Martin Kreiswirth (Baltimore: Johns Hopkins University Press, 1994), 534-40; and Stephen Greenblatt, "Culture," in *Critical Terms for Literary Study*, eds. Frank Lentricchia and Thomas McLaughlin, 2d ed. (Chicago: University of Chicago Press, 1995), 230-31, who states, "works of art are not neutral relay stations in the circulation of cultural materials. Something happens to objects, beliefs, and practices when they are represented, reimagined, and performed in literary texts. . . . That 'something' is the sign both of the power of art and of the embededness of culture in the contingencies of history."

[17] John Steinbeck, introduction to *The World of Li'l Abner*, by Al Capp (New York: Ballantine with Farrar, Straus and Young, 1953), ii (hereafter cited as *WLA*). For more on my advocacy of Steinbeck's fugitive pieces, see the introduction in *A New Steinbeck Bibliography: 1971-1981*, by Tetsumaro Hayashi (Metuchen, NJ: Scarecrow Press, 1983), 104; the preface to *Your Only Weapon Is Your Work: A Letter by John Steinbeck to Dennis Murphy* (San Jose, CA: Steinbeck Research Center, 1985); "The Best-Brewed Plans of Malt and Hop: Steinbeck's Minimalist Elegy for Ballantine Ale," *Steinbeck Newsletter* 3 (Winter 1990): 6-7; and "'Steinbeck on the Novel': A 1954 Interview," *Steinbeck Newsletter* 5 (Spring 1992): 6-7.

[18] Linda Hutcheon, *Narcissistic Narrative*, 24. See also Alistair Fowler, *Kinds of Literature: An Introduction to the Theory of Genres and Modes* (Cambridge: Harvard University Press, 1982), 123, who, in a comment applicable to *Sweet Thursday* (and the earlier *East of Eden* as well), notes that "in the

poioumenon or work-in-progress novel," where "at least one narrator or character is engaged in writing," there are often autobiographical materials, texts within texts, that represent "the creative process." "The inset works of art remind us that what we are reading is itself a work of fiction, and provide occasions for treating a principal theme of the genre: the relation of art to life."

[19] Quoted by Fred Allen in foreword to his *Much Ado About Me* (Boston: Little, Brown, 1956), n.p.

[20] Eighteen months earlier, around the time Benson's biography was originally set to appear, the Steinbeck sons, armed with copies of the unrevised galley sheets of Benson's book, threatened to sue Benson and Viking Press for libel. Eventually, in a process that took many months, Benson and his editor at Viking, Bill Strachan, made several changes in the allegedly offensive sections of the text and *The True Adventures of John Steinbeck* was published, much-delayed, in January 1984 to uniformly positive reviews. Benson was never sued, but the tempest kept brewing in the print media, fueled by irresponsible reporters such as Gene Detro, "Gripes of Wrath: Why the Steinbeck Inner-Circle is Trashing the New Biography," *San Francisco Sunday Examiner and Chronicle California Living Magazine* 22 January 1984, 12. When I visited Thom that day nine months later I was aware of the controversy, but, though I got an earfull on many other topics, this issue did not become part of our conversation; whether that was due to politeness, fastidiousness, common sense, or some legal caution on his part, I could not then ascertain, though the nearness of the whole affair made me wary of being drawn into a fiasco concerning various libelous claims. Benson waited four years to publish his side of the story and to reveal his sources (Steinbeck's agents and confidantes, Elizabeth Otis, Mavis McIntosh, and Shirley Fisher). That emotional scene in Otis's Manhattan apartment, Benson's angry reaction to being threatened with a libel suit, and his disatisfaction with the "boys" may be seen in Benson's autobiography, *Looking for Steinbeck's Ghost* (Norman: University of Oklahoma Press, 1988), 161-81, 199-201.

[21] The fact that John Steinbeck IV died a few years later, on 7 February 1991, following a routine back operation, only seems to highlight the folly of refracted and tenuous assessment. Ironically, he had nearly completed his confessional autobiography, *Legacy*, in which he had at last cleaned up and made peace with his own life and had reached a measured acceptance of his father's influence. See his reminiscences in Judith Moore, Abe Opincar, and Bob Shanbrom, "John Steinbeck Was My Father," *San Diego Weekly Reader* 30 March 1989, 26-29; also revealing is Judith Moore, "Destiny Manifest," *San Diego Weekly Reader* 7 March 1991, 5, 9-10.

[22] See Bill Scanlon, "Steinbeck Silver Sale Ironic," *Boulder Camera*, 22 September 1985, 1A, 12A; David McQuay, "Steinbeck Possessions Going on Sale to Public," *Denver Post*, 20 May 1988, 1F-2F; and Susan Shillinglaw, "The Denver Steinbeck Sale," *Steinbeck Newsletter* 2 (Fall 1988): 3.

[23] John Steinbeck, *Travels with Charley in Search of America* (New York: Viking Press, 1962, reprint, New York: Penguin Books, 1986), 11: "I thought I might do some writing along the way, perhaps essays, surely notes, certainly letters. I took paper, carbon, typewriter, pencils, notebooks. . . ."

PART FOUR:
A BIBLIOGRAPHY OF BOOKS BY AND ABOUT JOHN STEINBECK

". . . the bibliography is leaping. . . ."
—John Steinbeck to Chase Horton, 26 April 1957

"The catalogue is, then, both immoderate and inadequate."
—Debra A. Castillo, *The Translated World: A Postmodern Tour of Libraries in Literature* (1984)

"So much is no more than the truth: Casanova ended his life as a librarian."
—Jack Matthews, *Booking in the Heartland* (1986)

A Bibliography of Books by and about John Steinbeck

Originally, this bibliography (I use the term in its most generous sense) was a plain abbreviated list of books by and about John Steinbeck. Like the *East of Eden* bibliography in Part Two of *Steinbeck's Typewriter*, this one also began as a mimeographed handout distributed to students in my occasional Steinbeck elective at Ohio University in the late 1970s and early 1980s and in my regular Steinbeck course at San Jose State University, where I taught as a visiting professor for two years in the mid-1980s and directed its Steinbeck Research Center. The checklist also served as a modest memento to be given away to visitors and guests who found their way to the Steinbeck Center on the secluded sixth floor of San Jose State's "old" library—the partly vacated Wahlquist—and it doubled as a gift in 1984 and 1985 to participants and attendees at Steinbeck Festivals V and VI in Salinas, California, where I was an invited speaker.

In its earliest form, all entries were lumped into two main categories—primary works and secondary works—with only the broadest attempts at further differentiation by genre, contents, topic, or type. I also made a stab at a more comprehensive and abundant listing (incorporating periodicals and contributions to books), which appeared as "A Selective Bibliography" appended to *Steinbeck's Reading*. Inevitably, these lists began to grow, merge, mutate, divide, and recombine; somewhere along the line, one version introduced that most self-referring of categories, the bibliography of bibliographies. With the addition of that little hall of mirrors my classificatory endeavor took a turn toward inclusiveness, after which there seemed to be no going back. Indeed, this bibliography was updated, expanded, refined, and appended so often to keep abreast of its times that it seemed to take on a life of its own and came to be implicated in my existence, as I was implicated in its.

My initial purpose was simply to supply an accessible, conveniently grouped, and clearly organized inventory of books published in English that would provide students with a basic research tool for further study and offer visitors to "Steinbeck Country" a sense of the cumulative number of titles published by and about him. I hoped the free checklist, along with two special retail items, would stimulate increased interest in California's only Nobel Laureate in Literature and help set straight the quantitative dimensions of a career that had often been misrepresented at its most basic level or had been erroneously, even egregiously, mythologized. (Well-meaning visitors to the center sometimes wanted to see a first edition of his "dirty" novel *Tobacco Road*, and journalists, cranking out local interest stories in area papers, often mangled the details of his life and career.)

Directing the Steinbeck Center was the first and only "administrative" position I have held. Primarily a classroom teacher by temperament and by choice, I discovered my new position could be a maverick's dream, requiring the skills and energies of a teacher, as well as those of a scholar, bibliographer, resource person, literary detective, secretary, purchasing agent, archivist, tour guide, curator, fund raiser, and librarian, sometimes nearly all at once. As a result, my official "half-time" position as director quickly became, unofficially, a full-time job. If, like everyone else on San Jose's campus, I could be crushed under the weight of the bureaucratic paper avalanche or the day-to-day grindings of an especially busy urban institution (whose upper-echelon administrators seemed to pride themselves on maintaining strict accountability and a ruthless bottom line mentality), wearing several hats granted a certain freedom of movement and often delivered the days from routineness.

There were frequent queries from high school students in the San Jose community to answer concerning Steinbeck's life and work. There were undergraduates to confer with about this or that assigned project in English 167 (SJSU's Steinbeck course, which I taught three of my four semesters, never to fewer than thirty students). There were odd requests too intriguing to ignore, like the telephone call from an East San Jose Chicano, a former stoop laborer in the Salinas lettuce fields, who claimed to own Steinbeck's '48 Chevy, still in running condition. (He didn't want to sell the car, having entered a period of relative prosperity, but when I showed up at a mutually arranged rendezvous point to see it, the place was empty, and I never heard from him again.)

Acquisition (in its most benign sense) was one of the job's chief endeavors, so it was necessary to search book dealer's catalogs in order to purchase books, manuscripts, and letters to enhance the center's considerable collection. (At 128 pages in length, Robert Woodward's excellent catalog is only a *selective* description of the center's holdings.) This I did with gusto, managing to spend $85,000 in two years, aided in the center's lavish good fortune by a wholly cooperative and supportive director of libraries who shared my newly found enthusiasm for big ticket acquisitions. While some blue chip items naturally became focal points of the collection—Steinbeck's *Long Valley* notebook acquired by Martha H. Cox (the center's founding director from 1971-83), or, during my tenure, his unpublished letters to Wanda van Brunt—the real heart of the collection was always the incomparable library of primary and secondary works.

My days at the Steinbeck Center had an eminently practical cast, too, for I was in close proximity to every title ever published by or about Steinbeck. Examining firsthand each separate title listed here—from crude hand-stapled mimeographed or photocopied pamphlets to fine letter-press limited editions to signed and inscribed leather-bound volumes—transformed an otherwise mechanical task into a pleasurable experience, though even the most lovingly or obsessively compiled bibliography cannot convey what Argentine novelist Jorge Luis Borges called "the gravitation of the books," the physical palpability, the incredible variety, and the rich presence of the best of the books themselves. Not to wax too dilettantish here, there was something extremely gratifying—almost luxuriously sinful—in the sensuous glories, say, of the Pynson Printers handmade edition of *The Red Pony*.

Context certainly helped define the moment: there were rare times, working alone, when the center's monastic quiet, its bookcases—indeed, the whole room—curtained against the deleterious effects of the California sun's baking heat and ultraviolet rays, seemed an appropriate sanctuary from the ubiquitous white noise and unrelenting fractiousness of life in Silicon Valley. Occasionally I experienced connectedness too, and a sense of immediacy. For although Steinbeck, champion of the rights of the economically dispossessed, never thought of himself as a rare book collector (in the teeth of the Depression he stated he "wouldn't pay ten dollars for a Gutenberg Bible"), the fact remains that, in a life of unforeseen twists and unplotted contradictions, he eventually became an appreciator of fine press books, especially those he considered "perfectly beautiful" jobs of "book making," such as Armando Sapori's *Merchant and Companies in Ancient Florence,* a "prize" he purchased in Italy in 1957 and brought back to New York to round out his research library on the Middle Ages. I choose to regard that not merely as a welcome change on Steinbeck's part but as an auspicious sign as well.

Even a routine critical book, examined closely, holds surprises. Many only know the first full-length study of Steinbeck, Harry Thornton Moore's *The Novels of John Steinbeck,* through its 1969 Kennikat Press reissue, with its serviceable yellow cloth cover and Moore's appended contemporary epilogue (which documents his complete reversal of earlier enthusiasm —"Steinbeck does not wear well," he confesses). The original, however, published in an edition of one thousand copies by the Black Cat Press for Chicago's Normandie House in 1939, has an understated elegance and eye appeal. It also concludes with a "Bibliographical Checklist of First Editions" and "A Note Concerning the Map" (of "Steinbeck Country") which were dropped in the later version. The "Note" includes excerpts from a revealing letter by Steinbeck to Moore explaining the novelist's habit of creating composite geographical places in his fiction. The letter indicates that Steinbeck, far from deprecating all critics as "lice" or "sucker fish," was actually complicit in the early construction of his reputation. (The original letter, too, is now at the Steinbeck Center.)

But beyond the sometimes resplendent—and perhaps almost erotic—property of books and allure of manuscripts, there is the sad knowledge that print-based lists, bibliographies, and catalogs, by their very nature, are outdated—and therefore forever incomplete—as soon as they are published. With that awareness the Sisyphean absurdity surrounding the compiler's task begins to emerge. And yet despite, or perhaps because of, that frustrating absurdity (compounded by the bibliographer's twin seductions—the illusion of authority and the chimera of completeness), the urge to catalog persists, speaks to something disarmingly compulsive, if not neat, in the psyche. This too has compensations, however, for viewed from another angle, a bibliography, which as a form lends itself to endless tinkering and intercession, also can be considered a paradigm of interrelatedness, a web of interlacings; it is as much a whole structure of inviting beginnings and potential linkages as it is a system of accomplishments.

If processing a proliferating series of titles is, at least partly, its own perverse reward, a kind of testing of limits and patience one gets bellying up to an immoderate task—shoveling sand against the tide, let's say, or casting an inadequately weighted fly rod into a ferocious wind—then the other part, the larger part, I imagine—like Nick Carraway's list of Gatsby's party guests—is furnished by an evocative sense of the potential poetry of names, titles, relations, distinguishing signs and linguistic markers, all of them casting shadows on the mind's landscape or creating resonances on its inner ear. "Each item of a list," Robert Harbison claims in his marvelous book *Eccentric Spaces* (1977) "is repetition and novelty at once, conflates the past and the future, makes things co-present." Perhaps a bibliography, then, can itself be considered an apt text for our postmodern age: always on the verge of deconstructing itself, collapsing inward, it invites intervention by requiring constant updating; entereable at any point, it can be scanned forward or backward, up or down, without regard to traditional narrative necessities, such as the unity of plot. In this way, paradoxically, as with so many other things in life, a bibliographical catalog becomes a site of despair and promise, ignorance and knowledge, a system of containment and liberation, a dialogic of product and process. Amid such maddening but negotiable contradictions, it seems to say, we exist. Not for nothing, Melville laments in *Moby-Dick*, even the best intentioned "systems" remain unfinished, so that all our efforts are but "the draught of a draught."

In the decade since this checklist appeared in its second major embodiment as a limited edition chapbook printed handsomely by Robert Hanson's Opuscula Press (1987), the number of relevant Steinbeck titles has increased enormously. My 1987 checklist contained 169 titles, while this one has 230 items—a 36 percent leap in entries. Some of this increase is accounted for by recently published primary Steinbeck titles (*Working Days, Zapata*) or by reprints (*The Harvest Gypsies, Conversations with John Steinbeck*) and by the newly launched Library of America series. The increase in this version of the checklist also is influenced by my decision, prompted by Preston Beyer, Robert Harmon, and James Dourgarian, to considerably expand the Fine

Press and Limited Edition section. But without question the largest boost stems from the addition of new secondary titles in criticism, biography, bibliography, and reference.

As the centenary of Steinbeck's birth approaches in 2002, it seems that the man and his writing are being accorded the sustained, informed, and more or less even-handed treatment he always hoped for but never quite received. Never received, that is, except by a relative handful of committed specialists and enthusiasts who believe that Steinbeck is a more complex and deserving writer than he has ever given credit for being. If the books published by Hadella, Parini, Railsback, Simmonds, and jointly by McElrath, Crissler, and Shillinglaw—just to mention some of 1995's and 1996's output—are any gauge, perhaps the desire to see Steinbeck be given nothing more or less than a fair critical shake is what stands behind the work of many of the other following scholars too. Many of those writers' names appear here over and over—their titles provide the basis for continuing critical conversation and a reminder that, far from being the product of blind zealotry, a bibliography is a record of sustained advocacy and enduring attentiveness.

Combinatory fantasy or not, then, this bibliography, carried on for the most part in the plain style and unadorned by interpretative annotation (some primary items include descriptive comments), is both a tangible index of that attentive dialogue, as well as an instigation to further development in Steinbeck studies. For the reader, student, teacher, scholar, collector, librarian, or archivist of John Steinbeck's books, the following entries should provide a working introduction to a subject not only already far larger than many realize, but one which—happily, I should add—in these times of polarized aesthetic sensibilities, warring critical theories, and complicated issues of canon formation, shows few signs of diminishing. As a case in point, during the fall of 1996 a second volume of Steinbeck's work is scheduled to appear in the Library of America project. It will include *The Long Valley* and the narrative portion of *Sea of Cortez* (an appendix will carry "The Harvest Gypsies") and will feature as its centerpiece Gila Bercovitch's newly edited, corrected text of *The Grapes of Wrath*, which collates all known stages of the book—manuscript, typescript, galleys, and page proofs—to resurrect for the first time in over fifty years Steinbeck's original novel as closely as possible and to restore its censored language, skipped sentences, and hard edges.

Finally, though he would not have considered himself a traditional scholar, Steinbeck understood the necessity to map his fields of interest, and he remained fascinated by works of information, reference, and general knowledge, including all kinds of catalogs, dictionaries, lexicons, and encyclopedias. In fact he became an amateur bibliographer at least twice in his life: first, when he participated with Ed Ricketts in compiling and annotating the general reference books for their collaborative *Sea of Cortez;* and then when, with Chase Horton, he constructed a scrupulous bibliography of works by and about Sir Thomas Malory and his times in preparation for writing *Acts of King Arthur.* Moreover, Steinbeck's willingness to be bibliographed—"very flattering" he said of Lawrence Clark Powell's pioneering effort in *The Colophon* in 1938—adds a further delicious note of historical and catalogical precedence to this final chapter of *Steinbeck's Typewriter.*

1. PRIMARY WORKS

Note: Steinbeck's books, with the exception of *The Forgotten Village, Bombs Away, A Russian Journal, America and Americans*, and the posthumous *The Acts of King Arthur* (published in paper by Noonday), are available as trade paperbacks in Great Britain from Mandarin (M) and in the United States from Penguin Books (P). Since 1992 selected Steinbeck titles, some with original introductions by various scholars and writers, have been appearing in Penguin's uniform Twentieth-Century Classics format (PTC). Acting editions of Steinbeck's plays are available from Dramatists Play Service (DPS). Byron Press Multimedia, in conjunction with Penguin's electronic publishing division, has launched a John Steinbeck CD-ROM Library to provide self-contained multimedia experiences of major works (BPM).

A. FICTION

Cup of Gold. New York: Robert McBride, 1929. (P.)

The Pastures of Heaven. New York: Brewer, Warren & Putnam, 1932. (PTC, introduction by James Nagel.)

To a God Unknown. New York: Robert O. Ballou, 1933. (M; PTC, introduction by Robert DeMott.)

Tortilla Flat. New York: Covici-Friede, 1935. (M; P.)

In Dubious Battle. New York: Covici-Friede, 1936. (M; PTC, introduction by Warren French.)
Of Mice and Men. New York: Covici-Friede, 1937. (M; BPM; PTC, introduction by Susan Shillinglaw.)
The Long Valley. New York: Viking Press, 1938. (M; PTC, introduction by John H. Timmerman.)
The Grapes of Wrath. New York: Viking Press, 1939. (M; PTC, introduction by Robert DeMott; also available in revised Penguin Critical Library edition [1996], with text and criticism, eds. Peter Lisca and Kevin Hearle.)
The Moon is Down. New York: Viking Press, 1942. (M; PTC, introduction by Donald V. Coers.)
The Red Pony. Illustrations by Wesley Dennis. New York: Viking Press, 1945. (M; PTC, introduction by John Seelye.)
Cannery Row. New York: Viking Press, 1945. (M, introduction by Elaine Steinbeck; PTC, introduction by Susan Shillinglaw.)
The Wayward Bus. New York: Viking Press, 1947. (P.)
The Pearl. Drawings by Jose Clemente Orozco. New York: Viking Press, 1947. (PTC, introduction by Linda Wagner-Martin.)
Burning Bright: A Play in Story Form. New York: Viking Press, 1950. (P.)
East of Eden. New York: Viking Press, 1952. (M; PTC, introduction by David Wyatt.)
Sweet Thursday. New York: Viking Press, 1954. (M; P.)
The Short Reign of Pippin IV: A Fabrication. New York: Viking Press, 1957. (M; P.)
The Winter of Our Discontent. New York: Viking Press, 1961. (M; P.)
The Acts of King Arthur and His Noble Knights. Ed. Chase Horton. New York: Farrar, Straus & Giroux, 1976. (Includes introduction by Steinbeck, and appendix of 72 letters, written 1956-65, many in excised form, to Horton and Elizabeth Otis, selected from the 108 letters, cards, and notes housed at Ball State University's Bracken Library.)
Uncollected Stories of John Steinbeck. Ed. Kiyoshi Nakayama. Tokyo: Nan' un-do Company, 1986. (Includes "His Father," "The Summer Before," "How Edith McGillcuddy Met R. L. Stevenson," "Reunion at the Quiet Hotel," "The Miracle of Tepayac," "The Time Wolves Ate the Vice-Principal.")

B. DRAMA

Of Mice and Men: Play in Three Acts. New York: Covici-Friede, 1937. (DPS.)

The Moon is Down: Play in Two Parts. New York: Viking Press, 1942. (DPS.)

Burning Bright: Play in Three Acts. New York: Dramatists Play Service, 1951.

C. FILMSCRIPTS

The Forgotten Village. New York: Viking Press, 1941.

Viva Zapata! Ed. Robert E. Morsberger. New York: Viking Press, 1975.

Zapata. Ed. Robert E. Morsberger. New York: Penguin Books, 1993. (Extended preparatory narrative treatment "in dramatic form of the life of Emiliano Zapata," together with filmscript *Viva Zapata!*) (P.)

D. NONFICTION

Their Blood Is Strong. San Francisco: Simon J. Lubin Society, 1938. (Articles first published as "The Harvest Gypsies" in San Francisco *News*, 5-12 October 1936, with new epilogue.)

Sea of Cortez: A Leisurely Journal of Travel and Research. New York: Viking Press, 1941. (Written with Edward F. Ricketts.)

Bombs Away: The Story of a Bomber Team. New York: Viking Press, 1942. (With 60 photographs by John Swope.)

A Russian Journal. New York: Viking Press, 1948. (With photographs and single chapter by Robert Capa.)

The Log from the "Sea of Cortez." New York: Viking Press, 1951. (Contains introduction and narrative section from 1941 *Sea of Cortez* and memorial profile, "About Ed Ricketts.") (M; PTC, introduction by Richard Astro.)

Once There Was a War. New York: Viking Press, 1958. (Collection of World War II dispatches written in 1943 to New York *Herald-Tribune*, plus new introduction.) (M; P.)

Un Américain à New-York et à Paris. French translation by Jean-Francois Rozan. Paris: Rene Juillard, 1956. (Contains 17 essays and 1 story from French, British, and American periodicals, 1954-56.)

Travels with Charley in Search of America. New York: Viking Press, 1962. (M; P.)

Speech Accepting the Nobel Prize for Literature. New York: Viking Press, 1962. (Pamphlet; 3,200 copies.)

America and Americans. New York: Viking Press, 1966. (With photographs.)

Selected Essays of John Steinbeck. Eds. Hidekazu Hirose and Kiyoshi Nakayama. Tokyo: Shinozaki Shorin Press, 1983. (Includes "Autobiography: Making of a New Yorker," "A Primer on the 30s," "Jalopies I Cursed and Loved," "How to Tell Good Guys from Bad Guys," "My War with the Ospreys," "Conversation at Sag Harbor," "I Go Back to Ireland.")

The Harvest Gypsies: On the Road to "The Grapes of Wrath." Introduction by Charles Wollenberg. Berkeley, CA: Heyday Books, 1988.

E. CORRESPONDENCE, JOURNALS, INTERVIEWS

Journal of a Novel: The "East of Eden" Letters. New York: Viking Press, 1969. (Steinbeck's daily journal—covering 29 January to 1 November 1951—addressed to his editor, Pascal Covici.) (M; P.)

Steinbeck: A Life in Letters. Eds. Elaine Steinbeck and Robert Wallsten. New York: Viking Press, 1975. (P.)

Letters to Elizabeth: A Selection of Letters from John Steinbeck to Elizabeth Otis. Eds. Florian J. Shasky and Susan F. Riggs. Foreword by Carlton Sheffield. San Francisco: Book Club of California, 1978. (Publishes 44 letters, written between 1938-65, from the approximately 600 by Steinbeck to Otis at Stanford University; limited edition of 500 copies.)

Fensch, Thomas. *Steinbeck and Covici: The Story of a Friendship.* Middlebury, VT: Paul S. Eriksson, 1979. (Text includes generous selection of Steinbeck's 350 letters and cards to Pascal Covici, written 1937-63, at the University of Texas' Harry Ransom Humanities Research Center.)

Conversations with John Steinbeck. Ed. Thomas Fensch. Literary Conversations Series. Jackson: University Press of Mississippi, 1988. (Reprints 25 interviews published between 1935-72.)

Working Days: The Journal of "The Grapes of Wrath," 1938-1941. Ed. Robert DeMott. New York: Viking Press, 1989. (Provides 123 entries from February 1938 through January 1941, chronicling Steinbeck's composition of *The Grapes of Wrath* and its aftermath.) (P.)

F. COLLECTIONS AND ANTHOLOGIES

The Viking Portable Library Steinbeck. Ed. Pascal Covici. New York: Viking Press, 1943. (Includes selections from *The Long Valley, The Pastures of Heaven, Tortilla Flat, In Dubious Battle, Of Mice and Men, The Red Pony, The Grapes of Wrath, Sea of Cortez, The Moon is Down, Bombs Away.*)

The Steinbeck Pocket Book. Philadelphia: Blakiston, 1943; distributed by Pocket Books. (Briefer version of above.)

The Portable Steinbeck. Selected by Pascal Covici. Introduction by Lewis Gannett. New York: Viking Press, 1946. (Enlarged edition includes new additions from *Herald-Tribune* war dispatches, *Cannery Row,* and *How Edith McGillcuddy Met R. L. S.;* English version published as *The Steinbeck Omnibus* [1950].)

The Short Novels of John Steinbeck. Introduction by Joseph Henry Jackson. New York: Viking Press, 1953. (Includes *Tortilla Flat, The Red Pony, Of Mice and Men, The Moon is Down, Cannery Row, The Pearl.*)

The Portable Steinbeck. Ed. Pascal Covici, Jr. New York: Viking Press, 1971. (Revised, updated edition includes selections from *The Long Valley, The Pastures of Heaven, Tortilla Flat, In Dubious Battle, The Grapes of Wrath, Sea of Cortez,* "About Ed Ricketts," *East of Eden, Travels with Charley,* and complete "The Affair at 7, rue de M—," "How Mr. Hogan Robbed a Bank," *Of Mice and Men, The Red Pony,* Nobel Prize acceptance speech.) (P.)

The Complete Works of John Steinbeck. Ed. Yasuo Hashiguchi. 20 vols. Kyoto, Japan: Rinsen, 1985.

The John Steinbeck Collection. New York: Mallard Press, 1989. (Reprint of collection first published by Steinbeck's British publisher, Heinemann; includes *Of Mice and Men, The Grapes of Wrath, The Moon is Down, Cannery Row, East of Eden.*)

The Essential Steinbeck. New York: Seafarer Books, 1994. (Includes *Tortilla Flat, Of Mice and Men, The Grapes of Wrath,* and *Cannery Row.*)

John Steinbeck: Novels and Stories 1932-1937. Ed. Robert DeMott and Elaine Steinbeck. New York: Library of America, 1994. (Inaugural volume of multivolume uniform edition of Steinbeck's selected works; includes *The Pastures of Heaven, To a God Unknown, Tortilla Flat,*

In Dubious Battle, Of Mice and Men.)

John Steinbeck: "The Grapes of Wrath" and Other Writings 1936-1941. Ed. Robert DeMott and Elaine Steinbeck. New York: Library of America, 1996. (Includes "The Harvest Gypsies," *The Long Valley, The Grapes of Wrath, Sea of Cortez.*)

G. FINE PRESS, LIMITED EDITION, SPECIAL REPRINT PUBLICATIONS

In Dubious Battle. New York: Covici-Friede, 1936. (Edition of 99 numbered and signed copies.)

Saint Katy the Virgin. New York: Covici-Friede, 1936. (Edition of 199 copies printed by Golden Eagle Press.)

Nothing So Monstrous. New York: Pynson Printers, 1936. (Edition of 370 copies for Elmer Adler and others.)

The Red Pony. New York: Covici-Friede, 1937. (Edition of 699 numbered and 26[?] lettered copies; includes "The Gift," "The Great Mountains," "The Promise.")

The Grapes of Wrath. Illustrated by Thomas Hart Benton. 2 vols. New York: Limited Editions Club, 1940.

John Steinbeck Replies. New York: L. M. Birkhead, 1940. (Mimeographed leaflet; one folded sheet.)

A Letter Written in Reply to a Request for a Statement about His Ancestry. Together with the Letter Originally Submitted by the Friends of Democracy. Stamford, CT: Overbrook Press, 1940. (Same as above, but 350 copies in brown paper boards.)

How Edith McGillcuddy Met R. L. S. Cleveland, OH: The Rowfant Club, 1943. (Edition of 152 copies printed by Grabhorn Press.)

The First Watch. Los Angeles: Ward Ritchie Press, 1947. (Edition of 60 numbered copies, initiated by Marguerite and Louis Henry Cohn.)

Vanderbilt Clinic. Photographs by Victor Keppler. New York: Presbyterian Hospital, 1947.

Foreword to "Between Pacific Tides." Stanford, CA: Printed by Stanford University Press for Nathan Van Patten, 1948. (Printing of 10[?] copies of Steinbeck's foreword to revised edition of book by Ed Rickets and Jack Calvin published by Stanford.)

East of Eden. New York: Viking Press, 1952. (Edition of 1,500 signed copies, in slipcase.)

Positano. Salerno, Italy: Ente Provinciale Per Il Turismo, [1954]. (Pamphlet; reprint of essay from *Harper's Bazaar* [May 1953]; Italian and French versions, 1955.)

The Winter of Our Discontent. New York: Viking Press, 1961. (Edition of 500 copies "specially printed and bound for friends of the author and the publishers.")

A Letter from John Steinbeck Explaining Why He Could Not Write an Introduction for this Book. New York: Random House, 1964. (Pamphlet; separate publication of introduction to Ted Patrick's *The Thinking Dog's Man*.)

A Letter from John Steinbeck. San Francisco and Los Angeles: Roxburghe and Zamorano Clubs, 1964. (Edition of 150 copies printed by Grace Hoper Press.)

John Steinbeck His Language. Introduction by James B. Hart. Aptos, CA: Grace Hoper Press, 1970. (Edition of 150 copies printed for Roxburghe and Zamorano Clubs.)

Of Mice and Men. Illustrated by Fletcher Martin. Introduction by John T. Winterich. New York: Limited Editions Club, 1970.

Journal of a Novel: The "East of Eden" Letters. New York: Viking Press, 1969. (Edition of 600 copies in slipcase, specially printed and bound, with 8 fascimile pages of the manuscript.)

Cannery Row by John Steinbeck. Stanford, CA: Stanford University Libraries, 1975. (Chapbook commemorating acquisition of *The Complete Archive of Cannery Row*.)

Flight a Story by John Steinbeck. Illustrations by Karin Wickstrom. Afterword by Wallace Stegner. Covelo, CA: Yolla Bolly Press, 1984. (Edition of 260 copies of story reproduced from *The Long Valley* [1938].)

Your Only Weapon Is Your Work: A Letter by John Steinbeck to Dennis Murphy. Introduction by Robert DeMott. San Jose, CA: Steinbeck Research Center, 1985. (Chapbook of 500 copies of unpublished letter to young novelist and family friend.)

Always Something to Do in Salinas. Bradenton, FL: Opuscula Press, 1986. (Edition of 300 copies; essay reprinted from *Holiday* magazine [June 1955].)

Breakfast: A Short Story. Wood engravings and afterword by Colleen Dwire Weaver. Petaluma, CA: Anchor Acorn Press, 1990. (Edition of 100 copies of story reproduced from *The Long Valley* [1938].)

Zapata. 18 woodcuts by Karin Wickstrom. Covello, CA: Yolla Bolly Press, 1991. (First publication of Steinbeck's 1949 narrative on Zapata; limited edition of 40 copies [portfolio version] and 130 copies [slipcased version].)

H. ADAPTATIONS

Pipe Dreams. Music by Richard Rodgers; book and lyrics by Oscar Hammerstein II. New York: Viking Press, 1956. (Musical adaptation of *Sweet Thursday*.)

Of Mice and Men: A Musical Drama in Three Acts. By Carlisle Floyd. New York: Belwin-Mills, 1971.

John Steinbeck's The Grapes of Wrath. By Frank Galati. New York: Penguin Books, 1991. (DPS.)

2. SECONDARY WORKS

A. BIBLIOGRAPHIES

Note: In addition to the books listed in the first three sections below, consult the bio-bibliographical entries in the annual *American Literary Scholarship; Dictionary of Literary Biography:* Volume 7, *Twentieth Century American Dramatists;* and Volume 9, *American Novelists*, 1910-1945; *Dictionary of Literary Biography, Documentary Series*, Volume 2; *Fifty Western Writers*; Warren French's chapters in Jackson Bryer, ed., *Sixteen Modern American Authors*, Volumes I (1973) and II (1989) and his annotated "Selected Bibliography" in *John Steinbeck's Fiction Revisited* (1994); and the "Comprehensive Checklist of Criticism" in Jackson Benson, ed., *The Short Novels of John Steinbeck* (1990). Also, a comprehensive research guide, *The John Steinbeck Encyclopedia*, ed. Brian Railsback, is forthcoming from Greenwood Press.

DeMott, Robert. *John Steinbeck: A Checklist of Books By and About*. Bradenton, FL: Opuscula Press, 1987.

Goldstone, Adrian, and John R. Payne. *John Steinbeck: A Bibliographical Catalogue of the Adrian H. Goldstone Collection*. Austin, TX: Humanities Research Center, 1974.

Harmon, Robert B. *Steinbeck Bibliographies: An Annotated Guide*. Metuchen, NJ: Scarecrow Press, 1987.

—. *"The Grapes of Wrath": A Fifty Year Bibliographical Survey.* With John F. Early. Introduction by Susan Shillinglaw. San Jose, CA: Steinbeck Research Center, 1990.

—. *"Cannery Row": A Selected Fifty Year Bibliographic Survey,* San Jose, CA: Dibco Press, 1995.

—. *John Steinbeck: Annotated Guide to Biographical Sources.* Lanham, MD: Scarecrow Press, 1996.

Hayashi, Tetsumaro. *John Steinbeck: A Concise Bibliography (1930-1963).* Metuchen, NJ: Scarecrow Press, 1967.

—. *A New Steinbeck Bibliography, 1927-1971.* Metuchen, NJ: Scarecrow Press, 1973.

—. *A New Steinbeck Bibliography. Supplement I: 1971-1981.* Introduction by Robert DeMott. Metuchen, NJ: Scarecrow Press, 1983.

B. RESEARCH AND ARCHIVE GUIDES

Gross, John, and Lee Richard Hayman. *John Steinbeck: A Guide to the Collection of the Salinas Public Library.* Salinas, CA: Salinas Public Library, 1979.

Hashiguchi, Yasuo, and Koichi Kaida, comps. *A Catalogue of the Maurice Dunbar John Steinbeck Collection at Fukuoka University.* Okayama, Japan: Mikado Printing Office, 1992.

Hayashi, Tetsumaro, ed. *John Steinbeck: A Guide to the Doctoral Dissertations.* Steinbeck Monograph Series, no. 1. Muncie, IN: John Steinbeck Society of America/Ball State University, 1971.

—, and Donald Seifker, comps. *The Special Steinbeck Collection of the Ball State University Library: A Bibliographical Handbook.* Muncie, IN: John Steinbeck Society of America/Ball State University, 1972.

—, ed. *Steinbeck Criticism: A Review of Book-Length Studies (1939-1973).* Steinbeck Monograph Series, no. 4. Muncie, IN: John Steinbeck Society of America/Ball State University, 1974.

—, ed. *Steinbeck and Hemingway: Dissertation Abstracts and Research Opportunities.* Introduction by Warren French. Metuchen, NJ: Scarecrow Press, 1980.

—. *A Student's Guide to Steinbeck's Literature: Primary and Secondary Sources.* Steinbeck Bibliography Series, no. 1. Muncie, IN: Steinbeck Research Institute/Ball State University, 1986.

—, and Beverly K. Simpson, comps. *John Steinbeck: Dissertation Abstracts and Research Opportunities.* Introduction by John H. Timmerman. Metuchen, NJ: Scarecrow Press, 1994.

Hieb, Louis. *John Steinbeck.* Tucson: University of Arizona Library, 1987.

Riggs, Susan F. *A Catalogue of the John Steinbeck Collection at Stanford University.* Introduction by Jackson J. Benson. Stanford, CA: Stanford University Libraries, 1980.

Seifker, Donald L., Tetsumaro Hayashi, and Thomas J. Moore, eds. *The Steinbeck Quarterly: A Cumulative Index of Volumes XI-XX (1978-1987).* Introduction by Robert DeMott. Steinbeck Bibliography Series, no. 2. Muncie, IN: Steinbeck Research Institute/Ball State University, 1989.

Todd, William B. *John Steinbeck: An Exhibition of American and Foreign Editions.* Austin, TX: Humanities Research Center, 1963.

Woodward, Robert H. *The Steinbeck Research Center at San Jose State University: A Descriptive Catalogue.* Foreword by Robert DeMott. San Jose, CA: San Jose State University. (Also *San Jose Studies* 11 [Winter 1985].)

C. REFERENCE WORKS

Hayashi, Tetsumaro, ed. *John Steinbeck: A Dictionary of His Fictional Characters.* Metuchen, NJ: Scarecrow Press, 1976.

—, ed. *John Steinbeck on Writing.* Introduction by Reloy Garcia. Steinbeck Essay Series, no. 2. Muncie, IN: Steinbeck Research Institute/Ball State University, 1988.

McElrath, Joseph, Jessie Crissler, and Susan Shillinglaw, eds. *John Steinbeck: The Contemporary Reviews.* Contemporary Reviews Series. New York: Cambridge University Press, 1996.

D. GUIDES TO COLLECTING AND ACQUISTION CATALOGS

Barker, David. *John Steinbeck: A Checklist.* Salem, OR: David and Judy Barker, Booksellers, 1984.

Beyer, Preston, comp. *Essays on Collecting John Steinbeck Books.* Bradenton, FL: Opuscula Press, 1989.

Dunbar, Maurice. *Collecting Steinbeck.* Venice, FL: Opuscula Press, 1983.

Harmon, Robert B. *The First Editions of John Steinbeck.* Los Altos, CA: Hermes Publications, 1978.

—. *A Collector's Guide to the First Editions of John Steinbeck.* Bradenton, FL: Opuscula Press, 1985.

—. *The Collectible John Steinbeck: A Practical Guide.* Jefferson, NC: McFarland, 1986.

—. *Steinbeck Editions: A Bibliographic Checklist.* San Jose, CA: Bibliographic Research Services, 1992.

Hayashi, Tetsumaro, ed. *A Handbook for Steinbeck Collectors, Librarians, and Scholars.* Steinbeck Monograph Series, no. 11. Muncie, IN: John Steinbeck Society of America/Ball State University, 1981.

Mitchell, John. *John Steinbeck.* Pasadena, CA: Mitchell Books, 1982. (Mitchell Books Catalog 6.)

Morrow, Bradford. *John Steinbeck: A Collection of Books and Manuscripts Formed by Harry Valentine of Pacific Grove, California.* Foreword by John R. Payne. Santa Barbara, CA: Bradford Morrow, Bookseller, 1980. (Bradford Morrow Catalog 8.)

Peterson, Diane. *John Steinbeck: The Alexander Summers Collection with Additions.* Foreword by Alexander Summers. Atherton, CA: Diane Peterson, 1991. (Diane Peterson Book Lady Catalog 11.)

E. CRITICAL STUDIES: BOOKS, MONOGRAPHS, AND PAMPHLETS

Benson, Jackson J. *Steinbeck's "Cannery Row": A Reconsideration.* Steinbeck Essay Series, no. 4. Muncie, IN: Steinbeck Research Institute/Ball State University, 1991.

Burrows, Michael. *John Steinbeck and His Films.* St. Austell, Cornwall, England: Primestyle, 1970.

Chada, Rajni. *Social Realism in the Novels of John Steinbeck.* New Delhi, India: Harman Publishing House, 1990.

Coers, Donald V. *John Steinbeck as Propagandist: "The Moon is Down" Goes to War.* Tuscaloosa: University of Alabama Press, 1991.

Ditsky, John. *Essays on "East of Eden."* Steinbeck Monograph Series, no. 7. Muncie, IN: John Steinbeck Society of America/Ball State University, 1977.

—. *John Steinbeck: Life, Work, and Criticism.* Fredericton, New Brunswick: York Press, 1985.

Fontenrose, Joseph. *John Steinbeck: An Introduction and Interpretation.* American Authors and Critics Series. New York: Barnes and Noble, 1963.

—. *Steinbeck's Unhappy Valley: A Study of "The Pastures of Heaven."* Berkeley, CA: Privately printed, 1981.

French, Warren. *Film Guide to "The Grapes of Wrath."* Indiana University Press Filmguide Series. Bloomington: University of Indiana Press, 1973.

—. *John Steinbeck.* Twayne's United States Authors Series, no. 2. New York: Twayne Publishers, 1961.

—. *John Steinbeck.* Twayne's United States Authors Series, no. 2. Rev. ed. Boston: G. K. Hall, 1975.

—. *John Steinbeck's Fiction Revisited.* Twayne's United States Author Series, no. 638. New York: Twayne Publishers, 1994.

Garcia, Reloy. *Steinbeck and D. H. Lawrence: Fictive Voices and the Ethical Imperative.* Steinbeck Monograph Series, no. 2. Muncie, IN: John Steinbeck Society of America/Ball State University, 1972.

Gladstein, Mimi Reisel. *The Indestructable Woman in the Works of Faulkner, Hemingway, and Steinbeck.* Studies in Modern Literature, no. 45. Ann Arbor, MI: UMI Research Press, 1986.

Gray, James. *John Steinbeck.* Minnesota Pamphlets on American Writers. Minneapolis: University of Minnesota Press, 1971.

Hadella, Charlotte Cook. *"Of Mice and Men": A Kinship of Powerlessness.* Twayne's Masterwork Studies, no. 147. New York: Twayne Publishers, 1995.

Hayashi, Tetsumaro. *John Steinbeck and the Vietnam War (Part I).* Introduction by Reloy Garcia. Steinbeck Monograph Series, no. 12. Muncie, IN: John Steinbeck Society of America/Ball State University, 1986.

—. *Steinbeck's World War II Fiction, "The Moon is Down": Three Explications.* Introduction by Reloy Garcia. Steinbeck Essay Series no. 1. Muncie, IN: Steinbeck Research Institute/Ball State University, 1986.

Hughes, R. S. *Beyond "The Red Pony": A Reader's Companion to Steinbeck's Complete Short Stories.* Metuchen, NJ: Scarecrow Press, 1987.

—. *John Steinbeck: A Study of the Short Fiction.* Twayne's Studies in Short Fiction Series, no. 5. Boston: Twayne Publishers, 1989.

Jain, Sunita. *Steinbeck's Concept of Man: A Critical Study of His Novels*. New Delhi, India: New Statesman Publishing, 1979.

Jones, Lawrence William. *John Steinbeck as Fabulist*. Ed. Marston LaFrance. Steinbeck Monograph Series, no. 3. Muncie, IN: John Steinbeck Society of America/Ball State University, 1973.

Levant, Howard. *The Novels of John Steinbeck: A Critical Study*. Introduction by Warren French. Columbia: University of Missouri Press, 1974.

Lisca, Peter. *The Wide World of John Steinbeck*. New Brunswick, NJ: Rutgers University Press, 1958; reprint, with new afterword, New York: Gordian Press, 1981.

—. *John Steinbeck: Nature and Myth*. New York: Thomas Y. Crowell, 1978.

Marks, Lester. *Thematic Design in the Novels of John Steinbeck*. Studies in American Literature, vol. 11. The Hague: Mouton, 1969.

Martin, Stoddard. *California Writers: Jack London, John Steinbeck, the Tough Guys*. London: Macmillan, 1983.

McCarthy, Paul. *John Steinbeck*. Modern Literature Monographs Series. New York: Frederick Ungar, 1979.

Millichap, Joseph. *Steinbeck and Film*. New York: Frederick Ungar, 1983.

Moore, Harry Thornton. *The Novels of John Steinbeck: A First Critical Study*. Chicago: Normandie House, 1939; reprint, with contemporary epilogue, Port Washington, NY: Kennikat Press, 1969.

Owens, Louis. *John Steinbeck's Re-Vision of America*. Athens: University of Georgia Press, 1985.

—. *"The Grapes of Wrath": Trouble in the Promised Land*. Twayne's Masterwork Studies, no. 27. Boston: Twayne Publishers, 1989.

Prabhakar, S. S. *John Steinbeck: A Study*. Hyderabad, India: Academic Publishers, 1976.

Pratt, John Clark. *John Steinbeck: A Critical Essay*. Contemporary Writers in Christian Perspective Series. Grand Rapids, MI: William B. Eerdmans, 1970.

Satyanarayana, M. R. *John Steinbeck: A Study in the Theme of Compassion*. Hyderabad, India: Osmania University Press, 1977.

Shimomura, Noboru. *A Study of John Steinbeck: Mysticism in His Novels*. Tokyo: Hokuseido Press, 1982.

Simmonds, Roy S. *Steinbeck's Literary Achievement*. Steinbeck Monograph Series, no. 6. Muncie, IN: John Steinbeck Society of America/Ball State University, 1976.

—. *John Steinbeck: The War Years, 1939-1945*. Lewisburg, PA: Bucknell University Press, 1996.

Sreenivasan, K. *John Steinbeck: A Study of His Novels*. Trivandrum, India: College Book House, 1980.

Timmerman, John H. *John Steinbeck's Fiction: The Aesthetics of the Road Taken*. Norman: University of Oklahoma Press, 1986.

—. *The Dramatic Landscape of Steinbeck's Short Stories*. Norman: University of Oklahoma Press, 1990.

Watt, F. W. *Steinbeck*. Writers and Critics Series. Edinburgh: Oliver and Boyd, 1962; New York: Grove Press, 1963.

Williams, A. Susan. *John Steinbeck*. East Sussex, England: Wayland Ltd., 1990.

Yano, Shigeharu. *The Current of Steinbeck's World. Volumes I-IV*. Tokyo: Seibido Press, 1978-82.

F. COLLECTIONS OF SCHOLARLY ESSAYS

Astro, Richard, and Tetsumaro Hayashi, eds. *Steinbeck: The Man and His Work*. Corvallis: Oregon State University Press, 1971.

Benson, Jackson J., ed. *The Short Novels of John Steinbeck: Critical Essays with a Checklist to Steinbeck Criticism*. Durham, NC: Duke University Press, 1990.

Bloom, Harold, ed. *John Steinbeck*. Modern Critical Views Series. New York: Chelsea House Publishers, 1987.

—, ed. *John Steinbeck's "The Grapes of Wrath."* Modern Critical Interpretations Series. New York: Chelsea House Publishers, 1988.

Coers, Donald V., Paul C. Ruffin, and Robert J. DeMott, eds. *After "The Grapes of Wrath": Essays on John Steinbeck in Honor of Tetsumaro Hayashi*. Introduction by Warren G. French. Athens: Ohio University Press, 1995.

Davis, Robert Con, ed. *Twentieth Century Interpretations of "The Grapes of Wrath."* Englewood Cliffs, NJ: Prentice Hall, 1982.

Davis, Robert Murray, ed. *Steinbeck: A Collection of Critical Essays*. Twentieth Century Views Series. Englewood Cliffs, NJ: Prentice Hall, 1972.

Ditsky, John ed. *Critical Essays on "The Grapes of Wrath."* Critical Essays on Modern Literature Series. Boston: G. K. Hall, 1989.

Donohue, Agnes McNeill, ed. *A Casebook on "The Grapes of Wrath."* New York: Thomas Y. Crowell, 1968.

French, Warren, ed. *A Companion to "The Grapes of Wrath."* New York: Viking Press, 1963; reprint, Clifton, NJ: Augustus Kelley, 1972. (Includes Steinbeck's *Their Blood is Strong.*)

Hayashi, Tetsumaro, ed. *Steinbeck's Literary Dimension: A Guide to Comparative Studies.* Metuchen, NJ: Scarecrow Press, 1973.

—, ed. *A Study Guide to Steinbeck: A Handbook to His Major Works.* Metuchen, NJ: Scarecrow Press, 1974.

—, ed. *Steinbeck and the Arthurian Theme.* Steinbeck Monograph Series, no. 5. Muncie, IN: John Steinbeck Society of America/Ball State University, 1975.

—, ed. *A Study Guide to "The Long Valley."* Introduction by Reloy Garcia. Ann Arbor, MI: Pierian Press, 1976.

—, and Kenneth D. Swan, eds. *Steinbeck's Prophetic Vision of America.* Proceedings of the Bicentennial Steinbeck Seminar. Upland, IN: Taylor University for the John Steinbeck Society of America, 1976.

—, Yasuo Hashiguchi, and Richard F. Peterson, eds. *John Steinbeck: East and West.* Proceedings of the First International Steinbeck Congress, Kyushu University, Japan, August 1976. Steinbeck Monograph Series, no. 8. Muncie, IN: John Steinbeck Society of America/Ball State University, 1978.

—, ed. *Steinbeck's Women: Essays in Criticism.* Steinbeck Monograph Series, no. 9. Muncie, IN: John Steinbeck Society of America/Ball State University, 1979.

—, ed. *A Study Guide to Steinbeck, Part II.* Metuchen, NJ: Scarecrow Press, 1979.

—, ed. *Steinbeck's Travel Literature: Essays in Criticism.* Steinbeck Monograph Series, no. 10. Muncie, IN: John Steinbeck Society of America/Ball State University, 1980.

—, and Thomas J. Moore, eds. *Steinbeck's "The Red Pony": Essays in Criticism.* Steinbeck Monograph Series, no. 13.

Muncie, IN: John Steinbeck Society of America/Ball State University, 1988.
—, and Thomas J. Moore, eds. *Steinbeck's Posthumous Work: Essays in Criticism.* Steinbeck Monograph Series, no. 14. Muncie, IN: John Steinbeck Society of America/Ball State University, 1989.
—, ed. *Steinbeck's "The Grapes of Wrath": Essays in Criticism.* Introduction by John H. Timmerman. Steinbeck Essay Series, no. 3. Muncie, IN: Steinbeck Research Institute/Ball State University, 1990.
—, ed. *Steinbeck's Literary Dimension: A Guide to Comparative Studies Series II.* Introduction by Reloy Garcia. Metuchen, NJ: Scarecrow Press, 1991.
—, ed. *Steinbeck's Short Stories in "The Long Valley": Essays in Criticism.* Introduction by Warren French. Steinbeck Monograph Series, no. 15. Muncie, IN: John Steinbeck Society of America/Ball State University, 1991.
—, ed. *John Steinbeck: The Years of Greatness, 1936-1939.* Introduction by John H. Timmerman. Proceedings of the Third International Steinbeck Congress, Honolulu, HI, May 1991. Tuscaloosa: University of Alabama Press, 1993.
—, ed. *A New Study Guide to Steinbeck: Major Works, with Critical Explications.* Introduction by Reloy Garcia. Metuchen, NJ: Scarecrow Press, 1993.
Lewis, Cliff, and Carroll Britch, eds. *Rediscovering Steinbeck—Revisionist Views of His Art, Politics, and Intellect.* Studies in American Literature, vol. 3. Lewiston, NY: Edwin Mellen Press, 1989.
Nakayama, Kiyoshi, Scott Pugh, and Shigeharu Yano, eds. *Steinbeck: Asian Perspectives.* Proceedings of the Third International Steinbeck Congress, Honolulu, HI, May 1991. Osaka, Japan: Osaka Kyoiku Tosho, 1992.
Noble, Donald R., ed. *The Steinbeck Question: New Essays in Criticism.* Troy, NY: Whitston Publishing, 1993.
Sharma, R. K., ed. *Indian Responses to Steinbeck: Essays Presented to Warren French.* Foreword by Yasuo Hashiguchi. Jaipur, India: Rachana Prakashan, 1984.
Tedlock, E. W., and C. V. Wicker, eds. *Steinbeck and His Critics: A Record of Twenty-Five Years.* Albuquerque: University of New Mexico Press, 1957.
Wyatt, David, ed. *New Essays on "The Grapes of Wrath."* The

American Novel Series. New York: Cambridge University Press, 1990.

Yano, Shigeru, Tetsumaro Hayashi, Richard F. Peterson, and Yasuo Hashiguchi, eds. *John Steinbeck: From Salinas to the World.* Proceedings of the Second International Steinbeck Congress, Salinas, CA, August 1984. Tokyo: Gaku Shobo Press, 1986.

G. BIOGRAPHIES, MEMOIRS, AND PERSONAL REMINISCENCES

Ariss, Bruce. *Inside Cannery Row: Sketches from the Steinbeck Era.* San Francisco: Lexikos, 1988.

Bennett, Robert. *The Wrath of John Steinbeck or St. John Goes to Church.* Foreword by Lawrence Clark Powell. Los Angeles: Albertson Press, 1939.

Benson, Jackson J. *The True Adventures of John Steinbeck, Writer.* New York: Viking Press, 1984. (P.)

—. *Looking for Steinbeck's Ghost.* Norman: University of Oklahoma Press, 1988.

Enea, Sparky, as told to Audry Lynch. *With Steinbeck in the Sea of Cortez.* Los Osos, CA: Sand River Press, 1991.

Farrell, Keith. *John Steinbeck. The Voice of the Land.* New York: M. Evans and Company, 1986.

Guy, Betty. *Surprise for Steinbeck.* San Francisco: Fania Press, 1992.

Kiernan, Thomas. *The Intricate Music: A Biography of John Steinbeck.* Boston: Little, Brown, 1979.

O'Connor, Richard. *John Steinbeck.* New York: McGraw Hill, 1970.

Parini, Jay. *John Steinbeck: A Biography.* London: William Heinemann, 1994; New York: Henry Holt, 1995.

Sheffield, Carlton. *Steinbeck: The Good Companion.* Introduction by Richard Blum. Portola Valley, CA: American Lives Endowment, 1983.

St. Pierre, Brian. *John Steinbeck: The California Years.* The Literary West Series. San Francisco: Chronicle Books, 1983.

Valjean, Nelson. *John Steinbeck: The Errant Knight.* San Francisco: Chronicle Books, 1975.

H. INTELLECTUAL BACKGROUND AND CREATIVE (RE)SOURCES

Astro, Richard. *John Steinbeck and Edward F. Ricketts: The Shaping of a Novelist.* Minneapolis: University of Minnesota Press, 1973.

—, and Joel W. Hedgepeth, eds. *Steinbeck and the Sea*. Proceedings of a May 1974 Conference at the Marine Science Center, Newport, OR. Corvallis: Oregon State University Sea Grant College Program, 1975.

DeMott, Robert. *Steinbeck's Reading: A Catalogue of Books Owned and Borrowed*. Garland Reference Library of the Humanities, vol. 246. New York: Garland Publishing, 1984.

Gannett, Lewis. *John Steinbeck: Personal and Bibliographical Notes*. New York: Viking Press, 1939.

Hedgepeth, Joel. *The Outer Shore. Part I. Ed Ricketts and John Steinbeck Explore the Pacific Coast*. Eureka, CA: Mad River Press, 1978.

—, ed. *The Outer Shores. Part II. Breaking Through*. Eureka, CA: Mad River Press, 1979. (Includes Rickett's previously unpublished essays, "The Philosophy of Breaking Through," "A Spiritual Morphology of Poetry," "The Log of the Western Flyer," "Essays on Non-Teleological Thinking," "Notes from the *Sea of Cortez*.")

Railsback, Brian E. *Parallel Expeditions: Charles Darwin and the Art of John Steinbeck*. Moscow: University of Idaho Press, 1995.

I. ADAPTATION AND TRANSLATION

Auld, Louis E., ed. *"Burning Bright": The Genesis of an Opera. An Interview with Composer Frank Lewin*. Guilford, CT: Lyrica Society, 1985.

Liedloff, Helmut. *Steinbeck in German Translation: A Study of Translational Practices*. Carbondale: Southern Illinois University, 1965.

Whitebrook, Peter. *Staging Steinbeck. Dramatising "The Grapes of Wrath."* London: Cassell, 1988.

J. CULTURAL AND GEOGRAPHICAL CONTEXTS

Crouch, Steve. *Steinbeck Country*. Palo Alto, CA: American West Publishing, 1973.

Hanson, Robert F. *132 Central Avenue*. Bradenton, FL: Opuscula Press, 1985.

Hilleary, Roger. *A Grand Place. John Steinbeck's Homes in Pacific Grove and Monterey*. Monterey, CA: Hilleary and Petko, 1979.

Knox, Maxine, and Mary Rodriguez. *Steinbeck's Street: Cannery Row*. San Rafael, CA: Presidio Press, 1980.

Larsh, Edward B. *Doc's Lab: Myths and Legends of Cannery Row.* Monterey, CA: PBL Press, 1995.

Mangelsdorf, Tom. *A History of Steinbeck's Cannery Row.* Santa Cruz, CA: Western Tanager Press, 1986.

Messner, Mike. *Steinbeck Country in Dubious Homage.* Salinas, CA: Mike Messner, 1979.

Pearson, Pauline, comp. *Guide to Steinbeck Country.* Salinas, CA: John Steinbeck Library, 1984.

Schmitz, Anne-Marie. *In Search of Steinbeck.* Los Altos, CA: Hermes Publications, 1978.

The Valley Guild. *The Steinbeck House Cookbook.* Preface by Elaine Steinbeck. Foreword and introduction by Lee Richard Hayman. Salinas, CA: The Valley Guild, 1984.

Weber, Tom. *All the Heroes Are Dead: The Ecology of John Steinbeck's Cannery Row.* San Francisco, CA: Ramparts Press, 1974.

—. *John Steinbeck's Cannery Row: A Time to Remember.* Foreword by John Gross. Monterey, CA: Orenda/Unity Press, 1983.

K. JOURNALS: SPECIAL STEINBECK ISSUES

The American Examiner: A Forum of Ideas (Michigan State University), 6 (Fall-Winter 1978-79).

Modern Fiction Studies (Purdue University), 11 (Spring 1965).

San Jose Studies (San Jose State University), 1 (November 1975); 11 (Winter 1985); and 16 (Winter 1990).

The Steinbeck Collector (San Jose, CA), 1 (August 1979)-4 (April 1981).

Steinbeck Newsletter (San Jose State University), 1 (Fall 1987)-present.

Steinbeck Quarterly (Ball State University), 1 (Spring 1968)-26 (Summer-Fall 1993).

The University of Windsor Review (Canada), 8 (Spring 1973).

Index

Abramson, Ben 3
The Acts of King Arthur and His Noble Knights (Steinbeck) 36, 117
Adamic, Louis, *My America* 192
Addison, Joseph 32
"L'Affaire Lettuceberg" (Steinbeck) 154, 166, 168-69
Agee, James and Walker Evans, *Let Us Now Praise Famous Men* 192
Ainsworth, Elizabeth 6
Albee, George 10, 30, 108, 112, 117, 124, 136, 142, 149, 168
Allee, W. C., *Animal Aggregations* 13
Allen, Fred 309
Alter, Robert 77, 103; *The Pleasures of Reading in an Ideological Age* 51, 102
America and Americans (Steinbeck) 6, 31-32, 48, 100
Ames, Cathy 279
Anderson, Sherwood 12, 21, 25; *Winesburg, Ohio, Main Street* 49
Angoff, Charles 190
Armitage, Merle 175
Arvin, Newton 102
Arvin Sanitary Camp 160
The Associated Farmers, Inc. 154, 190, 199
Astro, Richard 50, 52, 141, 195, 287, 292, 315
Atkins, G. Douglas xvii, xxiii
Aurelius, Marcus 31, 86; *Meditations* 22, 24, 59-60
Auster, Paul xvii
"The Author Meets the Critics" 289
Bach, Johann Sebastion, *Art of the Fugue* 126
Bachelard, Gaston 287
Baker, Carlos 291, 315
Bakhtin, Mikhail xxi-xxii, 219, 316
"Ballad of Quid Pro Quo" 253
Ballou, Robert O. 117, 127, 132, 135-38, 143
Barbour, James 105
Barney, Virginia 137
Barry, John 155
Barry, Michael G. 196
Barthes, Roland xxii, 92, 106, 215, 218, 316
Bedford, Richard C. 53
Bellow, Saul 6
Bennett, Joseph 290-93, 309
Benson, Jackson J. 12, 27, 42, 50, 57, 74, 114, 154, 161, 162, 192, 195, 197-98, 201, 211, 215, 222, 236, 252, 259, 261, 264, 292-93, 311, 317
Bentley, Richard 90
Bercaw, Mary K. 105
Bercovitch, Gila 204, 325
Beswick, Katherine 12, 119-20, 122, 134, 235
Between Pacific Tides 16
The Bible 7, 22-3, 42, 57, 86, 97, 173, 303
Bidwell, Martin 16
Black Marigolds 18, 20, 255
Blaine, Mahlon 117
Bloom, Harold 26, 78, 103, 131, 191, 205, 211; *The Anxiety of Influence: A Theory of Poetry* 50-1; *A Map of Misreading* 50, 53, 103

Boileau-Despreaux, Nicolas, *The Art of the Poetic* 135, 176
Boodin, John Elof 14-5, 115; *A Realistic Universe* 15, 42, 115; *Three Interpretations of the Universe* 15
Borges, Jorge Luis 322
Boyle, Robert H. 291, 315
Boyle, T. Coraghessan 153
Braley, Berton 4
Brautigan, Richard 288
Bristol, Horace 165
Brodhead, Richard H. 104
Brodtkorb, Paul 104
Brooks, Peter 262
Brophy, Robert J. 143
Browning, Robert 7
Buell, Lawrence 105
Bunyon, Paul, *Pilgrims Progress* 7, 16
Burke, John 270
Burning Bright (Steinbeck) 35, 56, 245, 260, 295
Byer, Preston 324
Byrne, Donn 10, 111

Cabell, James Branch 9, 10, 111, 124
Cadzow, Hunter 316
Caldwell, Erskine, *Tobacco Road* 16
Cameron, Tom 188
Campbell, Joseph 13, 44, 129-132, 142; *The Hero with a Thousand Faces* 129
Cannery Row (Steinbeck) 6, 11, 14, 18, 20, 56, 114, 128, 193, 294, 296, 299-303, 307
Cannon, Gerald 202
Capp, Al, *The World of Li'l Abner* and influences on *Sweet Thursday* 303-309
Captain Ahab 82, 86-7, 92, 97-8, 135
Carlson, Eric W. 202
Carradine, John 153
Carroll, Lewis, *Alice's Adventures in Wonderland* 21-2, 42; *Through the Looking Glass* 303
Caswell, Paul 28
Casy, Jim 185; *The Grapes of Wrath* 157
Cathcart, Robert 119
Cather, Willa 48; *My Antonia* 113
Cervantes Saavedra, de Miguel 21, 32; *Don Quixote* 26, 31
Chambers, Rose 314
Chandler, Marilyn 196
Chaplin, Charlie 180
Chase, Richard 102, 104
Chavez, Cesar 178
"The Chrysanthemums" (Steinbeck) 253, 272
Clayton, Jay 316
Cohen, Michael 54
The Cold War 19, 79, 102, 218
Collins, Thomas 5, 152, 155, 157, 160-65, 167, 170, 199, 201
Conrad, Joseph 12
Cook, Sylvia J. 203
Coulton, C. G. 38
Covici, Pascal 41, 52, 56, 74, 81, 85, 100, 139, 152, 188, 285, 289-91, 293, 309
Covici, Pascal, Jr. 214, 312
Covici-Friede Publishing 139, 180, 198
Cowley, Malcolm 15, 173
Cox, Martha Heasley 141, 144, 201-02, 322
Crane, Stephen 48
Crawford, Broderick 180
"Critics, Critics, Burning Bright" (Steinbeck) xxii
Crockett, H. Kelly 202
Crystal, Bernard R. 261
Cup of Gold (Steinbeck) 5, 10-11, 110, 112, 150, 235

Danford, Merle 51, 174
Darwell, Jane 153
Dauber, Kenneth 103
Davis, Robert Con 191, 205
Davis, Robert Murray 72
Dawson, Margaret Cheney 138
De Schweinitz, George 202
The Depression 13, 112, 152, 174, 194, 322
Derrida, Jacques 218
Dickson, Sarah Eldredge 75
Dickson, Walter 75-6
Diem, Judith 263
Dircks, Phyllis T. 201

Discove Cottage 41
Ditsky, John 53, 72, 99, 106, 202, 204-05, 212, 217, 222, 235-36, 261-62
Doc (*Sweet Thursday*) 288, 296-302, 305, 307, 309, 312-13
Dos Passos, John 172; *USA* 16, 192
Dostoevsky, Fëdor, *Crime and Punishment* 3, 16
Doughty, Charles Montague, *Travels in Arabia Deserta* 19, 202
Dourgarian, James 324
Dr. Gunn's Family Medicine 22
Drake, Windsor (Thomas Collins) 198; *Bringing in the Sheaves* 161-62, 167, 185
Dreiser, Theodore, *An American Tragedy* 49
Dryden, Edgar A. 105
Dust Bowl 154, 156, 160, 164, 173, 176
Duyckinck, Evert 84; *Literary World* 100

East of Eden (Steinbeck) xix, xxi, 7, 11, 19, 20-3, 25-7, 35, 55-74, 76, 117, 193, 206, 235, 245, 260, 266-67, 274-76, 278-84, 294-96, 298, 302-03, 308, 311, 320; literary influences in 20-30
Eliot, George 3
Eliot, T. S., *The Waste Land* 42, 127, 270
Ellis, William 103
Emerson, Ralph Waldo 21-22, 46, 48, 51, 102, 172
Engle, Paul 208
Etheridge, Charles 212
Evans, Walker and James Agee, *Let Us Now Praise Famous Men* 192
Everson, William 143

Farm Security Administration 156, 162, 167
Faulkner, William 3, 4, 6, 10, 33, 77, 110, 114, 173, 300; *As I Lay Dying* 16, 49
Fauna (*Sweet Thursday*) 301-02
Faure, Raoul, *Lady Godiva and Master Tom* 30, 74
Fedallah 86
Fensch, Thomas 145, 290
Fiedler, Leslie 190, 205
Fisher, Shirley 317
Fitzgerald, F. Scott, *The Great Gatsby* 49
"Flight" (Steinbeck) 272
Fonda, Henry 153
Fontenrose, Joseph 74, 142, 213, 277
Ford, John 153
Ford, Wallace 180
The Forgotten Village (Steinbeck) 235, 246, 254
Fowler, Alistair 316
Fowles, John, *The French Lieutenant's Woman* 251
Frazer, Sir James, *The Golden Bough* 11, 127-28
French, Warren 87, 104-05, 116, 141, 153, 197, 202, 209, 213, 215, 277, 292-93, 315
Frere, Alexander 40
Friedman, Susan Stanford xxii
Fromm, Erich 86; *Psychoanalysis and Religion* 30

Galati, Frank 153
Gamble, Mary Jean S. 261
Gannett, Lewis 290-91, 311
Garcia, Reloy 53
Geertz, Clifford 161
Gemmell, Margaret 235
Genesis 25, 70, 90, 92, 126, 275
Genette, Gerard, *The Architext: An Introduction* xxiii
Gibbon, Edward 5
Gide, André 21; *The Counterfeitors* 26, 207, 214, 301
Gill, Brendan 291, 315
Ginsberg, Allen 288
Gladstein, Mimi Reisel 74, 197, 253, 262, 293, 315
Goldstone, Adrian H. 145
Gordon, Max 28
Govoni, Mark W. 104
Graham, Ellwood 263
Grail 40, 46
The Grapes of Wrath (Steinbeck) xx, 5, 14-8, 49, 76, 90, 114, 117, 139, 206, 218, 236, 246-48, 253, 281, 290,

The Grapes of Wrath (continued) 308, 325
Graubard, Mark, *Man the Slave and Master* 58
Graves, Robert 44; *The White Goddess* 37
Great Aunt Deborah (*The Winter of Our Discontent*) 45
"The Green Lady" (Steinbeck) 121-22
Greenblatt, Stephen 316
Guerard, Albert, *France: A Short History* 32
Gunn, Dr. John C. 55; *New Family Physician* 30, 55-74

Hadella, Charlotte 261
Hader, Elmer 152
Hall, Donald 6
Hall, George, *Plain Points on Personal Purity* 58
Halladay, Terry G. 239; "'The Closest Witness': The Autobiographical Reminiscenes of Gwyndolyn Conger Steinbeck" 50, 239
Hamilton, Samuel (*East of Eden*) 7, 11, 22-4, 30, 45, 55, 64, 68, 80, 86, 279; (*East of Eden*) as reader 59-61
Hamilton, Tom 276
Hanson, Robert 324
Harbison, Robert, *Eccentric Spaces* 324
Hardy, Thomas, *The Return of the Native* 3
Hargrave, John, *Summer Time Ends* 16
Harmon, Robert B. 197, 324
Harry Ransom Humanities Research Center 52-3, 73, 141-42, 236, 282, 285
"The Harvest Gypsies" (Steinbeck) 154, 162-63, 168
Haslam, Gerald 194
Hawley, Ellen (*The Winter of Our Discontent*) 46
Hawley, Ethan Allen (*The Winter of Our Discontent*) 43, 44-7, 100
Hawthorne, Nathaniel 4, 84, 91, 99, 135, 301
Hayashi, Tetsumaro 74, 212, 221, 287
Hayes, Albert, *The Science of Life; or Self-Preservation* 57-8
Hayford, Harrison 104
Hedgpeth, Joel 52, 144
Heflin, Wilson 96
Heller, Joseph, *Catch-22* 33
Hemingway, Ernest 3, 4, 12, 25, 33, 110, 207-08; *The Old Man and the Sea* 32
Hermes portable typewriter, "The Beast Within" 311-314
Herodotus 5, 7, 26-8, 31-2, 86, 97
Hirsch, E. D. 218
Hollander, John 50, 105
Holman, Hugh 292
Hopkins, Karen 211, 218
Horn, Helen 162
Horsford, Howard C. 101
Horton, Chase 13, 37, 40-1, 53, 326
"How Mr. Hogan Robbed a Bank" (Steinbeck) 42
Howard, Leon 96, 102
Howarth, William 178, 200
Howe, Julia Ward, "Battle Hymn" 152, 157, 170
Howe, Susan 105
Hudson Review 290
Hunter, J. Paul 203
Hutcheon, Linda 291, 314, 316

In Dubious Battle (Steinbeck) 5, 14, 114, 139, 156, 163, 180, 182, 193, 236, 272-73, 290
Intercalary chapters 26, 174
Ishmael 92, 96, 98

Jackson, Joseph Henry 110, 194, 197, 199; Interview with Steinbeck 176, 194
Jacobs, Will, *The Beaver Papers: The Story of the "Lost Season"* 153
James, Henry 5, 221
James, William 86; *Principles of Psychology* 22-3, 59-60; *Psychology: A Brief Course* 23
Jeffers, Robinson 14-15, 114, 136, 138, 253, 309; influence on *To a God Unknown* 130-134; "Roan

Jeffers, Robinson (continued) Stallion" 14, 131-32
Jesus Christ 19, 126
Joad, C. E. M. 198; *Guide to Philosophy* 198
Joad, Ma (*The Grapes of Wrath*) 160, 254
Joad, Tom (*The Grapes of Wrath*) 184, 186
Joan of Arc 40
Johnson, Nunnally 153
Jones, Gerard, *The Beaver Papers: The Story of the "Lost Season"* 153
Jones, Lawrence William 72
Journal of a Novel (Steinbeck) 25, 30, 61, 81, 84, 193, 214, 216-18, 223, 281, 283, 287
Joyce, James, *The Portrait of the Artist as a Young Man* 269
Jung, Carl 11, 44-5, 128; *The Psychology of Dementia Praecox* 11

Kaufman, George S. 156
Kazan, Elia 294
Keats, John 7; negative capability 137
Kennedy, William 191, 205
Kerouac, Jack 188
Kesey, Ken, *One Flew Over the Cuckoo's Nest* 151
Kiernan, Thomas 211, 261
Kimball, Margaret J. 260
Kristeva, Julia xxii
Krutch, Joseph Wood 208
Kunitz, Stanley 176

La Follette, Senator Robert M. 190
"A Lady in Infra-Red" (Steinbeck) 112
Lake Tahoe 112
Lancelot 40, 44
Lange, Dorothea 163-64, 173, 192, 199
Larsen, Robin and Stephen, *A Fire in the Mind: The Life of Joseph Campbell* 143, 263-64
Larsen, Stephen and Robin, *A Fire in the Mind: The Life of Joseph Campbell* 143, 263-64
"Leader of the People" (Steinbeck) 14
Lee (*East of Eden*) 23-24, 46, 64, 86, 88
Lee, Robert 103
Leithauser, Brad 200
Levant, Howard 106, 115-16, 141, 213, 292, 315
Lewis, R. W. B. 80, 209
Lewis, Sinclair (*Main Street*) 32
Leyda, Jay 101
The Library of America 50, 204, 220, 325
Lisca, Peter 74, 196, 201, 204, 213, 277-78, 298, 316
Loftis, Anne 160, 198-99
The Long Valley (Steinbeck) 115, 170, 182, 223, 271-72, 325
Longfellow, Henry Wadsworth 7
Lorentz, Pare 156, 180, 182, 197, 202, 246; *Ecce Homo!* 157, 172; *The Plow that Broke the Plains* 173; *The River* 173
Los Gatos 160, 166, 178, 180, 189, 239, 245, 247, 254, 311
Lovejoy, Ritch xvii, 152, 180
Lyman, Mildred 252

Macauley, Thomas Babington 5
Mack (*Cannery Row* and *Sweet Thursday*) 294, 297, 302, 305-07
Madame Bovary 3
Malory, Sir Thomas, *Acts of King Arthur* 326; *Morte d'Arthur* 2, 5, 7, 31, 35-6, 38, 45
Margary, Ivan, *Roman Roads in Britain* 37
Martin, Stoddard 292, 315
McBride, Robert N. 123
McCarthy, Paul 292
McIntosh, Mavis 119, 125, 244, 249, 262, 317
McWilliams, Carey 164, 204; *Factories in the Field* 178, 190, 192
Melville, Herman 10, 21, 101, 301; *The Confidence Man* 76; "Hawthorne and His Mosses" 101; *Journal of a Visit to Europe and the Levant* 76, 101; *Moby-Dick* 25, 57, 75-106, 135, 207, 324;

Melville, Herman (continued)
Pierre 93, 100; *Redburn* 79; *White-Jacket* 79
Mercer, Charles 56
Metcalf, Mrs. Eleanor Melville 96
Metzger, Charles 292, 315
Meyer, Michael J. 53-4, 221
Miller, Amassa 119, 123-25, 128, 142
Milton, John, *Paradise Lost* 3
Mirriliees, Edith 123
Mitchell, Ruth Comfort, *Of Human Kindness* 190
Mizener, Arthur 100, 209, 295
Monterey County 111, 116, 120
The Moon is Down (Steinbeck) 11
Moore, Harry Thornton 144, 166, 174, 277, 323
Morewood, Sarah Huyler 93
Mulder, Steven 105, 215
"Murder at Full Moon" (Steinbeck) 11
Murphy, Dennis 111, 309; *The Sergeant* 33, 309

Nakayama, Kiyoshi 261
Nantucket 85, 94-5, 106, 144
Needham, Wilbur 127, 138-39
New Belletrism xxiii
New Deal 151, 160, 162
Noble, Donald 212
Nolan, Jim (*In Dubious Battle*) 5

O. Henry's Full House (Steinbeck) 33
O'Hara, John 19, 206, 216, 295
O'Shea, Michael 270
Of Mice and Men (Steinbeck) 5, 18, 114, 139, 155-56, 193, 223, 236, 270, 272, 281, 298
"The Oklahomans" (Steinbeck) 154, 165, 167-68
Old and New Testament themes 173
Olson, Charles 86, 105
Once There Was a War (Steinbeck) 18, 265
Origo, Iris, *The Merchant of Prato* 37
Osborne, Mrs. Frances T. 96
Otis, Elizabeth 30, 41, 119, 189, 217, 317
Owens, Louis 73, 103, 105-06, 136, 144, 177, 196, 201-03, 212-14, 219, 292-93, 315

Pacific Biological Laboratories 13, 111, 128, 198
Pacific Grove 12, 111, 116, 120, 131, 235, 244, 305
Palace Flophouse 297, 305, 307
Parini, Jay 154, 197, 220, 261, 264, 293; *John Steinbeck: A Biography* 105, 143, 145, 263
Parks, Robert 261
Participates 215
Participating 306
Participation 52, 149
Participatory 174, 195
The Pastures of Heaven (Steinbeck) 6, 7, 12-3, 113, 115, 117, 121, 125, 139, 235, 272-73
Paul, Louis 154
Payne, John R. 145
The Pearl (Steinbeck) 19, 46, 297
Pearson, Michael 205
Pearson, Pauline 143
Pease, Donald E. 103
Peterkin, Julia 117
Peterson, Richard 73, 212
Phalanx theory 79, 128, 165, 183, 195, 295
Pierpont Morgan Library 38, 54, 235-36, 316
Plato 5
The Plow That Broke the Plains 156
Plutarch 86; *Lives* 26
Poe, Edgar Allan 11
Pope, James S. 300
Poulet, Georges 287
Powell, Lawrence Clark 133, 143, 192, 326
Prindle, Dennis 142

Queequeg 86, 88, 91, 98
Quinones, Ricardo 74
Quirk, Tom xxiii
"Quotation and Originality" (Ralph Waldo Emerson) 21, 48, 51, 102

Rahv, Philip 190
Railsback, Brian 50, 144, 261
Railton, Stephen 105, 194, 202

"Rationale" (Steinbeck) xvii, xix, xxii-iii
Rawley, Jim 160; *The Grapes of Wrath* 157
The Red Pony (Steinbeck) 5, 18, 253, 281, 322
Renza, Louis A. 50
Resettlement Administration 156, 160, 163
Rice, John C. 156
Ricketts, Edward F. 13-4, 15, 16, 18, 37, 79, 81, 111, 123, 143, 148, 173, 180, 218, 246, 258-59, 296, 299, 300, 313, 326
Riddel, Joseph N. 54, 103
The River 156
Robertson, James 234
Rogin, Michael Paul 104
Rombold, Tamara 202
Roosevelt, Eleanor 190
Roosevelt, President Franklin D. 156
Rose of Sharon (*The Grapes of Wrath*) 90, 172, 184-85, 189, 254
Rosenblatt, Louise 53
Rugoff, Milton 291

Sag Harbor's Old Whalers Festival 99
Sale, Roger 211
Salinas, California 6, 9, 111, 168, 253
Salinas Valley 56-7, 59, 82, 88, 114, 121, 213, 277
San Francisco News 155, 162, 199
Sapori, Armando, *Merchants and Companies in Ancient Florence* 37-8, 323
Schaub, Thomas Hill 103
Schloss, Carol 199
Schmitz, Anne-Marie 239
Schmitz, Edwin 239
Schopenhauer, Arthur 5
Schorer, Mark 209
Schulberg, Budd 33
Scott, Elaine Anderson 110
Scott, Sir Walter 2
Sea of Cortez: A Leisurely Journal of Travel and Research 14, 16-8, 128, 193, 246, 249, 263, 325-26
Sealts, Merton 105
Seelye, John 287
Self-character 38, 45-6, 135
Shakespeare, William 7; *Richard III* 42
Shaw, George Bernard, *Caesar and Cleopatra* 4
Sheehan, Ed xx
Sheffield, Carlton A. 14, 16, 115, 141, 180, 253
Shelley, Percy Bysshe 7
Shillinglaw, Susan 52, 197-98, 204, 258
Shirer, William (*The Rise and Fall of the Third Reich*) 32
Shockley, Martin 202
The Short Reign of Pippin IV (Steinbeck) 35
Simmonds, Roy S. 74, 105, 188, 201, 212, 220, 261, 292, 315
Simon J. Lubin Society 164
Simpson, Hassell A. 53
Sinise, Gary 153
"Some Random and Randy Thoughts on Books" (Steinbeck) 20
Soule, Frederick R. 162
Spanos, William V. 103
Spengler, Oswald 136; *Decline of the West* 111, 128
Springsteen, Bruce 153
St. Pierre, Brian 292
Stackpole, Edouard 96
Starr, Kevin 199
"Steinbeck Country" 115, 211, 321
Steinbeck Quarterly 287, 289
Steinbeck Research Center 235, 265, 311, 320, 322
Steinbeck, Carol (nee Henning) 12, 111, 122-23, 128-30, 139, 143, 152, 155, 160, 179-80, 182, 184, 188-89, 201, 236, 239, 244, 246, , 248-52, 254-55, 258
Steinbeck, Elaine 32, 41, 48, 73-4, 94, 106, 140, 196, 216, 223, 290, 298
Steinbeck, Gwyn (nee Conger) xxi, 17, 19, 69, 79, 157, 193, 217-18, 236, 238-40, 243-46, 248-52, 254-55, 258, 260, 297
Steinbeck, John, and fictive *architexture* xiii, 47, 56, 182-83, 186, 295-

Steinbeck, John (continued)
96, 306, 308; and imagination xix-xx, 47-48, 65-66, 72, 116-17, 149, 155, 172, 176, 185, 201, 308, 312-14; and intertextuality xxii, 42, 62, 77, 86, 97, 115, 133-34, 303; and theme of "The Creative" 296-302; and theory of participation in reading 17-18, 23, 56, 92-93, 149, 174, 195-96, 215, 294, 306; and writing process xvi-xviii, 60-61, 64, 79-80, 82, 89-90, 94, 111, 130-36, 178-79, 206, 216-17, 222-23, 248-49, 283-84; "Argument of Phalanx" 195; background, composition and reception of *The Grapes of Wrath,* 148-205; composition *To a God Unknown* 108; "Critics, Critics, Burning Bright" 293, 296, 315; *East of Eden* 55-106; *East of Eden* bibliography 224-232; *East of Eden* critical reception, 206-223; *The Grapes of Wrath* sales 152-53; "The Green Lady" 120; "In Awe of Words" 52; "A Letter on Criticism" 204; "Letters to Alicia" 102; literary readings 1924-26 10; Noble Prize Acceptance Speech 76; Phalanx research 13-14; reading of contemporary writers 33-5; readings in Malorian scholarship 37; Stanford University courses 9; "Suggestions for an Interview with Joseph Henry Jackson" 154, 195; teenage reading preferences 9; 17-18, 23; "To the Unknown God" 123
Steinbeck, John IV 51, 69, 81, 94, 239, 262, 290, 303, 310, 317,
Steinbeck, John Ernst 7
Steinbeck: A Life in Letters 238, 254, 261
Steinbeck, Mary 7
Steinbeck, Olive Hamilton 7
Steinbeck, Thom 69, 81-2, 88, 94, 104-05, 239, 262, 289, 290, 303, 309, 310-11
Sterne, Laurence, *Tristam Shandy* 26
Stevenson, Robert Louis 2, 9; *Child's Garden of Verses* 303; *Prince Otto* 108; *Travels with a Donkey* 32
Stinnett, Caskie 186
Stone, Geoffrey 102
Stowe, Harriet Beecher 4; *Uncle Tom's Cabin* 151
Strachan, William 196, 317
Stravinsky, Igor, *Symphony of Psalms* 175
Strecker, Geralyn 53
Street, Webster F. 118-19, 122, 141, 245
Sturz, Herbert 174, 192, 201
Suetonius 7
Suzy (*Sweet Thursday*) 297, 302, 305, 307
Sweet Thursday (Steinbeck) xix, 35, 193, 245, 260, 288-94-304, 306, 308-10, 314
Sypher, Wylie 293

Tacitus 7
Tanselle, G. Thomas 104
Tao Teh Ching 20
Taylor, Paul Schuster 164; *An American Exodus: A Record of Human Erosion* 192
Tchaikovsky, Pëtr Ilich, *The Swan Lake* 175
Tennyson, Lord Alfred 9
Their Blood Is Strong (Steinbeck) 170
Theory 79, 128
Thomsen, Eric H. 162
Thomson, J. A. K. 27
Thoreau, Henry David 46, 287; *Walden* 289
Thorp, Willard 96, 102
Thucydides 7, 31, 35, 48; *Peloponnesian Wars* 35
Timmerman, John H. 50, 74, 104, 202, 212, 214, 222, 293, 315
timshel/timshol (*East of Eden*) 24-5, 27, 70, 81, 88, 277, 314
To a God Unknown (Steinbeck) 5, 7, 11, 13, 15, , 45, 108-145, 223, 235, 272-73
Todorov, Tzvetan xxi
Tolstoy, Leo, *War and Peace* 16, 174

Torres, Hector 201
Tortilla Flat (Steinbeck) 5, 13, 110, 112-13, 139, 270, 281, 303
Trask, Adam (*East of Eden*) 24, 28, 62, 67-8, 70, 78, 80, 88, 92-3, 98, 277
Trask, Alice (*East of Eden*) 62
Trask, Aron (*East of Eden*) 311
Trask, Cal (*East of Eden*) 311
Trask, Caleb and Aron (*East of Eden*) 23
Trask, Cyrus (*East of Eden*) 62, 70
Trask, Kate/Cathy Ames (*East of Eden*) 28, 30, 60-4, 67-8, 80, 86-8, 93, 97-8, 275-76
Travels with Charley (Steinbeck) 6, 32, 42, 271, 274, 311
Twain, Mark 4, 25, 59; *Adventures of Huckleberry Finn* 49, 59, 151

United States Film Service 182

Valenti, Peter 54
Valentine, Harry 141, 144
Valjean, Nelson 141, 261
Van Brunt, Wanda 235, 259, 322
Varese, Edgar 202
The Vatican 38
Vedic Hymns 124, 127
"The Vigilante" (Steinbeck) 14
Vinaver, Eugène 13, 37, 40-1
Vincent, Howard 102, 289
Virgil 7; *Georgics* 113
Visalia, California 148, 166-68, 184-85, 199-200
Viser, Nicholas 194
Viva Zapata! (Steinbeck) 35, 235, 295
Voice of America 218
Voice of America radio interview 167

Wagner, Max 238, 250
Walker, Alice, *The Color Purple* 151
Walther, Louis 165, 199
Watkins, Floyd C. 197
Watt, F. W. 277
Waugh, Alec, *Island in the Sun* 36
Wayne, Benjy (*To a God Unknown*) 130
Wayne, Joseph 113-5, 116, 119, 122, 126, 128-29, 135-36, 139-41, 273; (*To a God Unknown*) 111
The Wayward Bus (Steinbeck) 19, 235, 272, 297
Webster, Harvey Curtis 208, 221, 291, 315
West, Anthony 208
West, George 162-63
Western Flyer 16-7
Weston, Jessie, *From Ritual to Romance* 127
Wharton, Edith 4
White, Ray Lewis 205
White, T. H., *The Once and Future King* 41
Whitman, Walt 9, 25, 46, 132, 154
Wilde, Oscar, *Lady Windemere's Fan* 245
Wilhelmson, Carl 116, 125
Williams, Annie Laurie 157, 169
Wilson, Edmund 209, 295
The Winter of Our Discontent (Steinbeck) xix, 31-2, 41-3, 45, 48, 193, 271, 100
Wolfe, Thomas 77
Wood, C. E. S. 32
Woodward, Robert 322
"The Word" (*Cannery Row*) 18
Wordsworth, William 7
Working Days (Steinbeck) xvi, 16, 148, 151, 154, 165-66, 191, 194, 202, 223, 235-36, 238, 245, 247, 254-55, 324
Wright, Harold Bell, *The Winning of Barbara Worth* 22
Wright, Richard, *Native Son* 192
Wyatt, David 105, 144, 203, 220, 292
Wylie, James Hamilton, *The Reign of Henry the Fifth* 38

Xenophon 7

Yardley, Jonathan 222

Zane, Nancy 216
Zanuck, Darryl F. 153